Making a World after Empire

This series of publications on Africa, Latin America, Southeast Asia, and Global and Comparative Studies is designed to present significant research, translation, and opinion to area specialists and to a wide community of persons interested in world affairs. The editor seeks manuscripts of quality on any subject and can usually make a decision regarding publication within three months of receipt of the original work. Production methods generally permit a work to appear within one year of acceptance. The editor works closely with authors to produce a high-quality book. The series appears in a paperback format and is distributed worldwide. For more information, contact the executive editor at Ohio University Press, 19 Circle Drive, The Ridges, Athens, Ohio 45701.

Executive editor: Gillian Berchowitz
AREA CONSULTANTS
Africa: Diane M. Ciekawy
Latin America: Brad Jokisch, Patrick Barr-Melej, and Rafael Obregon
Southeast Asia: William H. Frederick

The Ohio University Research in International Studies series is published for the Center for International Studies by Ohio University Press. The views expressed in individual volumes are those of the authors and should not be considered to represent the policies or beliefs of the Center for International Studies, Ohio University Press, or Ohio University.

Making a World after Empire

THE BANDUNG MOMENT AND
ITS POLITICAL AFTERLIVES

Christopher J. Lee

Ohio University Research in International Studies
Global and Comparative Studies Series No. 11
Ohio University Press
Athens

To obtain permission to quote, reprint, or otherwise reproduce or distribute material from Ohio University Press publications, please contact our rights and permissions department at (740) 593-1154 or (740) 593-4536 (fax).

Front cover images: Jawaharlal Nehru of India and Gamal Abdel Nasser of Egypt (top photo) and Zhou Enlai of China (bottom photo) walking to the conference hall in Bandung, Indonesia, April 1955. Reprinted courtesy of the Museum of the Asian-African Conference.

Some of the chapters published in this book have appeared elsewhere and are reprinted with permission:

Dipesh Chakrabarty, "The Legacies of Bandung: Decolonization and the Politics of Culture," *Economic and Political Weekly*, Vol. 40, No. 46, 12 November 2005.

Michael Adas, "Contested Hegemony: The Great War and the Afro-Asian Assault on the Civilizing Mission Ideology," *Journal of World History*, Vol. 15, No. 1 (2004): 31–63.

Denis M. Tull, "China's Engagement in Africa: Scope, Significance and Consequences," *Journal of Modern African Studies*, Vol. 44, No. 3 (2006): 459–479.

20 19 18 17 16 15 14 13 12 11 10   5 4 3 2 1

Printed in the United States of America
The books in the Ohio University Research in International Studies Series are printed on acid-free paper. ∞ ™

Library of Congress Cataloging-in-Publication Data

Lee, Christopher J.
   Making a world after empire : the Bandung moment and its political afterlives / Christopher J. Lee.
      p. cm. — (Ohio University research in international studies. Global and comparative studies series ; no 11)
   Includes bibliographical references and index.
   ISBN 978-0-89680-277-3 (pbk. : alk. paper) — ISBN 978-0-89680-468-5 (electronic)
   1. Asian-African Conference (1st : 1955 : Bandung, Indonesia) 2. Asian-African Conference (1st : 1955 : Bandung, Indonesia)—Influence. 3. Afro-Asian politics. 4. Asia—Relations—Africa. 5. Africa—Relations—Asia. 6. Imperialism—History—20th century. 7. Decolonization—Asia—History—20th century. 8. Decolonization—Africa—History—20th century. I. Title.
   DS35.2.L44 2010

327.1'16—dc22   2009053610

Contents

Illustrations

Acknowledgments

This volume originated with a workshop entitled "Bandung and Beyond: Rethinking Afro-Asian Connections During the Twentieth Century" held at the Stanford Humanities Center, Stanford University, in May 2005. Sponsored by the Empires and Cultures Workshop at the Center, a number of sources provided funding for this event, including the Mellon-Sawyer Program, the department of history at Stanford, the Stanford Society of Fellows in Japanese Studies, the department of philosophy at the University of San Francisco (USF), the Fleischhacker Family Fund (USF), the Yuchengco Philippines Studies Program (USF), the African-American Studies Program at USF, and the Asian-American Studies Program at USF. I would particularly like to thank David Kim, who was the co-organizer, and, in addition to his fundraising at USF, made significant intellectual and personal contributions to the spirit of the meeting. Others who helped make the workshop possible include Richard Roberts, Richard White, Kären Wigen, Zephyr Frank, Ronald Sundstrom, Emily Burrill, Sean Hanretta, Peter Hudson, and Monica Wheeler.

Having evolved over several years, this resulting volume represents a different collection of ideas and research from that presented in 2005. Nevertheless, I would like to draw attention to the work of participants Chris Connery, Judy Wu, Gaurav Desai, Jonathan Greenberg, Minkah Makalani, and, especially, John de Boer, whose research on Japanese diplomatic history deserves a wide readership. The 2007 Decolonization Seminar at the National History Center offered a later period of research support and an ideal audience to test ideas found in the introduction. I am grateful to Roger Louis, Philippa Levine, Dane Kennedy, and Jason Parker, as well as fellow seminar participants, for their support, insights, and time. A fellowship at the Centre for Research in the Arts, Social Sciences, and Humanities (CRASSH) at Cambridge University provided another period of work, reflection, and revision. I thank its director, Mary Jacobus, as well as my fellow visitors for their questions and encouragement. Megan Vaughan, Harri Englund, Arne Westad, and Derek Peterson also supplied conversation and support at Cambridge, as well as critically engaged readings of some of the ideas here. Barbara Harlow offered early inspiration, and Luise White gave advice at different moments along the way. In addition to those already mentioned, Fred Cooper, Marilyn Young, Antoinette Burton, Sarah Shields, Lisa Lindsay, Michael Tsin, and Jim Brennan read penultimate drafts of the introduction to great effect.

Gillian Berchowitz at Ohio has been unusually patient, supportive, and helpful to a first-time author. I am indebted to her and her sense of confidence and trust. I thank Isman Pasha, the director, and his staff at the Museum of the Asian-African Conference in Bandung for their warm hospitality and permission to reprint photos of the 1955 meeting. Finally, I would like to thank my contributors for their inspiring scholarship, and for keeping a kind of secular faith throughout this venture.

Contributors

Michael Adas is the Abraham E. Voorhees Professor and Board of Governor's Chair at Rutgers University, New Brunswick. His recent books include *Machines as the Measure of Men: Science, Technology, and Ideologies of Western Dominance* (1989) and *Dominance by Design: Technology, Social Engineering and America's Civilizing Mission* (2006).

Laura Bier is an assistant professor of history at Georgia Tech. She received her PhD from the departments of history and Middle Eastern studies at New York University in 2006. She has published widely on the politics of gender and state socialism in postcolonial Egypt.

James R. Brennan is an assistant professor of history at the University of Illinois and a research fellow at SOAS, University of London. He has published widely on East African history and is coeditor of *Dar es Salaam: Histories from an Emerging African Metropolis* (2007). He is also author of a manuscript tentatively entitled "Taifa: Africa, India, and the Making of Nation and Race in Urban Tanzania."

G. Thomas Burgess is an assistant professor of history at the United States Naval Academy in Annapolis. He is the author of *Race, Revolution, and the Struggle for Human Rights in Zanzibar: The Memoirs of Ali Sultan Issa and Seif Sharif Hamad* (2009).

Antoinette Burton teaches at the University of Illinois where she is Bastian Professor of Global and Transnational Studies. Her most recent work includes *The Postcolonial Careers of Santha Rama Rau* (2007) and (with Tony Ballantyne) *Empires and Imperial Encounters,*

1875–1955 (forthcoming, Harvard University Press). She is beginning a project on Afro-Asian solidarity in 20th-century India and South Africa.

Dipesh Chakrabarty is the Lawrence A. Kimpton Distinguished Service Professor in History and South Asian Languages and Civilizations at the University of Chicago. He is the author of *Provincializing Europe: Postcolonial Thought and Historical Difference* (2000) and *Habitations of Modernity: Essays in the Wake of Subaltern Studies* (2002), among other books.

Julian Go is an associate professor of sociology at Boston University. He is editor of the annual journal *Political Power and Social Theory*. His most recent book is *American Empire and the Politics of Meaning: Elite Political Cultures in Puerto Rico and the Philippines* (2008). He is currently completing a book comparing US and British imperial formations between 1688 and 2003.

Christopher J. Lee is an assistant professor of history at the University of North Carolina, Chapel Hill. He has published widely on the history of southern Africa, with articles appearing in the *Journal of African History, Politique Africaine, Transition, Radical History Review,* the *South African Historical Journal,* and *Interventions: International Journal of Postcolonial Studies.* He has recently completed a regional history of race and political culture in British Central Africa. His current project is a social and diplomatic history of the Bandung Conference.

Jamie Monson is a professor of history at Macalester College. She is the author of *Africa's Freedom Railway: How a Chinese Development Project Changed Lives and Livelihoods in Tanzania* (2009).

Jeremy Prestholdt is an associate professor of history at the University of California, San Diego. He is the author of *Domesticating the World: African Consumerism and the Genealogies of Globalization* (2008). His current work addresses the intersections of politics and consumerism in the appeal of popular icons.

Denis M. Tull is a senior researcher at the German Institute for International and Security Affairs in Berlin. He received his PhD from the University of Hamburg in 2004. His areas of research include Africa's international relations, state transformation and state building in Africa, and violent conflict and peacekeeping in Africa. His articles have appeared in *International Security, International Peacekeeping, African Affairs,* and the *Journal of Modern African Studies.*

Introduction

Between a Moment and an Era:
The Origins and Afterlives of Bandung

Christopher J. Lee

At the Rendezvous of Decolonization

No race possesses the monopoly of beauty, intelligence, force
and there is room for all of us at the rendezvous of victory.

—Aimé Césaire, *Cahier d'un retour au pays natal* (1939)

IN NOVEMBER 2006, China hosted a summit of forty-eight political leaders from countries across Africa, the third in a series sponsored by the Forum on China–Africa Cooperation (FOCAC) since
2000. Widely covered in the international media, this three-day event
in Beijing aimed to crystallize a common agenda between China, with
its burgeoning global role in the post-cold war world, and Africa, a
continent described on posters in Beijing as "the land of myth and
miracles."[1] Publicized as a benevolent occasion with promises of aid
and trade agreements reflective of a novel global partnership outside
the West, this meeting equally marked a new and ambivalent turn
for many observers in Europe and North America concerned with
China's increasing influence on a continent that has been perceived by
Chinese leaders as "up for grabs." That China's intentions are unsur-
prising and historically familiar—many have cited its aggressiveness

as reminiscent of European colonialism—has not mitigated these anxieties. Consumer markets and resources such as oil have been key incentives for recent Chinese attention. In particular, international criticism following the 1989 Tiananmen Square Massacre, the rise of US hegemony after the cold war, and the 1997 Asian financial crisis have forced China to reconsider its foreign policy, with Sino-African relations forming a central component of this shift toward restoring its global presence and power. Unrestricted foreign aid from China has in turn been attractive for a number of African nation-states, especially governments such as Zimbabwe's and Sudan's that have fallen into disfavor with the IMF, the World Bank, and Western governments generally. China's respect for sovereignty and noninterference has characterized this approach. Since 2005, China has consequently become Africa's third most important trading partner following the US and France, thus superseding Great Britain. The Forum's slogan of "Peace, Friendship, Cooperation, Development" therefore sums up the working sensibility found between both sides, though it also conceals a complex set of unsteady power relations that currently undergird this alignment.[2]

The rhetoric of newness surrounding the Forum also obscures an equally complicated past, not only between China and Africa but between Asia and Africa generally. The present collection seeks to amend this empirical and conceptual gap, to restore a chronology and trajectory of historical experience that have been marginalized by conventional area-studies analysis. Like many projects preceding it, this volume is concerned with the complex foundations, experiences, and aftereffects of the modern history of colonization and decolonization during the 20th century. As such, it builds upon work published over the past thirty years that has sought to respond to and redress the frameworks of political economy and social knowledge produced by global imperialism. Unlike many of its predecessors, however, this volume departs from a metropole-colony focus, asserting the impact and consequent importance of connections within the global South in the making of this history. It specifically uses the 1955 Afro-Asian Conference in Bandung, Indonesia, as a central point of orientation, being an occasion—diplomatic and symbolic—

when twenty-nine African and Asian countries met to discuss the possible futures of the postcolonial world. Indeed, a recent resurgence of interest in Afro-Asian relations and the fiftieth anniversary of the conference—which established the New Asian-African Strategic Partnership (NAASP), whose official declaration reinstated the Ten Principles of the Bandung Communiqué—have revived focus on the meeting.[3] This restoration, however, has also risked simplifying the complexities of 1955. From one point of view, the conference constituted a foundational moment of the early postcolonial era, manifesting the rendezvous of victory presaged metaphorically by Aimé Césaire. But from another vantage point, it equally contained the existential predicaments of newfound sovereignty and the internal and external political claims and responsibilities that would soon challenge it, particularly those generated by the cold war. In sum, Bandung comprised a complex intersection of "imagined communities"—in the influential nation-making sense as defined by Benedict Anderson—but also a set of politically constrained "represented communities" as described more recently by John Kelly and Martha Kaplan, being constituted and limited by institutionalized acts of law, diplomacy, and the structural legacies of colonial rule. Bandung contained both the residual romance of revolution, as well as the *realpolitik* of a new world order in the making.[4]

This volume is therefore poised between several interrelated but often disparate fields: cold war history and postcolonial studies, global history and area studies, diplomatic history and sociocultural history. The attraction of Bandung as an event is its capacity to bring these subjects into conversation with one another, presenting a historical moment and site generative of intersecting vantage points and their storied outcomes. Indeed, the contributions to this volume speak from and to these different academic audiences through a variety of social themes—gender, law, technology, labor, ideologies of development, foreign aid, and religion among them. Yet they are unified by a concern for community formation—or, more specifically, a geopolitical *communitas*, as discussed later—beyond the reaches of political, geographic, and historical convention. The case studies on offer here do not seek to reconstitute a triumphal narrative of postcolonial autonomy and assertion—a tact that has animated many recent discussions of Afro-Asian relations thus far—but instead recuperate a more usable past by identifying the varied locations and complex, situated meanings of "Afro-Asianism," an ill-defined term that has signaled both a cold war-era ideology of diplomatic solidarity as well as a more general phenomenon of intercontinental exchange and interracial connection. This volume does not pretend to cover every aspect of this history, nor does it emphasize one meaning of this expression over another. Given the still-early stage of this research field at present, we are more focused on identifying the occasions, archives, thematic realms, and analytic techniques for addressing this history. If Bandung in retrospect offered a "diplomatic revolution" for the postcolonial world, a subsequent question emerges as to how a sociocultural turn can be applied to this diplomatic history, to connect this event to preexisting area-studies agendas that have privileged the agency of local people and communities.

The essays that follow, in sum, explore these scales of power and geography not only to examine the ramifications of Bandung itself, but to add greater empirical depth to meanings of the postcolonial, a stronger area-studies perspective to cold war scholarship, and, at the broadest level, a more concerted emphasis on how political projects based in the "majority world" shaped global history during the latter half of the 20th century. But why this specific historical moment, and, furthermore, how might Bandung be situated and understood from the point of view of the present? In what ways does the Bandung conference complicate conventional exit-and-entry narratives of decolonization and generalized assertions about "the postcolony" by highlighting new forms of "political community" beyond the nation-state? In short, how does this history speak to concerns expressed with growing frequency regarding the disjunctures between 20th-century decolonization, postcolonial criticism, and the political problems of sovereignty in the global present by charting the possibilities and predicaments of the early postcolonial period? To answer these crucial questions, it is appropriate to start with a discussion of the precursors and afterlives of the Bandung moment.[5]

A Brief History of the Future, circa 1955

> For many generations our peoples have been the voiceless ones in the world. We have been the unregarded, the peoples for whom decisions were made by others whose interests were paramount, the peoples who lived in poverty and humiliation. Then our nations demanded, nay fought for independence, and achieved independence, and with that independence came responsibility. We have heavy responsibilities to ourselves, and to the world, and to the yet-unborn generations. But we do not regret them.
> —President Ahmed Sukarno of Indonesia, Opening Address of the Asian-African Conference, April 18, 1955

Decolonization poses fundamental challenges for the historian. From an empirical standpoint, it is both a contingent moment of political independence *and* a long-standing process with deep roots, at times originating with the act of initial colonization itself. It is an experience that is at once uniquely individual in scope—to people, communities, and nation-states alike—and in retrospect seemingly universal: the world witnessed a momentous wave of newly independent nation-states during the second half of the 20th century, more than doubling the number of members in the United Nations. Yet despite its relative ubiquity as a political process for many parts of the world, it is not easily contained within uniform frames of analysis, or time. The early episodes of decolonization in the Western hemisphere preceded that of Africa and Asia by almost two centuries, with the American Revolution (1776–83) and the Haitian Revolution (1791–1804) subverting the imperial presence of Great Britain and France respectively in the New World. Indeed, the early modern political independence of nation-states in North and South America antedated the formal colonization of Africa and in ways influenced this new shift in political direction for Europe during the late 19th century. Asia similarly experienced European imperialism within a time frame of its own, with initial Western intrusion concurrent to parallel endeavors in the Americas during the early modern era and the final vestiges of this process relinquished as late as Great Britain's handover of Hong Kong

Introd.1. Prime Minister Jawaharlal Nehru of India and President Gamal Abdel Nasser of Egypt arrive in Bandung

to China in 1997. Thus, the precolonial period in Africa does not overlap chronologically with Asia's precolonial period, in the same sense that Latin America's postcolonial period has existed for some time whereas it is still just starting for parts of Asia and Africa. Our schematic frames of chronological reference—the precolonial, colonial, and postcolonial eras—accordingly face the challenge of synchronicity. The timing of decolonization can be out of joint when transnational and transregional comparisons are made. Further complicating such matters have been trends of subimperialism, the rise of former colonies such as the United States, South Africa, and China, for example, into roles of regional and global dominance, a development that decenters Europe as a point of reference but introduces new complications in the chronological placement and meaning of decolonization in world history. Imperialism has reproduced itself in various changing forms over time and continues to do so to the present.[6]

Decolonization consequently presents a problem of narrative and analysis. It is not an expression that is easily transferred between contexts with a common definition intact. Like the nation-state with which it is intrinsically connected, decolonization on the surface lends itself wide use, as a process and baseline for narratives of autonomous economic development and political modernization. However, as with these issues, the outcomes are more often assumed than achieved, with a persistent risk being recourse to historical teleology to provide an explanatory structure.[7] Mindful of this problem, social historians for the most part have focused on explorations of nationalism, interrogating its claims of representation, but venturing little beyond the boundaries of the nation-state at hand or chronologically further into the postcolonial period to follow its changing meanings.[8] Recent work has attempted to address the internal, qualitative differences between settler and nonsettler colonies, but, as underscored by the insights of diplomatic historians, other geopolitical contexts—the cold war in particular—must also be pointed to as crucial external factors in shaping and at times prolonging decolonization, as in Southeast Asia and southern Africa.[9] From the vantage point of another involved field, postcolonial studies, the term "postcolonial" itself—to which decolonization is also intrinsically tied—has often been essentialized through interpretive assertions that have sought to read and inscribe a common set of experiences across much of the former colonial world.[10] The universality of condition imparted by such terminology therefore deserves critical vigilance as well. Decolonization and its correlative expressions, in sum, present an ongoing predicament, enabling comparison while equally posing the concession of oversimplification. Furthermore, they underscore the disjunctive manner by which these issues are currently addressed among political scientists, economists, anthropologists, historians, and literature scholars. It is best approached as a situated process that requires attention to local case studies as well as broader patterns of event and meaning across space and time. Rather than simply signaling a linear, diplomatic transfer of power from colonial to postcolonial status, decolonization equally constitutes a complex dialectical intersection of competing views and claims over colonial pasts, transitional presents, and inchoate futures.

Opportunities are provided in this set of tensions as well. If empirical generalization is to be avoided, processes of decolonization offer an entry point for rethinking the specific conditions and local causes for political change, in addition to more broadly experienced continuities that have attended such shifts. As observed with the political dilemmas of many postcolonial leaders, the transition from colonial to postcolonial status was often thin on autonomy and thick with ongoing entanglements. Political sovereignty did not automatically translate into economic self-sufficiency or cultural independence, as seen in the writing of such figures as Kwame Nkrumah, Julius Nyerere, and Jawaharlal Nehru.[11] Revisiting moments of decolonization consequently presents an opportunity for recapturing the senses of optimism, frustration, and uncertainty that characterized such occasions. Such emotive qualities found in the speeches and writings of figures who attended Bandung in 1955 reflect a lack of comfort through the absence of any stable trajectory, and they explain in part why contemporary narratives of anticolonialism and decolonization have often resorted to forms of romance, as David Scott has recently argued. In Scott's view, anticolonial histories

> have tended to be narratives of overcoming, often narratives of vindication; they have tended to enact a distinctive rhythm and pacing, a distinctive direction, and to tell stories of salvation and redemption. They have largely depended upon a certain (utopian) horizon toward which the emancipationist history is imagined to be moving.[12]

This interpretive situation has in turn created a sense of disconnection between the failures of the postcolonial present and the complex visions of postcolonial futures expressed during moments of decolonization. Frederick Cooper, for example, has pointed to empirical

Introd.2. Local popular reception of the arrival of international delegations in Bandung

gaps in recent critical work that has assigned postcolonial blame on past colonial projects, a common approach that can often obscure the importance of the late colonial and early postcolonial period in shaping the era that followed.[13] In this way, it is important to reexamine the events and features of decolonization in order to restore the competing strategies and complex visions that not only sought to achieve future outcomes, but at the time sought to inventively reshape the legacies of the past to serve such present endeavors.

Bandung was such an occasion. In retrospect, it can be seen as a pivotal moment placed in mid-century between colonial and postcolonial periods, between the era of modern European imperialism and the era of the cold war. It summarized an alternative chronology of world events organized by intellectuals and activists of color who had been subjected to forms of colonialism, racism, and class oppression. This historical sequence includes such precursors as the series of Pan-African Congresses that took place beginning in 1900, the 1911

Universal Races Congress in London, the League Against Imperialism meeting held in Brussels in 1927, and the two Pan-Asian People's Conferences held in Nagasaki (1926) and Shanghai (1927).[14] At a deeper level, Bandung also served as a culmination of connections and relationships that had crossed the Indian Ocean world for centuries.[15] The common ground shared and frequently cited at the conference was the history of Western imperialism in Asia, Africa, and the Middle East since the sixteenth century. These claims similarly extended to a broader set of thematic experiences including racism and cultural discrimination, which further attracted such noted observers as Richard Wright, the African American novelist.[16] The meeting therefore captured and represented a complex global present, one that signaled political achievement but also future uncertainty. Of the twenty-nine countries that sent official delegations, many had attained independence, though there were others, particularly from Sub-Saharan Africa, which still remained under the last remnants of colonial rule. Not all were former colonies either. Constituting a diverse spectrum, participants included leading lights of the postcolonial world, such as India and Egypt, as well as countries that had recent imperial legacies of their own, namely Japan.[17] From cultural, religious, and linguistic standpoints, the differences between attendees were equally pronounced. And yet, it is essential to recognize that the organizers themselves acknowledged such factors of division, resting their contingent solidarity and sense of purpose on a shared history of Western aggression.[18]

The immediate backdrop to the conference were two meetings in 1954 between Indonesia, Burma (Myanmar), Ceylon (Sri Lanka), India, and Pakistan—often referred to collectively as the Colombo Powers. Concerned with cold war tensions in Vietnam and Southeast Asia generally, one meeting was held in Colombo, Sri Lanka, in April with a second held in Bogor, Indonesia, in December. Prime Minister Ali Sastroamidjojo of Indonesia, a vocal critic of Western intervention in Asia, originally proposed the idea of an Asian-African conference as a response to the 1954 founding of the Southeast Asia Treaty Organization (SEATO) sponsored by the United States. Delegations were to be drawn from the existing Afro-Asian group within the United Nations. However,

Introd.3. Premier Zhou Enlai of China with Prime Minister Ali Sastroami-djojo of Indonesia at the Bandung Airport

the invitation list soon expanded, reflecting a diplomatic, rather than strictly continental, logic. Jawaharlal Nehru of India, for example, insisted that China be included as part of his foreign policy agenda to foster productive regional relations despite the forced acquisition of neighboring Tibet by China in 1950. This move eliminated Taiwan as a possible participant, given the tense Strait Crisis which then remained unresolved. Apartheid South Africa was also eventually excluded, as were North and South Korea which still maintained a cease-fire following the Korean War (1950–53). Israel was also voted down for fear that Arab and Muslim countries would not attend. Invitations ultimately were sent to Egypt, Turkey, Japan, Libya, Lebanon, Jordan, Syria, Iran, Iraq, Saudi Arabia, Yemen, Afghanistan, Nepal, Laos, Cambodia, Thailand, North and South Vietnam, the Philippines, Ethiopia, the Gold Coast (Ghana), Sudan, Liberia, and the Central African Federation.[19] With China and the Colombo Powers included, twenty-nine countries in total attended, comprising a group nearly half the size of the U.N. and ostensibly representing an estimated 1.5 billion people, thus underscoring the numeric significance of the meeting. But of these countries, only six were from Africa, which tilted much of the agenda toward concerns found in Asia, including the Middle East.

The conference took place between April 18 and 24, 1955. The location of Bandung was significant, as it was one of the most important cities in Indonesia. Indonesian President Ahmed Sukarno had received his university education and started his career as a political activist there, publishing the journal *Indonesia Muda* and helping found the Partai Nasional Indonesia.[20] More importantly, the choice of a metropole outside the West marked a symbolic departure from its Pan-African and League Against Imperialism antecedents, underscoring the new geographic sphere of autonomy found in the nascent postcolonial world. Although a certain diplomatic complexity undergirded the meeting, the public atmosphere achieved at the conference evinced this sensibility of a new era in world history. Social activities, panels, and receptions scheduled throughout the week contributed to this mood of excitement, with the centerpiece of the conference being the opening addresses given by various heads of state, a who's who of postcolonial leaders.[21] It was also this platform through which political tensions and opportunism emerged, posing immediate questions about the viability and longevity of Afro-Asianism as a political ideology and front. As with Sukarno, Bandung offered an unparalleled occasion for Nehru to consolidate his position as a recognized world leader, providing a diplomatic stage for his vision of nonalignment from the U.S. and Soviet Union, an idea that would gain traction in the years that followed. For Gamal Abdel Nasser of Egypt, it enabled him to ascend to a status equivalent to that of Nehru—a position soon consolidated by the 1956 Suez Crisis—in spite of the ambiguities of the coup that placed him in power in 1952. Given its exclusion from the U.N., Zhou Enlai, China's foreign minister, similarly perceived Bandung as a moment of legitimating China in the purview of its regional neighbors. Despite tensions with the US over Taiwan and North Korea and its concurrent alliance with the USSR, the Bandung meeting presented a forum through which China could state its peaceful intentions and overcome a sense of isolation within the international community.

Introd.4. Premier Zhou Enlai, who was also China's foreign minister, delivering his address at the Bandung Conference

However, beyond this "great men" perspective on the conference were issues and situations that underscored not only competing visions of the future, but how such visions were informed and supported by the new global order being established by the United States and Soviet Union. In a recent acclaimed survey of the cold war, Odd Arne Westad has contended that this period's greatest impact was on the Third World—not the theater of Europe as so often assumed— since American and Soviet policies ultimately formed a continued pattern of colonialism, if by revised means, with aspirations of political, economic, and ideological control.[22] In many cases, the imperial "man on the spot" had been replaced by a member of the new postcolonial elite, as famously warned by Frantz Fanon. Among the participants, Communist China, with its then-close relations with the Soviet Union, was perhaps the most widely viewed proxy for superpower interests, although other countries maintained similar sets of connections. Iran, Iraq, Pakistan, and Turkey, a member of NATO, had recently signed the Baghdad Pact with Great Britain on February 24, 1955 to form the Central Treaty Organization (CENTO) with the direct intention of limiting Soviet interests in the Middle East. In parallel, SEATO—with its members Thailand, the Philippines, and again Pakistan in attendance—had been formed in 1954 with the same intent. Japan and Saudi Arabia similarly had strong unilateral ties with the US. Yet, the most visible cold war fault line existed between North and South Vietnam, both of which took their opening addresses as an opportunity to accuse the other of escalating tensions within Indochina.[23] Following the French defeat at Dien Bien Phu, the 1954 Geneva Accords had granted independence to Vietnam, albeit dividing it into a pro-communist North and anti-communist South, eventually leading to the Vietnam War involving the US. Other speeches identified similar ongoing and future conflicts, perhaps most conspicuously the Palestinian and anti-apartheid struggles.

The conference thus captured a complex set of individual and group aims. The immediate outcome of the conference was a final communiqué that reinstated the desire for greater economic cooperation and cultural exchange, recognition for human rights and self-determination, the condemnation of new and future forms of imperialism, and the

Introd.5. The Liberian delegation in attendance

need to pursue policies that would promote world peace. It is important to recognize that nonalignment as a stated principle shared by all in attendance was not an outcome of the Bandung meeting, yet again a reflection of the formal and informal security agreements that many participants had already arranged and, moreover, the priority placed on individual sovereignty. Indeed, only India, Burma, and Indonesia supported the idea explicitly. However, the more momentous result was the *feeling* of political possibility presented through this first occasion of "Third World" solidarity, what was soon referred to as the Bandung Spirit. In defining this sentiment of a new future that transcended the bounds of member states, Vijay Prashad writes

> What they meant was simple: that the colonized world had now emerged to claim its space in world affairs, not just as an adjunct of the First or Second Worlds, but as a player in its own right. Furthermore, the Bandung Spirit was a refusal of both economic subordination and cultural suppression—two of the major policies of imperialism. The audacity of Bandung produced its own image.[24]

The Bandung Conference of 1955 consequently generated what has often been taken as self-evident: the idea of a Third World. Furthermore, in contrast to many contemporary understandings of this expression, the Third World was embraced as a positive term and virtue, an alternative to past imperialism and the political economies and power of the US and the Soviet Union. It represented a coalition of new nations that possessed the autonomy to enact a novel world order committed to human rights, self-determination, and world peace. It set the stage for a new historical agency, to envision and make the world anew. The recent history of imperialism and colonialism across Africa and Asia had informed these ideals. Although the 1952 origins of this expression preceded the conference by three years, Bandung captured in palpable form the potential of what this global coalition and its political imagination might mean.[25]

Still, the elusiveness of solidarity suggested by the word "spirit" equally characterized the aftermath of the conference. Indeed, although the sense of unity caught the Eisenhower administration off guard, the tense balance of cooperation and respect for individual

Introd.6. Members of the Gold Coast (Ghana) and Indian delegations during a recess

sovereignty among the delegates became more pronounced in the years that followed.[26] Unilateral and regional security arrangements such as SEATO and CENTO remained unchanged with few exceptions, as with the departure of Iraq from CENTO in 1958. The United States and Soviet Union continued to make regional inroads during the 1950s, escalating tensions particularly in the Middle East and Southeast Asia. The Vietnam War alone demonstrated an inability of Afro-Asian nations to dispel foreign geopolitical influence and guaranteed that peace, as aspired to in the Bandung communiqué, would not be the prevailing norm in Asia during the cold war. The Arab-Israeli conflict and the late decline of white minority rule in southern Africa—in Southern Rhodesia, Angola, Mozambique, and apartheid South Africa—would pose equally persistent challenges. Perhaps more politically damaging to the Bandung Spirit than these externally influenced cases were episodes of delegate nations themselves coming into conflict, at times violently. The Sino-Indian Border Conflict of 1962 as well as similar disputes between India and Pakistan undermined the possibility of solidarity within the subcontinent. The Sino-Soviet split also presented a diplomatic complexity for former Bandung participants, despite the surface suggestion of a new nonalignment. A final setback to the principles of the communiqué was the gradual testing and acquisition of nuclear arsenals by China (1964), India (1974), and eventually Pakistan (1998).

Such factors accumulated over time, however, and the vision of future opportunities articulated at Bandung was not foreclosed in the short term. Nasser became an early beneficiary by quickly moving to position himself as a leader of the Third World, a status enhanced by the global support Egypt garnered during the 1956 Suez Crisis, when Great Britain and France failed, under international pressure, to regain control over the Suez Canal. In December 1957, the Afro-Asian Peoples' Solidarity Organization (AAPSO) was established in Cairo, marking a new endeavor in the wake of Bandung. The Soviet Union and China both became involved in its activities. AAPSO proved to have even wider reach than the Bandung meeting itself, by including a range of political and cultural organizations as opposed to official delegates from African and Asian states. The conferences it organized between 1958 and 1965 continued the Bandung Spirit by emphasizing professional exchange, cultural connections, women's coalitions, and youth participation (see the chapters by Bier and Brennan in this volume for the prominent role of Egypt). Furthermore, meetings were held within an expanding range of locales including Guinea, Ghana, and Tanzania. The most important post-Bandung development, however, was the institutionalization of nonalignment through the founding of the Non-Aligned Movement (NAM). The Belgrade Conference of Non-Aligned Nations convened in September 1961 by Yugoslavia's Josip Tito, who sought greater autonomy from the USSR, initiated this formal alliance, revising once again the meaning of Afro-Asianism. The second conference held in Cairo in October 1964 had delegations from forty-seven states in attendance, a growth attributable to the wave of decolonization in Sub-Saharan Africa. Combined, these two mutual, if at times competitive, efforts at sustaining a Third World bloc manifested a high point for Afro-Asian solidarity by 1964. However, this trend was dramatically cut short a year later with the failure to coalesce the proposed second Afro-Asian meeting to be held in Algiers in 1965, the result of unresolved differences between China, Indonesia, India, and the Soviet Union, whose involvement in the intervening years had become ineluctable.[27]

With the period of colonial rule receding and the individual options and abilities of postcolonial political autonomy better understood, the original fervor of Afro-Asianism as an ideology shifted and declined thereafter, though it did not entirely disappear. The Vietnam War, the late decolonization of southern Africa, the antiapartheid struggle in South Africa, and the Arab-Israeli conflict continued to offer reasons for protest against continuing forms of imperialism and Western intervention. In parallel, the "development" and "modernization" aspects of solidarity discourse gained ground aside the political, taking root in local contexts and leading to debates, struggles, and continued speculation over the viability of transposing certain ideas, like Maoism, beyond their place of origin (see chapters by Burgess, Monson, and Lee). Translation, in its pragmatic and ideological forms, was a constant issue. Still, new connections were also fostered, particularly in Latin America with the 1966 founding of the Organization of Solidarity with the People of Asia, Africa and Latin America in Havana, Cuba, and the emergence of a broader tricontinentalism. If the reach of such projects embody in organizational form the kind of problematic essentialism of "the postcolonial" as addressed earlier, it is nevertheless important to recognize their institutional legacies that still continue today. In addition to the NAM, the Group of 77—established within the UN in 1964 to aggregate the interests of developing countries—has since enlarged to include 130 countries. The NAM itself continues, if in a weakened and less certain form after the cold war, to provide a forum for leaders and nation-states in Africa, Asia, and Latin America.[28]

A more decisive failure on the part of the original "Bandung regimes"—as Samir Amin has called them—and their successors has been within the political realm internal to their borders, rather than the version of late internationalism they sought to define and mobilize.[29] One-party states, authoritarian regimes, abuse of human rights, and economic discrepancies between elites, workers, and peasants have all too often characterized the social and political conditions of nation-states within the Third World, contributing to its pejorative valence in expression. Although such conditions can be traced in many cases to the political influence and financial backing of the United States and the Soviet Union, they nevertheless point to failures of leadership and inherited structural legacies of rule—what Frederick Cooper has referred to as the "gatekeeper" state, wherein power is highly centralized and vertically structured, such that political participation is strictly regulated.[30] Combined, such elements have undermined the core ideals of the Bandung communiqué. What Frantz Fanon warned in *The Wretched of the Earth* (1961) regarding the rise of a new comprador bourgeoisie in postcolonial countries has been consummated too often in too many places.[31] Working from this horizon, David Scott has asked if our postcolonial present of "less developed countries" (LDCs)— whether located in Africa, Asia, or Latin America—is characterized by forms of failure, how might this condition be traced to the moment of decolonization? What alternative futures were present at the time, and why have so many been rendered moribund? He argues that such questions return us to a set of fundamental political foundations and serve to re-engage academic scholarship with the conditions and problems of the present.[32] In a stimulating critique of Benedict Anderson, John Kelly and Martha Kaplan similarly have suggested that answers to the present may rest in the difference between "imagined communities" and "represented communities," that decolonization was not so much an exit but instead an entry into a global political scenario that shared structures and protocols with the preceding colonial era.[33] These concluding observations therefore highlight the analytic and political need for ongoing empirical investigation and critical vigilance; to develop more fully integrated conversations between diplomatic history, social history, and postcolonial criticism; and, in sum, to acknowledge the possibilities and contradictions of Bandung—its placement between constituting a moment and representing an era. The next section outlines how this volume intersects with this broad endeavor.

Imagined Communitas—Rethinking
"Political Community" along the Afro-Asian Divide

Prasenjit Duara has written that there are "remarkably few historical studies of decolonization as a whole, despite the importance of
the subject."[34] In a similar vein, Stephen Ellis has admonished historians of Africa for continuing to focus on the precolonial and colonial
periods even though the postcolonial period and its history are continuing apace fifty years hence.[35] Speaking to a Latin American audience, Gilbert Joseph has similarly cited the need for bringing Latin
American studies—and, by extension, area studies—into better conversation with scholarship on the cold war, to achieve an intellectual
rapprochement that recognizes their shared history and disciplinary
origins.[36] At the most fundamental level, the following essays aim to
amend this research situation by contributing a set of case studies that
help to outline the possible parameters of these related fields. In short,
the scope of this volume is panoramic, extending beyond the event of
the Bandung meeting to consider the locations, practices, and politics
that created senses of community across the Afro-Asian divide. The
history of connections between both continents, if not exactly hidden, has often been occluded by what have become the conventional
concerns of area-studies scholars since the 1960s. Beyond occasional
comparative studies, Afro-Asian relations have been marginalized
until quite recently by conceptual frameworks that have either centered historical change as emanating from Europe—world-systems
theory being a key example—or emphasized the local and regional
dynamics of African and Asian communities making their own history, if not always under conditions of their choosing.[37] Yet, as the
Bandung meeting itself emphasized, the backdrop to these contrasting approaches has been the history of modern imperialism on both
continents. Not only did acts of Western intervention serve as defining
experiences in many locales, but they also left durable intellectual legacies that have shaped how such acts would be interpreted after their
denouement. Area-studies scholars, who have been poised between
such legacies and the possibility of their critique, have undertaken
a range of efforts, both theoretical and empirical, to challenge the

uncritical reproduction of imperial knowledge. This endeavor has not only interrogated the internal contradictions of the colonial archive, but has variously sought to articulate countermodernities, alternative modernities, decolonial thought, and the "provincialization" of Europe—a sequence of related projects that have shared a common purpose designed to recover a space of agency, history, and social knowledge beyond Western influence.[38]

Attempting a shift away from such West-Rest dialectics, research on Afro-Asian relations has blossomed recently among a number of scholars drawn from cultural, literary, and American studies. In part, this research turn has been an outgrowth of multiculturalism in the American academy since the 1980s, further intersecting with contemporary concerns over US imperial ambitions during the 20th century. Within a brief space of time, this effort has underscored the historical importance of transracial coalitions in the making of modern social movements.[39] However, a striking absence in this developing subfield is the presence of area-studies scholars and their views on intercontinental, rather than solely interethnic, Afro-Asian connections. Africa and Asia are symbolically invoked, but often empirically absent. In parallel, recent scholarship on the Indian Ocean world has made substantial headway in defining a new framework analogous to the Black Atlantic, thus creating a geographic and thematic space for reconsidering the histories of Africa and Asia in mutually constitutive ways. But these studies so far have centered on the precolonial and colonial periods, leaving open questions as to the shifting contours and meaning of this setting for the postcolonial period.[40] Finally, a third agenda of interest—related to the critical projects mentioned previously, albeit with a stronger empirical focus—has been the writing of new imperial histories. Building upon the prescient insights of such thinkers as Hannah Arendt, Aimé Césaire, and Edward Said, this turn has helped account for interregional dynamics by examining the circuits of knowledge and experience that transformed European and colonial worlds alike.[41] Similar to Indian Ocean studies, this field by its very nature has remained entrenched in the colonial era, exploring the tensions of empire but leaving the tensions of postcoloniality aside. Overall, these loosely related agendas have shared a common purpose to work against conventional analytic binaries and to push geographic boundaries through critical explorations of how political space is defined. Even the contours and dynamics of continental thinking having come under scrutiny, with questions as to how the geographies that define our expertise have intellectual structures that furtively limit our spatial frames of reference and interpretation.[42]

This collection is situated amid these multilayered conversations. Its key distinctions from these existing projects are, first, its active attempt to move chronologically into the postcolonial and cold war periods— thus departing from the new imperial agenda and current work on the Indian Ocean—and second, to locate more firmly an intercontinental geography of historical agency and meaning, in order to avoid certain risks of parochialism found in area studies as well as the existing US-centered Afro-Asian literature. Indeed, to interrogate the area-studies paradigm is to readdress an enduring intellectual legacy of the cold war era that is still with us, a critical task of which we are quite conscious. But beyond these concerns over time, place, and disciplinary knowledge rests, at the center of our agenda, the question of "political community"—specifically, what its contours, content, and viability have been in the context of the postcolonial world beyond the archetype of the nation-state. This basic question dwelled at the heart of the Bandung meeting as the preceding section suggests, yet it is an idea that has animated a number of events and political formations of the modern era, from ideologies of Pan-Africanism and Pan-Arabism to more recent intergovernmental organizations at regional and global levels such as the Southern African Development Community (SADC), the Organization of the Petroleum Exporting Countries (OPEC), and the Nonaligned Movement itself. For sure, these ideas and bodies are diverse in their outlooks—serving varying degrees of cultural, economic, and political intent—and, although transnational in principle, they have typically been instruments at the service of individual state agendas. However, despite these limitations, which evince the risks of overdetermining their import, these bodies do outline a realm of community politics situated between the nation-state as such and outsized global political entities, namely the United Nations. Indeed, the continued use and dependence on political units—in particular, the nation-state and empire—which matured during the 19th and 20th centuries marks a distinct analytic constraint in contemporary scholarship, given the proliferation of these alternative political models. These new structures are not entirely defined by these existing categories, nor do they approximate alternative community forms, such as diaspora, that have been anchored by descent-based identities. In this view, political conditions have outpaced the evolution of our mainstream analytic vocabulary. The recent imperial turn to explain contemporary US foreign policy appears to be an all-too-clear reflection of this state of categorical impasse, making presumptive conclusions of behavior instead of raising new questions of definition and practice.[43]

Rethinking political community requires, then, a removal from this safety of terminology. A better strategy is needed beyond labeling multipolar phenomena as transnational. This proposal does not necessarily mean inventing new language per se. Rather, recourse to empiricism and social process—how such terminology is understood and redefined on the ground—is needed. Attention to the relationships between decolonization, the rise of interregional bodies, and the interpersonal, sociopolitical practices that constituted such efforts is required. The term "community," of course, is generic enough for wide application. But it does possess a deep genealogy and an existing set of distinct uses. In his classic study *Gemeinschaft und Gesellschaft* (1887), Ferdinand Tönnies drew a distinction between "community" (*Gemeinschaft*) and "society" (*Gesellschaft*), the former organized around a shared set of values and the latter characterized by self-interest.[44] These elements for thinking through the dynamics of community have carried over in contemporary employment of the expression. The most influential recent use of the term "community" has arguably been in relation to nationalism and the nation-state, as outlined by Benedict Anderson in *Imagined Communities* (1983). Anderson's argument contains a compelling focus on the role of popular imagination as a political practice, enabled through the rise of print media. This approach has sparked debate, though, with critics such as Partha Chatterjee and Manu Goswami drawing attention to the structural role of colonialism and global capital in the making of national territorial spaces and, more generally, a functional nation-state system in the wake of mid-20th century decolonization.[45]

Other scholars have embraced Anderson's intervention, but have also cited a need to expand the parameters of his expression. Extending Chatterjee's question of *whose* imagined community, Dipesh Chakrabarty, for example, has suggested that scholars should "breathe heterogeneity into the word 'imagination'" in order to open its wide-ranging sites and expressive possibilities.[46] Taking a different angle, Frederick Cooper has similarly decried two prevailing misuses of "community": first, its synonymous relationship with the nation-state, which reduces the diverse meanings of the term and the complex scale of relations they have inhabited; and second, how "community" is often employed to capture a sociohistorical alternative or counterpoint to Western modernity and its claims to universalism, rather than being mobilized to create a link between the two. Simplification in both cases has reproduced categorical norms that fail to highlight examples of innovation and entanglement that have animated connections between individuals, organizations, and states.[47] Returning to the question of representation, Martha Kaplan and John Kelly have cited the related insufficiency of "imagination" as a means for explaining community formation during the colonial and postcolonial periods. A better grasp of the institutional limitations and the ritual practices of community legitimation is needed to understand the political and material obstacles that postcolonial countries have faced.

These comments that derive primarily from research on the colonial and early postcolonial periods equally pertain to the present. Contemporary globalization has generated wide-ranging discussion about the function and meanings of community in a context increasingly defined and managed by nonstate actors. Arjun Appadurai has pointed to how states have sought "to monopolize the moral resources of community" through heritage projects and equating "state" with "nation," in order to counter competing trends of transnational separatist movements.[48] Michael Hardt and Antonio Negri, echoing Cooper, have criticized how "the nation becomes the only way to imagine community," that too often the "imagination of a community becomes overcoded as a nation, and hence our conception of community is severely impoverished."[49]

Meanwhile, David Held has contended that national governments are not the arbiters of power they once were, since the contemporary rise of "political communities of fate"—which he defines as "a self-determining collectivity which forms its own agenda and life conditions"—increasingly transcend their boundaries of control.[50] Recent changes in the global scale of political interaction therefore do not herald the deterioration or end of "community" as such but have only escalated its role and stature. This "return to community"—through incipient nationalisms, indigenous-people movements, and the mobilization of religious identities—has refreshed questions of individual-versus-group interests in determining the viability of political ideals of equitable justice and democratic practice.[51]

This volume takes such contemporary developments seriously, as highlighted at the start. But it seeks to flesh out the history between late colonialism and these observations of the global present.[52] Indeed, this book does not seek to overdetermine Bandung as a direct precursor to current political trends or suggest that contemporary China-Africa relations have assumed without revision the mantle of mid-20th-century Afro-Asianism. Instead, it aims to articulate a complex history composed of a constellation of political communities that have cut across the Asia–Africa divide during the 20th and early 21st centuries. These communities have been inspired by ideas that transcend conventional political geographies. But they have also been made by individuals who have been both empowered and limited by political resources, language, and other day-to-day realities (see Bier, Brennan, Burgess, Monson, Lee, and Prestholdt in this volume).

As proposed here, uniting these diverse and challenging conditions and the way people managed them is not only the question of "community" but the practices and habits of *communitas*. This expression is most closely associated with the ethnographic work of Victor Turner on social custom and ritual. But taken as a political process, it offers several compelling features that apply to the concerns of this volume. First, *communitas* is related to, but also distinct from, community, which Turner describes as grounded in a particular geography. Instead, *communitas* is defined by "social relatedness" that comprises a "community of feeling." Turner references Tönnies's use of

Gemeinschaft as a point of orientation, with this expression's argument for community based on sentiment, not locality or blood. The second important feature of *communitas* is its transitory, liminal status and subsequently antistructural character. Unlike the more generic and static expression "community," which conveys a ready-made quality, *communitas* is in movement, an interval moment of creative possibility and innovation, and therefore an active rite of passage thought to be necessary, yet equally perceived as destabilizing. It embraces what Andrew Apter has called "critical agency," a capacity to mobilize social discourse and challenge existing norms.[53]

Applied here, *communitas*—and its existential, normative, and ideological forms—provides a term for capturing the complex dimensions and meaning of decolonization and the diverse political communities inaugurated by it.[54] It cites the demands and rituals of what it takes to be a community—nation-state or otherwise—on the world stage, as well as the potential for challenging those rules. Of particular use is its emphasis on political feeling rather than a structured community per se, which relates to the spirit of Bandung, but also its inventive, transitional qualities that reflect the cold war fluidity of political alignments and nonalignments. Employing Turner's taxonomy to its full extent, one can argue that an existential *communitas*—based on a shared experience of Western imperialism—informed an ideological *communitas* that intended to provide a distinct, even utopian alternative to the preceding era through a discourse of Afro-Asian solidarity. Indeed, as the previous section noted, the US and Soviet Union were quick to intervene to mitigate the possibility of a permanent and influential Afro-Asian bloc from taking hold—what Turner would call a normative *communitas*. The idea of an imagined *communitas* proposed here, therefore, conjoins Turner and Anderson with the intent of advancing a more active notion of "community," one emphasizing elements of movement and innovation in the face of existing structures of a global nation-state system. It aims to step beyond the subjective and often rhetorical qualities of "imagination" to represent both the strong sense of political purpose postcolonial communities had as well as the practical limitations they faced, diplomatic and otherwise. Embracing *communitas* as a political phenomenon at this level therefore asks what it takes to be a viable community international in scope, the diplomatic rituals of recognition as well as the more local practices of self-constitution involved. It demands examination of the strengths and weaknesses of such communities, with their potential for alternative views that provide forms of critical authority, but also the challenges they face based on political feelings that could shift and subside.

These observations intimate the constraints of the translocal communities that followed Bandung and, at a broader level, the improbability of long-term Afro-Asian solidarity. Yet their histories, if at times ephemeral in nature, offer another angle as well: that significant patterns of interaction can be pointed to, addressed, and explored in depth. The chapters that follow present case studies that examine the grounded ways this interaction took place and held influence, charting a history intended to flesh out empirically the period between Bandung and the global present. They are at once social and intellectual, diplomatic and cultural, and are defined as much by strategic intention as they are by geographic obstacle. They reveal not tensions of empire, but tensions of postcoloniality—the complex and at-times contradictory set of aims and conditions situated between the rhetoric of revolution and the pragmatism of governance, defiance of the West and continued forms of economic and political need. Tensions of postcoloniality, in sum, refer to inherited colonial legacies and possible postcolonial futures that African and Asian countries had to negotiate. Whether in "strong" or "weak" form, the political communities described here serve to reposition how the term "community" itself might be understood against the paradigms of empire and the nation-state, by working through variable modes of *communitas* as a means of understanding the opportunities and impediments for alternative communities of fate and the realm of political futures they have had to offer.

Tensions of Postcoloniality—Locations, Practices, Politics

This edited volume works at three levels. First, it aims to enhance developing discussions on this neglected aspect of world history through focused case studies—from South Africa, to Tanzania, to Egypt, to Southeast Asia, to Central Asia—that demonstrate the variety, complexity, and wide-ranging geography of Afro-Asian relations during the last century. It should be emphasized that, with several key exceptions (see Chakrabarty, Go, Adas, and Burton), this topic is approached from the vantage point of scholars working within Africa. In this regard, the essays here intend to speak to contemporary Afro-Asian relations, particularly those with China, as suggested at the start of this introduction. Yet this volume also seeks to de-center a narrow emphasis on China, pointing to multiple histories of connection between both continents. This relates to a second level. Through a case-study approach, the essays of this book equally demonstrate the research and methodological possibilities of this field: from empirically based examples that locate the state and nonstate archives of such history, to more conceptually driven pieces that provide ways of interpreting and thinking about the Afro-Asian world. As stated before, the precursors and afterlives of the Bandung moment present an opportunity to rethink the interactions between social history, cultural history, intellectual history, and diplomatic history—the latter in particular a genre that remains underdeveloped within area studies, especially for Africa.

At the broadest level, this collection aspires to address and contribute to contemporary debates over transnationalism, globalization, and the crossing of area-studies boundaries—to articulate the meaning of these expressions and agendas through grounded illustrations. We do not propose an autonomous realm of knowledge or experience beyond the West—a turn that continues to reemerge, whether under the rubric of "alternative modernities" or "decolonial" thought—but rather we seek to interrogate the historical relations of power at micro- and macro-levels that make such agendas at best limited. Such positions not only risk simplifying the spatial dimensions of political and cultural power to generic locations of "inside" and "outside," but in the same manner they reinstate rather than dissolve the very perception of such boundaries that were first established through histories of imperialism, and later redeployed by cold war politics. This third dimension of the book therefore encapsulates the thrust of the project as a whole: to identify the contours of a new research agenda that speak to, and build upon, existing discussions in area studies, global history, and postcolonial studies that are critical of such preexisting conventions of geography and power and their genealogical origins. This volume does not pretend to offer complete coverage or conclusively answer the questions it raises. It does not chart a sequence of diplomatic events typical of many cold war histories. Rather, it positions the Bandung meeting as a means of bringing the aforementioned issues and disciplines together. Straddling the colonial and postcolonial worlds, Bandung provides a new chronology and an event-centered focus for examining the postcolonial period.

The volume is divided into three parts. The first section—entitled "Framings: Concepts, Politics, History"—is devoted to a conceptual and empirical stage setting for the essays that follow. Dipesh Chakrabarty leads off with a study of three key concepts—anticolonialism, postcolonialism, and globalization—by examining their genealogical origins and interrelations in various decolonization projects, including Bandung. This chapter is an effort at outlining and unifying these interrelated, though often separate, ideas that have defined a broad agenda shared by many area-studies scholars working today. It furthermore offers a useful historical and theoretical structure for the essays that follow. Michael Adas, for example, examines the effects that World War I had on the genesis of anticolonialism during the interwar years. As his wide-ranging chapter underscores, these effects were not isolated but formed a broader pattern of experience and meaning across Africa and Asia against the effects of European imperialism. In sum, his essay outlines the political terrain and intellectual origins of rationales that would lead to Bandung in 1955. Julian Go follows with a similar set of political questions posed after World War II, examining how postcolonial independence in Africa and Asia can be fruitfully understood through a lens informed by constitutional law, thus serving to separate the rhetoric of autonomy from the demands of legal *realpolitik*. Go's essay therefore refrains from uncritically valorizing the spirit of Bandung by instead situating the development and reconfiguration of the post–World War II global order from the perspective of constitutional practices that typically underscored continuity, rather than departure, from Western practices. In sum, these essays examine the early challenges of community formation faced in the Afro-Asian world.

With this foundation, the second section—entitled "Alignments and Nonalignments: Movements, Projects, Outcomes"—transitions to the multiple afterlives of the Bandung moment, with particular attention to the role of local contexts, practices, and meanings in the articulation of this broader geography. Laura Bier's essay explores how Afro-Asianism intersected with a nascent Third World feminist movement based in Cairo through AAPSO during the late 1950s and 1960s. Despite the open embrace of these two ideologies as a common front, Bier underscores how cultural challenges remained, with prevailing views that were often informed by Western cultural discourse inherited from the colonial period. James Brennan similarly examines the importance of Cairo, offering a detailed discussion of how the Egyptian government under Nasser mediated discourses of anticolonialism and pan-Islamism in East Africa during the 1950s and 1960s through the Swahili broadcasting of Radio Cairo. His essay underlines the technological means of diplomatic engagement that states and anticolonial movements had at their disposal for communicating ideas of Third World solidarity, yet also the local dynamics of race and nationalism that complicated any easy acceptance of Afro-Asian solidarity. Venturing further in this geographic direction, the next two chapters explore Chinese-sponsored "development" projects in East Africa. Gary Burgess investigates the exchange of students, official visitors, and "modernization" experts between Zanzibar and China during the 1960s, along with the corresponding complexity of the ideological connections between Mao, Nyerere, and Abdulrahman Mohamed Babu, each of whom aspired to a "usable future." In parallel, Jamie Monson discusses the history of Chinese development experts and African workers on the TAZARA railway in postcolonial Tanzania and Zambia during the 1960s and 1970s. Complementing Burgess's chapter, this essay points to the more practical demands and day-to-day aspects of Afro-Asian interaction beyond rhetorical gestures toward "modernization," as well as the deep history of cooperation with China that has reemerged today. Moving to a different context, Christopher Lee's biographical essay on father–son activists James and Alex La Guma examines the role travel had in fostering diplomatic relationships between South African activists and the Soviet government over the course of the 20th century. Central Asia proved to be a particularly important site of these travels, illustrating the development possibilities that a socialist South Africa might experience as described by Alex in his memoir *A Soviet Journey* (1978).

The final section of the volume—"The Present: Predicaments, Practices, Speculation"—builds upon the empiricism of the previous section and returns to the conceptual questions in the first. Moving beyond state-and-social-history narratives, the chapters of this section address present challenges developing between Africa and Asia, exploring issues of continuity and change in relations between both continents since the end of the cold war. Denis Tull's essay provides a useful overview of China's growing involvement in Africa and how it suggests more problems than benefits for African nation-states, thus marking a decisive shift in Afro-Asianism as an ideology of solidarity since Bandung. Focusing on a separate set of politics that are equally important, Jeremy Prestholdt offers a parallel analysis of the rise of Osama bin Laden as an icon of anti-Western revolution among communities in the Indian Ocean region, especially coastal Kenya, today. Building upon recent work by Mahmood Mamdani and others, he questions whether bin Laden has joined the symbolic ranks of Mao and Che Guevara and what the implications this discourse has for understanding Afro-Asian political ideologies of the present.[55] Combined, both essays suggest the continued growth of regional interaction with patterns that recall the past as well as signal different visions of the future.

In sum, this volume considers the past, present, and future of political communities in this contingent world. It intimates an alternative history and geography of the 20th century that challenges not only Eurocentric accounts, but also contributes to ongoing discussions of transnationalism and globalization in a committed empirical fashion. It presses for a reconfiguration of viewpoint and consequently a reassessment of conventional accounts of the 20th century. Indeed, as Antoinette Burton suggests in her insightful epilogue, the occasion of Bandung forces a reorientation not only with how the fields of postcolonial and cold war studies might be readdressed chronologically and empirically, but also how the mobility and redefinition of race, class, and gender in the wake of Bandung subsequently demand a thorough reappraisal of how these categories were transformed in variable ways between the receding experience of modern imperialism and our global present.

To those who were present and those who observed from afar, the 1955 Bandung Conference was a watershed moment, a historical juncture that served as a summary point for previous anticolonial activism and a new baseline by which the accomplishments of the postcolonial world were to be measured. Although essays found here address pertinent theoretical issues connected to this moment, the majority provide historical case studies that lend substantive empirical weight to the premises of the volume. The net effect of these strengths is that we can start to move beyond the theory-driven conventions of postcolonial studies and, armed with evidence, begin to think more concretely and extensively about how to sharpen our reconception of postcolonial history and that of the 20th century. Bandung must not be understood as an isolated moment, but instead be situated within a rich and varied history of intercontinental exchange that it shaped and still continues today.

Notes

1. Joseph Kahn, "China Opens Summit for African Leaders," *New York Times*, November 2, 2006.

2. It should be noted that as this volume went to press, a Fourth Forum meeting was to be held in November 2009 in Egypt. For an overview of the past and present of this relationship, see, for example, Jan S. Prybyla, "Communist China's Economic Relations with Africa, 1960–64," *Asian Survey* 4, no. 11 (1964): 1135–43; George T. Yu, "Sino-African Relations: A Survey," *Asian Survey* 5, no. 7 (1965): 321–32; George T. Yu, "China's Failure in Africa," *Asian Survey* 6, no. 8 (1966): 461–68; Harish Kapur, *China and the Afro-Asian World* (New Delhi: Prabhakar Padhye, 1966); George T. Yu, "Dragon in the Bush: Peking's Presence in Africa," *Asian Survey* 8, no. 12 (1968): 1018–26; John K. Cooley, *East Wind Over Africa: Red China's African Offensive* (New York: Walker, 1965); Bruce D.

Larkin, *China and Africa, 1949–70: The Foreign Policy of the People's Republic of China* (Berkeley: University of California Press, 1971); Tareq Y. Ismael, "The People's Republic of China and Africa," *Journal of Modern African Studies* 9, no. 4 (1971): 507–29; Alaba Ogunsanwo, *China's Policy in Africa, 1958–71* (London: Cambridge University Press, 1974); George T. Yu, *China's African Policy: A Study of Tanzania* (New York: Praeger, 1975); Alan Hutchison, *China's African Revolution* (Boulder: Westview Press, 1976); Warren Weinstein, ed., *Chinese and Soviet Aid to Africa* (New York: Praeger, 1975); Alvin Z. Rubenstein, ed., *Soviet and Chinese Influence in the Third World* (New York: Praeger, 1975); Martin Bailey, "Tanzania and China," *African Affairs* 74, no. 294 (1975): 39–50; Martin Bailey, *Freedom Railway: China and the Tanzania–Zambia Link* (London: Collings, 1976); Richard Hall and Hugh Peyman, *The Great Uhuru Railway: China's Showpiece in Africa* (London: Victor Gollancz, 1976); Gao Jinyuan, "China and Africa: The Development of Relations Over Many Centuries," *African Affairs* 83, no. 331 (1984): 241–50; Philip Snow, *The Star Raft: China's Encounter with Africa* (London: Weidenfeld and Nicolson, 1988); George T. Yu, "Africa in Chinese Foreign Policy," *Asian Survey* 28, no. 8 (1988): 849–62; Ian Taylor, "China's Foreign Policy towards Africa in the 1990s," *Journal of Modern African Studies* 36, no. 3 (1998): 443–60; Deborah Bräutigam, "Close Encounters: Chinese Business Networks as Industrial Catalysts in Sub-Saharan Africa," *African Affairs* 102, no. 408 (2003): 447–67; Chris Alden, "Red Star, Black Gold," *Review of African Political Economy*, nos. 104/5 (2005): 415–19; Lindsey Hilsum, "Re-enter the Dragon: China's New Mission in Africa," *Review of African Political Economy*, nos. 104/5 (2005): 419–25; Michael Klare and Daniel Volman, "America, China and the Scramble for Africa's Oil," *Review of African Political Economy*, no. 108 (2006): 297–309; Denis M. Tull, "China's Engagement in Africa: Scope, Significance and Consequences," *Journal of Modern African Studies* 44, 3 (2006): 459–79; Ian Taylor, *China and Africa: Engagement and Compromise* (London: Routledge, 2006); Chris Alden, *China in Africa* (London: Zed, 2007); Daniel Large, "Beyond 'Dragon in the Bush': The Study of China–Africa Relations," *African Affairs* 107, no. 426 (2008): 45–61.

3. For recent work on Afro-Asianism, which has been unusually, if not entirely, American-focused, see, for example, Vijay Prashad, *Everybody Was Kung-Fu Fighting: Afro-Asian Connections and the Myth of Cultural Purity* (Boston: Beacon Press, 2001); Robin D. G. Kelley, *Freedom Dreams: The Black Radical Imagination* (Boston: Beacon Press, 2002), chapter 3; Andrew F. Jones and Nikhil Pal Singh, eds., *The Afro-Asian Century*, special issue of *Positions* 11, no. 1 (2003); Bill V. Mullen, *Afro-Orientalism* (Minneapolis: University of Minnesota Press, 2004); Heike Raphael-Hernandez and Shannon Steen, eds., *Afro-Asian Encounters: Culture, History, Politics* (New York: New York University

Press, 2006); Vijay Prashad, *The Darker Nations: A People's History of the Third World* (New York: New Press, 2007); Fred Ho and Bill V. Mullen, eds., *Afro Asia: Revolutionary Political and Cultural Connections between African Americans and Asian Americans* (Durham: Duke University Press, 2008). On the fiftieth anniversary of the Bandung meeting, see R. M. Marty M. Natalegawa, ed., *Asia, Africa, Africa, Asia: Bandung, towards the First Century* (Jakarta: Department of Foreign Affairs, Republic of Indonesia, 2005); John Mackie, *Bandung 1955: Non-alignment and Afro-Asian Solidarity* (Singapore: Editions Didier Millet, 2005). For the NAASP, which South Africa, a country that did not officially participate in the original Bandung meeting, has taken a lead in overseeing, consult: <http://www.naasp.gov.za/index.html>.

4. Benedict Anderson, *Imagined Communities: Reflections on the Origin and Spread of Nationalism* (London: Verso, 1983); John D. Kelly and Martha Kaplan, *Represented Communities: Fiji and World Decolonization* (Chicago: University of Chicago Press, 2001), 22, 23.

5. On these disjunctures, see Arif Dirlik, *The Postcolonial Aura: Third World Criticism in the Age of Global Capitalism* (Boulder: Westview Press, 1997); David Scott, *Refashioning Futures: Criticism after Postcoloniality* (Princeton: Princeton University Press, 1999); Ania Loomba, et. al., eds., *Postcolonial Studies and Beyond* (Durham: Duke University Press, 2005). On generalized assertions about the postcolony, see Achille Mbembe, *On the Postcolony* (Berkeley: University of California Press, 2001).

6. On modern decolonization and its variability, see, for example, Prosser Gifford and William Roger Louis, eds., *The Transfer of Power in Africa: Decolonization, 1940–1960* (New Haven: Yale University Press, 1982); Prosser Gifford and William Roger Louis, eds., *Decolonization and African Independence: The Transfers of Power, 1960–1980* (New Haven: Yale University Press, 1988); John Darwin, *Britain and Decolonisation: The Retreat from Empire in the Post-war World* (Basingstoke: Macmillan, 1988); Frederick Cooper, *Decolonization and African Society: The Labor Question in French and British Africa* (Cambridge: Cambridge University Press, 1996); M. E. Chamberlain, *Decolonization: The Fall of the European Empires* (Oxford: Blackwell, 1999); John Springhall, *Decolonization Since 1945: The Collapse of European Overseas Empires* (New York: Palgrave, 2001); James D. Le Sueur, ed., *The Decolonization Reader* (New York: Routledge, 2003); Prasenjit Duara, ed., *Decolonization: Perspectives from Now and Then* (New York: Routledge, 2004); Raymond F. Betts, *Decolonization* (New York: Routledge, 2004); Hendrik Spruyt, *Ending Empire: Contested Sovereignty and Territorial Partition* (Ithaca: Cornell University Press, 2005); David Luis-Brown, *Waves of Decolonization: Discourses on Race and Hemispheric Citizenship in Cuba, Mexico and the United States*

(Durham: Duke University Press, 2008); Frederick Cooper, "Possibility and Constraint: African Independence in Historical Perspective," *Journal of African History* 49, no. 2 (2008): 167–96. For various popular and academic studies of "empire" and its reproduction, see, in addition to works previously cited, Michael W. Doyle, *Empires* (Ithaca: Cornell University Press, 1986); Michael Hardt and Antonio Negri, *Empire* (Cambridge: Harvard University Press, 2000); Niall Ferguson, *Empire: The Rise and Demise of the British World Order and the Lessons for Global Power* (New York: Basic Books, 2003); Noam Chomsky, *Hegemony or Survival: America's Quest for Global Dominance* (Boston: Metropolitan Books, 2003); Chalmers Johnson, *The Sorrows of Empire: Militarism, Secrecy, and the End of the Republic* (Boston: Metropolitan Books, 2004); Rashid Khalidi, *Resurrecting Empire: Western Footprints and America's Perilous Path in the Middle East* (Boston: Beacon Press, 2004); Frederick Cooper, "Empire Multiplied," *Comparative Studies in Society and History* 46, no. 2 (2004): 247–72; Frederick Cooper, *Colonialism in Question: Theory, Knowledge, History* (Berkeley: University of California Press, 2005), especially chapter 6.

7. For recent critiques of development teleologies, see, for example, James Ferguson, *The Anti-Politics Machine: "Development," Depoliticization, and Bureaucratic Power in Lesotho* (Cambridge: Cambridge University Press, 1990); James Ferguson, *Expectations of Modernity: Myths and Meanings of Urban Life on the Zambian Copperbelt* (Berkeley: University of California Press, 1999); Arturo Escobar, *Encountering Development: The Making and Unmaking of the Third World* (Princeton: Princeton University Press, 1995); Akhil Gupta, *Postcolonial Developments: Agriculture in the Making of Modern India* (Durham: Duke University Press, 1998).

8. On the challenges of nationalism, see, variously, Partha Chatterjee, *Nationalist Thought and the Colonial World: A Derivative Discourse?* (London: Zed, 1986); Partha Chatterjee, *The Nation and Its Fragments: Colonial and Postcolonial Histories* (Princeton: Princeton University Press, 1993); Jean Marie Allman, *The Quills of the Porcupine: Asante Nationalism in an Emergent Ghana* (Madison: University of Wisconsin Press, 1993); Prasenjit Duara, *Rescuing History from the Nation: Questioning Narratives of Modern China* (Chicago: University of Chicago Press, 1995); B. A. Ogot and W. R. Ochieng, eds., *Decolonization and Independence in Kenya, 1940-93* (Athens: Ohio University Press, 1995); Geoff Eley, ed., *Becoming National: A Reader* (New York: Oxford University Press, 1996); Susan Geiger, *TANU Women: Gender and Culture in the Making of Tanganyikan Nationalism, 1955-1965* (Portsmouth, NH: Heinemann, 1997); E. S. Atieno Odhiambo and John Lonsdale, eds., *Mau Mau and Nationhood: Arms, Authority, and Narration* (Athens: Ohio University Press, 2003); Gregory H. Maddox and James L. Giblin, eds., *In Search of a Nation: Histories of Authority*

and Dissidence in Tanzania (Athens: Ohio University Press, 2005); Elizabeth Schmidt, *Mobilizing the Masses: Gender, Ethnicity, and Class in the Nationalist Movement in Guinea, 1939–1958* (Portsmouth, NH: Heinemann, 2005); Elizabeth Schmidt, *Cold War and Decolonization in Guinea, 1946–1958* (Athens: Ohio University Press, 2007). On the postcolonial challenges of nationalism and historiography, see Terence Ranger, "Nationalist Historiography, Patriotic History and the History of the Nation: The Struggle over the Past in Zimbabwe," *Journal of Southern African Studies,* 30, 2 (2004): 215–34.

9. On settler colonialism and its legacies, see Caroline Elkins and Susan Pedersen, eds., *Settler Colonialism in the Twentieth Century: Projects, Practices, Legacies* (New York: Routledge, 2005). On the intersection between decolonization and the cold war, see Robert J. McMahon, *Colonialism and the Cold War: The United States and the Struggle for Indonesian Independence, 1945–1949* (Ithaca: Cornell University Press, 1981); Matthew Connelly, *A Diplomatic Revolution: Algeria's Fight for Independence and the Origins of the Post–Cold War Era* (Oxford: Oxford University Press, 2002); Todd Shepard, *The Invention of Decolonization: The Algerian War and the Remaking of France* (Ithaca: Cornell University Press, 2006); Odd Arne Westad, *The Global Cold War: Third World Interventions and the Making of Our Times* (Cambridge: Cambridge University Press, 2005); Gary Baines and Peter Vale, eds., *Beyond the Border War: New Perspectives on Southern Africa's Late–Cold War Conflicts* (Pretoria: UNISA Press, 2008).

10. On critiques of the expression "postcolonial" and its use, see Ella Shohat, "Notes on the Postcolonial," *Social Text,* nos. 31/32 (1992): 99–113; Anne McClintock, "The Angel of Progress: Pitfalls of the Term 'Postcolonialism,'" *Social Text,* nos. 31/32 (1992): 84–98; Arif Dirlik, "The Postcolonial Aura: Third World Criticism in the Age of Global Capitalism," *Critical Inquiry* 20, no. 2 (1994): 328–56; Stuart Hall, "When was 'the Postcolonial'? Thinking at the Limit," in *The Post-Colonial Question: Common Skies, Divided Horizons,* ed. Iain Chambers and Lidia Curti (New York: Routledge, 1996): 242–60; Scott, *Refashioning Futures.* For an attempt at bridging an existing divide between imperial history and postcolonial studies, see Dane Kennedy, "Imperial History and Post-Colonial Theory," *Journal of Imperial and Commonwealth History* 24, no. 3 (1996): 345–63.

11. Kwame Nkrumah, *Neo-colonialism: The Last Stage of Imperialism* (New York: International Publishers, 1965); Kwame Nkrumah, *Consciencism: Philosophy and the Ideology for Decolonization* (New York: Monthly Review Press, 1970); Julius K. Nyerere, *Ujamaa: Essays on Socialism* (Oxford: Oxford University Press, 1968); Jawaharlal Nehru, *The Discovery of India* (New York: Penguin, 2004).

12. David Scott, *Conscripts of Modernity: The Tragedy of Colonial Enlightenment* (Durham: Duke University Press, 2004), 8.

13. Cooper's critique is directed primarily toward Mahmood Mamdani, *Citizen and Subject: Contemporary Africa and the Legacy of Late Colonialism* (Princeton: Princeton University Press, 1996). See Cooper, *Colonialism in Question*, ch. 1.

14. It should be noted that the First Congress as such was held in 1919, with the 1900 conference serving as a key precursor. See P. Olisanwuche Esedebe, *Pan-Africanism: The Idea and Movement, 1776–1991* (Washington, DC: Howard University Press, 1994). On the Universal Races Congress, see, for example, Universal Races Congress, *Record of the Proceedings of the First Universal Races Congress, Held at the University of London, July 26–29, 1911* (London: P. S. King and Son, 1911); Paul Rich, "'The Baptism of a New Era': The 1911 Universal Races Congress and the Liberal Ideology of Race," *Ethnic and Racial Studies*, 7, no. 4 (1984): 534–50; Susan D. Pennybacker, "The Universal Races Congress, London Political Culture, and Imperial Dissent, 1900–1939," *Radical History Review*, 92 (Spring 2005): 103–17; Mansour Bonakdarian, "Negotiating Universal Values and Cultural and National Parameters at the First Universal Races Congress," *Radical History Review*, 92 (2005): 118–32. On the League Against Imperialism, see, for example, Robert J. C. Young, *Postcolonialism: An Historical Introduction* (Oxford: Blackwell, 2001), 176–77; Vijay Prashad, *The Darker Nations* (New York: New Press, 2007), ch. 2. On Pan-Asianism—which, it must be noted, also contributed to Japan's imperial ambitions—see Prasenjit Duara, "The Discourse of Civilization and Pan-Asianism," *Journal of World History*, 12, no. 1 (2001): 99–130; Sven Saaler and J. Victor Koschmann, eds., *Pan-Asianism in Modern Japanese History: Colonialism, Regionalism and Borders* (London: Routledge, 2007); Cemil Aydin, *The Politics of Anti-Westernism in Asia: Visions of World Order in Pan-Islamic and Pan-Asian Thought* (New York: Columbia University Press, 2007). For a recent study of the "global color line," see Marilyn Lake and Henry Reynolds, *Drawing the Global Colour Line: White Men's Countries and the International Challenge of Racial Equality* (Cambridge: Cambridge University Press, 2008).

15. For past and present examples of this growing historiography, see Joseph E. Harris, *The African Presence in Asia: Consequences of the East African Slave Trade* (Evanston: Northwestern University Press, 1971); K. N. Chaudhuri, *Trade and Civilization in the Indian Ocean: An Economic History from the Rise of Islam to 1750* (Cambridge: Cambridge University Press, 1985); Sugata Bose, *A Hundred Horizons: The Indian Ocean in the Age of Global Empire* (Cambridge: Harvard University Press, 2006); Thomas R. Metcalf, *Imperial Connections: India in the Indian Ocean Arena, 1860-1920* (Berkeley: University of California Press, 2007).

16. Richard Wright, *The Color Curtain: A Report on the Bandung Conference* (New York: World Publishing Company, 1956).

17. Turkey and China also had imperial legacies, if not as recent as Japan's.

18. A number of studies on the conference exist in the fields of international relations, Southeast Asian studies, and diplomatic history. For a selection, see George McTurnan Kahin, *The African–Asian Conference: Bandung, Indonesia, April 1955* (Ithaca: Cornell University Press, 1956); A. Appadorai, *The Bandung Conference* (New Delhi: Indian Council of World Affairs, 1955); Carlos P. Romulo, *The Meaning of Bandung* (Chapel Hill: University of North Carolina Press, 1956); David Kimche, *The Afro-Asian Movement: Ideology and Foreign Policy of the Third World* (New York: Halstead Press, 1973); A. W. Singham and Tran Van Dinh, eds., *From Bandung to Colombo* (New York: Third Press Review, 1976); Robert A. Mortimer, *The Third World Coalition in International Politics* (New York: Praeger, 1980); Roeslan Abdulgani, *The Bandung Connection: The Asia–Africa Conference in Bandung in 1955*, trans. Molly Bondar (Singapore: Gunung Agung, 1981); Prashad, *The Darker Nations*, ch. 3.

19. The British Central African Federation—consisting of Northern Rhodesia (Zambia), Southern Rhodesia (Zimbabwe), and Nyasaland (Malawi)—did not send a delegation.

20. Prashad, *The Darker Nations*, 34, 35.

21. For speeches, see Asian–African Conference, *Asia–Africa Speaks from Bandung* (Jakarta: Ministry of Foreign Affairs, Republic of Indonesia, 1955).

22. Westad, *The Global Cold War*.

23. Asian–African Conference, *Asia–Africa Speaks from Bandung*, 146, 147, 150, 151.

24. Prashad, *The Darker Nations*, 45, 46.

25. On the 1952 origins of the expression "Third World," see ibid., 10, 11.

26. On the perspective of the Eisenhower administration, see Matthew Jones, "A 'Segregated' Asia? Race, the Bandung Conference, and Pan-Asianist Fears in American Thought and Policy, 1954–1955," *Diplomatic History*, 29, 5 (2005): 841–68; Jason Parker, "Cold War II: The Eisenhower Administration, the Bandung Conference, and the Reperiodization of the Postwar Era," *Diplomatic History*, 30, 5 (2006): 867–92. For another view of the Bandung moment from the viewpoint of African American activists, see Penny M. Von Eschen, *Race against Empire: Black Americans and Anticolonialism, 1937–1957* (Ithaca: Cornell University Press, 1997), ch. 8.

27. Prashad, *The Darker Nations*, 46, 47.

28. On the history of nonalignment, see, for example, Lawrence W. Martin, ed., *Neutralism and Nonalignment: The New States in World Affairs* (New York: Praeger, 1962); Cecil V. Crabb Jr., *The Elephants and the Grass: A Study of*

Nonalignment (New York: Praeger, 1965); G. H. Jansen, *Nonalignment and the Afro-Asian States* (New York: Praeger, 1966); J. W. Burton, ed., *Nonalignment* (London: Andre Deutsch, 1966); K. P. Misra, ed., *Non-Alignment Frontiers and Dynamics* (New Delhi: Vikas Publishing, 1982); A. W. Singham and Shirley Hune, *Non-Alignment in an Age of Alignments* (London: Zed, 1986); M. S. Rajan, V. S. Mani, and C. S. R. Murthy, eds., *The Nonaligned and the United Nations* (New Delhi: South Asian Publishers, 1987); Roy Allison, *The Soviet Union and the Strategy of Non-Alignment in the Third World* (Cambridge: Cambridge University Press, 1988).

29. Amin as cited in Scott, *Refashioning Futures*, 144. See also Samir Amin, *Re-reading the Postwar Period: An Intellectual Itinerary* (New York: Monthly Review Press, 1994).

30. Frederick Cooper, *Africa Since 1940: The Past of the Present* (Cambridge: Cambridge University Press, 2002).

31. Frantz Fanon, *The Wretched of the Earth*, trans. Constance Farrington (New York: Grove Press, 1963).

32. Scott, *Refashioning Futures*.

33. Kelly and Kaplan, *Represented Communities*, 5.

34. Duara, ed., *Decolonization*, 1.

35. Stephen Ellis, "Writing Histories of Contemporary Africa," *Journal of African History*, 43, no. 1 (2002): 1–26.

36. Gilbert Joseph, "What We Know and Should Know: Bringing Latin America More Meaningfully into Cold War Studies," in *In from the Cold: Latin America's New Encounter with the Cold War*, ed. Gilbert M. Joseph and Daniela Spenser (Durham: Duke University Press, 2008), 7.

37. For world-systems theory and its variants, see, for example, Andre Gunder Frank, *Crisis in the World Economy* (London: Heinemann, 1980); Giovanni Arrighi, *Chaos and Governance in the Modern World System* (Minneapolis: University of Minnesota Press, 1999); Immanuel Wallerstein, *World-Systems Analysis: An Introduction* (Durham: Duke University Press, 2004). An important critique is Frederick Cooper, et. al., *Confronting Historical Paradigms: Peasants, Labor, and the Capitalist World System in Africa and Latin America* (Madison: University of Wisconsin Press, 1993).

38. On countermodernities, see Paul Gilroy, *The Black Atlantic: Modernity and Double Consciousness* (Cambridge: Harvard University Press, 1993). On alternative modernities, see Dilip Parameshwar Gaonkar, ed., *Alternative Modernities* (Durham: Duke University Press, 2001); On decoloniality, see Walter D. Mignolo, *Local Histories/Global Designs: Essays on the Coloniality of Power, Subaltern Knowledges, and Border Thinking* (Princeton: Princeton University Press, 2000); Walter D. Mignolo, ed., *Coloniality of Power and*

De-colonial Thinking, special issue of *Cultural Studies*, 21, nos. 2–3 (2007). On "provincializing" Europe, see Dipesh Chakrabarty, *Provincializing Europe: Postcolonial Thought and Historical Difference* (Princeton: Princeton University Press, 2000).

39. In addition to the work of Bill Mullen and Robin Kelley cited in fn 3, see Cynthia A. Young, *Soul Power: Culture, Radicalism, and the Making of a U.S. Third World Left* (Durham: Duke University Press, 2006); Besenia Rodriguez, "'Long Live Third World Unity! Long Live Internationalism!': Huey P. Newton's Revolutionary Intercommunalism," *Souls: A Critical Journal of Black Politics, Culture and Society*, 8, no. 3 (2006): 119–41; Judy Tzu-Chun Wu, "Journeys for Peace and Liberation: Third World Internationalism and Radical Orientalism during the U.S. War in Vietnam," *Pacific Historical Review*, 76, no. 4 (2007): 575–84.

40. For more recent studies in addition to those mentioned above, see Patricia Risso, *Merchants and Faith: Muslim Commerce and Culture in the Indian Ocean* (Boulder: Westview Press, 1995); Shihan De S. Jayasuriya and Richard Pankhurst, eds., *The African Diaspora in the Indian Ocean* (Trenton: Africa World Press, 2003); Edward Alpers, Gwyn Campbell, and Michael Salman, eds, *Slavery and Resistance in Africa and Asia* (New York: Routledge, 2005); Eng-seng Ho, *The Graves of Tarim: Genealogy and Mobility across the Indian Ocean* (Berkeley: University of California Press, 2006); Edward Alpers, Gwyn Campbell, and Michael Salman, eds., *Resisting Bondage in Indian Ocean Africa and Asia* (New York: Routledge, 2007); Jeremy Prestholdt, *Domesticating the World: African Consumerism and the Genealogies of Globalization* (Berkeley: University of California Press, 2008). On the Black Atlantic, see, inter alia, John K. Thornton, *Africa and Africans in the Making of the Atlantic World, 1400–1680* (Cambridge: Cambridge University Press, 1992); Gilroy, *The Black Atlantic*; Brent Hayes Edwards, *The Practice of Diaspora: Literature, Translation, and the Rise of Black Internationalism* (Cambridge: Harvard University Press, 2003); Christopher L. Miller, *The French Atlantic Triangle: Literature and Culture of the Slave Trade* (Durham: Duke University Press, 2008).

41. See, for example, Hannah Arendt, *The Origins of Totalitarianism* (New York: Harcourt Brace, 1951); Aimé Césaire, *Discourse on Colonialism* (New York: Monthly Review Press, 2000 [1953]); Edward W. Said, *Culture and Imperialism* (New York: Vintage, 1993); Nicholas B. Dirks, ed., *Colonialism and Culture* (Ann Arbor: University of Michigan Press, 1992); Frederick Cooper and Ann Laura Stoler, eds., *Tensions of Empire: Colonial Cultures in a Bourgeois World* (Berkeley: University of California Press, 1997); Catherine Hall, ed., *Cultures of Empire: Colonizers in Britain and the Empire in the Nineteenth and Twentieth Centuries* (New York: Routledge, 2000); Antoinette Burton, ed., *After the*

Imperial Turn: Thinking with and through the Nation (Durham: Duke University Press, 2003); Kathleen Wilson, ed., *A New Imperial History: Culture, Identity and Modernity in Britain and the Empire, 1660–1840* (New York: Cambridge University Press, 2004).

42. For critiques of continental thinking, see V. Y. Mudimbe, *The Invention of Africa: Gnosis, Philosophy and the Order of Knowledge* (Bloomington: Indiana University Press, 1988); Walter D. Mignolo, *The Idea of Latin America* (London: Blackwell, 2005); Martin W. Lewis and Kären E. Wigen, *The Myth of Continents: A Critique of Metageography* (Berkeley: University of California Press, 1997). For texts that have engaged with the specific limitations of area studies, see Dirlik, *The Postcolonial Aura*; Arif Dirlik, Vinay Bahl, and Peter Gran, eds., *History after the Three Worlds: Post-Eurocentric Historiographies* (New York: Rowman and Littlefield, 2000); Masao Miyoshi, ed., *Learning Places: The Afterlives of Area Studies* (Durham: Duke University Press, 2002).

43. The trend of labeling the US as an imperial power is not entirely new, an earlier, influential view being William Appleman Williams, *Empire as a Way of Life* (Oxford: Oxford University Press, 1980); William Appleman Williams, *The Tragedy of American Diplomacy* (New York: Norton, 1988 [1959]). Recent studies that explore the deep history of this trajectory in the American case include Greg Grandin, *Empire's Workshop: Latin America, the United States, and the Rise of the New Imperialism* (New York: Metropolitan Books, 2006); Michael Adas, *Dominance by Design: Technological Imperatives and America's Civilizing Mission* (Cambridge: Harvard University Press, 2006); George C. Herring, *From Colony to Superpower: US Foreign Relations Since 1776* (Oxford: Oxford University Press, 2008). For another critical view of the category of "empire," see Cooper, "Empire Multiplied."

44. Ferdinand Tönnies, *Community and Civil Society*, ed. Jose Harris, trans. Jose Harris and Margaret Hollis (Cambridge: Cambridge University Press, 2001).

45. On the former, see Manu Goswami, "From *Swadeshi* to *Swaraj*: Nation, Economy, Territory in Colonial South Asia, 1870 to 1907," *Comparative Studies in Society and History,* 40, no. 4 (1998): 609–36; Manu Goswami, "Rethinking the Modular Nation Form: Toward a Sociohistorical Conception of Nationalism," *Comparative Studies in Society and History,* 44, no. 4 (2002): 770–99; Manu Goswami, *Producing India: From Colonial Economy to National Space* (Chicago: University of Chicago Press, 2004). On the nation-state system and decolonization, see Kelly and Kaplan, *Represented Communities*. For studies that followed Anderson, at times critiquing him, see Chatterjee, *Nationalist Thought and the Colonial World*; Chatterjee, *The Nation and Its Fragments*, especially chapter 1; E. J. Hobsbawm, *Nations and Nationalism since 1780: Programme, Myth, Reality*

(Cambridge: Cambridge University Press, 1992); Sara Castro-Klarén and John Charles Chasteen, eds., *Beyond Imagined Communities: Reading and Writing the Nation in Nineteenth-Century Latin America* (Baltimore: Johns Hopkins University Press, 2003).

46. Chakrabarty, *Provincializing Europe*, 149.

47. Cooper, *Colonialism in Question*, 20, 31, 140. See also Frederick Cooper, "Conflict and Connection: Rethinking Colonial African History," *American Historical Review*, 99, no. 5 (1994): 1516–45.

48. Arjun Appadurai, *Modernity at Large: Cultural Dimensions of Globalization* (Minneapolis: University of Minnesota Press, 1996), 39.

49. Hardt and Negri, *Empire*, 107. It should be emphasized although a common ground is cited here, Cooper has been sharply critical of Chakrabarty and of Hardt and Negri. See Cooper "Empire Multiplied"; Cooper, *Colonialism in Question*, ch. 1.

50. David Held, "Democracy and Globalization," in *Re-imagining Political Community: Studies in Cosmopolitan Democracy*, eds. Daniele Archibugi, David Held, and Martin Köhler (Stanford: Stanford University Press, 1998), 21, 24.

51. For discussion, see Janna Thompson, "Community Identity and World Citizenship," in *Re-imagining Political Community*, 179–97.

52. Cooper, *Colonialism in Question*, 17, 18.

53. Victor Turner, *Dramas, Fields, and Metaphors: Symbolic Action in Human Society* (Ithaca: Cornell University Press, 1974), 201–03; Andrew Apter, *Beyond Words: Discourse and Critical Agency in Africa* (Chicago: University of Chicago Press, 2007). For a separate exploration of *communitas*, see Roberto Esposito, *Bíos: Biopolitics and Philosophy*, trans. Timothy Campbell (Minneapolis: University of Minnesota Press, 2008), especially the translator's introduction.

54. On these different forms, see Victor Turner, *The Ritual Process: Structure and Anti-structure* (Chicago: Aldine, 1969), 132.

55. Mahmood Mamdani, *Good Muslim, Bad Muslim: America, the Cold War, and the Roots of Terror* (New York: Pantheon, 2004).

Part 1

Framings

Concepts, Politics, History

1

The Legacies of Bandung

Decolonization and the Politics of Culture

Dipesh Chakrabarty

THE URGE TO decolonize, to be rid of the colonizer in every possible way, was internal to all anticolonial criticism after the end of
World War I. Postcolonial critics of our times, on the other hand, have
emphasized how the colonial situation produced forms of hybridity or
mimicry that necessarily escaped the Manichean logic of the colonial
encounter.[1] It is not only this intellectual shift that separates anticolonial and postcolonial criticism. The two genres have also been separated by the political geographies and histories of their origins. After
all, the demand for political and intellectual decolonization arose
mainly in the colonized countries among the intellectuals of anticolonial movements. Postcolonial writing and criticism, on the other
hand, was born in the West. They were influenced by anticolonial
criticism but their audiences were at the beginning in the West itself,
for these writings have been an essential part of the struggle to make
the liberal-capitalist (and, initially, mainly Anglo-American) Western democracies more democratic with respect to their immigrant,
minority, and indigenous—though there have been tensions between
these groups—populations. Race has thus figured as a category central to postcolonial criticism whereas its position in anticolonial

45

discourse varies. The question of race is crucial to the formulations of Fanon, Césaire, or C. L. R. James, for example, but it is not as central to how a Gandhi or a Tagore thought about colonial domination. If historically, then, anticolonialism has been on the wane since the 1960s and displaced by postcolonial discourse in the closing decades of the 20th century, it has been further pointed out by more-recent critics of postcolonial theory and writing that even the postcolonial moment is now behind us, its critical clamor having been drowned in turn by the mighty tide of globalization.[2]

This seemingly easy periodization of the 20th century—anticolonialism giving way to postcolonial criticism giving way to globalization—is unsettled if we look closely at discussions about decolonization that marked the 1950s and the 1960s. Ideas regarding decolonization were dominated by two concerns. One was development. The other I will call "dialogue." Many anticolonial thinkers considered colonialism as something of a broken promise. European rule, it was said, promised modernization but did not deliver on it. As Césaire said in his *Discourse on Colonialism* (1953):

> [I]t is the indigenous peoples of Africa and Asia who are demanding schools, and colonialist Europe which refuses them . . . it is the African who is asking for ports and roads, and colonialist Europe which is niggardly on this score . . . it is the colonized man who wants to move forward, and the colonizer who holds things back.[3]

This was the developmentalist side of decolonization whereby anticolonial thinkers came to accept different versions of modernization theory that in turn made the West into a model for everyone to follow. This today may very well seem dated but it has not lost its relevance. One consequence of this developmentalism was a cultural style of politics that I call *pedagogical*. In the pedagogical mode, the very performance of politics reenacted civilizational or cultural hierarchies: between nations, between classes, or between the leaders and the masses. Those lower down in the hierarchy were meant to learn from those higher up. Leaders, when they spoke in this mode, were like teachers. But there was also another side to decolonization that has received less scholarly attention. Anticolonial thinkers often devoted a great deal of time to the question of whether or how a global conversation of humanity could genuinely acknowledge cultural diversity without distributing such diversity over a hierarchical scale of civilization—that is to say, an urge toward cross-cultural dialogue without the baggage of imperialism. Let me call it the dialogical side of decolonization. Here, unlike on the pedagogical side, there was no one model to follow. Different thinkers took different positions, and it is the richness of their contradictions that speaks directly to the fundamental concerns of both postcolonial criticism and globalization theory. That indeed may be where the global movement toward decolonization left us a heritage useful for the world, even today.

In what follows, I track these two aspects of the language of decolonization, starting with the historic conference in Bandung, where some six hundred leaders and delegates of twenty-nine newly independent countries from Asia and Africa met between April 18 and 24, 1955, to exchange views of the world at a time when the cold war and a new United Nations regime were already important factors in international relations. (On the conference itself, see also the introduction to this volume by Christopher Lee.)[4] It may be timely to remind ourselves of a recent moment in human history when the idea of nation was something people aspired to and the idea of empire wielded absolutely no moral force. Today the opposite rules: the theme of empire has made a triumphant return in historiography whereas the nation-state has fallen out of favor. Historians of Niall Ferguson's ilk even seem to recommend a return to imperial arrangements in the interest of a decent global future for mankind.[5] For some critics from the Left too, empire, variously understood, has become a key operative term for understanding global relations of domination as they exist at present.[6] It may be salutary today to revisit a time when both the category *empire* and actual, historical European empires truly seem to have seen the sun set over them.

Dateline: Bandung, April 1955

In 1955 when Richard Wright, the noted African American writer then resident in Paris, decided to attend the Bandung Conference,

many of his European friends thought this would be an occasion simply for criticizing the West. Even Gunner Myrdal, in contributing the
foreword to the book that Wright wrote as a result of his experience
at Bandung, ended up penning an indictment of what happened in
Bandung: "His [Wright's] interest was focused on the two powerful
urges far beyond Left and Right which he found at work there: Religion and Race. . . . Asia and Africa thus carry the irrationalism of both
East and West."[7] Both Myrdal and Wright's Parisian friends appear to
have misjudged what decolonization was all about. It was not a simple
project of cultivating a sense of disengagement with the West. There
was no reverse racism at work in Bandung. If anything, the aspira-
tion for political and economic freedom that the Conference stood for
entailed a long and troubled conversation with an imagined Europe or
the West. "I was discovering," wrote Wright, "that this Asian elite was,
in many ways, more Western than the West, their Westernness consisting in their having been made to break with the past in a manner
that but few Westerners could possible do."[8] It was in fact the newsmen
from his own country that attended the conference who, Wright felt,
"had no philosophy of history with which to understand Bandung."[9]

I will shortly come to this question of the philosophy of history
that marked the discourse of decolonization. For now, let me simply
note the historical moment when the conference met. The Bandung
Conference was held at a time when currents of deep and widespread
sympathy with the newly independent nations—or with those struggling to be independent (such as Algeria, Tunisia, Morocco, Central
Africa, etc.)—met those of the cold war. Treaties, unsatisfactory to
the United States, had been signed in Vietnam, Laos, and Cambodia.
The French had lost in Dien Bien Phu and the Korean War had ended.
Some of the Asian nations had joined defense pacts with the United
States: Pakistan, Thailand, and the Philippines. Some others belonged
to the Socialist Bloc. Bandung was attempting to sustain a sense of
Asian-African affinity in the face of such disagreements. This was not
easy as there was pressure from the Western countries to influence
the course of the conversation at Bandung by excluding China, for
example. Nehru's correspondence with the United Nations makes it
obvious that sometimes he had to stand his ground on the question

of neutrality in the cold war. A letter he wrote to the Secretary General of the United Nation dated December 18, 1954, on the subject of Bandung, reads:

> We have no desire to create a bad impression about anything in the US and the UK. But the world is somewhat larger than the US and the UK and we have to take into account what impressions we create in the rest of the world. . . . For us to be told, therefore, that the US and the UK will not like the inclusion of China in the Afro-Asian Conference is not very helpful. In fact, it is somewhat irritating. There are many things that the US and the UK have done which we do not like at all.[10]

The leaders who got together in Bandung thus came from a divided world. They were not of the same mind on questions of international politics, nor did they have the same understanding of what constituted imperialism. They did not even necessarily like each other. The representative of the Philippines, Carlos Romulo, for example, found Nehru to be a "highly cultivated intellect" but full of "pedantry" (and one might add opposed—as a believer in nonalignment—to the Manila Pact of which the Philippines were a member). "His pronounced propensity to be dogmatic, impatient, irascible, and unyielding . . . alienated the goodwill of many delegates," writes Romulo. Nehru "typified" for him "the affectations of cultural superiority induced by a conscious identification with an ancient civilization which has come to be the hallmark of Indian representatives to international conferences. He also showed an anti-American complex, which is characteristic of Indian representations at international diplomatic meetings." India, Romulo judged, was "not so much anti-West as it is anti-American."[11]

The memoir of Dr. Roeslan Abdulgani, once Jakarta's ambassador to the United States and an organizer of the conference, reflects some of the competitive currents that characterized the relationship between the Indian and the Indonesian leadership and officials. "The cleverness of the Indian delegation," he writes, "lay in the fact that they had thoroughly mastered the English language, and had very much experience in negotiations with the British. . . . Some of them were even arrogant as for instance . . . Krishna Menon, and, at times, Prime Minister Nehru himself."[12] Nehru, in turn, had trouble trusting the Indonesians with the responsibility of organizing the conference. He wrote to B. F. H. B. Tyabji, the Indian Ambassador to Indonesia, on February 20, 1955: "I am rather anxious about this Asian-African Conference and, more especially, about the arrangements. I wonder if the people in Indonesia have any full realization of what this Conference is going to be. All the world's eyes will be turned upon it. . . . Because of all this, we cannot take the slightest risk of lack of adequate arrangements. . . . You have been pointing out that the Indonesians are sensitive. We should respect their sensitiveness. But we cannot afford to have anything messed up because they are sensitive. . . ."[13] His particular concern, it turns out, were the arrangements for bathrooms and lavatories. It is hard to know whether he was being merely anxious or expressing a peculiar Brahmanical obsession with ritual purity and cleanliness when he went on to say: "I have learnt that it is proposed to crowd numbers of people in single rooms. . . . your Joint Secretariat will not get much praise from anybody if delegates are herded up like cattle. . . . Above all, one fact should be remembered, and this is usually forgotten in Indonesia. This fact is an adequate provision for bathrooms and lavatories. People can do without drawing rooms, but they cannot do without bathrooms and lavatories."[14]

Apart from the lack of mutual trust and respect, the conference, so opposed to imperialism, had no operative definition of the term. This was so mainly because there were deep and irreconcilable differences among the nations represented. The Prime Minister of Ceylon (Sri Lanka), Sir John Kotelawala, caused some tension in the Political Committee of the conference—and shocked Nehru—when on the afternoon of Thursday, April 21, 1955, referring to the Eastern European countries he asked, "Are not these colonies as much as any of the colonial territories in Africa or Asia? . . . Should it not be our duty openly to declare opposition to Soviet colonialism as much as Western imperialism?"[15] The compromise prose drafted by the conference in trying to accommodate the spirit of Sir John's question clearly reveals the shallow intellectual unity on which the conference was based. Rather than refer directly to "the form of the colonialism of the Soviet Union," the Founding Committee eventually agreed on a statement that called for an end to "colonialism in all its manifestation."[16]

What then held the conference together? Appadorai, the Indian member of the joint secretariat set up for the conference and a member of the Indian Foreign Service, was right in saying that "[i]n the realm of ideas . . . not much that is significantly new can be found in the Bandung Declaration. Most of the points of the historical declaration are found in the United Nations Charter."[17] Bandung surely helped the newly independent states become parts of the UN system. But it brought into the imagination of that system a shared anti-imperial ethic. Whatever the meaning of the term *imperialism,* there was an absolute unanimity among the participants of the conference that they were all opposed to "it." From Nehru to Romulo, the message was clear. As Romulo put it in his statement to the conference: "The age of empire is being helped into oblivion by the aroused will and action of the people determined to be masters of their own fate." He was confident that "the old structure of Western empire will and must pass from the scene."[18] Many of the speakers at the conference inserted Bandung into a line of other international conferences held in the first half of the 20th century that signaled the spirit of anti-imperialist self-determination among the emergent new nations in Asia or elsewhere. Thus President Sukarno, in his welcoming speech made at the opening of the conference on April 18, referred to "the conference of the 'League Against Imperialism and Colonialism,' which was held in Brussels almost thirty years ago."[19] Writing soon after the conference Appadorai mentions "the first [ever] expression of an Asian sentiment" which he "traced to August 1926 when the Asian delegations to the non-official International Conference for Peace held at Bierville declared in a memorandum that Asia must have its rightful place in the consideration of world problems." The Asian Relations Conference in Delhi in March–April 1947, under the auspices of the Indian Council of World Affairs, was mentioned as yet another precedence.[20]

A pictorial album produced soon after the conference from the Netherlands on the theme nationalism and colonialism in Africa and Asia thus characterized the meeting at Bandung: "The end of Western supremacy has never been demonstrated more clearly."[21] Even the Chinese Premier Zhou Enlai's much anticipated and controversial participation in the conference succeeded since his speeches partook of this spirit of anti-imperialism. His message that China had no plans for dominating her neighbors and did not intend to spread her influence through the overseas Chinese community, "that the small nations of Asia had nothing to fear from their great neighbour, China," resonated with the spirit that held the conference together.[22] This was indeed a time when, whatever its meaning, any conscious project of imperialism had no takers.

The organizers went to some trouble to make sure that the anti-imperialism undergirding the conference was open to political ideologies on both sides of the cold war divide. Even the opening day of the conference was chosen with American sensitivity in mind. The planning conference at Bogor had decided that the conference would be held in the last week of April in 1955. In the meanwhile, says Abdulgani, news was received from the US indicating that the Americans feared "that Western colonialism would be subjected to attack [at Bandung] and would be the main target. Especially so with the attendance of the People's Republic of China." Abdulgani writes:

> I and my staff thought and puzzled for a long time about how to get rid of, or how to neutralize American fears. Suddenly, we recalled the date of 18 April in the history of the American Revolution; exactly what it was, we didn't remember. . . . I telephoned American Ambassador Hugh Cummings [and] . . . asked him for data about the American Revolution around the month of April. On the following day, Ambassador Cummings sent several books of reference. . . . It turned out that . . . [o]n 18 April 1775 . . . amidst the upheaval of the American Revolution for independence against British colonialism, a young patriot named Paul Revere rode at midnight from Boston harbour ro the town of Concord, arousing the spirit of opposition to British troops, who were landing at that time. . . . It was clear that 18 April 1775 was an historic day for the American nation in their struggle against colonialism. Why should we not simply link these two events, the date of which was the same, the spirit of which was the same, only the years were different?[23]

Indeed, President Sukarno made this American connection on the very first day of the conference. Armed with the information provided by the American Embassy and his own staff, he said: "The battle against colonialism has been a long one, and do you know that today is a famous anniversary of that battle? On April 18th, 1775, Paul Revere rode at midnight through the New England countryside warning of the approach of the British troops and the opening of the American war of Independence, the first successful anti-colonial war in history."[24]

The Pedagogical Style of Developmental Politics

The discourse and politics of decolonization in the nations that met in Bandung often displayed an uncritical emphasis on modernization. Sustaining this attitude was a clear and conscious desire to "catch up" with the West. As Nehru would often say in the 1950s, "What Europe did in a hundred or a hundred and fifty years, we must do in ten or fifteen years." Or as is reflected in the very title of a 1971 biography of Tanzanian leader Julius Nyerere: *We Must Run while They Walk.*[25] The accent on modernization made the figure of the engineer one of the most eroticized figures of the postcolonial developmentalist imagination. Even the cursory prose of a stray remark by Richard Wright to a friend in Indonesia catches this precedence of the engineer over the poet or the prophet in the very imagination of decolonization. "Indonesia has taken power away from the Dutch," Wright said, "but she does not know how to use it." This, he thought, "need not be a Right or Left issue," but wondered: "Where is the *engineer* who can build a project out of eighty million human lives, a project that can nourish them, sustain them, and yet have their voluntary loyalty?"[26]

This emphasis on development as a catching-up-with-the-West produced a particular split that marked both the relationship between elite nations and their subaltern counterparts as well as that between elites and subalterns within national boundaries. Just as the emergent nations demanded *political* equality with the Euro-American nations while wanting to catch up with them on the economic front, similarly their leaders thought of their peasants and workers simultaneously as people who were *already* full citizens—in that they had the associated rights—but also as people who were not quite full citizens in that they needed to be educated in the habits and manners of citizens.

This produced a style of politics on the part of the leaders that could only be called *pedagogical*. From Nasser and Nyerere to Sukarno and Nehru, decolonization produced a crop of leaders who saw themselves, fundamentally, as teachers to their nations.

There are two remarkably similar incidents in Nehru's and Nyerere's lives that illustrate this pedagogical style of leadership. Both incidents involve them speaking to their countrymen on the subject of singing the national anthem. The similarities are striking. Here is Nehru speaking at a public meeting in Dibrugarh on August 29, 1955. Mark the teacherly voice and the disciplinary insistence on military bodily postures when singing the national anthem. Nehru could have been speaking at a school assembly:

> Now we shall have the national anthem. Please listen carefully to what I have to say. One, nobody should start singing until the word is given. I have found that in Dibrugarh people start singing even while I am speaking. It is all wrong, you must start only when I say so, not until then. Two, *Jana gana mana* is our national anthem. So it must be sung in loud and clear voices, with eyes open. You must stand erect like soldiers and sing, not hum it under our breath. Thirdly, you must remember that *Jana gana mana* . . . has been selected to be our national anthem. . . . It is given great honour abroad. So . . . everybody must stand up when the national anthem is sung because it is the voice of the nation, of *Bharat Mata*. We must stand erect like soldiers and not shuffle around while it is being sung. I would like to tell you that everyone must learn to sing the national anthem. When the girls sing just now all of you must join in. It does not matter if you do not know the words. The girls will sing one line at a time and you will repeat it. Have you understood? All right, stand up, everybody. Let us start.[27]

Compare this with what Nyerere said at a mass rally on July 7, 1963, explaining the vice of "pomposity" in the new nation. It is not difficult to hear the same teacherly voice of the leader trying to instill in his audience the proper habits of citizenship: "When we became independent," Nyerere said, "we started by singing the national anthem every time the Prime Minister arrived anywhere, even at supposedly informal dinner parties."

This, already, was rather unnecessary; but, as a little over-enthusiasm was understandable just at first. I had hoped that in time we should learn to reserve the anthem for the really ceremonial functions at which its playing is appropriate. It seems I was too hopeful; for now we sing it whenever a Minister, a Parliamentary Secretary, a regional Commissioner or an Area Commissioner arrives at a gathering of any kind anywhere in Tanganyika! Nothing could be more disrespectful to our national anthem than to treat it as a popular song-hit, or a "signature-tune" to be "plugged" the moment any member of the Government appears on the scene. . . . It is customary in every country in the world for visiting foreigners, as well as the local public, to show their respect by standing to attention while the anthem is being played. But it is not customary in other countries to play or sing their national anthem without any warning, just because some official of the government happens to have dropped in unexpectedly at a small gathering, or landed at an airstrip on a visit to his mother-in-law![28]

Even as these two excerpts from Nehru's and Nyerere's speeches confirm, the pedagogical aspect of their politics had to do with their desire to see their respective nations take their pride of place in the global order of nations. This is why there is the reference to "abroad" or "every country in the world" in these speeches. The "voice" of Bharatmata (Mother India) and the "inter-national" world had its audience. Behind the idea of pedagogical politics was the emergent and territorial nation-state putting development ahead of diversity.

Deterritorialization and the Displacement of Pedagogical Politics

If decolonization was thus generally predicated on a worldwide urge on the part of the formerly colonized countries to catch up with Europe (or more broadly the West), one could say that this was a discourse that saw an imaginary Europe as the major agentive force in the world. Decolonization thus may be thought of as the last phase in the history of what Martin Heidegger once called "the Europeanization" of the earth.[29] I say "the last phase" since all this was to change from the late 1960s on, and the pace of change would hasten in the decades to follow.

Some of these changes may be easily tracked from the history of "identity politics" in India since the 1980s and particularly in the last decade. The pedagogical politics of the likes of Nehru, Nasser, or Nyerere, were firmly based on the territorial idea of the nation-state and on the assumption that names and identities involved in politics had clear and discernible historical-cultural references. Words such as *Muslim, Scheduled caste, tribal* were backed up in India of the British period or in the early years of Independence by academic studies in disciplines such as history and anthropology. It could be said, in other words, that the politics favored by decolonization was modernist in its understanding of representation.[30] This entire assumption is now under challenge. Politics of being *dalit* (ex-untouchable or low caste) or "tribal" no longer seek sanction from the realist prose of academic social sciences. Instead, certain deterritorialized, global imaginations of identity have come to be operative, challenging the connections once made between signs and their references.[31]

Two handy examples come from recent Indian debates around the ways leaders of the so-called Dalitbahujan (a coalition of ex-untouchable and low caste) groups and indigenous peoples in India have sought in the last two decades to globalize the politics of caste-oppression and indigeneity. A significant debate on caste broke in the Indian press months before the UN-sponsored "World Conference Against Racism, Racial Discrimination, Xenophobia and Related Intolerance" was held in Durban on August 31, to September 2, 2001. Many of the leaders of the Dalitbahujan groups wanted to use this forum to draw global attention to their problems by declaring that caste-oppression was no different from the oppression related to race; that caste, in effect, was the same as race. Andre Beteille, a respected and liberal anthropologist who sat on the preparatory committee the government of India had set up, resigned in protest arguing that this was "mischievous," and that all his life-long training in anthropology had taught him that race and caste were very different and unrelated phenomena. A storm of protest was raised by intellectuals sympathetic to the *dalit* cause, their arguments ranging from the proposition that a "conservative" thinker like Beteille could not appreciate the pragmatics of this globalizing strategy, to the idea that the *dalit* "experience" of caste-oppression was a better source of knowledge than academic "expertise" on the subject.[32]

Beteille has also been at the center of arguments related to indigeneity. Whereas tribal groups in India have increasingly sought the appellation "indigenous" in order to make use of the UN Charter on Indigenous Peoples' Right (which includes the right of self-definition), Beteille (and some other anthropologists) have raised academic objections, arguing that the category *indigenous,* although useful and right in the context of settler-colonial countries, is rendered problematic by facts specific and particular to Indian history. Intellectuals on the other side, however, have pointed out that the political and pragmatic benefits of globalizing these issues far outweigh considerations of historical accuracies. Beteille's positions in either case, as may be easily imagined, have not endeared him to intellectual supporters of *dalit* or indigenous politics. But even without taking sides, it could be said that whereas Beteille is looking for certain connections between identity tags—*indigenous, untouchables*—and the historical claims they implicitly make, his opponents are clearly engaged in developing global and deterritorialized forms of political imagination that precisely breach these connections between signs and their assumed historical/social referents. In other words, one may say that although Beteille still subscribes to a modernist view of representation, the *dalits* and the tribal leaders have found it to their advantage, in these particular cases, to base their quest for further democratization of Indian society politics on premises that are reminiscent of what globalization theorists have said about deterritorialization of identities.[33] Here, clearly, the very democratizing of politics in India has moved it away from the pedagogical model of politics that the Nehruvian vision of decolonization promoted even into the early 1960s. This is not to say that the Nehruvian vision has lost all relevance. But that vision was part of the Europeanization of the earth. The "global" that *dalit* or indigenous politics partake of today no longer conjures a monolithic Europe or the West as the most important agentive force in the world. Under conditions of globalization, the clash is often between certain norms of modernization or modernity—which took a Western model for granted—and the very global momentum of the forces of democratization. Political leaders are no longer looked upon as "engineers" of their societies.

Why all this has come about in the last few decades is for a future historian to determine. But clearly the theme of European imperialism died a global death about the same time as scholars date the beginnings of the contemporary forms of globalization: the 1970s.[34] Vietnam was perhaps the last war for "national liberation" that was seen as delivering a blow to a weak link in an imperial chain that was Western. Other long-term struggles—such as those of the Kurds, the Kashmiris, the Nagas, the Tibetans for self-determination that occurred in a "national" context—would never produce the depth of anticolonial and cross-cultural enthusiasm in the world that Vietnam did. The 1960s and later were also a period of some profoundly democratic changes in the West (some of which have since been reversed). Anticolonial discourse (Fanon, Gandhi, et al.) traveled back to the West at the same time as civil-liberties movements and antiwar demonstrations broke out, alongside movements of indigenous peoples and immigrant groups for cultural sovereignty and recognition. Racist policies on immigration were lifted or modified in countries such as the US and Australia in this period. Battles were joined against racism in the West in the name of multiculturalism (both official and nonofficial). Postcolonial theory emerges from this recirculation of decolonization texts within the West. It cannot be an insignificant fact that Homi Bhabha, Stuart Hall, and Isaac Julien, for instance, came together to read Fanon in England of the 1970s and 1980s in the context of a struggle against British racism.[35] This was also the period of the rise of poststructuralist and postmodern theories in the West, theories that were, in any case, opposed to the territorial imagination of the nation-state. It was as part of this process that debates began in Anglo-American universities about questioning the canonical texts that had represented the nation or the West, resulting in the emergence of fields such as postcolonial and cultural studies.[36]

The Dialogical Side of Decolonization

It is our contemporary interests in the circulation of humans, objects, and practices across and beyond the boundaries of the nation-state that makes this other side of decolonization—representing the thoughts of the colonized on conversation across differences—relevant to the concerns of both globalization and postcolonial theory. However, what was said by theorists of decolonization about "dialogue across difference" was often contradictory. But precisely because their debate was of necessity unfinished, it leaves us a rich body of ideas that speak to the concept of cosmopolitanism without seeking any overall mastery over the untamable diversity of human culture.

Long before academics began to talk about "global English," Bandung brought Richard Wright a premonition of the global future of this language that was once, as Gauri Viswanathan and others have shown, very much a part of the colonizing mission. "I felt while at Bandung," as Wright says,

> that the English language was about to undergo one of the most severe tests in its long and glorious history. Not only was English becoming the common, dominant tongue of the globe, but it was evident that soon there would be more people speaking English than there were people whose native tongue was English. . . . H.L. Mencken has traced the origins of many of our American words and phrases that went to modify English to an extent that we now regard our English tongue in America as the American language. What will happen when millions upon millions of new people in the tropics begin to speak English? Alien pressures and structures of thought and feeling will be brought to bear upon this mother tongue and we shall be hearing some strange and twisted expressions. . . . But this is all the good; a language is useless unless it can be used for the vital purposes of life, and to use a language in new situations is, inevitably, to change it.[37]

Clearly ahead of his time, Wright glimpsed a future that would be visible much later only to the generations that would come after Rushdie. Wright's was a vision of anticolonial cosmopolitanism. English would cease to be the master's language. Learning it would no longer be a matter of the colonized Caliban talking back to Prospero, the master. Instead, the vision was that as other languages gradually died into it, English would become plural from within so that it could become the new Babel of the world. The Nigerian writer Chinua Achebe would echo this vision in ten years after Wright articulated it: "Is it right that a man should abandon his mother tongue for someone else's? It looks like a dreadful betrayal and produces a guilty feeling. But for me there is no other choice. I have been given the [English] language and I intend to use it. . . . I felt that the English language will be able to carry the weight of my African experience. But it will have to be a new English, still in full communication with its ancestral home but altered to suit new African surroundings."[38]

Yet, delivering the Robb lectures—later published as *Decolonising the Mind: The Politics of Language in African Literature* (1986) at the University of Auckland in New Zealand some twenty years after these words were spoken—Ngũgĩ wa Thiongo, the Kenyan writer, adopted a position exactly the opposite of that spelled out by Wright and Achebe. An essay by the Nigerian writer Gabriel Okara in the Africanist journal *Transition* illustrated for Ngũgĩ the "lengths to which we were prepared to go in our mission of enriching foreign languages by injecting Senghorian 'black blood' into their rusty joints." Okara has written:

> [I]n order to capture the vivid images of African speech, I had to eschew the habit of expressing my thoughts first in English. It was difficult at first, but I had to learn. I had to study each jaw expression I used and to discover the probable situation in which it was used in order to bring out their nearest meaning in English. I found it a fascinating exercise.

Ngũgĩ disagreed. "Why," he asks, "should an African writer, or any writer, become so obsessed with taking from his mother-tongue to enrich other tongues? . . . What seemed to worry us more was this: after all this literary gymnastics of preying on our languages to add life and vigour to English and other foreign languages, would the result still be accepted as good English or good French?"[39] He for one experienced this as a "neocolonial situation" and went on to describe the book resulting from his lectures as his "farewell to English as a vehicle for any of [his] writing": "From now on it is Gikuyu and Kiswahili all the way."[40]

It is not my purpose to use the positions of Wright and Ngũgĩ to cancel each other out. I think they anticipate two familiar and legitimate responses to possibilities inherent in global conversation: globalization as liberation and globalization as subjugation. Globalization is no one homogeneous thing. It could indeed be both. Leopold Senghor on the other hand—of whose love of French, the reader will remember, Ngũgĩ was no fan—points us in directions that remind us that the ambiguities and the richness of the moment of decolonization were never exhausted by the antinomies set up here by what we have excerpted from Wright and Ngũgĩ. Senghor's thoughts, even in what he wrote on the (somewhat unpopular) topic of "assimilation" to French culture in 1945, have much to say to us about what it might mean to inflect our global conversation by a genuine appreciation of human diversity. Clearly, Senghor was not for nativist isolation. He wrote, for instance, "mathematics and the exact sciences . . . by definition have no frontiers and appeal to a faculty of reason which is found in all peoples." This, he thought, was true for even "History and Geography" which had "attained a universal value." But what about languages such as "Greek, Latin and French?" He writes: "I know the advantages of these languages because I was brought up on them." But "the teaching of the classical languages is not an end in itself. It is a tool for discovering human truths in oneself and for expressing them under their various aspects." There follows Senghor's argument for diversity in the humanities:

> [I]t would be good in African secondary schools to make it compulsory to study a vernacular language along with French. We have heard for decades about the "modern humanities." Why should there not be "African humanities?" Every language, which means every civilization, can provide material for the humanities, because every civilization is the expression, with its own peculiar emphasis, of certain characteristics of humanity. . . . This then is where the real aim of colonization lies. A moral and intellectual cross-fertilization, a spiritual graft.[41]

In other words, there is no cross-fertilization without an engagement with difference. Senghor's thoughts received an even sharper focus when, writing in 1961 on the question of Marxism, he made a passionate plea against overlooking the always-situated human being—humankind in its concrete affiliations to the past—in favor of the figure of the abstract human, so favored by the modernizers, or some globalizers of today, from both the Left and the Right. "Man is not without a homeland," writes Senghor,

> He is not a man without colour or history or country or civilization. He is West African man, our neighbour, precisely determined by his time and his place: the Malian, the Mauritian, the Ivory-Coaster; the Wolof, the Tuareg, the Hausa, the Fon, the Mossi, a man of flesh and bone and blood, who feeds on milk and millet and rice and yam, a man humiliated for centuries less perhaps in his hunger and nakedness than in his colour and civilization, in his dignity as incarnate man.[42]

"Incarnate man"—or man as always-already incarnate—is how Senghor imagines the world's heritage of historical and cultural diversity. It was not a diversity that got in the way of cross-cultural communication, nor was it a diversity that did not matter. For Senghor, one way that diversity could be harnessed in the cause of development is by deliberately creating a plural and yet thriving tradition of humanities in the teaching institutions of the world.

The vision was different from those of Wright or Ngũgĩ. Neither "global" English (or French) nor a return to one's native language was the option Senghor outlined. The way forward was a world of multilingual individuals who would appreciate language both as means of communication and as repositories of difference. A philologist's utopia perhaps, but how far from the vision of anticolonial modernizers who, in their single-minded pursuit of science and technology in order to catch up with the West, ended up leaving to the West itself the task of preserving and nurturing the world's plural heritage of the humanities.

Senghor's voice also militates against the tendency in much that is written on globalization today to celebrate "placelessness" as the ultimate goal of human life. Hardt and Negri's argument in their justly celebrated book *Empire* (2000) often assumes this position: contemporary capitalism makes labor placeless, so let labor use its placelessness to wrest from capital a global right of passage as a preliminary step toward global governance.[43] The argument has much to commend in it but it forgets what Senghor reminds us of: the fact that global passage may not define the ends of life for many. We may indeed all want the same rights—and this may very well include the right of global passage—but we may want these rights in order to pursue precisely those diverse "meanings of life" that make the history of one part of the world debate issues that may not resonate in another corner of humanity. If Hardt and Negri's analysis takes its bearing from the tradition of the social sciences, Senghor's thoughts speak squarely to the role that the humanities ought to play in the age of globalization. For it is within the humanities that we study texts for what they tell us about how the "ends of human life" have been debates in different parts of the world. There is nothing essentialist in this exercise. For the argument is not that the "ends of life" are given in a fixed form, once and for all, for a group or a people. The purpose of life is what a group or a people debate endlessly over generations, and in the process they, of course, listen to "outsiders" precisely to find out what is peculiar about themselves. In India, the epics, the *Ramayana* and the *Mahabharata* may be cited as two such texts that have had many recensions over the centuries—pro-women, anti-women, pro-lower-caste, anti-lower-caste and so on—where a certain set of moral issues, endlessly debated, help in the end to create a sense of shared and common past and place. It is the role of the humanities to make these diverse debates and their hermeneutics a part of every person's citizenly repertoire. Without that there is no cosmopolitanism.

However, the humanities have generally suffered in the modernizing nations of the world—my generation of Indians could testify to the cult of engineering and management that went hand-in-hand with discussions of development—while at least surviving in some of the elite universities of the West in the form of area studies. This is not an argument against area studies in the West. For it may very well be a sad fact today that it is only in the West that modern, non-Western humanities are pursued with some seriousness.[44] But there is a risk here. As the late Edward Said demonstrates, the West has seldom performed this task in a manner that transcends its own geopolitical interests. This is why it is all the more important that the developing parts of the world take the humanities seriously. And that is where Senghor's call for a plural tradition of the humanities remains a living legacy for all postcolonial intellectuals both inside and outside the West. The "dialogical" side of the discourse of decolonization, which rings through the writings of Wright, Ngũgĩ, Senghor, and others, helps us to raise for our times the question of the role that the humanities should play in a globalizing world.

Acknowledgments

This paper was presented initially as a keynote lecture at the conference "Bandung and Beyond: Rethinking Afro-Asian Connections During the Twentieth Century" held at Stanford University on May 14 to 15, 2005. I am grateful to the participants at the conference and to Christopher Lee, David Kim, and Rochona Majumdar for comments. Thanks to Arvind Elangovan and Sunit Singh for assistance with research.

Notes

1. The classic statement of this is Homi K. Bhabha, *The Location of Culture* (London: Routledge, 1994).

2. See, for instance, Michael Hardt and Antonio Negri, *Empire* (Cambridge: Harvard University Press, 2000), 143–59.

3. Aimé Césaire, *Discourse on Colonialism*, trans. Joan Pinkham (New York: Monthly Review Press, 2000), 25.

4. On the conference and its participants, see also *Selected Documents of the Bandung Conference* (New York: Institute of Pacific Relations, 1955), 29. It should be noted that Israel was invited to participate in the Asian Relations Conference of 1947 but, as noted elsewhere in this book, the delegation was called the "Jewish delegation from Palestine." See *Asian Relations: Report of the Proceedings and Documentation of the First Asian Relations Conference, New Delhi, March–April, 1947*, introduced by Professor D. Gopal (Delhi: Authorspress, 2003). Bandung, however, excluded Israel, mainly because of "strong opposition" from Arab countries. See *Selected Works of Jawaharlal Nehru* [here-

after *SWJN*], Second Series, vol. 27, eds. Ravinder Kumar and H. Y. Sharada Prasad (Delhi: JN Memorial Fund, 2000), 109, 566.

5. Niall Ferguson, *Empire: How Britain Made the Modern World* (London: Penguin, 2003). See in particular the conclusion.

6. Hardt and Negri, *Empire*; David Harvey, *The New Imperialism* (Oxford: Oxford University Press, 2003).

7. Gunner Myrdal, foreword, to Richard Wright, *The Color Curtain: A Report on the Bandung Conference* (New York: World Publishing, 1956), 7.

8. Wright, *Color Curtain*, 71. This point is underscored in a review of the book by Merze Tate of Howard University in *The Journal of Negro History*, 41, no. 3 (July 1956), 263–65. Tate quotes the following lines from Wright: "Bandung was the last call of Westernized Asians to the moral conscience of the West" (p.265).

9. Wright, *Color Curtain*, 82.

10. *SWJN*, second series, vol. 27, 106.

11. Carlos P. Romulo, *The Meaning of Bandung* (Chapel Hill: University of North Carolina Press, 1956), 11–12.

12. Roeslan Abdulgani, *The Bandung Connection: The Asia-Africa Conference in Bandung in 1955* (Singapore: Gunung Agung, 1981), 26. To be fair to Abdulgani, however, it needs to be said that he also expressed much admiration for Nehru's speech at a closed meeting of the political committee of the conference on April 22, 1955: "The influence of that speech was very great indeed. [Nehru] was a fighter, well-on in years, his hair going white, his voice strong, speaking in fluent English, without pretence, full of idealism and valuable ideas. . . . I can never forget those moments. Everyone present listened spell-bound," ibid., 143. Abdulgani also presented the following evaluation of Nehru: "He was very wealthy, but he lived simply full of discipline. Every morning, he did physical exercises, in the form of yoga. For a dozen minutes, he stood on his hand, with two feet in the air. In order to guard [sic] the easy coursing of blood in his veins. And in this way to clear his thoughts, he said," ibid.

13. *SWJN*, second series, vol. 28, ed. Ravinder Kumar and H.Y. Sharada Prasad (Delhi: Jawaharlal Nehru Memorial Fund, 2001), 98.

14. Ibid., 99.

15. Abdulgani, *Bandung Connection*, 115, 117. See also John Kotelawala, *An Asian Prime Minister's Story* (London: George G. Harrap and Co., 1956).

16. Abdulgani, *Bandung Connection*, 119. It should be noted that the Bandung conference was not to make any "majority" decisions or raise divisive, controversial issues. See *SWJN*, second series, vol. 28, 97–98.

17. A. Appadorai, *The Bandung Conference* (New Delhi: Indian Council of World Affairs, 1955), 29. See also A. W. Stargardt, "The Emergence of the Asian Systems of Power," *Modern Asian Studies* 23, no. 3 (1989): 561–95.

18. Romulo, *Meaning of Bandung*, 66.

19. See *Selected Documents of the Bandung Conference* (New York: Institute of Pacific Relations, 1955), 1. The foreword states:"The texts have been reproduced from those published in the *New York Times* or issued by the Indonesian Mission to the United Nations, New York."

20. Appadorai, *Bandung Conference*, 1. For the details and the proceedings of the Asian Relations Conference held in Delhi in 1947 see *Asian Relations: Report of the Proceedings and Documentation of the First Asian Relations Conference, New Delhi, March–April, 1947.*

21. *A World on the Move: A History of Colonialism and Nationalism in Asia and North Africa from the Turn of the Century to the Bandung Conference* (Amsterdam: Djambaten, 1956), 246. A review of this book in *The Bulletin of the School of Oriental and African Studies,* University of London, vol.22, no.1/3, 1959, 198–99 remarked: "The real value of this book lies in the clear picture it will give to the Western students of the way Asian thinkers feel about 'colonialism.'"

22. Appadorai, *Bandung Conference*, 30.

23. Abdulgani, *Bandung Connection*, 46–48.

24. *Select Documents*, 3.

25. *SWJN*, vol. 28, "Speech inaugurating the new building of the Punjab High Court, Chandigarh, March 19, 1955," 30; William Edgett Smith, *We Must Run While They Walk: A Portrait of Africa's Julius Nyerere* (New York: Random House, 1971).

26. Wright, *Color Curtain*, 132.

27. *SWJN*, vol. 29 (Delhi: Jawaharlal Nehru Memorial Fund, 2001), 67.

28. Julius K. Nyerere, *Freedom and Unity* (London: Oxford University Press, 1967), lecture on "Pomposity" on July 7, 1963, at a mass rally to celebrate the formation of his political party TANU (7 July 1954), 223–24.

29. This, roughly, was the argument of my essay "Postcoloniality and the Artifice of History: Who Speaks for 'Indian' Pasts?" first published in 1992 and then incorporated with modifications in my book *Provincializing Europe: Postcolonial Thought and Historical Difference* (Princeton: Princeton University Press, 2000). For Heidegger's statement, see "A Dialogue on Language" in Martin Heidegger, *On the Way to Language,* trans. Peter D. Hertz (New York: Harper and Row, 1982), 15. Césaire in *Discourse on Colonialism* also discusses the world in terms of its "Europeanization."

30. One of the best available discussions of the relationship between colonial rule and modernist practices of representation is in the first chapter of Timothy Mitchell's *Colonising Egypt* (Berkeley: University of California Press, 1991), chapter 1.

31. I am not saying one has completely displaced the other; it is the nature of contestation that I focus on here.

32. See, for example, Yogendra Yadav, "Barna, Jati, o Kancha Ilaiah: The Golden Stag [Mirage] of International Cooperation," *Anandabajar Patrika*, September 20, 2001; Naunidhi Kaur, "Caste and Race" in *Frontline*, 18 (13), June 23, to July 6, 2001; Andre Beteille, "Race and Caste", *The Hindu*, March 10, 2001; Ambrose Pinto, "Caste is a Variety of Race," *The Hindu*, March 24, 2001; Susan Shahin, "Caste is a word India just doesn't want to hear," *Asia Times*, April 25, 2001. See also my essay "Globalization, Democratization, and the Evacuation of History" in *At Home in the Diaspora: South Asian Scholars in the West*, eds. Veronique Benei and Jackie Assayag (Bloomington: Indiana University Press, 2003), 127–47.

33. I should not be read as saying that deterritorialization always and only helps subaltern groups or that the modernist idea of the political was only for the elite. There are counterexamples for both propositions. For a discussion on deterritorialization, see Arjun Appadurai, *Modernity at Large: Cultural Aspects of Globalization* (Minneapolis: University of Minnesota Press, 1996). On the debates Beteille and others have argued about tribal politics in India, see Bengt G. Karlsson and Tanka B. Subba, eds., *The Politics of Indigeneity in India* (London: Kegan Paul, 2006) as well as my essay "Politics Unlimited: The Global *Adivasi* and Debates about the Political" in the same volume.

34. Arjun Appadurai, *Modernity at Large*, chapter 2 dates contemporary globalization from the 1970s. David Harvey, *The Condition of Postmodernity* (Oxford: Blackwell, 2000), chapter 9 dates what he calls "flexible accumulation" from the same period.

35. See David Morley and Kuan-Hsing Chen, eds., *Stuart Hall: Critical Dialogue and Cultural Studies* (London: Routledge, 1996), 477; Alan Read, ed., *The Fact of Blackness: Frantz Fanon and Visual Representation* (Seattle: Bay Press, 1996).

36. See Simon During, "Introduction," in *The Cultural Studies Reader*, ed. Simon During, 2nd ed. (London and New York: Routledge, 2000), 1–28.

37. Wright, *Color Curtain*, 200.

38. Chinua Achebe's 1964 lecture on "The African Writer and the English Language" cited in Ngũgĩ wa Thiongo, *Decolonising the Mind: The Politics of Language in African Literature* (London: James Curry, 1986), 7.

39. Ibid., 7–8.

40. Ibid., xii, xiv.

41. Léopold Sédar Senghor, *Prose and Poetry*, selected and translated by John Reed and Clive Wake (Oxford: Oxford University Press, 1965), 53–55.

42. Ibid., 59.

43. Hardt and Negri, *Empire, passim*.

44. In saying this, I exclude the field of postcolonial studies for that field, as

I have already said, had its origins in the West. Postcolonial writers from outside the West are absorbed in that global field that still tilts toward the West. Nor do I mean to denigrate or deny the value of the work in modern, non-Western humanities that emanates from countries like India, for instance, for a wider audience. But voices from the world of non-Western scholarship in the humanities command much less global presence than voices from the social sciences in India and elsewhere. The humanities one comes across in global forums today are much more parochially Western than the social sciences: that is my point. And that, I think, was the gap Senghor also was pointing to.

2

Contested Hegemony

The Great War and the Afro-Asian Assault
on the Civilizing Mission

Michael Adas

THE CIVILIZING MISSION has been traditionally seen as an ideology by which late 19th-century Europeans rationalized their colonial domination of the rest of humankind. Formulations of this ideology varied widely from those of thinkers or colonial administrators who stressed the internal pacification and political order that European colonization extended to "barbaric" and "savage" peoples suffering from incessant warfare and despotic rule, to those of missionaries and reformers who saw religious conversion and education as the keys to European efforts to "uplift" "ignorant" and "backward" peoples. But by the late 1800s, most variations on the civilizing mission were grounded in presuppositions that suggest that it had become a good deal more than salving the conscience of those engaged in the imperial enterprise. Those who advocated colonial expansion as a way of promoting good government, economic improvement, or Christianity agreed that a vast and ever-widening gap had opened between the level of development achieved by Western European societies (and their North American offshoots) and that attained by any other peoples of the globe. Variations on the civilizing mission theme became the premier means by which European politicians and colonial officials, as well as popularizers and propagandists, identified the areas of human endeavor in which European superiority had been incontestably established, and calibrated the varying degrees to which different non-European societies lagged behind those of Western Europe. Those who contributed to the civilizing mission discourse, whether through official-policy statements or in novels and other fictional works, also sought to identify the reasons for Europe's superior advance relative to African backwardness or Asian stagnation and the implications of these findings for international relations and colonial policy.

Much of the civilizing mission discourse was obviously self-serving. But the perceived gap between Western Europe's material development and that of the rest of the world appeared to validate the pronouncements of the colonial civilizers. Late Victorians were convinced that the standards by which they gauged their superiority and justified their global hegemony were both empirically verifiable and increasingly obvious. Before the outbreak of the Great War in 1914, these measures of human achievement were contested only by dissident (and marginalized) intellectuals, and occasionally by disaffected colonial officials. The overwhelming majority of thinkers and political leaders who concerned themselves with colonial issues had little doubt that the scientific and industrial revolutions—at that point still confined to Europe and North America—*had* elevated Western societies far above all others in the understanding and mastery of the material world. Gauges of superiority and inferiority, such as differences in physical appearance and religious beliefs, which had dominated European thinking in the early centuries of overseas expansion remained important. But by the second half of the 19th century, European thinkers, whether they were racists or antiracists, expansionists or anti-imperialists, or on the political left or right, shared the conviction that through their scientific discoveries and inventions Westerners had gained an understanding of the workings of the physical world and an ability to tap its resources that were vastly superior to anything achieved by other peoples, past or present.[1]

Many advocates of the civilizing-mission ideology sought to capture the attributes that separated industrialized Western societies from those of the colonized peoples by contrasting Europeans (or Americans) against the dominated "others" with reference to a standard set of binary opposites that had racial, gender, and class dimensions. Europeans were, for example, seen to be scientific, energetic, disciplined, progressive, and punctual, whereas Africans and Asians were dismissed as superstitious, indolent, reactionary, out of control, and oblivious to time. These dichotomous comparisons were, of course, blatantly essentialist. But the late Victorians were prone to generalizing and stereotyping. They were also determined to classify and categorize all manner of things in the mundane world, and fond of constructing elaborate hypothetical hierarchies of humankind.

For virtually all late Victorian champions of the civilizing mission, the more colonized peoples and cultures were seen to exhibit such traits as fatalism, passivity, and excessive emotionalism, the further down they were placed on imaginary scales of human capacity and evolutionary development, and thus the greater the challenge of civilizing them. For even the best-intentioned Western social theorists and colonial administrators, difference meant inferiority. But there was considerable disagreement between a rather substantial racist majority, who viewed these attributes as innate and permanent (or at least requiring long periods of time for evolutionary remediation), and a minority of colonial reformers, who believed that substantial progress could be made in civilizing stagnant or barbarian peoples such as the Chinese or Indians within a generation, and that even savage peoples such as the Africans or Amerindians could advance over several generations.[2] Those who held to the social-evolutionist dogmas interpolated from rather dubious readings of Darwin's writings were convinced that the most benighted of the savage races were doomed to extinction. Some observers, like the Reverend Frederick Farrar, thought the demise of these lowly peoples who had "not added one iota to the knowledge, the arts, the sciences, the manufactures, the morals of the world," were quite consistent with the workings of nature and God.[3]

Whatever their level of material advancement, "races," such as the Sikhs of India or the Bedouin peoples of the African Sahel, which were deemed to be martial—thus, presumably energetic, active, disciplined, in control, expansive, and adaptive—were ranked high in late-Victorian hierarchies of human types. The colonizers' valorization of martial peoples underscores the decidedly masculine bias of the desirable attributes associated with the civilizing-mission ideology. Colonial administrations, like the legendary Indian Civil Service, were staffed entirely by males until World War II, when a shortage of manpower pushed at least the British to recruit women into the colonial service for the first time.[4] The club-centric, sports-obsessed, hard-drinking enclave culture of the European colonizers celebrated muscular, self-controlled, direct, and energetic males. Wives and eligible young females were allowed into these masculine bastions. But their behavior was controlled and their activities constricted by the fiercely enforced social conventions and the physical layout of European quarters that metaphorically and literally set the boundaries of European communities in colonized areas. Within the colonizers' enclaves, the logic of the separate spheres for men and women prevailed, undergirded by a set of paired, dichotomous attributes similar to that associated with the civilizing mission ideology. Thus, such lionized colonial proconsuls as Evelyn Baring (the first earl of Cromer), who ruled Egypt like a monarch for over two decades, saw no contradiction between their efforts "to liberate" Muslim women from the veil and purdah in the colonies and the influential support that they gave to antisuffragist organizations in Great Britain.[5]

As T. B. Macaulay's oft-quoted 1840 caricature of the Bengalis as soft, devious, servile, indolent, and effeminate suggests, feminine qualities were often associated in colonial thinking with dominated, inferior races.[6] Some writers stressed the similarities in the mental makeup of European women and Africans or other colonized peoples; others argued that key female attributes corresponded to those ascribed to the lower orders of humanity. Again, the paired oppositions central to the civilizing mission ideology figured prominently in the comparisons. Though clearly (and necessarily) superior in moral attributes, European women—like the colonized peoples—were intuitive, emotional, passive, bound to tradition, and always late.[7] In addition, the assumption that scientific discovery and invention had been historically monopolized by males (despite the accomplishments of contemporaries such as Marie Curie) was taken as proof that women were temperamentally and intellectually unsuited to pursuits, such as engineering and scientific research, that advocates of the civilizing mission ideology viewed as key indicators of the level of societal development. These views not only served to fix the image and position of the European *memsahib* as passive, domestic, apolitical, and vulnerable, they made it all-but impossible for indigenous women in colonized societies to obtain serious education in the sciences or technical training. As Ester Boserup and others have demonstrated, institutions and instruction designed to disseminate Western scientific knowledge or tools and techniques among colonized peoples were directed almost totally toward the male portion of subject populations.[8]

The attributes that the colonizers valorized through the civilizing mission ideology were overwhelmingly bourgeois. Rationality, empiricism, progressivism, systematic (hence scientific) inquiry, industriousness, and adaptability were all hallmarks of the capitalist industrial order. New conceptions of time and space that had made possible and were reinforced by that order informed such key civilizing mission attributes as hard work, discipline, curiosity, punctuality, honest dealing, and taking control—the latter rather distinct from the self-control so valued by aristocrats. Implicit in the valorization of these bourgeois traits was approbation of a wider range of processes, attitudes, and behavior that was not usually explicitly discussed in the tomes and tracts of the colonial proponents of the civilizing mission ideology. Ubiquitous complaints by colonial officials regarding the colonized's lack of foresight, their penchant for "squandering" earnings on rites-of-passage ceremonies or religious devotion, and their resistance to work discipline and overtime suggested they lacked proclivities and abilities that were essential to the mastery of the industrial, capitalist order of the West. Implicitly then, and occasionally explicitly, advocates of the civilizing-mission ideology identified the accumulation and reinvestment of wealth, the capacity to anticipate and forecast future trends, and the drive for unbounded productivity and the provision of material abundance, as key attributes of the "energetic, reliable, improving" Western bourgeoisie, which had been mainly responsible for the scientific and industrial revolutions and European global hegemony.[9]

In the decades before the Great War, white European males reached the pinnacle of their power and global influence. The civilizing-mission ideology both celebrated their ascendancy and set the agenda they intended to pursue for dominated peoples throughout the world. The attributes that male European colonizers ascribed to themselves and sought—to widely varying degrees in different colonial settings and at different social levels—to inculcate in their African or Asian subjects were informed by the underlying scientific and technological gauges of human capacity and social development that were central to the civilizing-mission ideology. Both the attributes and the ideology of the dominant in turn shaped European perceptions of and interaction with the colonized peoples of Africa and Asia in a variety of ways. Many apologists for colonial expansion, for example, argued that it was the duty of the more inventive and inquisitive Europeans to conquer and develop the lands of backward or primitive peoples who did not have the knowledge or the tools to exploit the vast resources that surrounded them.[10] Having achieved political control, it was incumbent upon the Western colonizers to replace corrupt and wasteful indigenous regimes with honest and efficient bureaucracies, to reorganize the societies of subjugated peoples in ways the Europeans deemed more rational and more nurturing of individual initiative and enterprise, and to restructure the physical environment of colonized lands in order to bring them into line with European conceptions of time and space.

The Europeans' superior inventiveness and understanding of the natural world also justified the allotment of tasks in the global economy envisioned by proponents of the civilizing mission. Industrialized Western nations would provide monetary and machine capital and entrepreneurial and managerial skills, while formally colonized and informally dominated overseas territories would supply the primary products, cheap labor, and abundant land that could be developed by Western machines, techniques, and enterprise. Apologists for imperialism argued that Western peoples were entrusted with a mission to civilize because they were active, energetic, and committed to efficiency and progress. It was therefore their duty to put indolent, tradition-bound, and fatalistic peoples to work, to discipline them (whether they be laborers, soldiers, domestic servants, or clerks), and to inculcate within them (insofar as their innate capacities permitted) the rationality, precision, and foresight that were seen as vital sources of Europe's rise to global hegemony. But efforts to fully convert the colonized to the virtues celebrated by the civilizing-mission ideology were normally reserved for the Western-educated classes. Through state-supported and missionary education, Western colonizers sought to propagate epistemologies, values, and modes of behavior that had originally served to justify their dominance and continued to be valorized in their rhetoric of governance.

The elite-to-elite emphasis of the transmission of the civilizing-mission ideology meant that it was hegemonic in a rather different sense than that envisioned by Antonio Gramsci's original formulation of the concept.[11] To begin with, it was inculcated across cultures by colonizer elites onto the bourgeois and petty-bourgeois classes that Western education and collaboration had brought into being. In addition, the proponents of the civilizing mission viewed it only marginally as an ideology that might be employed to achieve cultural hegemony over the mass of colonized peoples. Few of the latter had anything but the most rudimentary appreciation of the scientific and technological breakthroughs that were vital to Western dominance— as manifested in the colonizers' military power, transportation systems, and machines for extracting mineral and agrarian resources. Only the Western-educated classes among the colonized were exposed to the history of Europe's unprecedented political, economic, and social transformations; and only these groups were expected by their colonial overlords to emulate them by internalizing the tenets of the civilizing-mission ideology.

In the pre–World War era, the great majority of Western-educated collaborateur and comprador classes in the colonies readily conceded the West's scientific, technological, and overall material superiority. Spokesmen for these classes—often even those who had already begun to agitate for an end to colonial rule—clamored for more Western education and an acceleration of the process of diffusion of Western science and technology in colonized societies.[12] In Bengal, in eastern India in the 1860s, for example, a gathering of Indian notables heartily applauded K. M. Banerjea's call for the British to increase opportunities for Indians to receive advanced instruction in the Western sciences. Banerjea dismissed those who defended "Oriental" learning by asking which of them would trust the work of a doctor, engineer, or architect who knew only the mathematics and mechanics of the Sanskrit sutras.[13] What is noteworthy here is not only Banerjea's confusion of Buddhist (hence Pali) sutras and Sanskrit *shastras*, but his internalization of the Western Orientalists' essentialist conception of Asian thinking and learning as a single "Oriental" whole that had stagnated and fallen behind the West in science and mathematics. Just over two decades later, the prominent Bengali reformer and educator Keshub Chunder Sen acknowledged that the diffusion of Western science that had accompanied the British colonization of India had made it possible for the Indians to overcome "ignorance and error" and share the Europeans' quest to explore "the deepest mysteries of the physical world."[14]

Thus, despite the Hindu renaissance that was centered in these decades in Bengal, as S.K. Saha has observed, the presidency's capital, Calcutta, had been reduced to an intellectual outpost of Europe.[15] Perhaps a majority of English-educated Indians did not just revere Western scientific and technological achievements; they accepted their colonial masters' assumption that responsible, cultivated individuals privileged rationality, empiricism, punctuality, progress, and the other attributes deemed virtuous by proponents of the civilizing-mission ideology. Just how widely these values had been propagated in the Indian middle classes is suggested by anthropological research carried out among Indian merchant communities in central Africa in the 1960s. Responses to questions relating to the Indians' attitudes toward the African majority in the countries in which they resided revealed that the migrant merchants considered their hosts "illiterate and incomprehensible savages," who were lazy and without foresight, childlike in their thinking (and thus incapable of logical deductions), and self-indulgent and morally reprobate.[16] As the recollections of one of Zimbabwe's Western-educated, nationalist leaders, Ndabaningi Sithole, make clear, the colonized of sub-Saharan Africa were even more impressed by the Europeans' mastery of the material world than were their Indian counterparts. Because many African peoples had often been relatively isolated before the abrupt arrival of European explorers, missionaries, and conquerors in the last decades of the 19th century, early encounters with these agents of expansive, industrial societies were deeply disorienting and demoralizing:

> The first time he ever came into contact with the white man the African was overwhelmed, overawed, puzzled, perplexed, mystified, and dazzled. . . . Motor cars, motor cycles, bicycles, gramophones, telegraphy, the telephone, glittering Western clothes, new ways of ploughing and planting, added to the African's sense of curiosity and novelty. Never before had the African seen such things. They were beyond his comprehension; they were outside the realm of his experience. He saw. He wondered. He mused. Here then the African came into contact with two-legged gods who chose to dwell among people instead of in the distant mountains.[17]

In part because European observers took these responses by (what they perceived to be) materially impoverished African peoples as evidence of the latter's racial incapacity for rational thought, discipline, scientific investigation, and technological innovation, there were few opportunities before World War I for colonized Africans to pursue serious training in the sciences, medicine, or engineering, especially at the post-secondary level. Technological diffusion was also limited, and the technical training of Africans was confined largely to the operation and maintenance of the most elementary machines.[18] Nonetheless, the prescriptions offered by French- and English-educated Africans for the revival of a continent shattered by centuries of the slave trade shared the assumption of the European colonizers that extensive Western assistance would be essential for Africa's uplift. Abbé Boilat, for example, a mixed-race missionary and educator, worked for the establishment of a secondary school at St. Louis in Senegal, where Western mathematics and sciences would be taught to the sons of the local elite. Boilat also dreamed of an African college that would train indigenous doctors, magistrates, and engineers who would assist the French in extending their empire in the interior of the continent.[19]

Although the Edinburgh-educated surgeon J. A. Horton was less sanguine than Boilat about the aptitude of his fellow Africans for higher education in the Western sciences, he was equally convinced that European tutelage was essential if Africa was to be rescued from chaos and barbarism. Horton viewed "metallurgy and other useful arts" as the key to civilized development, and argued that if they wished to advance, Africans must acquire the learning and techniques of more advanced peoples like the Europeans.[20] Even the Caribbean-born Edward Blyden, one of the staunchest defenders of African culture and historical achievements in the prewar decades, conceded that Africa's recovery from the ravages of the slave trade depended upon assistance from nations "now foremost in civilization and science" and the return of educated blacks from the United States and Latin America. Blyden charged that if Africa had been integrated into the world-market system through regular commerce rather than the slave trade, it would have developed the sort of agriculture and manufacturing, and imported steam engines, printing presses, and other machines by which the "comfort, progress, and usefulness of mankind are secured."[21]

There were those who contested the self-satisfied, ethnocentric, and frequently arrogant presuppositions that informed the civilizing-mission ideology in the decades before World War I. The emergence of Japan as an industrial power undermined the widely held conviction that the Europeans' scientific and technological attainments were uniquely Western or dependent on the innate capacities of the white or Caucasian races. Conversely, the modernists' "discovery" of "primitive art" and the well-publicized conversion of a number of rather prominent European intellectuals to Hinduism, Buddhism, and other Asian religions suggested the possibility of viable alternatives to European epistemologies, modes of behavior, and ways of organizing societies and the natural world. Some European thinkers, perhaps most famously Paul Valéry and Hermann Hesse, actually questioned Western values themselves. They asked whether the obsessive drive for increased productivity and profits and the excessive consumerism that they saw as the hallmarks of Western civilization were leading humanity in directions that were conducive to social well-being and spiritual fulfillment.[22]

Before the outbreak of war in 1914, these critiques and alternative visions were largely marginalized, dismissed by mainstream politicians and the educated public as the rantings of gloomy radicals and eccentric mystics. But the coming of World War I and the appalling casualties that resulted from the trench stalemate on the Western Front made a mockery of the European conceit that discovery and invention were necessarily progressive and beneficial to humanity. The mechanized slaughter and the conditions under which the youth of Europe fought generated profound challenges to the ideals and assumptions upon which the Europeans had for over a century based their sense of racial superiority and from which they had fashioned that ideological testament to their unmatched hubris, the civilizing mission. Years of carnage in the very heartlands of European civilization demonstrated that Europeans were at least as susceptible to instinctual, irrational responses and primeval drives as the peoples they colonized. The savagery that the war unleashed within Europe, Sigmund Freud observed, should caution the Europeans against assuming that their "fellow-citizens" of the world had "sunk so low" as they had once believed, because the conflict had made it clear that the Europeans themselves had "never risen as high."[23]

Remarkably (or so it seemed to many at the time), the crisis passed, the empire survived, and the British and French emerged victorious from the war. In fact, in the years following the end of the conflict in 1918, the empires of both powers expanded considerably as Germany's colonies and Turkey's territories in the Levant were divided between them.[24] Although recruiting British youths into the Indian Civil Service and its African counterparts became more difficult, and such influential proponents of French expansionism as Henri Massis conceded that the Europeans' prestige as civilizers had fallen sharply among the colonized peoples, serious efforts were made to revive the badly battered civilizing-mission ideology.[25] Colonial apologists, such as Étienne Richet and Albert Bayet, employed new, less-obviously hegemonic slogans that emphasized the need for "mutual coopera-tion" between colonizers and colonized as well as programs for "devel-opment" based on "free exchanges of views" and "mutual respect." But the central tenets of the colonizers' ideology remained the same: European domination of African and Asian peoples was justified by the diffusion of the superior science, technology, epistemologies, and modes of organization that it facilitated. Though the engineer and the businessman may have replaced the district officer and the mission-ary as the chief agents of the mission to civilize, it continued to be envisioned as an unequal exchange between the advanced, rational, industrious, efficient, and mature societies of the West and the back-ward, ignorant, indolent, and childlike peoples of Africa, Asia, and the Pacific.[26]

For many European intellectuals and a handful of maverick poli-ticians, however, postwar efforts to restore credibility to the civiliz-ing-mission ideology were exercises in futility. These critics argued that the war had destroyed any pretense the Europeans might have of moral superiority or their conceit that they were innately more ratio-nal than non-Western peoples. They charged that the years of mas-sive and purposeless slaughter in the trenches had made a shambles of proofs of Western superiority based on claims to higher levels of scientific understanding and technological advancement. Though the literature in which this discourse unfolded is substantial, I would like to focus on the writings of Georges Duhamel, and in particular an incident that he relates in his first novel about the war and returns to repeatedly in his later essays, an incident that provides the focal point for his extensive critique of the civilizing-mission ideology.[27] That cri-tique in turn fed the growing doubts about European civilization and its global influence that African and Asian intellectuals and political leaders had begun to voice in the years before 1914. Though African and Asian writers rarely cited European authors for support in their assaults on the civilizing-mission ideology and colonialism more gen-erally, both metropolitan and colonial intellectuals were engaged in a common discourse in the decades after World War I, a discourse that proved deeply subversive of the colonizers' hegemonic rhetoric and thus a critical force in the liberation struggles of colonized peoples.

As its title, *Civilisation 1914–1918* suggests, Duhamel's autobiographical novel about a sergeant in the French medical corps on the Western Front is an exercise in irony.[28] Like many among the millions of young European males who were funneled into the trenches/tombs of the Western Front and lived long enough to tell about it, Duhamel was profoundly disoriented and disillusioned by his wartime experiences. They seemed to contradict all that he thought he knew or believed about Western civilization. Nothing was as it appeared to be or *ought* to be. As in a Max Ernst painting, reality was grotesquely deformed. Everything was bewilderingly inverted. The massive, mechanized, and increasingly senseless slaughter of young men that resulted from the trench stalemate transformed machines from objects of pride and symbols of advancement to barbarous instruments of shame and horror. From the masters of machines, European men had become their slaves, "bent under the burden of tedious or sorrowful work." Even the scientific breakthroughs that Duhamel, a highly trained surgeon and former laboratory technician, had once thought the most unique, noble, and exalted of Europe's achievements had been enlisted by the forces of hate and destruction to sustain the obscene and irrational combat that was destroying Europe from within.[29] The poet Paul Valéry, who shared Duhamel's assessment of the war, lamented the fact that the Europeans' greatest discoveries had been perverted by the need for so "much science to kill so many men, waste so many possessions, and annihilate so many towns in so little time."[30]

The conditions under which the soldiers and Duhamel's protagonist-surgeon lived and the wasteland their combat wrought in northern France made a mockery of the European conviction that their unprecedented mastery of nature was proof of their superiority over all contemporary peoples and past civilizations. The filthy, lice-ridden bodies of the youth of Europe, exposed for weeks on end to the cold and mud of winter in Flanders or the valley of the Somme, fighting with huge rats for their miserable rations or their very limbs, belied the prewar conviction that superior science had given Western humanity dominion over nature. For Duhamel the flies that swarmed about the open latrines, garbage heaps, and dismembered corpses and carcasses of the unclaimed dead in the no-man's-land moonscape provided an ever-present reminder of the Europeans' reversion to a state of savagery, where they were continually buffeted by the forces of nature. Duhamel's surgeon-protagonist in *Civilisation 1914–1918* is repelled by, but utterly incapable of fending off, the multitude of flies that suck the pus and blood of his patients and the larvae that multiply rapidly in their festering wounds.[31] But the soldiers' vulnerability to the forces of nature represents only one of the inversions that Duhamel and other chroniclers of the trench trauma associated with the colossal misuse of science and technology in the war. Duhamel concluded that the Western obsession with inventing new tools and discovering new ways to force nature to support material advancement for its own sake had inevitably led to the trench wasteland where "man had achieved this sad miracle of denaturing nature, of rendering it ignoble and criminal."[32]

The climax of the surgeon's ordeal in Duhamel's *Civilisation 1914–1918* comes in his first encounter with the Ambulance Chirurgical Automobile (ACA), "the most perfect thing in the line of an ambulance that has been invented . . . the last word in science; it follows the armies with motors, steam-engines, microscopes, laboratories. . . ."[33] The sergeant is assigned to minister to the casualties delivered to "the first great repair-shop the wounded man encounters." The wounded in question are fittingly cuirassiers—traditionally cavalrymen with shining breastplates and plumed helmets—fighting without their horses and sans plumes, since both had proved positively lethal, given the firepower of the opposing armies, in the first months of the war. The sergeant relates that these once "strong, magnificent creatures," have been shattered and wait "like broken statues" for admission to the ACA. In the midst of the mechanized trench battleground, the cuirassiers are anachronisms, pitiful vestiges of a lost chivalric ethos. They chatter "like well-trained children" about their wounds and fear of anesthesia. In contrast to the active, self-controlled, take-charge European male ideal of the prewar era, the cuirassiers have, as Sandra Gilbert argues for male combatants more generally, been transformed into "passive, dependent, immanent medical object[s]."[34]

In Gilbert's rendering, wounded males are opposed to European women who as nurses and ambulance drivers have become "active, autonomous, and transcendent." But Duhamel recounts an inversion that must have been even more unsettling for his French and British readers in the postwar decades. The cuirassiers are carried into the ACA by African stretcher-bearers, whom Duhamel initially depicts in some of the stock images of the dominant colonizers. With their "thin black necks, encircled by the [stretcher-bearers'] yokes" and their "shriveled fingers," the "little" Malagasies remind him of "sacred monkeys, trained to carry idols." The sergeant finds the Malagasies "timid," "docile," and "obedient," and compares them (curiously) to "black and serious embryos." But after the Malagasies place the wounded cuirassiers on the operating tables, a revelatory encounter occurs:

> At this moment my glance met that of one of the blacks and I had a sensation of sickness. It was a calm, profound gaze like that of a child or a young dog. The savage was turning his head gently from right to left and looking at the extraordinary beings and objects that surrounded him. His dark pupils lingered lightly over all the marvelous details of the workshop for repairing the human machine. And these eyes, which betrayed no thought, were none the less disquieting. For one moment I was stupid enough to think, "How astonished he must be!" But this silly thought left me, and I no longer felt anything but an insurmountable shame.[35]

The surgeon begins by depicting the African in terms—"child," "young dog," "savage"—which were standard epithets for racists and colonizers alike. But his complacent sense of superiority is shattered by his realization that rather than being impressed by the advanced science and technology that have been packed into the ACA, the "primitive" Malagasy must be appalled or at the very least bewildered by the desperate and costly efforts of the Europeans to repair the devastation wrought by their own civilization's suicidal war. The savage has the exalted doctor and the frenzied activity of the ACA in his "calm, profound gaze"; an exact reversal of the only permissible relationship between Europeans and "savage" or subordinate peoples according to postmodernist readings of European travel literature and colonial memoirs.[36] The surgeon is embarrassed and angered by his realization that the Malagasy is a witness to the Europeans' irrational, but very destructive, tribal war.

The reversion to barbarism and savagery that Duhamel associates with trench warfare is a pervasive theme in participants' accounts of the conflict. Combatants describe themselves as "wild beasts," "primitives," "bushmen," "ape-men," and "mere brutes." Soldiers at the front compare their mud-caked existence to that of prehistoric men who lived in caves or crude holes dug into the earth.[37] In the trenches or behind the lines, the refinements of civilization recede. Decorum is associated with death; modesty became irrelevant to soldiers who used crudely fabricated latrines as places to congregate, gossip, and curse their leaders. In battle, primal instincts—"the furtive cunning of a stoat or weasel"—were the key to survival. Europeans fought, as Frederic Manning observes in perfect social evolutionist tropes, like peoples at a "more primitive stage in their development, and . . . [became] nocturnal beasts of prey, hunting each other in packs."[38] Infantrymen were forced to listen rather than look for incoming shells, which were often fired from miles away and could not be seen until it was too late. Soldiers who lived long enough to become trench veterans did so by developing an acute sensitivity to the sounds of different sizes and sorts of projectiles and gauging by sound how close they would hit to where the soldiers were dug in. Thus, a refined sense of hearing, which the Europeans had associated with savage or primitive peoples since at least the 18th century, superseded sight, which had long been regarded as the most developed sense of civilized peoples like the Europeans.[39]

As these examples suggest, the reversion to savagery that the youth of Europe experienced was mainly of the degraded rather than the noble variety of primitivism that European artists and writers had been trying to sort out for centuries. In a moment that borders on black comedy, Duhamel's surgeon-protagonist fantasizes about escaping the horrors of the trench stalemate by fleeing to the mountains to live among the "savage" blacks. Envisioning, like the impulsive Ernest Psichari who fled to Africa from the Europe of "large stomachs and vain speeches" just before the outbreak of the war, a land where people still lived in a "state of nature," free from the mechanical outrages inflicted continually on those at the front, the sergeant is shocked to encounter Africans riding bicycles at Soissons, and later clamoring for war decorations.[40] Despondent, he concludes that there are no "real black people" left and no place on earth that has not been contaminated by European civilization.[41]

In the many works he published in the decades after the war, Duhamel elaborated and expanded upon the critique of European civilization and of the civilizing-mission ideology that had been initially fueled by his experiences on the Western Front.[42] Like many prominent European intellectuals, from Valéry, André Malraux, and René Guenon to Hermann Hesse, Hermann Keyserling, and E. M. Forster, Duhamel concluded that the war was the inevitable outcome of the Europeans' centuries-old obsession with scientific and industrial advance. They had been so captivated by mechanical progress and material increase that they had neglected the needs of the soul and spirit. They had allowed the spiritual ideals and moral dimensions of Western civilization to wither, while subordinating themselves to the machines they had created to serve them. They had confused industry and science with civilization, and become deluded by the conviction that progress, well-being, and goodness could be equated with the ability to go 100 miles per hour. These misunderstandings had led inexorably to the ruin of Europe in a war that had devastated its once-prosperous lands, thrown its societies into turmoil, and aroused the colonized peoples to resistance.

Although at times in his later years Duhamel felt compelled to come to Europe's defense in the face of rising challenges from the colonized world, he believed that the Great War had proved decisive in undermining the image of Europeans as "inscrutable masters," "dazzling and terrible demi-gods."[43] In supporting their colonial rulers in the war, Africans and Asians had discovered that the Europeans' claim that they possessed attributes that entitled them to dominate the rest of humankind was false. The "men of color" found that the Europeans inhabited only a small and divided continent, and that their overlords were not gods but "miserable, bleeding animal[s] (the most extreme of inversions from the Western perspective) . . . devoid of hope and pride." The war had taught the colonized peoples that, despite their claims to have mastered the forces of nature, the Europeans submitted to cold and heat, to epidemics, and to innumerable "perils without names." Not surprisingly, Duhamel argues, the colonized felt little pity for the once-proud masters whom they had grown increasingly determined to resist. But he believed that they must not resist European domination alone. They must also resist the spread of the "cruel" and "dangerous" civilization that the Europeans—and, after the war, their American progeny—sought to impose on the rest of humankind.[44] The war had revealed the unprecedented capacity for barbarity of this so-called civilization, as well as the perils of destructiveness and vacuousness that threatened those who sought to emulate its narrowly materialistic achievements. In the decades after the war, a number of Asian and African intellectuals took up Duhamel's call to resist with important consequences for liberation struggles in the colonized world.

Mounted by Asian and African thinkers and activists who often received little publicity in Europe or the United States, pre–World War I challenges to assumptions of Western superiority enshrined in the civilizing mission ideology were highly essentialist, mainly reactive rather than proactive, and framed by Western gauges of human achievement and worth. The most extensive and trenchant critiques in the case of India were articulated by the Hindu revivalist Swami Vivekananda (Naren Datta), who had won some measure of fame in the West with a brilliant lecture on Vedanta philosophy at the Conference of World Religions held in conjunction with the Chicago World's Fair in 1893. Vivekananda was fond of pitting a highly essentialized spiritual "East" against an equally essentialized materialistic "West." And like the earlier holy men activists of the Arya Dharm, he claimed that most of the scientific discoveries attributed to Western scientists in the modern era had been pioneered or at least anticipated by the sages of the Vedic age.[45] Vivekananda asserted that after mastering epistemologies devised to explore the mundane world, the ancient Indians (and by inference their modern descendants) had moved on to more exulted, transcendent realms, a line of argument that clearly influenced the thinking of the French philosopher René Guenon in the postwar decades.[46] Vivekananda cautioned his Indian countrymen against the indiscriminate adoption of the values, ways, and material culture of the West, a warning that was powerfully echoed at another level by the writings of Ananda Coomaraswamy, who, like William Morris and his circle in England, called for a concerted effort to preserve and restore the ancient craft skills of the Indian peoples, which he likened to those of Medieval Europe.[47] In what has been seen as a premonition of the coming global conflict, Vivekananda predicted, decades before 1914, that unless the West tempered its obsessive materialistic pursuits by adopting the spiritualism of the East, it would "degenerate and fall to pieces."[48]

Many of Vivekananda's themes had been taken up in the prewar years by two rather different sage-philosophers, Rabindranath Tagore and Aurobindo Ghose, who, like Vivekananda, were both Bengalis that had been extensively exposed to Western learning and culture in their youths. Tagore emerged during the war years as the most eloquent and influential critic of the West, and a gentle advocate of Indian alternatives to remedy the profound distortions and excesses in Western culture that the war had so painfully revealed. But in the prewar decades, knowledge in the West of the concerns of the Hindu revivalists regarding the directions that European civilization was leading the rest of humanity was confined largely to literary and artistic circles, particularly to those, such as the theosophists, which were organized around efforts to acquire and propagate ancient Indian philosophies. Popularists like Hermann Keyserling had begun in the years before the war to disseminate a rather garbled version of Hinduism to a growing audience in the West. But few Europeans gave credence to the notion that Indian or Chinese learning or values, or those of any other non-Western culture for that matter, might provide meaningful correctives or alternatives to the epistemologies and modes of organization and social interaction dominant in the West. The war changed all of this rather dramatically. Shocked by the self-destructive frenzy that gripped European civilization, Western intellectuals sought answers to what had gone wrong, and some—albeit a small but influential minority—turned to Indian thinkers like Tagore for tutelage.

In many ways Tagore was the model guru. Born into one of the most intellectually distinguished of modern Bengali families, he was educated privately and consequently allowed to blend Western and Indian learning in his youthful studies. From his father, Devendranath, the founder of the reformist Bramo Samaj, Rabindranath inherited a deep spiritualism and a sense of the social ills that needed to be combated in his colonized homeland. Both concerns were central to his prolific writings that included poems, novels, plays, and essays. Though more of a mystic than an activist, Tagore promoted community-development projects on his family estates. And he later founded an experimental school and university at Shantiniketan, his country refuge, which visitors from the West likened to a holy man's ashram. Although Tagore had attracted a number of artistic friends in Europe and America during his travels abroad in the decades before the war, and although his poetry and novels were admired by Yeats, Auden, and other prominent Western authors, he received international recognition only after winning the Nobel Prize for literature in 1913—the first Asian or African author to be so honored.

The timing was fortuitous. When the war broke out in the following year, Tagore was well positioned to express the dismay and disbelief that so many Western-educated Africans and Asians felt regarding Europe's bitter and seemingly endless intertribal slaughter. He expressed this disenchantment as a loyal subject of King George and the British Empire, which may also help to explain why he received such a careful hearing from educated British, French, and American audiences during and after the war. During the first months of the war, Tagore learned that he had made a bit of money on one of the poems he had sent to his friend William Rothenstein to be published in London. He instructed Rothenstein to use the proceeds to "buy something" for "our" soldiers in France; a gesture he hoped would "remind them of the anxious love of their countrymen in the distant home."[49] But loyalty to the British did not deter Tagore from speaking out against the irrationality and cruelty of the conflict, and using it as the starting point for a wide-ranging critique of the values and institutions of the West. The more perceptive of Tagore's Western readers and the more attentive members of the audiences who attended his well-publicized lectures in Europe, the United States, and Japan, could not miss his much-more subversive subtexts: such a civilization was not fit to govern and decide the future of most of the rest of humanity.

The colonized peoples must draw on their own cultural resources and take charge of their own destinies.

In his reflections on the meanings of the war Tagore returned again and again to the ways in which it had undermined the civilizing-mission ideology that had justified and often determined the course of Western global hegemony. Like Valéry, Hesse, and other critics of the West from within, Tagore explored the ways in which the war had inverted the attributes of the dominant and revealed what the colonizers had trumpeted as unprecedented virtues to be fatal vices. Some of the inversions were incidental, such as Tagore's characterization of the damage to the cathedral town of Rheims as "savage," and others were little more than brief allusions, for example, to science as feminine (the direct antithesis of the masculine metaphors employed in the West) and to Europe as a woman and a child.[50] But many of the inversions were explored in some detail. In a number of his essays and lectures, Tagore scrutinized at some length the colonizers' frequent invocation of material achievement as empirical proof of their racial superiority and fitness to rule less-advanced peoples. He charged that the moral and spiritual side of the Europeans' nature had been sapped by their material self-indulgence. As a result, they had lost all sense of restraint (or self-control), as was amply evidenced by the barbaric excesses of trench warfare. Because improvement had come for the Europeans to mean little more than material increase, they could not begin to understand—or teach others—how to lead genuinely fulfilling lives. The much-touted discipline that was thought to be exemplified by their educational systems produced, he averred, little more than dull repetition and stunted minds. The unceasing scramble for profit and material gain that drove Western societies had resulted in a "winning at any cost" mentality that abrogated ethical principles and made a victim of truth, as wartime propaganda had so dramatically demonstrated.

Like Mohandas Gandhi in roughly the same period, Rabindranath Tagore expressed considerable discomfort with railways and other Western devices that advocates of the civilizing mission had celebrated as the key agents of the Europeans' victory over time and space.[51] Forced to rush his meal at a railway restaurant and bewildered by the fast pace at which cinema images flickered across the screen, Tagore concluded that the accelerated pace of living made possible by Western machines contributed to disorientation and constant frustration, to individuals and societies out of sync with the rhythms of nature, each other, and their own bodies. He reversed the familiar, environmental determinists' notion that the fast-thinking-and-acting—hence decisive and aggressive—peoples of the colder Northern regions were superior to the languid, congenitally unpunctual peoples of the South. The former, Tagore maintained, had lost the capacity for aesthetic appreciation, contemplation, and self-reflection. Without these, they were not fit to shape the future course of human development, much less rule the rest of humankind.

In two allegorical plays written in 1922, Tagore built a more general critique of the science- and industry-dominated societies of the West. The first, titled *Muktadhara*, was translated into French as *La Machine* and published in 1929 with a lengthy introduction, filled with anti-industrial polemic, by Marc Elmer. The second, *Raketh Karabi*, was translated into English as *Red Oleanders*. Both plays detail the sorry plight of small kingdoms that come to be dominated by machines. In each case, the misery and oppression they cause spark revolts aimed at destroying the machines and the evil ministers who direct their operations. Like Vivekananda before him, Tagore warned that science and technology alone were not capable of sustaining civilized life. Like Vivekananda, he cautioned his Indian countrymen against an uncritical adoption of all that was Western, and insisted that the West needed to learn patience and self-restraint from India, to acquire the spirituality that India had historically nurtured and shared with all humankind. With the other major holy men activists of the Hindu revival, Tagore pitted the oneness and cosmopolitanism of Indian civilization against the arrogance and chauvinism of European nationalism. He argued that the nationalist mode of political organization that the Europeans had long seen as one of the key sources of their global dominion had proved to be the tragic flaw that had sealed their descent into war. Unlike Gandhi, Tagore did not reject the industrial civilization of Europe and North America per se, but concluded that if it was to endure, the West must draw on the learning of the "East," which had so much to share. He urged his countrymen to give generously and to recognize the homage that the Europeans paid to India by turning to it for succor in a time of great crisis.

In sharp contrast to Tagore, Aurobindo Ghose felt no obligation to support the British in the Great War. Educated in the best English-language schools in India and later at St. Paul's School and Cambridge University in Britain, Ghose's life had veered from brilliant student and a stint as a petty bureaucrat in one of India's princely states, to a meteoric career as a revolutionary nationalist that ended with a two-year prison sentence, and finally to an ashram in (French-controlled) Pondicherry on India's southeastern coast. Finding refuge in the latter, he began his lifelong quest for realization and soon established himself as one of India's most prolific philosophers and revered holy men. Aurobindo was convinced that the war would bring an end to European political domination and cultural hegemony throughout Asia.[52] In his view, the conflict had laid bare, for all humanity to see, the moral and intellectual bankruptcy of the West. Fixing on the trope of disease, he depicted Europe as "weak," "dissolute," "delirious," "impotent," and "broken." He believed that the war had dealt a "death blow" to Europe's moral authority, but that its physical capacity to dominate had not yet dissipated. With the alternative for humanity represented by the militarist, materialist West discredited, Aurobindo reasoned, a new world was waiting to be born. And India—with its rich and ancient spiritual legacy—would play a pivotal role in bringing that world into being.

Of all of the Indian critics of the West, Aurobindo was the only one to probe explicitly the capitalist underpinnings of its insatiable drive for power and wealth, and the contradictions that had brought on the war and ensuing global crisis. Aurobindo mocked Woodrow Wilson's version of a new world order with its betrayal of wartime promises of self-determination for the colonized peoples. Though he felt that the Bolshevik Revolution had the potential to correct some of the worse abuses of capitalism, Aurobindo concluded that socialism alone could not bring about the process of regeneration that humanity needed to escape the *kali yuga* or age of decline and destruction in which it was ensnared. Only Indian spiritualism and a "resurgent Asia" could check the socialist tendency to increase the "mechanical burden of humanity" and usher in a new age of international peace and social harmony.[53]

Although he was soon to become the pivotal leader of India's drive for independence, Gandhi was not a major contributor to the cross-cultural discourse on the meanings of World War I for European global dominance. Despite his emergence in the decade before the war as major protest leader in the civil-disobedience struggles against the pass laws in South Africa, Gandhi, like Tagore, felt that he must "do his bit" to support the imperial war effort. He served for some months as an ambulance driver, and later sought to assist British efforts to recruit Indians into the military. When the contradiction between his support of the war and his advocacy of nonviolent resistance was pointed out, Gandhi simply replied that he could not expect to enjoy the benefits of being a citizen of the British Empire without coming to its defense in a time of crisis.[54] But he clearly saw that the war had brutally revealed the limits of Western civilization as a model for the rest of humanity. Even before the war, particularly in a 1909 pamphlet titled "Hind Swaraj," he had begun to dismiss Western industrial civilization in the absolute terms that were characteristic of his youthful thinking on these issues. Like the holy men activists who had come before him, such as Vivekananda and Aurobindo, and drawing on prominent critics of industrialism and materialism, such as Tolstoy and Thoreau, Gandhi concluded that it was folly to confuse material advance with social or personal progress.[55] But he went beyond his predecessors in detailing alternative modes of production, social organization, and approaches to nature that might replace those associated with the dominant West. The war strengthened his resolve to resist the spread of industrialization in India, and turned him into a staunch advocate of handicraft revival and village-focused community development. Though often neglected in works that focus on his remarkable impact on India's drive for independence, these commitments—fed by his witness of the catastrophic Great War—were central to Gandhi's own sense of mission. As he made clear in an article in *Young India* in 1926, freedom would be illusory if the Indian people merely drove away their British rulers and adopted their fervently nationalistic, industrial civilization wholesale. He urged his countrymen to see that

India's destiny lies not along the bloody way of the West . . . but along the bloodless way of peace that comes from a simple and godly life. India is in danger of losing her soul. She cannot lose it and live. She must not, therefore, lazily and helplessly say: "I cannot escape the onrush from the West." She must be strong enough to resist it for her own sake and that of the world.[56]

Because most of sub-Saharan Africa had come under European colonial rule only a matter of decades before 1914, the Western-educated classes of the continent were a good deal smaller than their counterparts in India. With important exceptions, such as the Senegalese of the *Quatre Communes*, African professionals and intellectuals tended to have fewer avenues of access to institutions of higher learning in Europe and fewer opportunities for artistic and literary collaboration with their British, French, or German counterparts than the Indians.[57] For these reasons, and because the new Western-educated classes of Africa were fragmented like the patchwork of colonial preserves that the continent had become by the end of the Europeans' late 19th-century scramble for territory, African responses to the Great War were initially less focused and forceful than those of Indian thinkers such as Tagore and Aurobindo. Only well over a decade after the conflict had ended did they coalesce in a sustained and cogent interrogation of the imperialist apologetics of the civilizing-mission ideology. But the delay in the African response cannot be attributed to an absence of popular discontent or disillusioned intellectuals in either the British or French colonies. In the years following the war, anthropologists serving as colonial administrators and European journalists warned of "a most alarming" loss of confidence in their European overlords on the part of the Africans. They reported widespread bitterness over the post-Versailles denial of promises made to the colonized peoples under the duress of war and a general sense that the mad spectacle of the conflict had disabused the Africans of their prewar assumption that the Europeans were more rational and in control—hence more civilized.[58]

These frustrations and a bitter satire of the Europeans' pretensions to superior civilization were evident in René Maran's novel *Batouala*, which was published in 1921 and was the first novel by an author of

African descent to win the prestigious Prix Goncourt in the follow-ing year. An *évolué* from Martinique, Maran had been educated from childhood in French schools and had served for decades in the French colonial service. His account of the lives of the people of Ubangui-Shari, the locale in central Africa where the novel takes place, tends to vacillate between highly romanticized vignettes of the lives of African villagers and essentialized depictions of the "natives" as lazy, promis-cuous, and fatalistic that are worthy of a European *colon*. But Maran's skillful exposé of the empty promises of civilizing colonizers added an influential African voice to the chorus of dissent that began to drown out Europeans' trumpeting of the global mission in the post-war years.

Although Maran's protagonist, Batouala, admits to an "admiring terror" of the Europeans' technology—including their bicycles and false teeth—he clearly regards them as flawed humans rather than demigods with supernatural powers. In a series of daring inversions, Maran's characters compare their superior bodily hygiene to the sweaty, smelly bodies of the colonizers; their affinity with their natu-ral surroundings to the Europeans' "worry about everything which lives, crawls, or moves around [them]"; and their "white" lies to the exploitative falsehoods of the colonizers:

> The 'boundjous' (white people) are worth nothing. They don't like us. They came to our land just to suppress us. They treat us like liars! Our lies don't hurt anybody. Yes, at times we elaborate on the truth; that's because truth almost always needs to be embellished; it is because cassava without salt doesn't have any taste. Them, they lie for nothing. They lie as one breathes, with method and memory. And by their lies they establish their superiority over us.[59]

In the rest of the tale that Maran relates, the vaunted colonizers' mission to civilize is revealed as little more than a string of conscious deceptions and broken promises. In exchange for corvée labor and increasingly heavy taxes, Batouala and his people have been promised "roads, bridges, and machines which move by fire on iron rails." But the people of Ubangui-Shari have seen none of these improvements; taxes, Batouala grumbles, have gone only to fill the "pockets of our commandants." The colonizers have done little more than exploit the Africans, whom they contemptuously regard as slaves or beasts of burden. In their arrogant efforts to suppress the exuberant celebrations and sensual pleasures enjoyed by Batouala and his fellow villagers, the Europeans are destroying the paradisiacal existence that the African villagers had once enjoyed.[60]

Maran's essentialized treatment of Africa and Africans is more or less a 20th-century rendition of the noble-savage trope that had long been employed by European travelers and intellectuals. In many ways a testament to the thoroughness of his assimilation to French culture, Maran's depiction of the "natives" of Ubangui-Shari might have been written by a compassionate colonial official who had dabbled in ethnology during his tour of duty. In fact, it is probable that he was influenced by the work of anthropologist colleagues in the colonial civil service, and the pioneering studies of the Sierra Leonean James Africanus Horton and his West Indian-born countryman Edward Blyden. He would certainly have been familiar with the West African ethnologies compiled by the French anthropologist Maurice Delafosse. Delafosse's works in particular had done much to force a rethinking of Western (and Western-educated African) attitudes toward Africa in the decades before and after World War I.[61] The revision of earlier assessments of African achievement was also powerfully influenced by the "discovery" of African art in the prewar decades by avant-garde European artists of the stature of Derain, Braque, Matisse, and Picasso. The powerful impact of African masks and sculpture on cubism, abstract expressionism, and other modernist movements bolstered once-despairing African intellectuals in their efforts to fight the racist dismissals of African culture and achievement that had been commonplace in 19th-century accounts of the "Dark Continent." The accolades of the European arbiters of high culture energized the delegates who journeyed to Paris from all the lands of the slave diaspora and Africa itself for the Second Pan-African Congress, convened by W. E. B. DuBois in 1919.[62] Though most of those attending from colonized areas urged a conciliatory and decidedly moderate approach to the postwar settlement, many took up DuBois's call to combat racism and linked that struggle to the need to remake the image of Africa that had long been dominant in the West.[63] With its explicit challenges to the assumptions of the civilizing-mission ideology and its acclaim by the French literary establishment, Maran's *Batouala* proved a pivotal, if somewhat eccentric, work.

The extent of René Maran's influence on the progenitors of the Négritude movement that dominated the thinking of African intellectuals in French-speaking colonies from the late 1930s onward has been a matter of some dispute.[64] But both Maran's efforts to reconstruct precolonial life and culture and his challenges to the colonizers' arguments for continuing their domination in Africa, which were grounded in the civilizing-mission ideology, figure importantly in the work of the most influential of the Négritude poets. Maran's background as an *évolué* and a scion of the slave diaspora also reflected the convergence of transcontinental influences, energy, and creativity that merged in the Pan-African Congresses in the 1920s and in the Négritude movement in the following decade.

As Léopold Senghor fondly recalls in his reflections on his intellectual development and philosophical concerns, the circle of Négritude writers began to coalesce in Paris in the early 1930s.[65] He credits Aimé Césaire, a poet from Martinique, for the name of the movement, and sees its genesis in the contributions to the short-lived journal *L'Étudiant noir* and the lively exchanges among the expatriate students and intellectuals drawn to the great universities of Paris from throughout the empire in the interwar decades. Most of the poems that articulated the major themes of Négritude were published after World War II, beginning with the seminal 1948 *Anthologie de la nouvelle poésie négre et malgache de langue française*. But a number of works that were privately circulated in the late 1930s and Aimé Césaire's *Cahier d'un retour au pays natal*, first published in fragments in 1938, suggest the continuing power of recollections of the trauma of World War I in the African awakening.

In Senghor's evocative "Neige sur Paris," the poet wakes up to find the city covered with newly fallen snow.[66] Though encouraged by the thought that the pure white snow might help to soften the deep divisions that threaten to plunge Europe once again into war and heal the wounds of a Spain already "torn apart" by civil war, Senghor conjures up the "white hands" that conquered Africa, enslaved its peoples, and cut down its forests for "railway sleepers." He mocks the mission of the colonizers as indifferent to the destruction of the great forests as they are to the suffering they have inflicted on the African people:

> They cut down the forests of Africa to save Civilization, for
>   there was a shortage
> of human raw-material.

And he laments the betrayal of his people by those posing as peace-makers, suggesting the ignoble machinations of the Western leaders at Versailles:

> Lord, I know I will not bring out my store of hatred against
>   the diplomats who flash their long teeth
>   And tomorrow will barter black flesh.

In "For Koras and Balafong," which he dedicated to René Maran, Senghor flees from the factory chimneys and violent conflict of Europe to the refuge of his childhood home, the land of the Serer, south of Dakar along the coast of Senegal. Throughout the poem he celebrates the music and dance, the sensuality and beauty of his people and their communion with the natural world—all central themes in the corpus of Négritude writings. But like Maran, he turns these into inversions of the European societies from which he has fled and that have been defiled by the violence of the Great War. His journey to the land of his ancestors is

> guided through thorns and signs by Verdun, yes Verdun the
>   dog that kept
> guard over the innocence of Europe.

In his travels, Senghor passes the Somme, the Seine, the Rhine, and the "savage Slav rivers" all "red under the Archangel's sword." Amid the rhythmic sounds of African celebration, he hears:

> Like the summons to judgment, the burst of the trumpet
>   over the snowy
> graveyards of Europe.

He implores the earth of his desert land to wash him clean "from all contagions of civilized man," and prays to the black African night to deliver him from

> arguments and sophistries of salons, from pirouetting pre-
> texts, from calculated
> hatred and humane butchery.

These final passages recall the powerful inversions that provide some of the most memorable passages in the verse of Senghor's collaborators and cofounders of the Négritude movement in the 1930s. There is Léon Damas's iconoclastic rejection of the costume of his assimilated self:

> I feel ridiculous
> in their shoes
> in their evening suits,
> in their starched shirts,
> in their hard collars
> in their monocles
> in their bowler hats.[67]

And in Aimé Césaire's *Cahier d'un retour au pays natal,* perhaps the most stirring of the Négritude writers' defiant mockeries of the standards by which the Europeans had for centuries disparaged their people and justified their dominance over them one reads:

> Heia [praise] for those who have never invented anything
> those who never explored anything
> those who never tamed anything
> those who give themselves up to the essence of all things
> ignorant of surfaces but struck by the movement of all
>   things
> free of the desire to tame but familiar with the play of the
>   world.[68]

The discourse centered on the meanings of the Great War for the future of the science and technology oriented civilization pioneered in the West was, I believe, the first genuinely global intellectual exchange. Though the African slave trade had prompted intellectual responses from throughout the Atlantic basin, the post–World War I discourse was the product of the interchange between thinkers from the Americas, Europe, Africa, and Asia. At one level, the postwar discourse became a site for the contestation of the presuppositions of the civilizing mission ideology that had undergirded the global hegemony of the West. At another, it raised fundamental questions about the effects of industrialization in the West itself as well as the ways in which that process was being transferred to colonized areas in Asia and Africa. For nearly two decades, philosophers, social commentators, and political activists scrutinized the ends to which scientific learning and technological innovation had been put since the industrial watershed. Their profound doubts about the long-term effects of the process itself on human development would not be matched until the rise of the global environmentalist discourse that began in the 1960s and continues to the present.

Although unprecedented in its global dimensions, in the colonized areas of Africa and Asia postwar challenges to the industrial order and the civilizing-mission ideology were confined largely to the Western-educated elite. Colonized intellectuals, with such notable (and partial) exceptions as Tagore and Aurobindo, critiqued the hegemonic assumptions of the West in European languages for audiences that consisted largely of Western-educated professionals, politicians, and academics.[69] Even those who wrote in Asian or African languages were also compelled to publish and speak in "strong"[70] languages such as English or French if they wished to participate in the postwar discourse. And as Ngũgĩ wa Thiong'o reminds us, the cage of language set the limits and had much to do with fixing the agenda of that interchange.[71] Not only did Indian and African intellectuals draw on the arguments of Western thinkers such as Tolstoy, Bergson, Thoreau, and Valéry, but the issues they addressed were largely defined by European and, to a lesser extent, American participants in the global discourse. In this sense, the postwar Indian and African assault on the civilizing mission was as reactive as Antenor Firmin's 19th-century refutations of "scientific" proofs for African racial inferiority or Edward Blyden's defense of African culture. Even the essentialized stress on the spirituality of Indian civilization or the naturalness of African culture was grounded in tropes employed for centuries by European travelers, novelists, and Orientalists. As the reception of Maran and Tagore (or Vivekananda before them and Senghor afterward) also suggests, Robert Hughes's "cultural cringe" was very much in evidence.[72] European approbation had much to do with the hearing that Asian or African thinkers received not only in the West, but among the Western-educated, elite circles they addressed in colonial settings.

Although the terms of the discourse between colonizer and colonized remained the same in many respects, the Great War had done much to alter its tone and meaning for Indian and African participants. The crisis of the West and the appalling flaws in Western civilization that it revealed did much to break the psychological bondage of the colonized elite, which, as Ashis Nandy argues, was at once the most insidious and demoralizing of the colonizers' hegemonic devices.[73] World War I provided myriad openings for the reassertion—often in the guise of reinvention—of colonized cultures that were dramatically manifested in the inversions in the postwar writings of Indian and African thinkers of the attributes valorized by the prewar champions of the civilizing mission. The crisis of the Great War gave credence to Gandhi's contention that the path for humanity cleared by the industrial West was neither morally nor socially enabling, nor ultimately sustainable. And though the circle in which the postwar discourse unfolded was initially small, in the following decades it contributed much to the counterhegemonic ideas of the Western-educated intellectuals of Asia and Africa, ideas that were taken up by the peasants and urban laborers who joined them in the revolt against the European colonial order.

Notes

1. For examples of leftist, anti-imperialist acceptance of these convictions, see Martine Loutfi's discussion of the views of Jean Jaures in *Littérature et colonialisme* (Paris: Mouton, 1971), 119; and Raoul Giradet, *L'Idée coloniale en France, 1871–1962* (Paris: La Table Ronde, 1972), 96–98, 104–111.

2. For representative racist views on these issues, see John Crawfurd, "On the Physical and Mental Characteristics of the European and Asiatic Races,"

Transactions of the Ethnological Society of London, 5 (1867): 58–81; and Robert Knox, *The Races of Men: A Philosophical Enquiry into the Influence of Race Over the Destinies of Nations* (London: H. Renshaw, 1862). For samples of long-term evolutionist thinking, see Gustave Le Bon, *The Psychology of Peoples* (London: T. Fisher, 1899); and C. S. Wake, "The Psychological Unity of Mankind," *Memoirs Read before the Anthropological Society of London*, 3 (1867–68): 134–47. Late 19th-century non-racist or antiracist improvers included Jacques Novicov [*L'Avenir de la race blanche* (Paris, 1897)] and Henry Maine [*Short Essays and Reviews on the Educational Policy of the Government of India from the "Englishman"* (Calcutta, 1866)].

3. Reverend Frederick Farrar, "Aptitudes of the Races," *Transactions of the Ethnological Society of London*, 5 (1867), 120. For a less-celebratory view of this process that was closely tied to evolutionary thinking, see Alfred Russel Wallace, "The Development of Human Races under the Law of Natural Selection," *Anthropological Review* (1865).

4. Helen Callaway, *Gender, Culture and Empire: European Women in Colonial Nigeria* (Urbana: University of Illinois Press, 1987), especially 139–45.

5. Leila Ahmed, *Women and Gender in Islam* (New Haven: Yale University Press, 1992), 153–54.

6. In his essay "On Clive," in Macaulay, *Poetry and Prose*, ed. G. M. Young (Cambridge: Harvard University Press, 1970).

7. For examples of these comparisons, see Arthur de Gobineau, *Essai sur l'inégalité des races humaines* (Paris, 1853), vol. 1, 150–52; James Hunt, "On the Negro's Place in Nature," *Memoirs Read before the Anthropological Society of London* (1863–64), 10; and Le Bon, *Psychology of Peoples*, 35–36.

8. Ester Boserup, *Women's Role in Economic Development* (New York: St. Martin's Press, 1979), ch. 3.

9. William Greg as quoted in John C. Greene, *Science, Ideology and World View* (Berkeley: University of California Press, 1981), 108. A stimulating and contentious exploration of these connections can be found in Thomas Haskell, "Capitalism and the Origins of the Humanitarian Sensibility," part 1, *American Historical Review*, 90, no. 2 (1985): 339–61; Thomas Haskell, "Capitalism and the Origins of the Humanitarian Sensibility," part 2, *American Historical Review*, 90, no. 3 (1985): 547–66.

10. See, for examples, Benjamin Kidd, *The Control of the Tropics* (London: Macmillan, 1898), 14, 39, 52–55, 58, 83–84, 88–90; H. H. Johnson, "British West Africa and the Trade of the Interior," *Proceedings of the Royal Colonial Institute*, 20 (1888–89), 91; and Arthur Girault, *Principes de colonisation et de legislation coloniale* (Paris: Larose, 1895), 31.

11. Antonio Gramsci, *Selections from Prison Notebooks*, ed. and trans. Q. Hoare and G. Smith (New York, 1971), 12–14, 55–63, 275–76.

12. See, for example, Ira Klein, "Indian Nationalism and Anti-industrialization: The Roots of Gandhian Economics," *South Asia*, 3 (1973): 93–104; and Bade Onimode, *A Political Economy of the African Crisis* (London: Zed, 1988), 14–22 and ch. 6, 9, and 11.

13. K. M. Banerjea, "The Proper Place of Oriental Literature in Indian Collegiate Education," *Proceedings of the Bethune Society* (February 1868), 149, 154.

14. Keshub Chunder Sen, "Asia's Message to Europe," in *Keshub Sen's Chunder Lectures in India*, vol. 2 (London: Cassell, 1901), 51, 61.

15. S. K. Saha, "Social Contest of Bengal Renaissance," in *Reflections on the Bengal Renaissance*, eds. David Kopf and Joaarder Safiuddin (Dacca: Institute of Bangladesh Studies, 1977), 140.

16. Floyd and Lillian Dotson, *The Indian Minority of Zambia, Rhodesia, and Malawi* (New Haven: Yale University Press, 1968), 262–68, 320.

17. Ndabaningi Sithole, *African Nationalism* (London: Oxford University Press, 1969), 157.

18. On British and French educational policies in 19th-century Africa and their racist underpinnings, see Michael Adas, *Machines as the Measure of Men: Science, Technology and Ideologies of Western Dominance* (Ithaca: Cornell University Press, 1989), ch. 5.

19. Abbé Boilat, *Esquisses sénégalaises* (Paris: Bertrand, 1853), 9–13, 478; and André Villard, *Histoire du Sénégal* (Dakar: M. Viale, 1943), 98.

20. J. A. Horton, *West African Countries and Peoples* (London: W. J. Johnson, 1868), 1–4; and *Letters on the Political Condition of the Gold Coast* (London: W. J. Johnson, 1870), i–iii.

21. Edward Blyden, "Hope for Africa: A Discourse," *Colonization Journal* (August 1861), 7–8; and "The Negro in Ancient History," in *The People of Africa* (New York, 1871), 23–24, 34.

22. For a discussion of these divergent challenges to the underlying assumptions of the civilizing mission, see Adas, *Machines as the Measure of Men*, 345–65.

23. Sigmund Freud, "Reflections on War and Death," (1915), reprinted in Philip Reiff, ed., *Character and Culture* (New York: Collier, 1963), 118. For a fuller discussion of these themes, see Adas, *Machines as the Measure of Men*, ch. 6.

24. On the postwar expansion of the French colonial empire, see Christopher M. Andrew and A. S. Kanya-Forstner, *France Overseas: The Great War and the Climax of French Imperialism* (London: Thames and Hudson, 1981); and for British expansion in the Middle East, see John Darwin, *The British in the Middle East 1918–1922* (London: Macmillan, 1981).

25. Hugh Tinker, "Structure of the British Imperial Heritage," in *Asian Bureaucratic Systems Emergent from the British Imperial Tradition*, ed. Ralph

Braibanti (Durham: Duke University Press, 1966), 61–63; and Henri Massis, *Defense of the West* (London: Faber, 1927), 6, 9, 134. For an insightful discussion of the demoralized state of colonial officialdom in Africa in the post–World War I years, see Robert Delavignette, *Freedom and Authority in French West Africa* (London: Oxford University Press, 1950), 149–50.

26. For discussions of efforts to revive the civilizing-mission ideology in the postwar era, see Girardet, *L'Idée coloniale en France*, 117–32 and ch. 5; and Thomas August, *The Selling of Empire: British and French Imperialist Propaganda, 1890–1940* (Westport, CT: Greenwood, 1985), 126–40. For a thorough exploration of shifts in colonial policy in the 1920s and 1930s, see Frederick Cooper, *Decolonization and African Society: The Labor Question in British and French Africa* (Cambridge: Cambridge University Press, 1996).

27. For a fuller discussion of these themes, see Adas, *Machines as the Measure of Men*, ch. 6.

28. The novel was originally published in 1917. The first English translation appeared in 1919 (London: Century Company) with the same title as the original. Direct quotations in this essay are taken from the 1919 translation, and so numbered; otherwise page numbers refer to the 1922 Paris edition, published by Mercure de France.

29. Duhamel, *Civilisation*, 257–58, 268–69; *Entretien sur l'esprit européen* (Paris: Mercure de France, 1928), 17–18, 36–39; *La Pensée des âmes*, (Paris: Mercure de France, 1949); and *La possession du monde* (Paris: Mercure de France, 1919), 18–19, 140, 242–45.

30. Paul Valéry, "Letters from France I: The Spiritual Crisis," *The Athenaeum* (11 April 1919), 182.

31. Duhamel, *Civilisation*, 11–12.

32. *Possession du monde*, 99. One is reminded here of Celine's obsessive fear of trees, "since [he] had known them to conceal an enemy. Every tree meant a dead man," (*Journey to the End of Night* [New York: New Directions, 1960], 53); or Remarque's tortured account of wounded horses who died in no-man's-land "wild with anguish, filled with terror, and groaning." (*All Quiet on the Western Front* [New York: Fawcett Crest, 1975], 61).

33. Quoted passages in the following are taken from the English translation of *Civilisation 1914–1918*, ch. 16, unless otherwise noted.

34. Sandra Gilbert, "Soldier's Heart: Literary Men, Literary Women, and the Great War," *Signs* 8, no. 3 (1983): 435.

35. Duhamel, *Civilisation*, 282–83.

36. See, for examples, Mary Louise Pratt, *Imperial Eyes: Travel Writing and Transculturation* (London: Routledge, 1992).

37. For samples of the use of these metaphors by infantrymen from each of

the major combatant nations on the Western Front, see Roland Rorgelès, *Les Croix de Bois* (Paris: Albin Michel, 1919), 62, 113; Henri Barbusse, *Under Fire: The Story of a Squad* (London, 1916); Remarque, *All Quiet*, 103–04, 236–37; and Richard Aldington, *The Death of a Hero* (London, 1984), 255, 264, 267.

38. Quoted portions from Manning's *Middle Parts of Fortune* (New York: St. Martins, 1972), 8, 12, 39–40. Other references to Remarque, *All Quiet*, 12–13, 124–25, 236–37; Aldington, *Death of a Hero*, 362; and Ludwig Renn, *War* (London: Antony Mott, 1984), 110–11.

39. Léon-François Hoffman, *Le Nègre romantique: Personnage littéraire et obsession collective* (Paris: Payot, 1973); and Eric J. Leed, *No Man's Land: Combat and Identity in World War I* (Cambridge: Cambridge University Press, 1979), 126–27.

40. Robert Wohl, *The Generation of 1914* (Cambridge: Harvard University Press, 1979), 12–13.

41. Duhamel, *Civilisation*, 268; quoted phrases, *Civilisation*, 272.

42. The following discussion is based heavily on relevant sections from *La Possession du monde*, especially 140, 242–46, 254–56, 264–65; and *Entretien sur l'esprit Européen*, 17–18, 20–22, 29–37, 40–46, 50.

43. See, for example, *Les Espoirs et les Épreuves* (Paris: Mercure de France, 1953), 135–36, 186–87.

44. Duhamel visited America in the late 1920s and came away with decidedly negative impressions that are detailed in his *America the Menace: Scenes from the Life of the Future* (London: Allen and Unwin, 1931).

45. See Mal, *Dayanand* (1962), 66–68, 73, 216; Dayanda, *Satyarth Prakash*, 292–93; Vivekananda, *Collected Works*, vol. 1, 13, 134; vol. 2, 124, 140–41.

46. Ibid., 121, 365. For Guenon's celebration of the higher levels of thinking achieved by Indian philosophers, see *The Crisis of the Modern World* (London, 1924), 24–26, 66–67, 125–26; and *East and West* (London, 1941), 23–26, 36–39, 43–44, 57–62, 68.

47. Vivekananda, *Collected Works*, vol. 2, 410–11. For Coomaraswamy, see *The Dance of Shiva* (London: Sunrise Turn Press, 1924). For an appreciation of Coomarswamy's message by an influential European thinker, see Romain Rolland's introduction to this edition of the work. Among the many works on Morris and the English arts-and-crafts revival, two of the best are E.P. Thompson, *William Morris: Romantic to Revolutionary* (London: Lawrence and Wisehart, 1955), and Peter Stansky, *Redesigning the World: William Morris, the 1880s, and the Arts and Crafts* (Princeton: Princeton University Press, 1985).

48. From his *Lectures from Colombo to Almora*, as quoted in V. S. Narvane, *Modern Indian Thought* (Bombay: Asia Publishing House, 1964), 106. See also *Collected Works*, vol. 4, 410–11.

49. Mary M. Lago, ed., *Imperfect Encounter: Letters of William Rothenstein and Rabindranath Tagore* (New Haven: Yale University Press, 1972), 189, 191.

50. Carolyn Merchant has convincingly demonstrated this in *The Death of Nature* (New York: Harper and Row, 1983). This discussion of Tagore's responses to the war is based upon the following sources: *Diary of a Westward Voyage* (Bombay: Asia Publishing House, 1962), 68–69, 71–74, 96–97; *Letters from Abroad* (Madras: Ganesan, 1924), 18, 56, 66, 83–85, 130; *Personality* (London: Macmillan, 1917), 50, 52, 169–75, 181–82; and *Nationalism* (London: Macmillan, 1917), 33, 37, 44–45, 77, 91–92. Only additional references and quoted portions of Tagore's writings will be individually cited below.

51. See Gandhi's writings in *Young India* during the war years. Also Adas, *Machines as the Measure of Men*, 221–236.

52. Aurobindo's responses to the war are set forth in the most detail in his essays on *War and Self-determination* [Calcutta: Sarojini Chose, n.d. (c. 1924)]; and *After the War* (Pondicherry: Shri Aurobindo Ashram, 1949).

53. Quoted portions from "After the War," 10, 13.

54. For Gandhi's activities during the war and justifications of his support for the British, see *The Story of My Experiments with Truth: The Autobiography of Mahatma Gandhi* (Boston: Beacon, 1957 ed.), 346–48; and Louis Fischer, *The Life of Mahatma Gandhi* (New York: Collier, 1962), 133, 164–65, 180, 288–90.

55. See, for example, his address to the YMCA at Colombo in Ceylon (Sri Lanka), which was reprinted in *Young India*, December 8, 1927.

56. *Young India*, October 7, 1926.

57. See Michael Crowder, *Senegal: A Study in French Assimilationist Policy* (London: Methuen, 1967), ch. 1 and 2.

58. See, for example, John A. Harris, "The 'New Attitude' of the African," *Fortnightly Review* 108 (1920), 953–60, and G. St. John Orde-Browne, *The Vanishing Tribes of Kenya* (London: Seeley, Service, 1925), 271.

59. René Maran, *Batouala*, trans. Barbara Beck and Alexandre Mboukou (London: Heinemann, 1973), 74.

60. Ibid., 29–31, 47–50, 75–76.

61. See, for example, his monumental survey *The Negroes of Africa*, first published in 1921. On his impact, see Gérard Leclerc, *Anthropologie et colonialisme: essai sur l'histoire de l'Africainisme* (Paris: Fayard, 1972), 43–52; and Girardet, *L'Idée coloniale*, 158–64.

62. On these connections, see S. Okechukwu Mezu, *Léopold Sedar Senghor et la défense et illustration de la civilisation noire* (Paris: M. Didier, 1968), especially 32–36.

63. Crowder, *Colonial West Africa*, 408–12.

64. Dorothy S. Blair, *African Literature in French* (Cambridge: Cambridge University Press, 1976), 18–20.

65. See Senghor, *Ce que je crois: négritude, francité et civilisation de l'universel* (Paris: B. Grasset, 1988), 136–52.

66. Quoted portions are taken from the superb translation of "Snow upon Paris," by John Reed and Clive Wake in Senghor, *Selected Poems* (Oxford: Oxford University Press, 1964).

67. From "Solde," published in Léon-Gontran Damas, *Pigments* (Paris: Présence Africaine, 1962) and quoted in Abiola Irele, "Négritude—Literature and Ideology," *Journal of Modern African Studies*, 3, no. 4 (1965): 503.

68. From *Cahier d'un retour au pays natal*, translated as *Return to My Native Land* by John Berger and Anna Bostock (Harmondsworth, England: Penguin, 1969), 75.

69. These patterns are stressed by Paul Sorum in his treatment of the origins of Négritude in *Intellectuals and Decolonization in France* (Chapel Hill: University of North Carolina Press, 1977), 213–14.

70. For a discussion of this useful concept, see Talal Asad, "Two European Images of Non-European Rule," in *Anthropology and the Colonial Encounter*, ed. Talal Asad (New York: Humanities Press, 1973), 103–18.

71. *Decolonising the Mind: The Politics of Language in African Literature* (London: Heinemann, 1986).

72. "The Decline of the City of Mahagonny," *New Republic*, June 28, 1990, 27–28.

73. Ashis Nandy, *The Intimate Enemy: Loss and Recovery of Self Under Colonialism* (Delhi: Oxford University Press, 1983), esp. xi–xiii.

3

Modeling States and Sovereignty

Postcolonial Constitutions in Asia and Africa

Julian Go

THE DECOLONIZATION OF Asia and Africa since World War II appears at once as a novel and yet banal historical process. On the one hand, it was an intensified moment of state-building and frenzied constitutional activity. As Western empires crumbled, they left behind a multitude of nascent states seeking to institute new constitutional orders. The number of these new states, and especially their impact upon the configuration of the global political map, is staggering. In 1910 there were fifty-six independent countries in the world. By 1970, the number had increased to one hundred and forty-two. In 1973 Ivo D. Duchacek thus noted that "Over two-thirds of the [world's] existing national constitutions were drafted and promulgated in the last three decades."[1] On the other hand, there is also a sense in which decolonization marked less a historical change than continuity. Similar to the anticolonial nationalism that Partha Chatterjee has theorized elsewhere, the independence constitutions of Asia and Africa have been haunted by the specter of appearing unoriginal.[2] According to existing views, these constitutions were little else than imitations of Western constitutions. More specifically, they appear as dysfunctional duplications of the constitutions of former imperial masters. New African states, according to Francois Perrin, "yielded to the temptation of trying to adopt the [constitutional] institutions of the erstwhile imperial power."[3] E. Brausch similarly asserted in 1963 that the constitutions of Africa were "too close to their Western models."[4] R. N. Spann has made parallel claims for Asia: constitutions there reflect the unflattering "mark of uninventiveness."[5] It would seem that the more things change the more they stay the same. Postcolonial constitutions may have marked a historical novelty by their sheer number but, according to the existing literature, they merely imitated and thereby reproduced the constitutional models of former colonial powers.

This story of intraimperial isomorphism in independence constitutions, though, remains largely a proposition. As yet there are no macrolevel studies of all of the independence constitutions in Asia and Africa.[6] Furthermore, most existing scholarship was written in the immediate wake of decolonization. Retrospective studies on independence constitutions, or works that synthesize the extant literature to compare across cases remain forthcoming tasks. Certainly this gap makes sense. Many independence constitutions were altered or overturned completely after the first few years of their promulgation, and scholars since have directed their attention to issues of constitutional change, whereas others have interrogated the apparent failure of constitutionalism more generally. Indeed, the strength of constitutionalism in postcolonial societies remains a debated question.

The present essay makes one step toward bridging this gap. I return to the proposition that there was isomorphism between the constitutions of postcolonial state and former colonial powers, but I do so through an analysis of all of the independence constitutions of Asia and Africa since World War II.[7] Looking across different countries—and therefore across different empires, regions, and specific local conditions—to what extent can we maintain the claim that constitution-makers mapped their postcolonial states in accordance with the constitutional models of former imperial states? Given the scope, this analysis is extensive rather than intensive, exploratory rather than definitive. Constitutions are complex things. They are replete with subtle legal intricacies and they bear the mark of various historical conditions and processes. To narrow the focus, I restrict the analysis to four basic elements of the constitutions: governmental form, provisions for religion, political parties, and fundamental rights. On these counts I look for patterns across the independence constitutions and ask whether or not these patterns can be explained by the imperial factor.[8]

The analysis reveals two general processes at work. First, at the register of governmental form, there was indeed a trend toward intraimperial isomorphism. When it came to choosing monarchical, parliamentary, or presidential forms, a great majority of postcolonial states—regardless of geographic location or particular colonial history—modeled their constitutions after that of their former colonial ruler. But such intraimperial isomorphism is not the whole story. Constitutional provisions for religion, parties, and human rights in at least half of the independence constitutions show influences that cannot be traced to former colonial powers. I argue that in these cases, postcolonial states turned to models that circulated across, rather than within, empires and regions. Such models often belied the models of the Western empires. They evidence a nascent set of transimperial, cross-colonial, and thus potentially globalizing influences.

Questions of Governmental Form: Imposition, Imitation, and Isomorphism

Of course, there are a number of good reasons for thinking that the independence constitutions in Asia and Africa were isomorphic with metropolitan constitutions. One reason has to do with direct imperialist imposition.[9] According to MacKenzie and Robinson, imperial powers had a vital interest in ensuring that the independence constitutions followed their own constitutional model: "When the time comes to transfer power, the colonizer inevitably satisfies his conscience as to the integrity of his act by implanting a system modeled upon the democratic values and their structural embodiment which are cherished at home."[10] Young has noted similarly that "both colonial administrators and metropolitan opinion demanded that departure, if it had to come, should be honorable. Inevitably, honor was measured by the closeness of the apparent approximation of metropolitan institutions."[11] Imperial powers thus used various means to ensure constitutional isomorphism. Even a cursory examination of the processes by which independence constitutions were written is suggestive of this influence. For example, while some of the independence constitutions of the former British empire were written by constituent assemblies, they ultimately had to be approved by the British for independence to be granted. This was especially true for those African countries that joined the Commonwealth: the constitutions of Ghana, Kenya, Nigeria, and Tanganyika had to be signed by the British monarch with the same stroke that granted independence.[12] Similarly, the constitutions of the former British colonies in Asia were partially written by the British themselves, or at least by British appointees. The independence constitution of Malaysia was drafted by a committee appointed by the British Crown and chaired by the British jurist Lord Reid. There had been no constituent assembly.[13] The independence constitution of India was drafted in part by an Indian Constituent Assembly, and Indian elites attended constitutional conferences in London, but the critical decisions were made by policy-makers in England.[14] Other imperial powers also seem to have played a hand in the drafting of independence constitutions. American authorities allowed Filipinos to draft a constitution, but according to the Philippine Independence Act of 1934 it had to be approved by the US President.[15]

Besides imperial imposition, another reason for predicting isomorphism has to do with imitation on the part of the colonized. According to this argument, the native political elite who took part in constitution-making or lent their support to the new constitutions were themselves eager to draw upon metropolitan models. This is what Carl Friedrich once called, in reference to African constitutions, the "hidden impulse of a foreign (colonial) constituent power working through small groups of converts to Western constitutionalism."[16] Indeed, when the makers of the constitution were not representatives of the former imperial power, they were typically members of the colonial elite who were well-educated in (or at least exposed to) the political idioms of their former mother country. And they often saw much value in the metropolitan political forms.[17]

The story, in short, is that imposition and imitation led to intraimperial isomorphism. This story bears out when we examine the governmental forms proscribed in the independence constitutions. By governmental form I refer to the basic institutions of state and the functional distribution of power among them, particularly the relations between the executive and legislative powers. All of the imperial powers at the time of decolonization had constitutions dictating one of three forms: (1) parliamentary, (2) constitutional monarchy, or (3) presidential.[18] England has the prototypical parliamentary form, with the head of government dependent upon the confidence of the legislature. Alternatively, Belgium and the Netherlands have constitutional monarchies: the head of state is hereditary and exercises real legislative or executive powers, as opposed to merely ceremonial powers. Finally, France, the United States, and Portugal each has a presidential system. The president, as both the head of state and head of government, is elected by popular vote for a fixed term of office. The French system is somewhat unique. The constitution of the Fifth French Republic (1958) mixed some elements of both the parliamentary and presidential systems. Nonetheless, in this constitution the leaning was more clearly towards the presidential.[19]

Independence constitutions in Asia and Africa imitated these governmental forms, and most of them were direct imitations. Indicative are the constitutions of the earliest colonies to obtain independence. In Africa, for example, Ghana was the first to achieve independence, and as a member of the British Commonwealth, its 1957 independence constitution made the Queen of England the official head of state who, in turn, acted through a governor. The head of government was a prime minister responsible to an elected parliament.[20] This was an exact duplicate of the Westminster system. In Asia, we find that the independence constitutions of Burma (1947) and India (1950) also followed the Westminster model, however with slight modifications. For example, the executive in both countries was referred to as a President, but the President was elected by Parliament and was responsible to it.[21] The deviation was not enough to categorize these constitutions as presidential; they remain squarely within the Westminster model. Notably, we find a parallel to this in Africa with the 1966 Botswana constitution and with Zambia's 1963 constitution. It named Kenneth Kaunda as president, but the next president was to be elected by parliament. Kaunda fashioned this constitution as "essentially our own—designed to suit our own needs and conditions and our own way of life." Still, as even he later admitted, it was largely inspired by the British system.[22]

A preliminary look at other constitutions also reveals imperial influence, despite variations in timing, region, and the conditions under which the constitution was written. Even Algeria, which was somewhat unique in the French empire in that it won its independence through a protracted and violent struggle, imitated the French presidential system.[23] The independence constitution of the Ivory Coast (1959) also imitated the French presidential system and, more specifically, the constitution of the Fifth Republic, which incorporated parliamentary and presidential elements but placed most emphasis on the latter.[24] The constitution of the Philippines (1935) also had a presidential system, though it was modeled after the US rather than the French system as, indeed, the Philippines had been the only US colony in Asia.[25] In Burundi there was isomorphism also. There the precolonial-monarchical system found resonance with the Belgian monarchy: the 1962 constitution called for a king—"in direct, natural and legitimate descendence of S. M. Mwambutsa IV"—to serve as constitutional monarch.[26] All of these cases therefore imply a larger pattern of intraimperial imposition and imitation, with some exceptions. However, even a case like Cambodia—which established a constitutional monarchy in 1947 that approximated the British or Belgian systems more than the French—is an exception that nonetheless proves the rule. Coding the independent constitutions of the former French and British colonies into three categories—monarchical, parliamentary, or presidential—and cross-tabulating these by former empire, we find that the majority of independence constitutions followed the model of their former imperial ruler (see Table 1).[27]

Table 1. Independence Constitutions: Governmental Form
in the Former British and French Colonies

	Monarchy	Parliamentary	Presidential	TOTAL
Former British Colonies	0	20	0	20
Former French Colonies	3	1	18	22

All of the independence constitutions of the former British colonies followed the British pattern and called for parliamentary systems. Of the former French colonies, four deviated from the French model.[28] Besides Cambodia, two others also deviated from the French model by adopting a monarchical system rather a presidential one: Morocco and Laos. The fourth deviation is North Vietnam, which had a parliamentary system. In the 1959 constitution, there was a President but he was responsible to the legislative assembly. This is primarily due to the socialist ideology behind the constitution: the legislative assembly was actually the base of the Vietnam Workers' Party, and the president chosen by the assembly was therefore an organ of the party.[29] But again, these stand as exceptions. The other French colonies, eighty percent of them, adopted the presidential system.

The Influence of Religion

Although most independence constitutions explicitly adopted the governmental form of their former imperial master, there is evidence of a counterlogic: many had peculiar provisions regarding religion. Fifteen, constituting twenty-eight percent in toto, either: (1) explicitly name a specific religion as the official state religion, (2) make reference to a specific religion as providing certain legal principles, (3) have some kind of provisions that directly elevate a particular religion, or (4) have some combination of these. None of the religions named is the religion of the former imperial master. They are either Buddhism or Islam. These cases thereby show the work of cultural influences on independence constitutions besides that of the former colonial power.

The constitution of Pakistan is exemplary. On the one hand it was based after the British-constitutional model, incorporating key elements of the Westminster system even as it named the head of state "President." On the other hand, the constitution contained certain articles with references to Islam, thus deviating significantly from the British system. Article 32(2), for instance, lays out the qualifications for the President and states that Presidential candidates must be of the Muslim faith. Articles 197 and 198, under the heading "Islamic Provision," take the matter further. Article 197 states that the President must set up an organization for Islamic research and instruction in advanced studies to assist in the reconstruction of Pakistan society along Islamic lines. Article 198 calls for an appointed Commission of Experts to make recommendations "as to the measures for bringing existing laws into conformity with the Injunctions of Islam." Furthermore, the constitution makes the state responsible for enabling the Muslims "to order their lives according to the teachings of Islam, to make the teaching of the Koran compulsory, and to organize the collection and expenditure of the charitable religious tax (zakat)."[30]

These provisions have little parallel in the constitutions of any of the major Western imperial powers. True enough, there is a long history of religious influence upon written constitutions in the West. In fact, constitutionalism in Western civilization had always been intimately tied to Christianity, the traces of which are still seen in some modern European constitutions. Canon law, as Said Arjomand reminds us, was a critical factor in the emergence of Western constitutionalism.[31] Of course in England, Henry VIII established the Church of England and Parliament made him head. The traces of this religious history are still seen in some modern European constitutions. The Basic Law of the Federal Republic of Germany (1949) states that it is the work of the German People "conscious of its responsibility before God and Men." The constitution of Ireland, dating from 1937, states that it was enacted "in the Name of the Most Holy Trinity, from Whom is all authority and to Whom, as our final end, all actions both of men and States must be referred."[32] Still, the secularization of public law, and hence of constitutions, had been completed long before the 20th century. Whether one goes back to the social-contract theories of Hobbes and Locke or to Montesquieu's *Spirit of the Laws* (1748), reason had come to replace religion as the foundation of human laws. In Weber's classic formulation, written constitutions asserted rational-legal legitimacy over and above other forms of legitimacy, not least those associated with religious authority. Ultimately this process of legal-rational secularization led to the great importance given in most Western constitutions to the separation of Church and State.[33] The constitutional scholar Carl Friedrich in 1964, after tracing the religious origins of Western constitutions, was quite correct when he referred to this period (and therefore the time of decolonization) as "an age when the religious foundations of constitutionalism have almost vanished."[34]

The religious provisions in the constitution of Pakistan thus stand in contrast to the British model and to the constitutional models of the major imperial powers more generally. Indeed, the specification that the President has to be a Muslim was modeled on the constitutions of Aghanistan, Greece, Iran, Paraguay, Saudi Arabia, Syria, and Thailand. These constitutions had similar provisions for a religious executive. Perhaps more importantly, proponents argued on principle, claiming that it was "a fundamental principle of an Islamic Constitution that a person who did not believe in 'Allah' could not be expected to rule over Muslims."[35] The decision to name Pakistan an "Islamic Republic" was legitimated by reference to Islamic principle, as well as to the constitution of the Soviet Union. At the constituent assembly, Sardar Abdur Rab Nishtat explained:

> It is necessary to give some indication about the nature of our republic. According to the Objectives Resolution the character of *our constitution is to be based on principles of equality, democracy and tolerance as enunciated by Islam.* Therefore, it is quite natural that this Republic should be described as an Islamic Republic. Take the name of the great country U.S.S.R. It is described as Socialist Republics. . . . Islamic Republic of Pakistan means that this republic would be run in accordance with the principles laid down by Islam.[36]

One of the major goals animating the framers of the Pakistan independence constitution, then, was that it should incorporate the dictates of Islam, not the principles of British law.

Of course, it might not be surprising that many of Pakistan's constitutional provisions were influenced by sources other than those emanating from the British. After all, its separation from India was in large part predicated upon the Islamic character of the majority of the population. Further, none of the drafters of the Pakistan constitution were representatives of England. By the time the first constitution was approved, it had been at least ten years since British rule. Nonetheless, even in those cases where British representatives had indeed played a hand in constitution-making, there were significant religious-influenced provisions. The independence constitution of Malaysia, for instance, was initially drafted by a five-member Royal Commission appointed by the Queen of England and headed by Lord Reid, a distinguished Judge of the House of Lords. Also on the commission were representatives from other parts of the British empire, namely Australia, India, and Pakistan.[37] It is not entirely surprising that the subsequent constitution of 1957 was inspired by the British system. However, despite this British influence, the constitution originally contained Islamic provisions. Part I, Article 3(1) states that "Islam is the religion of the Federation; but other religions may be practised in peace and harmony." Article 3(2) states further that each of the Federation Rulers has to serve as the "head of the Muslim religion in his State," whereas Article 3(3) says that the *Yang di Pertuan Agong* is to serve as "the Head of the Muslim religion" in the two other states of Malacca and Penang. Moreover, the Fourth Schedule of Part XIV, article 181, dictates that in his oath of office, the *Yang di Pertuan Agong* must declare that he shall "at all times protect the religion of Islam and uphold the rules of law and order in the country."[38]

These Islamic provisions were demanded by the Malaysian elite. The Royal Commission had spent a year traveling throughout the country to collect opinions and debate initial recommendations. It received 131 memoranda from various Malaysian organizations, held 81 hearings across the peninsula, and met with Malay officials.[39] During this time, the Alliance Party demanded that Islam be the state religion.[40] Lord Reid noted his disapproval in his report, but the Pakistani member of the Commission, Mr. Justice Abdul Hamid, felt that since the demand among the Malaysian elite seemed unanimous it should be included. Hamid legitimated the move not by referencing the British system but other constitutions:

> A provision like the one suggested above is innocuous. Not less than fifteen countries of the world have a provision of this type entrenched in their Constitutions. . . . Among the Muslim countries are Afghanistan (Art. 1), Iran (Article 1), Iraq (Art. 3), Jordan (Art. 2), Saudi Arabia (Art. 7), and Syria (Art. 3). Thailand is an instance where Buddhism has been enjoined to be the religion of the King who is required by the Constitution to uphold that religion. If in these countries a religion has been declared to be the religion of the State and that declaration has not been found to have caused hardships to anybody, no harm will ensue if such a declaration is included in the Constitution of Malaya.[41]

As with their Pakistan counterparts, the Malaysian writers found sources of influence other than that of their former imperial ruler. Indeed, the Islamic provisions could be traced, genealogically, all the way back to the period preceding British rule when Islam was having a strong impact upon Malaysian customary law.[42] Furthermore, the specific content of constitutional provisions can be traced to constitutional developments in the Ottoman empire during the late 19th century. In the 1870s, constitutional reformers in the Ottoman empire had hoped to create a new constitution modeled after the Belgian constitution but filled with Islamic content. The resulting Fundamental Law of 1876 declared Islam the religion of the state (Art. 11), just as Malaysia's constitution did later. Finally, the Sultan was declared the *padishah* (monarch) of the Ottoman state and the "protector of Islamic religion" in equal measure. This is similar to the Fourth Schedule of Part XIV, article 181, in the Malaysian constitution, which provides that the *Yang di Pertuan Agong* should declare himself "protector" of Islam.[43]

Evidence of Islamic influence is found in other constitutions and not just those of the British empire or of countries in Asia. The 1959 constitution of Tunisia, a former French protectorate, began with a Preamble declaring:

In the name of God, the merciful! We, the Representatives of the Tunisian people, meeting at the Constituent National Assembly, proclaim, that this people, who have liberated themselves from foreign domination . . . on remaining true to the teachings of Islam, to the ideal of a Union of the Great Maghreb, to their membership of the Arab Family, to their co-operation with the African peoples in building a better future and to all peoples struggling for justice and freedom.

Thus, as Romdhane argues, the Tunisian independence constitution was not strongly influenced by the French constitution.[44] Its sources must rather be traced back to constitutional ideas of Islamic intellectuals who had been part of the Nahda reformist movement, a movement that once embraced Turkey, Egypt, and Tunisia alike.

Other African countries with Islamic provisions include Algeria, Libya, Morocco, Mauritania, the Comoros, and Somalia. All of these countries declared Islam their state religion. But Islam is not the only religious influence on independence constitutions. The constitutions of Cambodia and Laos, for example, proclaim Buddhism as their state religion. Both Cambodia and Laos were formerly of the French empire, and both were constitutional monarchies. Laos, however, went further than Cambodia in its Buddhist provisions.[45] Art. 7 of the Laos independence constitution declares Buddhism to be the religion of the state and the king as "its High Protector." Art. 8 states that "His person is sacred and inviolable. He must be a fervent Buddhist." Besides Cambodia and Laos, the constitution of Burma also had a religious provision. Although it did not declare Buddhism the official state religion, article 21(1) asserted: "The State recognizes the special position of Buddhism as the faith professed by the great majority of the citizens of the Union." This was a compromise between conservative leaders who wanted to make Buddhism the state religion and other Burmese leaders such as Bogyoke Aung San who wished the state to be secular.[46]

The narrative of imperial imposition and imitation cannot explain why all three of these Asian countries—Burma, Laos, and Cambodia—defied Western constitutional models by inserting religious provisions. They had been part of different empires: Burma had been a

British colony, whereas Cambodia and Laos had been French colonies. The important similarity they shared was not their former imperial ruler, but the fact that they were the only three postcolonial countries of Southeast Asia that had been historically subjected to the influence of Theravada Buddhism, which had originally traveled from Sri Lanka through Burma to Cambodia and Laos.[47] The diasporic factor, rather than imperial influence, thus becomes key. For example, while precise numbers are difficult to obtain, it is not entirely off the mark to state that all of the countries that had religious provisions in their constitutions also had a large proportion of inhabitants who adhered to the particular religion in question. Perhaps by the same token, what many of these countries shared was membership in particular subregions that then went into the making of a religious diasporic identity. For example, as Laos, Burma, and Cambodia were all Southeast Asian countries forming a geographic chain around Thailand, so too were Algeria, Morocco, Libya, and Mauritania countries that stretched across Northern Africa. These constitutions thereby reveal one critical way in which transnational influences, in this case religious influence, cross-cut any particular metropolitan-colony circuit to work against the logic of intraimperial isomorphism.

Socialist Ideology and One-party States

If religion formed one transimperial circuit of influence on constitutions, socialist ideology provided another. Whereas, as Ziyad Motala notes, comparably little attention has been paid to the potential influence of these ideologies on independence constitutions, their influence on some independence constitutions is indeed strong, lending toward the creation of novel constitutional forms.[48] In Algeria, for instance, the constitution (1963) begins with a Preamble declaring:

> Algerian people have waged an unceasing armed, moral and political struggle against the invader and all his forms of oppression. . . .
> In March 1962 the Algerian people emerged victorious from the seven and half years' struggle waged by the National Liberation Front. . . .

Faithful to the program adopted by the National Council of the Algerian Revolution in Tripoli, the democratic and popular Algerian Republic will direct its activities toward the creation of the country in accordance with the principles of socialism and with the effective exercise of power by the people, among whom the fellahs, the laboring masses and the revolutionary intellectuals shall constitute the vanguard.

Having attained the objective of national independence which the National Liberation Front undertook on November 1, 1954, the Algerian people will continue its march toward a democratic and popular revolution.

This intimates a constitutional type that belies the standard Western constitutional model. For one thing, rather than merely reflecting the structure of state power or mapping out state institutions and functions, as is the case for Western constitutions, the Algerian constitution also appears to be an instrument of social transformation. It incorporates ideological goals. Thus, it proclaims loudly that the people will follow the program of the National Council of the Algerian Revolution and direct their activities "toward the creation of the country in accordance with the principles of socialism." Later in the Preamble definite economic and social programs are laid out, such as "the creation of a national economy whose administration will be ensured by the workers"; "a social policy for the benefit of the masses to raise the standard of living of the workers, to accelerate the emancipation of women in order that they may take part in the direction of public affairs"; and so on. In related fashion, there is a strong historical aspect to the constitution. The Preamble narrates a long story about Algerian resistance to French rule, situating the present independence moment in Algerian history, and then projects a socialist future. Finally, at the center of it all is a single political party: the National Liberation Front. The party is defined as "the revolutionary force of the nation," a "powerful organ of impulsion." The party duties are likewise laid out: the party "will mobilize, form and educate the popular masses"; "perceive and reflect the aspirations of the masses"; "draw up and define the policy of the nation and supervise its implementation"; and so on. The party thus becomes the mover of history; its sovereignty replaces the sovereignty of the nation: "The National Liberation Front . . . will be the best guarantee of the conformity of the country's policy with the aspirations of the people." Accordingly, Article 23 declares it "the single vanguard party in Algeria." Articles 27 and 39.2 instruct the National Liberation Front to designate presidential candidates who are then elected through universal suffrage.[49]

Such constitutional features are traceable to a socialist or communist constitutional model exemplified in the constitutions of the former Soviet Union and China. In this model, constitutions are intended to map the historical progress of society, charting its movement toward the final state of communism. Accordingly, in this model new constitutions are to be written at each stage in the evolution, reflecting the particular historical moment and projecting a future.[50] This explains the strong temporal component in the language of the Algerian Preamble. It is remarkably similar to the Preamble to the constitution of the People's Republic of China (1954). That Preamble begins by discussing the "century of heroic struggle" and the "great victory in the people's revolution against imperialism, feudalism, and bureaucratic-capitalism." It proceeds to discuss how China is in "a period of transition" and then ends by pointing to the future and "the progress of humanity" which it will bring. Second, in the socialist-constitutional model, goals are explicitly laid out in the constitution, enumerating the projects, policies, and programs that need to be undertaken in order to evolve. Thus similarly, the Algerian constitution lists various social and economic policies (Preamble and also Article 10). Finally, in socialist political systems, constitutions are not so much intended to limit government as they are designed to express that the constitution is, in a sense, limited by the ruling party.[51] In the 1936 Soviet constitution, the Communist Party is "the leading and guiding force of Soviet society and the nucleus of its political system and of all state and social organizations."[52] Likewise, the Preamble to the Algerian constitution states that the FLN is the only vanguard party, leading the destiny of the nation. The Algerian constitution also has articles under the heading "National Liberation Front" that lay out the duties of the Party (Articles 23–26). Finally there are in the Algerian constitution articles to ensure that the party rules the executive and the government as a whole (e.g., Articles 27 and 39.2).

This is not to say that the Algerian constitution replicated the Soviet or Chinese constitutions exactly. To the contrary, the Algerian constitution incorporates some elements of the constitution of its former imperial master, France, primarily in regard to its presidential system. The constitution called for a President of Algeria and a National Assembly elected by universal suffrage (Articles 27 and 39). By contrast, in the Soviet model the closest thing to an "executive branch" is not a President but a Council of Ministers elected by the legislature cum "Supreme Soviet." The Algerian constitution thus forges a novel synthesis; for even though the constitution spells out a French-styled Presidential system, it contains provisions that give the Party full control over the Assembly and the President. The Party is given the power to nominate Assembly candidates and Presidential candidates and thus dominates both branches. As one Algerian deputy explained at the time: "Well disciplined, the assembly executes the party's orders."[53]

Other African countries whose constitutions were influenced by ideologies of socialism include former Portuguese colonies Angola, Cape Verde, Guinea-Bissau, Mozambique, and São Tome. All of these independence constitutions not only declared adherence to socialist principles but also provided for the dominance of a single party. The constitution of Mozambique (1975), for example, begins with Article 1 stating: "The People's Republic of Mozambique, the fruit of the Mozambican People's centuries-old resistance and their heroic and victorious struggle, under the leadership of FRELIMO, against Portuguese domination and imperialism, is a sovereign, independent, and democratic state." Party dominance is secured by Article 3, which declares FRELIMO as the official party, and by other provisions such as Article 47 which makes the President of the Party also the President of the Republic. In the Guinea-Bissau constitution (1973), Article 3 declares that "the State shall have as its objective . . . the building of a society that shall create the political, economic, and cultural conditions needed to eliminate the exploitation of man by man and all forms of subordination for the human being to degrading interests for the benefit of any individual, group, or class." This constitution therefore follows the Soviet and Chinese model more closely than did the constitution of Algeria. For instance, duplicating the Chinese constitution, the Guinea-Bissau constitution called for a Council of State elected by the People's National Assembly rather than a President elected by universal suffrage (Articles 36–41).[54]

The 1959 constitution of the Democratic Republic of Vietnam is another that adopted a socialist constitutional model, thereby revealing socialist influence on Asia.[55] The preamble to the VDR constitution narrates the anticolonial struggle and "the Vietnamese Revolution," which "advanced into a new stage" with the Indochinese Communist Party. The preamble then discusses the meddling of "French imperialists, assisted by the U.S. imperialists" over Vietnam in the early 1950s and declares: "The Vietnamese revolution has moved into a new position. Our people must endeavour to consolidate the North, taking it towards socialism; and to carry on the struggle for peaceful reunification of the country and completion of the tasks of the national people's democratic revolution throughout the country." Chapter II of the constitution, titled "Economic and Social System," lays out a plan for state-led socialist development (Articles 9–21). Article 9 introduces the plan by stating "The Democratic Republic of Vietnam is advancing step by step from people's democracy to socialism by developing and transforming the national economy along socialist lines, transforming its backward economy into a socialist economy with modern industry and agriculture, and an advanced science and technology." Finally, provisions for the organs of government mimic the Chinese system almost directly, at times merely changing the names of the institutions but nonetheless reproducing the language almost verbatim. For example, the 1954 Chinese Constitution has provisions for a National People's Congress, which is "the only legislative authority," a Chairman of the Republic elected by the Congress, and a State Council, which is "the highest administrative organ of state."[56] Likewise, in the Vietnamese constitution there are provisions for a National Assembly defined as "the only legislative authority," a President elected by the Assembly, and a Council of Ministers which, just like the State Council in China, is defined as "the highest administrative organ of state" (Articles 43, 44, 61, and 71).

The Vietnamese constitution shows that whereas all of the for-mer Portuguese colonies, winning their independence after 1970, adopted the socialist model of constitutions, there is no one-to-one relationship between former colonial power and socialist constitu-tions. The former colonies of Portugal adopted the socialist model, but so too did some of the former colonies of other imperial pow-ers. By a conservative estimate, at least two former French colonies (Algeria and Vietnam) and at least one former British colony (Sey-chelles) were strongly influenced by socialist-constitutional models. What all of these countries share is not any single former imperial master but a common history of resistance. Most if not all of them had strong communist movements prior to independence, and they could be said to have achieved independence through violent, pro-tracted struggle. This meant that during the struggle they formed revolutionary governments.[57] Furthermore, these constitutions are not the only ones that were influenced by socialist ideology. Certain aspects of other independence constitutions were also influenced to varying degrees by socialist models, even if these constitutions did not provide for single-party states. Elements of the constitutions of Egypt, Tanzania, and Guinea, as well as Mali, Benin, and Togo could all be traced to socialist influence.[58] Of course later, after the first years under their initial independence constitution, many other postcolo-nial states came to adopt one-party systems and advocate socialism.[59] Thus socialist ideology, like religion, served as a transnational force, which in some instances destabilized the logic of imperial imitation, imposition, and isomorphism.

Fundamental Rights

There has been a general trend over the past decades, evidenced around the globe, toward an increasing constitutional concern for rights. It has been noted by Lawrence Beer that by 1991, "168 of 173 states had a single-document national constitutions with substantial provisions about human rights."[60] The independent constitutions of Asia and Africa surely contributed to this trend. All but three of them had provisions mentioning or enumerating fundamental rights.[61] Of course the particulars are not uniform. Some of the constitutions cover more rights than others. Some enumerate rights in the preamble, whereas others enumerate them in particular articles or chapters. But there is a clear predominance of provisions for rights in these independence constitutions, as the overwhelming majority has them. To what extent did direct imperial influence play a hand in this trend?

Some cases reveal direct imperial influence quite clearly. One example is the 1935 constitution of the Philippines. Rights in that constitution were enumerated in Article III, known as *the Bill of Rights,* which closely resembled the first ten amendments of the US Constitution, also typically referred to as *the Bill of Rights.* Indeed, all of the rights enumerated in the US Constitution, from freedom of assembly to free speech and press, were reproduced in the Philippine Bill of Rights. In fact, much of the language is remarkably the same. Section 1(1), Article III, of the Philippine Constitution reproduces Amendment V of the US Constitution verbatim. Section 1(3) reproduces Amendment IV. The reasons for such direct influence have to do with the processes of imitation and imposition already noted above. For one thing, the Filipinos who drafted the constitution were well versed in US constitutional law and emulated the US system. The head of the committee was José P. Laurel, a graduate of Yale Law School; others had taken courses in American constitutional law taught by the American-constitutional scholar George A. Malcolm at the University of Philippines.[62] Thus as the President of the Philippine Constitutional Convention observed, all of the delegates to the convention believed that the US-constitutional system should serve as the model.[63] Further, many elements of the US Bill of Rights had already been incorporated into colonial law through various organic acts and official instructions since the beginning of US occupation.[64] Finally, there were direct constraints imposed by the colonialists that readily led to isomorphism. By the Philippine Independence Act of 1934, the constitution had to be approved by the US President who, in turn, had to certify that it provided for a republican form of government and contained a bill of rights.[65]

The constitutions of the former colonies of other imperial powers also reveal imperial influence on rights provisions. Some of the former French colonies borrow directly from the French Declaration of the Rights of Man of 1789. The preamble to the 1959 independence constitution of Upper Volta (before it became Burkina Faso) begins by stating explicitly: "The people of Upper Volta proclaims its attachment to the principles of democracy and the rights of man as defined by the Declaration of the Rights of Man and the Citizen of 1789." This phrasing is almost identical to the phrasing of the preamble to the 1964 independence constitution of Dahomey (Benin), another former French colony: "The People of Dahomey . . . solemnly proclaim their attachment to the principles of democracy and the rights of man as defined in the Declaration of Rights of Man and the Citizen of 1789." At least nine out of the twenty-two former French colonies explicitly refer to the French Declaration of 1789.[66]

Still, intraimperial imitation is not the only story. The constitutions of the former British colonies are the most indicative. As is well known among constitutional scholars, the British model of fundamental rights is unique. Unlike the US or France, human rights in Britain have arisen as common law or as statutory rights and have not been entrenched in a single-document written constitution. This is due to the principle of parliamentary sovereignty as laid out long ago by A. V. Dicey: Parliament has the right to make or unmake laws, which means that no courts can overrule Parliament and that, therefore, there is no urgent need to have a formal constitution with a bill of rights.[67] The same principle, and therefore the same absence of extensive constitutional guarantees for rights, applied as well to the older Commonwealth countries such as Canada, Australia, and New Zealand.[68] But if this is the British model, most of the British colonies did not follow it when formulating their independence constitutions. Except for three (Brunei, Singapore, and Tanzania), all of the former British colonies had provisions enumerating fundamental rights in single-document written constitutions.[69] This in itself is a deviation from the model of the imperial master. As Franck Moderne observes: "Great Britain introduced to its former colonies . . . constitutional guarantees of fundamental rights that it had not established at home."[70] In fact, unlike the US imperialists in the Philippines, many British imperialists opposed having constitutional guarantees of fundamental rights in both the preindependence constitutions of the British empire and the independence constitutions. Sir Ivor Jennings opposed constitutional guarantees of rights when drafting various preindependence and independence constitutions for former British colonies like Sri Lanka and Malaysia. He justifies this by saying that while Britain has no Bill of Rights, and while "we merely have liberty according to law . . . we think—truly I believe—that we do the job better than any country."[71] The rights provisions in the constitutions of the former British colonies, then, are not traceable to direct imperial influence by the British. They must rather be traced to other sources.

Consider the independence constitution of India (1949), one of the first former British colonies in Asia to have rights provisions. Fundamental rights are laid out in part 3 titled "Fundamental Rights," and are listed under headings such as the "Right to Equality," the "Right to Freedom," "Right to Freedom of Religion," "Right to Property," and "Right to Constitutional Remedies." The concern for these rights among India's political leaders stretches back to at least 1924, when the National Convention prepared the Commonwealth of India Bill that contained a "declaration of rights."[72] Later conventions and conferences among India's political leaders affirmed the demand for such a declaration of rights, despite British opposition. The influence throughout these conventions and conferences, including the meetings of the Constituent Assembly, which led to the formulation of India's independence constitution, was the United States model, not the British model. In 1947, for instance, Sir B. N. Rau, one of the key advisers to the Indian Constitution, traveled to the US and held meetings with several members of the Supreme Court and the Columbia Law School.[73] A year later, at the Indian Constituent Assembly, members of the Assembly consistently referred to the United States Constitution during the discussion of rights provisions.[74] Finally, when it came time to draft the rights provisions, the subcommittee in charge made more direct references to the US Constitution. One member, Sir Alladi, "advised the sub-committee to take the United States as model for the protection of the basic rights of citizens."[75] Thus, early drafts of the constitution as well as the final draft reveal the US influence. As Tripathi shows, "almost every fundamental right which was included in these [early] drafts and which finally became part of the Constitution of India has its counterpart in the United States Bill of Rights."[76]

The United States Constitution influenced other independence constitutions besides India. The "Fundamental Liberties" section of the Malaysian constitution was modeled after India's independence constitution, thereby adopting, however indirectly, the US model. Indeed, that section of the Malaysian constitution contained language very similar to the US Bill of Rights.[77] Part 2, article 5(1), for example, states that "no person shall be deprived of his life or personal liberty save in accordance with the law," whereas article 6(1) declares that "No person shall be held in slavery." The constitutional guarantees for rights in the 1945 independence constitution of Indonesia also had US influence, in this case as direct as the influence on the Indian constitution. Mohamed Yamin, one of the key framers, referred to various US documents in the midst of the drafting process: "Before me is the structure of the Republic of the United States of America, which time and again has been used as an example for several constitutions in the world, for this is the oldest constitution existing in the world and contains three elements: (1) Declaration of Rights in the city of Philadelphia (1774); (2) the Declaration of Independence of July 4, 1776; (3) and finally, the Constitution of the United States of America."[78] The fact that India, Malaysia, Indonesia, and the Philippines all followed the US model in drafting their constitutional guarantees for rights, despite that only one of them was a former US colony, thus attests to transimperial rather than intraimperial circuits of influence.[79]

Besides the United States Constitution, there were other nonimperial circuits of influence. The constitution of Nigeria is exemplary. Like India, the 1960 Nigerian constitution belied the British model by including provisions for fundamental rights. The concern for constitutional guarantees emerged out of the sociopolitical situation at the time. Nigeria had been fundamentally divided into three regions each with different ethnic groups, and each of the three major political parties represented one of the three regions. This situation meant that some Nigerian leaders were cautious of possible oppression by the other regional-ethnic groups upon the withdrawal of the British. Definite constitutional provisions for rights (along with federalism) became one of the solutions.[80] This is not unlike the situation in India, where communal minorities had desired some constitutional guarantees of rights to protect themselves.[81] Unlike India, though, the influence was not so much the US Constitution as it was the influence of a document forged by a transnational organization that had been unavailable to the Indian framers: the European Convention on Human Rights (1950), ratified under the auspices of the Council of Europe. Indeed, the Minorities Commission, appointed for the purpose of determining how to handle the fears of minority populations, stated explicitly that the European Convention of Human Rights should serve as the model.[82] Thus, the Nigerian Constitution and the European Convention share crucial similarities that together stand in contrast to the US Constitution. Both documents have provisions detailing freedom against torture and inhuman treatment, for instance; and both have provisions explicitly protecting the right to family life.[83] Furthermore, rather than working from concepts of equality before the law, equal protection, and due process, both incorporate guarantees of freedom from discrimination and lay out "the implications of due process in terms of explicit procedural safeguards and detailed substantive restrictions on the permissible content of legislation."[84]

The European Convention served as a model for rights provisions in the independence constitutions of many other African countries also, either through direct influence or indirectly through the Nigerian constitution serving as a precedent. These include, in chronological order after Nigeria: Sierra Leone, Uganda, Kenya, Malawi, Gambia, Botswana, Lesotho, Mauritius, Swaziland, the Seychelles, and Zimbabwe.[85] There seems to have been a strong diffusion effect: once Nigeria adopted the European Convention as a model, so too did many others.[86] Iain Mcleod, Secretary of State to the colonies, intimated this Nigerian influence already in 1960, noting that leaders from other British African colonies were already interested in using Nigeria as a model. The code of fundamental human rights in the Nigerian constitution, he said, "has been extremely useful because it has proved a model for many of the conferences I have presided over since [1958, when the code was first formulated]. I have found people from many countries ready to accept as, for example, the delegates from Kenya and Sierra Leone did, the Nigerian proposals as a model for the future."[87]

As the former British colonies drew upon transimperial influences, so too did former French colonies. As said already, many of the former French colonies imitated the French constitutions of the Fourth and Fifth Republics: their independence constitutions referred directly to the Declaration of the Rights of Man of 1789. But just as many French colonies also referred to the Universal Declaration of Human Rights of 1948. The preamble to the independence constitution of Niger (1959), for example, read: "The people of Niger proclaims its attachment to the principles of democracy and the Rights of Man as defined by the Declaration of the Rights of Man and the Citizen of 1789, by the Universal Declaration of 1948 and as they are guaranteed in this Constitution." The constitutions of Cameroon, Chad, Dahomey (a.k.a. Benin), the Ivory Coast, Mauritania, Niger, Senegal, and Upper Volta (a.k.a. Burkina Faso) had similar references. Meanwhile, other former French colonies eschewed reference to the French Declaration altogether and instead referred only to the Universal Declaration of Human Rights of 1948. One example is Algeria's constitution (1963). Article 11 states: "The Republic adheres to the Universal Declaration of the Rights of Man. Convinced of the necessity of international co-operation, it will give its support to any international organization which corresponds to the aspirations of the Algerian people." Other former French countries with constitutions that refer only to the Universal Declaration are Comoros (1975), Congo-Brazzaville (1958), Djibouti (1977), Guinea (1958), Madagascar (1958), and Mali (1958).

The impact of the Universal Declaration by the United Nations was indeed wide-ranging and not only restricted to former French colonies. Togo, which had been both a French and British colony, referred to it in its independence constitution. The independence constitutions of the former colonies of Belgium (Rwanda, Burundi, and Zaire/Congo) and Spain (Equatorial Guinea) explicitly refer to it also. One former colony of Italy (Somalia) refer to the Universal Declaration in its independence constitution, whereas the independence constitution of another former colony of Italy (Libya) was heavily influenced by it even though it did not refer to it directly.[88] In such manner, discourses of rights in the United States Constitution, the European Convention, and the United Nations—like religion and socialist ideology—all served as transimperial influences on independence constitutions, short-circuiting direct imperial influence.

Conclusion

My attempt to transcend existing studies and look comparatively has only been exploratory. There are a number of aspects to the independence constitutions that I have not been able to cover here. The provisions for court systems, for example, have yet to be examined. Future researchers might also pay closer attention to certain innovations such as synthetic or hybrid elements in them, which resulted from an interaction between localized and imperial influence. But despite its limits, my macrolevel analysis already shows that the story of intraimperial isomorphism needs to be amended. On the one hand, at the level of governmental form, constitution-makers indeed looked to the constitutional models of their imperial master, not least due to the constraints of imperial imposition and logics of imitation. On the other hand, constitution-makers at times looked elsewhere for certain provisions, circumventing direct imperial influence to find other sources that circulated in between and across countries, geographic regions, and empires. In this sense, these independence constitutions did in fact mark something new, for in them lie the marks of a post-imperial constitutional politics.[89]

Notes

1. Duchacek as quoted in Lawrence W. Beer, "Introduction: Constitutionalism in Asia and the United States," in *Constitutionalism in Asia: Asian Views of the American Influence*, ed. Lawrence W. Beer (Berkeley: University of California Press, 1979), 8.

2. Partha Chatterjee, *The Nation and Its Fragments* (Princeton: Princeton University Press, 1994).

3. Crawford Young, *Politics in the Congo: Decolonization and Independence.* (Princeton: Princeton University Press, 1965), 210.

4. G. E. J. Brausch, "African Ethnocracies: Some Sociological Implications of Constitutional Change in Emergent Territories of Africa," *Civilisations*, 13, nos. 1–2 (1963), 85.

5. R. N. Spann, "Notes on Some Asian Constitutions," in *Constitutionalism in Asia*, ed. R. N. Spann (Bombay: Asia Publishing House, 1963), 10.

6. The work of Nwabueze is an exception but nonetheless examines only African constitutions, not Asian ones. See Benjamin Obi Nwabueze, *Constitutionalism in the Emergent States* (London: C. Hurst and Company, 1973).

7. I focus upon the original independent constitutions of Asia and Africa. I exclude later versions of these constitutions and the independence constitutions of the countries in other regions (for example, Caribbean and the Pacific). This leaves a total of sixty-five constitutions. Copies of many of the constitutions are available in volumes compiled by Blaustein and Flanz (1971–94) and Peaselee (1966). Since these volumes publish constitutions only at specific intervals, some of the original independence constitutions are missing and thereby had to be tracked down in various secondary sources. See Albert P. Blaustein and Gisbert H. Flanz, eds., *Constitutions of the Countries of the World* (New York: Dobbs Ferry, 1971–94); Amos J. Peaselee, *Constitutions of Nations* (The Hague: Martinus Nijkoff, 1966).

8. The analysis is based upon a reading and coding of all independence constitutions in Africa and Asia since World War II supplemented and contextualized with secondary studies of one or another case. Below, I discuss in detail only a handful of constitutions within the larger database. These constitutions are selected either for their representative character, the fact that they were the earliest independence constitution of a particular region or former empire, or for comparative purposes (for example, comparing across regions, timing, empire, or conditions of constitutional enactment).

9. This argument as it applies to the independence constitutions in Africa has been raised by Yash P. Ghai, *Constitutions and the Political Order in East Africa* (Dar es Salaam: University College Dar es Salaam, 1970), 10–12; Nwabueze, *Constitutionalism in the Emergent States*, 23; and Julius K. Nyerere, "Reflections on Constitutions and the African Experience," in *Constitutions and National Identity*, ed. Thomas J. Barron, Owen Dudley Edwards, and Patricia J. Storey (Edinburgh: Quadriga, 1993), 9.

10. Quoted in Young, *Politics in the Congo*, 176.

11. Crawford Young, *The African Colonial State in Comparative Perspective* (New Haven: Yale University Press, 1994), 210.

12. On Ghana, see T. O. Elias, *Ghana and Sierra Leone: The Development of their Laws and Constitutions* (London: Steven and Sons, 1962). On Kenya, see James Nyamweya, "The Constitution of Kenya," *Civilisations*, 14, no. 4 (1964), 331. On Nigeria, see F. R. A. Williams, "The Making of the Nigerian Constitution," in *Constitution Makers on Constitution Making*, eds. Robert A. Goldwin and Art Kaufman (Washington, DC: American Enterprise Institute for Public Policy Research, 1983). On Tanganyika, see Kenneth Robinson, "Autochthony and the Transfer of Power," in *Essays in Imperial Government*, eds. Kenneth Robinson and Frederick Madden (Oxford: Basil Blackwell, 1963), 264–67.

13. Ahmad Ibrahim and M. P. Jain. "The Constitution of Malaysia and the American Constitutional Influence," in *Constitutional Systems in Late Twentieth Century Asia*, ed. Lawrence W. Beer (Seattle: University of Washington Press, 1992), 507.

14. Ivor Jennings, *The Commonwealth in Asia* (Oxford: Clarendon Press, 1949), 57.

15. Enrique M. Fernando, "The American Constitutional Impact on the Philippine Legal System," in *Constitutionalism in Asia: Asian Views of the American Influence*, ed. Lawrence W. Beer (Berkeley: University of California Press, 1979), 168.

16. Nwabueze, *Constitutionalism in the Emergent States*, 27. In the parlance of neo-institutional theory within sociology, we might call this a logic of "mimetic isomorphism" as opposed to "coercive isomorphism."

17. Besides, constitution-writing often took place under extreme conditions, which meant that constitution-makers did not always have the luxury of time to seriously consider other options. See M. G. Winton, "Decolonisation and the Westminster Model," in *Africa in the Colonial Period III. The Transfer of Power: The Colonial Administrators in the Age of Decolonization.*, ed. A. H. M. Kirk-Greene (Oxford: University of Oxford Inter-Faculty Committee for African Studies, 1979), 185.

18. Here I follow the criteria laid out by Arend Lijphart, "Introduction," in *Parliamentary Versus Presidential Government*, ed. Arend Lijphart (Oxford: Oxford University Press, 1992); Fred W. Riggs, "Bureaucratic Power and Administrative Change," *Administrative Change*, 11 (1984), 136; Benjamin Obi Nwabueze, *Presidentialism in Commonwealth Africa* (New York: St. Martin's, 1974), 28, 29; and Ivo D. Duchacek, *Power Maps: Comparative Politics of Constitutions* (Santa Barbara: American Bibliographical Center-Clio Press, Inc., 1973), ch. 6 and 7.

19. Maurice Duverger, "A New Political System Model: Semi-Presidential Government," in *Parliamentary Versus Presidential Government*, ed. Arend Lijphart (Oxford: Oxford University Press, 1992), 142; Stanley Hoffman, "The French Constitution of 1958: The Final Text and Its Prospects," *American Political Science Review*, 53 (1959), 332–57.

20. Elias, *Ghana and Sierra Leone*, 46.

21. Articles 45–84. See also U. Maung Maung, "The Search for Constitutionalism in Burma," in *Constitutionalism in Asia*, ed. R. N. Spann (Bombay: Asia Publishing House, 1963), 118–19.

22. Kenneth Kaunda, *Zambia Independence and Beyond. The Speeches of Kenneth Kaunda*, ed. and with an intro. by Colin Legum (London: Thomas Nelson and Sons, 1966), 86.

On how this system approximated the parliamentary form, see M. G. de Winton, "Decolonisation and the Westminster Model," 189–90.

23. David Ottoway and Marina Ottoway, *Algeria: The Politics of a Socialist Revolution* (Berkeley: University of California Press, 1970), 77–79.

24. Aristide Zolberg, *One-Party Government in the Ivory Coast* (Princeton: Princeton University Press, 1964).

25. The 1935 constitution was for the Commonwealth of the Philippines, but it was used also as the constitution when the Philippines officially obtained complete independence in 1946.

26. Article 51. See John Webster, *The Constitutions of Burundi, Malagasy and Rwanda* (Chicago: Program of East African Studies, 1964), 1, 2.

27. This coding scheme follows Riggs who analyzes differences in presidential, parliamentary, and monarchical regimes in the Third World more generally. See Fred W. Riggs, "Bureaucratic Power and Administrative Change," *Administrative Change*, 11 (1984): 105–58. Some countries, like Ghana, had a queen (in this case the Queen of England) but are coded as *parliamentary* rather than monarchical since the Queen is not the real executive power and is instead ceremonial only.

28. It is not my purpose here to explain why more former French colonies deviated than former British colonies. But it may have had to do with the different approaches between the French and the British to decolonization. See Smith for a good discussion of these different approaches. Tony Smith, "Patterns in the Transfer of Power: A Comparative Study of French and British Decolonization," in *The Transfer of Power in Africa: Decolonization 1940–1960*, ed. Prosser Gifford and William Roger Louis (New Haven: Yale University Press, 1982).

29. I discuss socialist constitutional models below.

30. Article 25. See also Said Amir Arjomand, "Religion and Constitutionalism in Western History and in Modern Iran and Pakistan," in *The Political*

Dimensions of Religion, ed. Said Amir Arjomand (Albany: State University of New York Press, 1993), 89.

31. Arjomand, "Religion and Constitutionalism in Western History and in Modern Iran and Pakistan," 76–77.

32. John Markoff and Daniel Regan, "Religion, the State and Political Legitimacy in the World's Constitutions," in *Church–State Relations: Tensions and Transitions*, eds. Thomas Robbins and Roland Robertson (New Brunswick: Transaction, 1987), 169.

33. Arjomand, "Religion and Constitutionalism in Western History and in Modern Iran and Pakistan," 76–77.

34. Carl J. Friedrich, *Transcendent Justice: The Religious Dimensions of Constitutionalism* (Durham: Duke University Press, 1964).

35. Javid Iqbal, "The Islamic State in Pakistan," in *Constitutionalism in Asia*, ed. R. N. Spann (Bombay: Asia Publishing House, 1960), 141.

36. Ibid., 142.

37. Tun Mohamed Suffian bin Hashim, "The Malaysian Constitution and the United States Constitution," in *Constitutionalism in Asia: Asian Views of the American Influence*, ed. Lawrence W. Beer (Berkeley: University of California Press, 1979), 132.

38. As translated in Ahmad Ibrahim and M. P. Jain, "The Constitution of Malaysia and the American Constitutional Influence," in *Constitutional Systems in Late Twentieth Century Asia*, ed. Lawrence W. Beer (Seattle: University of Washington Press, 1992), 521.

39. Harry E. Groves, *The Constitution of Malaysia* (Singapore: Malaysia Publications, 1964), 13.

40. Federation of Malaya, *Federation of Malaya Constitutional Proposals* (Kuala Lummpur: Government Press, 1957); Suffian bin Hashim, "The Malaysian Constitution and the United States Constitution," 132.

41. Ahmad Ibrahim, "The Position of Islam in the Constitution of Malaysia," in *The Constitution of Malaysia. Its Development: 1957–1977*, eds. Tun Mohamed Suffian, H. P. Lee, and F. A. Trindade (Kuala Lumpur: Oxford University Press, 1978), 48–49.

42. Groves, *Constitution of Malaysia*, 33.

43. On the Ottoman constitutions see Said Amir Arjomand, "Constitutions and the Struggle for Political Order," *Archives Europeennes de Sociologie/ Archives of European Sociology*, 33 (1992): 51–52.

44. Mahmoud Ben Romdhane, "Constitutionalism and Social Movements in Tunisia," (Working Paper Prepared for the African Regional Institute of the American Council of Learned Societies Comparative Constitutionalism Project, 1989), 5.

45. For a discussion of the formation of the Cambodian constitution, see David P. Chandler, *The Tragedy of Cambodian History* (New Haven: Yale University Press, 1991), 28–29.

46. U. Maung Maung, *Burma's Constitution* (The Hague: Martinus Nijhoff, 1959), 98.

47. Thailand has also been influenced by Theravada Buddhism, but it had not been colonized and therefore is not in my database. Vietnam had seen a different Buddhist sect, Mahayana Buddhism, and it occupied a less-prominent place in Vietnamese society than did Theravada Buddhism in Burma, Laos, and Cambodia. Joel Steinberg, ed., *In Search of Southeast Asia* (Honolulu: University of Hawai'i Press, 1985), 39.

48. Ziyad Motala, *Constitutional Options for a Democratic South Africa* (Washington, DC: Howard University Press, 1994), 120.

49. For more on the Algerian one-party constitution, see Arjomand, "Constitutions and the Struggle for Political Order," 62–64; Henry F. Jackson, *The FLN in Algeria: Party Development in a Revolutionary Society* (Westport: Greenwood Press, 1977), 95–97; Ottoway and Ottoway, *Algeria*, 77–79.

50. William J. Duiker, "Socialist Republic of Vietnam: The Constitutional System of the Socialist Republic of Vietnam," in *Constitutional Systems in Late Twentieth Century Asia*, ed. Lawrence W. Beer (Seattle: University of Washington Press, 1992), 331.

51. Jan F. Triska, "Introduction," in *Constitutions of the Community Party-States*, ed. Jan F. Triska (Palo Alto: Hoover Institution on War, Revolution, and Peace, 1968), xi.

52. Motala, *Constitutional Options for a Democratic South Africa*, 117–18.

53. Ottoway and Ottoway, *Algeria*, 77.

54. China had given aid to preindependence socialist movements in parts of Portuguese Africa. See Kenneth Maxwell, "Portugal and Africa: The Last Empire," in *The Transfer of Power in Africa: Decolonization 1940–1960*, eds. Prosser Gifford and William Roger Louis (New Haven: Yale University Press, 1982).

55. Vietnam had a provisional constitution in 1946 but it was intended to be temporary until a proper constitution was drafted.

56. Constitution of the People's Republic of China, Articles 21, 22, 39, and 47.

57. Seychelles is the unique case here. Independence was gained peacefully in 1976, but the first real independence was not promulgated until much later [1979] due to a coup soon after independence had been granted.

58. Motala, *Constitutional Options for a Democratic South Africa*, 120, 156.

59. There is a large literature on African states taking this path, but see,

for example, Onésimo Silveira, *Africa South of the Sahara: Party Systems and Ideologies of Socialism* (Stockholm: Rabén and Sjögren, 1976).

60. Lawrence W. Beer, "Conclusion: Towards Human Rights Constitutionalism in Asia and the United States?" in *Constitutional Systems in Late Twentieth Century Asia*, ed. Lawrence W. Beer (Seattle: University of Washington Press, 1992), 708.

61. The exceptions are Singapore, Tanganyika, and Vietnam.

62. Enrique M. Fernando, "The American Constitutional Impact on the Philippine Legal System," in *Constitutionalism in Asia: Asian Views of the American Influence*, ed. Lawrence W. Beer (Berkeley: University of California Press, 1979), 169.

63. A. Caesar Espiritu, "Constitutional Development in the Philippines," in *Constitutionalism and Rights: The Influence of the United States Constitution Abroad*, eds. Louis Henkin and Albert J. Rosenthal (New York: Columbia University Press, 1990), 266.

64. Ibid., 262.

65. Other former French colonies, while not referring explicitly to the French Declaration, nonetheless adopt the sequential form for rights in the French constitution. For example, the independence constitutions of the Central African Republic (1959), Madagscar (1959), and Gabon (1961), among others, follow the constitutions of the French Fourth and Fifth Republics by proclaiming attachment to rights and then enumerating them in the Preamble, as opposed to the US form whereby rights are enumerated in separate titles or chapters. Enrique M. Fernando, "The American Constitutional Impact on the Philippine Legal System," 168.

66. On this French practice, see Nwabueze, *Constitutionalism in the Emergent States*, 43.

67. On this see Anthony Lester, "Fundamental Rights: The United Kingdom Isolated?" *Public Law*, Spring (1984): 46–72. There are, though, documents such as the Bill of Rights (1689), the Magna Carta (1215), the Petition of Right (1628), and various Habeas Corpus Acts.

68. Stanley de Smith, *The New Commonwealth and Its Constitutions*. (London: Stevens and Sons, 1964), 170–71.

69. Brunei, rather than inserting rights provisions in its constitution (1959) seems to have adopted the British model in that rights have arisen from common law and statutory rights. See Ahmad Ibrahim and Valentine S. Winslow, "The Kingdom of Brunei: Constitution and Monarch in Brunei," in *Constitutional Systems in Late Twentieth Century Asia* (Seattle: University of Washington Press, 1992), 370.

70. Franck Moderne, "Human Rights and Postcolonial Constitutions

in Sub-Saharan Africa," in *Constitutionalism and Rights: The Influence of the United States Constitution Abroad*, eds. Louis Henkin and Albert J. Rosenthal (New York: Columbia University Press, 1990), 327.

71. Joseph Cooray, *Constitutional and Administrative Law of Sri Lanka* (Colombo: Hansa Publishers, 1973), 509–11.

72. P. K. Tripathi, "Perspectives on the American Constitutional Influence on the Constitution of India," in *Constitutionalism in Asia: Asian Views of the American Influence*, ed. Lawrence W. Beer (Berkeley: University of California Press, 1979), 74-75.

73. Albert P. Blaustein, *The Influence of the United States Constitution Abroad* (Washington, DC: Washington Institute for Values in Public Policy, 1986), 21.

74. Tripathi, "Perspectives on the American Constitutional Influence on the Constitution of India," 72–73.

75. Ibid.

76. Ibid., 80.

77. Harry E. Groves, *The Constitution of Malaysia* (Singapore: Malaysia Publications, 1964), 34; Suffian bin Hashim, "The Malaysian Constitution and the United States Constitution," 131.

78. Quoted in Oemar Seno Adji, "An Indonesian Perspective on the American Constitutional Influence," in *Constitutionalism in Asia: Asian Views of the American Influence*, ed. Lawrence W. Beer (Berkeley: University of California Press, 1979), 104.

79. The 1972 constitution of Bangladesh also contained rights provisions inspired heavily by the US Constitution. See Justice Abu Sayeed Chowdhury, "The Bangladesh Constitution in American Perspective," in *Constitutionalism in Asia: Asian Views of the American Influence*, ed. Lawrence W. Beer (Berkeley: University of California Press, 1979), 29–31.

80. T. O. Elias, *Nigeria: The Development of Its Laws and Constitution* (London: Stevens and Sons, 1967), 141–43; Smith, *The New Commonwealth and Its Constitutions*, 178–79.

81. Ralph H. Retzlaff, "The Problem of Communal Minorities in the Drafting of the Indian Constitution," in *Constitutionalism in Asia*, ed. R. N. Spann (Bombay: Asia Publishing House, 1960), 55–73.

82. Smith, *The New Commonwealth and Its Constitutions*, 180; Sir Udo Udoma, *History and the Law of the Constitution of Nigeria* (Lagos: Malthouse Press, 1994), 207. A discussion of the European Convention can be found in Moderne, "Human Rights and Postcolonial Constitutions in Sub-Saharan Africa," 324–27.

83. For torture and inhumane treatment, see Article 3 of the European Convention, Article 18 of the Nigerian Constitution. The US Constitution does not

have an article explicitly laying out freedom from torture or inhumane treatment. For right-to-family life, see Article 12 of the European Convention and Article 22 of the Nigerian Constitution.

84. Smith, *The New Commonwealth and Its Constitutions*, 184.

85. Moderne, "Human Rights and Postcolonial Constitutions in Sub-Saharan Africa," 326.

86. Smith, *The New Commonwealth and Its Constitutions*.

87. Quoted in D. J. Morgan, *The Official History of Colonial Development. Volume 5: Guidance Towards Self-Government in British Colonies, 1941–1971* (Atlantic Highlands, NJ: Humanities Press, 1980), 24.

88. For the influence on Libya, see especially United Nations Office of Public Information, *The Universal Declaration of Human Rights: A Standard of Achievement* (New York: United Nations Office of Public Information, 1962), 26–27.

89. For a telling analysis of how global political culture impacts new constitutions, see Arjomand, "Constitutions and the Struggle for Political Order." See also John Boli-Bennett, "The Expansion of Nation-States, 1870–1970," Ph.D. dissertation, Department of Sociology, Stanford University, 1976.

Part 2

_____

Alignments and Nonalignments

Movements, Projects, Outcomes

4

Feminism, Solidarity, and Identity in the Age of Bandung

Third World Women in the Egyptian Women's Press

Laura Bier

Four years after the Bandung Conference, the historic 1955 meeting that signaled the intentions of the colonized and formerly colonized world to challenge the emerging cold war global order by uniting under the banner of national liberation and anti-imperialism, the February issue of the Egyptian women's magazine *Hawwa'* [*Eve*] featured an interview with Sukina Kusima, a leading figure in the Indonesian women's movement. Kusima was in town at the invitation of Nahid Sirry, head of the women's section of the Egyptian state-sponsored Arab Socialist Union. According to the article, her mission was to bring life to the spirit of Bandung by promoting ties of sisterhood and solidarity between the women of Africa and Asia. She was asked questions ranging from her views of women combining political and domestic duties, to the extent of Indonesian women's advancement in comparison to Western women, to the role of the "Eastern Woman" in anti-imperialist struggles. Reflecting a set of political sentiments commonly felt at the time, she concluded the interview by declaring that the gains that Indonesian women had made over the previous decade "counted not only as victory for Indonesian women, but for Eastern women in general."[1]

The interview with Kusima was one of hundreds of articles that appeared in the Egyptian mainstream and women's press, which focused on the lives and conditions of non-Egyptian women in the eighteen years following the 1952 revolution that brought Gamal Abdel Nasser to power. Linked to the Nasser regime's attempts to forge a new social and political order in the wake of decolonization fostered by solidarities among formerly colonized and decolonizing nations, the proliferation of articles on women in China, India, Vietnam, Thailand, America, Algeria, Germany, Russia, Cameroon, and elsewhere during this period raise a compelling set of questions—about the historical trajectories of global feminism, identity, and the construction of political imaginaries in an era of (trans) national, anti-imperialist struggle. This essay therefore seeks to explore two central issues. First, it examines how this pattern of publication relocates the trajectories of global-feminist activism during the post–World War II period, specifically to locales and processes outside the West. Second, it considers the ways in which depictions of "Third World" and other women in the Egyptian women's press were a vehicle for the construction of gendered national and transnational identities and visions of a "new" society in the period following the 1952 revolution in Egypt. Combined, this essay argues that the consequences of decolonization after World War II—and its key occasions like the Bandung meeting—were not merely diplomatic in scope, but had social and cultural repercussions that serve to bridge the complex history between imperial discourses of womanhood to the contemporary politics of global feminism.

Third World Political Imaginaries

The Bandung conference was an inaugural moment in the formation of the Third World, not as a place on a map but as a project, a political imaginary that linked "the darker nations" of the world in common struggle for freedom.[2] The first large-scale meeting of Asian and African states in history, it brought together delegates and leaders from twenty-nine countries representing over half the world's population. Many were, like host country Indonesia, newly independent of colonial control. Its stated aims were to promote Afro-Asian economic and cultural cooperation and to oppose colonialism and imperialism, particularly attempts by the United States and the Soviet Union to extend their influence over the global South in the postwar global order. More than that, however, Bandung was an attempt to forge a common ideology among anticolonial nations, which could supersede the cold war system dominated by the ideological conflict between communism and capitalism and the aforementioned superpowers that were their standard bearers (see the introduction by Christopher Lee to this volume).[3]

In his now-famous address to conference delegates, Indonesian leader Sukarno laid out the basis of unity and cooperation between the disparate nations that made up the conference:

> All of us, I am certain, are united by more important things than those which superficially divide us. We are united by a common detestation of colonialism in whatever form it appears. We are united by a common detestation of racialism. And we are united by a common determination to preserve and stabilize peace in the world. . . . Relatively speaking, all of us gathered here today are neighbors. Almost all of us have ties of common experience, the experience of colonialism. Many of us have a common religion. Many of us have common cultural roots. Many of us, the so-called underdeveloped nations have similar economic problems, so that each can profit by the others' experience and help. And I think I may say that we all hold dear the ideals of national independence and freedom.[4]

These stated elements of unity comprised the "Bandung spirit," which came to define the Third World as an imagined political space of solidarity. The three key components of this "spirit" included support for national independence movements, opposition to the continued pernicious effects of colonialism in all of its postcolonial guises—intellectual and economic control, cultural influence, and indirect political interference—and, thirdly, mutual exchange and cooperation to address shared problems of economic, technological, and cultural underdevelopment. The resulting vision of the Third World was thus based neither on a rejection of national differences nor the articulation of essentialist claims to racial, cultural, or geographic commonalities; but rather on the overarching, yet contingent, idea that national self-definition and transnational unity could be mutually reinforcing when positioned against Western power.

This complex program initiated at a time of global political transition challenges many of the prevailing assumptions about mid-century decolonization. James Le Sueur, for example, has defined decolonization as "a process during which hard won battles were waged between nationalists and metropolitan colonial powers . . . the historical phase that bridged the gap between colonial and postcolonial worlds."[5] The neat temporal and spatial boundaries presumed by such a definition confines the process of decolonization to the achieving of formal political independence and situates it fundamentally within the activism and political imaginaries of anticolonial nationalist movements. However, the types of political movements and solidarities that Bandung enabled and inspired, as well as its symbolic relationship (in Egypt and elsewhere) to both national and transnational struggles for liberation from European rule, suggest that the processes of decolonization equally entailed the formation of other sorts of imaginaries that extended beyond the immediate effects of sovereignty and diplomatic change. The impact of Bandung on the politics of global feminism offers a case in point.

The Nasser regime's attempts to contribute to the forging of a new world political order under the rubric of nonalignment, socialism, and Arab nationalism were an integral part of its self-definition as a progressive, anti-imperialist nation in a newly postcolonial world. The 1952 revolution marked the beginning of Egypt's transition from a monarchy purportedly based on liberal-democratic principles to a republic, which, by the 1960s had adopted Arab Socialism as its official ideology. Central to this project of political and social engineering were attempts to fundamentally reorder gender and class relations by mobilizing previously marginalized groups, such as women, peasants, and the urban poor. The status of women, in particular, was held to be a measure of the extent to which Egypt had succeeded in becoming a modern, liberated nation after centuries of foreign occupation. With the 1956 nationalization of the Suez Canal, which stripped away the last vestiges of British colonial control, Egypt placed itself at the forefront of global opposition to Western hegemony over the formerly colonized world. Egypt's participation in the Nonaligned Movement, its increasingly close ties with the Soviet bloc, and its attempts to bring other progressive Arab regimes together under the rubric of Arab nationalism were intimately tied to domestic efforts to envision and create a new society that was both socialist and "authentically" Egyptian. The range of communities and solidarities invoked by depictions of non-Egyptian women both reflected and gave gendered meanings to this project of Arab modernity.

Bandung, which enabled Egypt to play a leading role, gave rise to a number of distinct but overlapping movements including the Nonaligned Movement mentioned before, but also the Afro-Asian Peoples' Solidarity Movement and the African Peoples Summit.[6] At the same time, the unification of Egypt with Syria in 1958 and the creation of the United Arab Republic gave impetus to Pan Arab aspirations in the region. The attention paid in the domestic Egyptian women's press to women in postcolonial Asia and Africa, the Arab world, and socialist countries like Yugoslavia, was a product of such shifts in Egypt's ideological orientation. But it also actively produced the creation of new spaces within the sphere of global politics through which new people, ideas, and discourses could circulate. As new alliances were forged in the international arena, groups of women activists, writers, students, and politicians participated within a postcolonial milieu of international conferences, visiting delegations, summits, and committee meetings. The resulting exchanges and networks formed an essential part of the complex imaginaries initiated by decolonization, which inevitably overflowed the boundaries of the nation-state.

Gendering Internationalisms and Contentious Histories: Egyptian Women's Engagement with International Feminism

By 1952, Egyptian women already had a long history of participation in transnational activism. Since the 1920s, members of the Egyptian Feminist Union (EFU) had been active members of various international organizations and congresses including the International League of Mothers and Educators for Peace, the Women's International League for Peace and Freedom, the International League for the Suppression of Traffic in Women and Children, and, most prominently, the International Alliance of Women for Equal Suffrage and Citizenship (IAW).[7] The EFU had joined the IAW when it changed its name from the International Woman Suffrage Alliance in 1923.[8] The change in name signaled the IAW's shift from a narrow focus on suffrage to a multitiered platform that encompassed multiple rights and a more fully enfranchised definition of citizenship.[9] However, prior to the 1950s the engagement of Egyptian women with international feminism was to be a story of disjuncture between the nationalist feminism of the colonized and the "universalism" of Western-dominated international feminism that masked the movement's imperial genealogy.[10]

The rhetoric of international feminism, as it developed in Britain and the United States, rejected ethnic and national differences between women in favor of a notion of solidarity on the basis of biological sex and a shared experience of oppression and disenfranchisement. A song of the International Women's Suffrage Alliance summed it up: "Whatever our race or country be . . . we are one nation/Womanhood."[11] Carrie Chapman Catt, the leader of the IWSA, rejected "local" (that is, nation-specific) patriotism as a male phenomenon. National feeling had to be sacrificed for the sake of female solidarity so the Suffrage movement could present a united front to the world. The inclusion of non-Western women within the movement was key if it were to be considered a truly global enterprise. In 1923, for example, along with the EFU, the IAW admitted the Indian Women's Association, the Jewish Women's Equal Rights Association from Palestine, and a Japanese women's association that joined the ranks of women's organizations from countries such as Greece and Turkey.

On the other hand, the ways in which non-Western women were included reveal the colonial assumptions upon which "global sisterhood" functioned within the context of Empire. In a letter written to an American magazine about the Egyptian women's movement in 1912, Catt praised the women of Egypt for "daring to refuse marriage" and demanding the right to education. Yet she attributed the beginnings of a women's movement in Egypt to the influence of British colonial control. "Great Britain has created a new Egypt," she declared. "It has awakened a sleeping race and held before it the dazzling achievements of Western progress."[12] Thus, non-Western women were to be absorbed into international feminism in a position of subordination. They were admitted not as leaders or equal partners with their Western "sisters," but as objects of tutelage. As Antoinette Burton has pointed out elsewhere, "British feminist internationalism—and more specifically, Anglo-American suffrage—was predicated on the assumption that Western women would lead the women of the East to freedom and British and American women would spearhead the charge."[13]

The rejection of nationalism as the antithesis of universalist female solidarity and the absorption of colonized and formerly colonized women into the IAW as objects of Western reform and tutelage remained defining features of international feminism throughout the 1920s, 1930s, and 1940s even as the movement challenged colonialism in other ways.[14] As expected, this created a sense of unstable, rather than common, ground. In particular, the 1939 meeting of IAW in Copenhagen graphically revealed the tensions in international feminism and lack of consensus between Western and non-Western women on what constituted feminism and gender solidarity. In its declaration of principles, IAW proposed to observe "absolute neutrality on all questions that were strictly national."[15] The failure of the IAW to put the nationalist, anticolonial concerns of colonized and formerly colonized women on its agenda was a source of deep-seated frustration to Egyptian and other feminists.

After the Copenhagen conference, the IAW and other international women's organizations largely ceased their activities due to the advent of World War II. When the IAW reconvened in 1946, the terrain of transnational women's activism had been dramatically reordered. The 1945 creation of the leftist Women's International Democratic Federation, which wedded gender and class struggle, signaled one major split in international feminism along the East-West axis of the cold war.[16] The creation of the Afro-Asian solidarity movement and the Non-aligned Movement in the 1950s and 1960s, which divided the movement along North-South lines, was the other. The first Asian-African

Conference on Women held in Colombo in 1958, for example, was confined to women's organizations from the twenty-nine countries of the Asian and African Region that were represented at Bandung. The first Afro-Asian Women's Conference, which was convened in Cairo in 1961 under United Arab Republic (UAR) sponsorship grew out of a resolution from the earlier Cairo-sponsored Afro-Asian Peoples' Solidarity Committee (AAPSC) meeting in 1957. Patterns of global feminism therefore shifted in accordance with the dramatic political changes that occurred during the early cold war and postcolonial periods. But these shifts were not mere reflections of geopolitical transitions then current. Rather, the role of "Third World" women and their organizations must be understood as active and therefore vital in the shaping of these new and evolving global orders.

The existence of a transnational women's movement encompassing the colonized and formerly colonized world led and driven by the concerns of non-Western women in the 1950s and 1960s challenges conventional historical narratives of international feminism. According to such narratives, international feminism, originating in the struggles for women's Suffrage in Europe and America at the turn of the century, largely ended when international connections between women were "severed" by World War II, only to reemerge in the 1970s and 1980s after a "lull" of some two decades.[17] Writing struggles for decolonization—and the transnational movements that emerged from them—out of histories of international feminism ignores the critical impact that the South-South exchanges and solidarities produced by the Bandung moment have had on feminist thought and praxis in the last two decades, most notably the emergence of postcolonial critiques of Western feminism from women in the global South. Moreover, the elision of such struggles tends to reproduce a historical trajectory of feminism that situates Europe and America as the origin and locus of feminist thought and practice, and the global South as passive consumer. Restoring Bandung as a formative moment in the history of global feminisms challenges both assumptions.

For the first time, occasions like the Bandung meeting provided colonized and formerly colonized women an alternative political and organizational space to the prewar, Western-dominated, imperial, international women's feminist movement. The novelty of the meeting location—and the connections that it enabled—was not lost on its participants. It continued to inform the sensibilities of future events. For example, Bahia Karam, secretary of the preparatory committee for the 1961 Cairo Women's Conference, wrote in her introduction to the 1961 proceedings:

> It is for the first time in modern history, feminine history that is, that such a gathering of Afro-Asian women has taken place . . . represent[ing] over 37 peoples, some of them participating for the first time in an international meeting. It was indeed a great pleasure, an encouragement to meet delegates from countries in Africa which the imperialists had never allowed before to leave the boundaries of their land. Delegates from Basutoland, [and the] Gambia, for example, had the chance for the first time to meet their sisters from other countries in Africa and Asia.[18]

In a similar spirit, Lakshmi Menon, leader of the Indian delegation to the 1958 Colombo Asian-African Conference of Women, had marveled several years earlier that women from Mongolia and Ghana would finally be able to meet their "sisters" from the Mediterranean to the Pacific.[19]

It was not only geographic location that separated transnational women's activism in the NAM and AAPSC from the activism of the IAW and organizations like it during the first part of the century. Despite the imperial assumptions and uneven power relationships that contradicted its founding premise, the IAW consistently asserted biology—and a common experience of exclusion based on that biology—as the basis for women's solidarity and a unified feminist program. Although not denying the importance of ties based on the purportedly "natural" division between the sexes, the activism of colonized and formerly colonized women stressed solidarity based on a common *history*, a shared experience of subjugation created and perpetuated by Western imperialism—what Chandra Mohanty has called "an imagined community of third world oppositional struggles . . . women with divergent histories and social locations woven together by the political threads of opposition to forms of domination that are not only pervasive but systematic."[20] African and Asian women "suffered from the same disabilities" and were thus "struggling for the same aims."[21] In her speech at the 1961 Cairo conference, UAR delegate Karima Sa'id evoked such a shared genealogy of suffering and resistance, stating: "We, Afro-Asian women, meet today representing two-thirds of the world population, tied by the unity of the great past, the struggling present and the glorious future—a unity of pains and aims—a unity of struggle for the rights and for the sake of freedom, peace and humanism."[22]

It was the explicit purpose of meetings like the 1961 Afro-Asian Women's Solidarity Conference to establish a framework for exchanges between women of the global South. One of the outcomes of these exchanges was articles on foreign women, which appeared during this period in the Egyptian women's press. The UAR delegates to the 1961 women's conference, for example, included Amina Sa'id, the editor-in-chief of *Hawwa'*, Fathia Bahij, a journalist for *Akhir sa'a* who often covered women's issues, and Sohayr Qalamawi, head of the Egyptian Press Syndicate and occasional contributor to the women's pages of various publications. Such occasions and the attendance of these women journalists soon resulted in a political-print culture focused on the gendered experience of Third World women. An article on Vietnamese women in *Hawwa'* was based on an interview with Nguyen Ty Banh, who visited Cairo as a delegate to the Plenary Committee of the Conference of Afro-Asian Solidarity.[23] A series of articles on women in Tanganyika was based on Sa'id's attendance of the third Afro-Asian Solidarity conference there. These articles on "other women" grew directly out of Egyptian women's presence at such conferences and the equal presence of foreign women in Cairo. The content of this organic-print culture that arose through such international meetings and contingent encounters both reflected and reinforced the escalation of postcolonial women's activism during the early decades of the cold war.

The Women's Press and "Global Sisterhood"

It is within the context of Bandung and the movements that grew out of it that we must place the hundreds of articles and profiles of non-Egyptian women that appeared in the mainstream and women's press during the eighteen years of Nasserist rule. Depictions of other women played a part in the construction of an idea of "global sisterhood" even as they highlighted the tensions inherent to such constructions. The images were multivalent and often contradictory. They could be deployed by Egyptian women journalists to make new claims for rights, but equally used to assert the liberated status of Egyptian women under socialist rule. By comparing the condition of women in other, more "backward," nations, these images and articles offered examples to readers of the progressive promises that becoming "modern" held for a recently decolonized nation as well as expressions of anxiety about the effects such a process could have on gender roles and society in general. They allowed Egyptian women readers to imagine certain kinds of forward-looking roles and lives for themselves, while foreclosing others deemed as too "traditional." In short, articles about "other women" were a vehicle through which Egyptian women negotiated and contested the boundaries of the nation, the national project, and their place within both.

Articles about foreign women were not a new feature of the women's press.[24] Since the beginning of the 20th century, women's magazines had featured articles about such individuals.[25] Often these took the form of what Marilyn Booth has termed "prescriptive biographies"—biographical sketches of notable women meant to impart lessons to female readers about proper gender roles.[26] After World War II, however, the prevalence of prescriptive biography in women's magazines had greatly declined, as had the actual number of women's magazines.[27] The gradual tightening of state control over the press, coupled with its subsidizing of media and cultural output, resulted in more words—and because of the impact of education, a larger readership—but fewer voices.[28] Comparisons of the women's press between the Nasser period and the 1920s are striking. During the latter decade, there had been no fewer than ten journals aimed at a primarily female readership. By 1958, the newly founded *Hawwa'* was the only remaining periodical of its kind.[29]

Amina Saʿid was appointed as *Hawwa*'s editor-in-chief when the magazine was established in 1957. Her background and political orientations were emblematic of other journalists and cultural producers of the Nasser period. The daughter of a physician who was active in nationalist politics, Saʿid was an early beneficiary of the 1930s educational expansion under liberal-nationalist rule. She became a journalist—a common career path for newly higher-educated women with professional aspirations—and in 1959 was appointed as the vice president of the Egyptian journalism syndicate. Saʿid was an outspoken advocate of the revolution and the vision of secular modernity that it embodied. The pages of *Hawwaʾ*, particularly its editorial content, reflected this perspective. However, while much of the content of the women's press at this time was thus consistent with the general vision and policies of the regime, it also became an important vehicle for the construction of and contests over the gendered meanings of Nasserism and state socialism. Unlike the earlier period, articles about foreign women published during the 1950s and 1960s increasingly took more intimate forms of interviews, multipage features with photos, or editorials. Consistent with the more general trends toward social realism in the visual arts, cinema, and literature, such articles made truth claims through the author's offer of accurate, eyewitness testimony of the condition of women in other countries. Under the editorial supervision of Saʿid and others like her, foreign datelines, the rhetoric of witness ("I was there and I saw with my own eyes"), and the author's assertion of having had expectations about a country that were changed through experience all provided ways in which this political journalism purported to give a real, unmediated picture of other women's lives.

Although articles about foreign women could be found outside of the sections of magazines designated as "the woman's page," they were most often to be found there or, in the case of women's magazines, in other specific locations. In *Hawwaʾ*, for example, articles about foreign women could regularly be found in a section called "*With Hawwaʾ*." In the weekly news magazine *Akhir saʿa* (Up to the Hour) they could be found in the segment entitled "*Hiyya*" (She) and in its competitor *al-Musawwar* (The Illustrated) in *al-Nifs al-hilwa* (The Charming Half).[30] These sections also featured news on the activities of local women's groups, announcements of visiting women dignitaries, and briefs on the participation of Egyptian women in various national and international conferences. With titles like "The Girls of Iran,"[31] "I Saw the Yemeni Woman With out a Veil!,"[32] "What Do You Know about the Yugoslavian Woman?,"[33] and "Thank God You're an Egyptian Woman,"[34] the articles implied the nation-state as primary locus of allegiance and identity. The editorial placement of the articles and their rhetorical strategies, however, suggested that the magazine's readers might envision themselves as belonging to other, transnational communities. The textual organization of *Hawwa'*, *Hiyya*, and *al-Nifs al-hilwa*—where reports on the international, national, and local contexts of women's activism intermingled and overlapped seemingly at random—in practice created a discursive space of "global sisterhood," the boundaries of which were shifting and contingent. The sense of kinship among women across national boundaries was further reinforced by the text of the articles themselves, which relied frequently on the trope of sisterhood and unity between women of different nationalities. An article about a meeting of Egyptian and other African women, for example, extolled the unity displayed by the "children of one continent."[35] Another piece claimed to inform its readers all about the lives of their "Iraqi sisters."[36] An article in *al-Musawwar* about Sudanese women asserted "women are women everywhere."[37] In addition, the prevalence of articles on women in countries undergoing or having recently emerged from wars of national liberation against European powers, such as Vietnam, Algeria, and Mozambique, stressed the solidarity of Egyptian women with colonized and formerly colonized women as victims of a common history of oppression and Western domination.

Although it is tempting to critique such rhetorical strategies from the vantage point of the present, I would argue that it is a mistake to view the various national and supranational communities invoked by articles on non-Egyptian women as essentializing or contradictory to claims of solidarity. To do so risks missing the fluid nature of subjectivity and self-definition at a time in Egyptian history when the primacy of the nation-state as the locus of identity was largely taken for granted. I would argue instead that representations of foreign women articulated the multiple layers of women's identity that were at play. Factors of context as well as the idea of transgressing boundaries to create shifting patterns of overlapping experience were both important. An Egyptian woman could be an Arab woman vis-à-vis non-Arab women, an Eastern woman vis-à-vis European women, a socialist woman vis-à-vis non-socialist women, an African woman vis-à-vis Asian women, or a woman vis-à-vis an Egyptian man. The identity of women thus moved beyond mere biology—as emphasized by feminist movements of the colonial period—to a more complex set of constructed coordinates defined by race, culture, geography, political ideology, and national identity.

It is important to note here that such coordinates also pose limitations. For example, the universalizing rhetoric of "sisterhood," unsurprisingly, was class-specific. Feminist theorizations of sisterhood and community as they appeared in these articles typically elided the class identity of both writers and subjects. Interviews with and representations of the largely middle- and upper-middle-class women from other countries, who were most often the focus of these articles, depicted them as proto-typical representatives of their respective national womanhoods. Unlike prescriptive biography, which purported to tell the life stories of *exemplary* women, these articles tend to portray the attitudes and experiences of middle-class women as tacitly those of the "normal" national female subject. In addition to class, the content of the women's press during this period more importantly reflect the generational orientations of its authors. Like Saʿid, the women that wrote and edited these articles were primarily educated, middle-class women that came of political age in the 1930s and 1940s. They were, in many cases, the first to benefit from the successes of the early Egyptian feminist movement in opening higher education and the professions to women. However, for many their own eventual political orientations constituted a conscious break with the liberal nationalist feminism of the previous generation.[38] They saw themselves as part of *al-jil al-jadid* (the new generation) whose political and social outlooks were shaped (ironically enough) by their rejection of the elitism of early feminists and the climate of radical political protest against British imperialism, the corruption of the monarchy, and the vast social ills that had beset Egypt since it gained initial independence in 1923. The new political and social movements that emerged during this period therefore challenged notions of identity based upon Egyptian territorial nationalism in favor of alternative visions of national belonging that incorporated supranational affiliations and orientations. Such generational distinctions are further evinced by examining more closely the print culture that they produced.[39]

Difference and Representation

If articles about "other women" can be seen as part of the Nasser regime's attempts to contribute to the forging of a new world political order, they should also be located within the more "local" project of national (self-) definition. In an article about women in the former West Germany, Amina Sa'id wrote: "Whenever I visit a foreign country for the first time . . . I compare between the status of women in it and the status of our women and then I work from this to extract a comparison . . . the place of the modern Egyptian woman in the pageant of world civilization." Compared to advanced societies *(mujtama'at mutaqadima)* such as Britain, France, and America, Egyptian women were still "at the bottom of the ladder."[40] However, compared to the conditions of most Asian and African women, she argues, Egyptian women were the pinnacle of culture and advancement. Such postcolonial practices of comparison echo a deeper history of cultural encounter and political translation. In her work on imperial feminism, Antoinette Burton has demonstrated how British feminist self-images were constructed through reading images of Indian women in the women's press. "Representing these women and making them topics of debate about femininity, emancipation and progress," she writes, "[British] feminists objectified women of the East into types of their own making."[41] I would argue that depictions of non-Egyptian women both subverted and reinscribed this imperial paradigm. Representations in the Egyptian women's press were simultaneously a project of identification and objectification.

On the one hand, the authors of these articles and, indeed the rhetorical strategies of the articles themselves, were the product of a postcolonial, explicitly anti-imperial context that stressed the solidarity and common struggle of non-Western women against Western oppression and domination. On the other hand, depictions of foreign women acted as a foil against which Egyptian women could exhibit their role as exemplary agents of civilization and the modernity of Egyptian society, especially in relation to other nations of Africa, Asia, and the Arab world. "Whenever I go to the region of our Arab brothers and sisters, I find afflicted women," wrote Sa'id. "They fervently desire to follow our example and would benefit greatly if we took them by the hand in their striving to achieve a better life. . . . If we want, truly, to preserve our leadership in our greater nation (the Arab world) it is not right to confine our efforts to ourselves."[42] In a similar vein, another author writes: "My impression of the Pakistani woman, from first to last, is that she is a backward woman (*imra'a mutakhalifa*) [but] I excuse her. Because the Pakistani woman is governed by tradition (*taqalid*) passed down for generations and centuries."[43] Among the social practices that marked Pakistani womanhood as backward were prevalence of adolescent marriage, uncontrolled reproduction, and the persistence of purdah. In other articles, practices such as veiling and sex segregation were commonly juxtaposed with the "new" activities women were undertaking in the public sphere, such as waged professional work and pursuit of higher education. The home as a locus of women's oppression and ossified tradition exemplified by polygamy, arranged marriages, and extended-kinship networks was posed against the more enlightened model of the nuclear family, companionate marriage, and bourgeois domesticity. The extent to which a nation was considered to be "advanced" depended on the extent to which it adhered to a particular constellation of social, political, and economic practices identified as modern. In sum, these women writers of the Egyptian press surreptitiously embraced identifiable criteria of Western modernity, despite their surface rejection of such influence.

The discourse of "underdevelopment" or "backwardness" as it appears in these articles frequently erase the complicated histories and relations of power among Egyptian women and between Egyptian women and foreign women. An article entitled "Your Sudanese Sister in Her Path to Liberation," for example, traces early girls' education as the beginning of women's emancipation in Sudan, and lauds the role of Egyptians that were among the first to establish girls' schools.[44] What it and every other article on Sudanese women surveyed for this chapter fails to mention is that the presence of Egyptian educators in Sudan was a direct result of British colonial policies there.[45] Other articles provide justification of Egyptian military involvement in a brutal civil war in Yemen on the side of Abdullah al-Sallal, an officer in the Yemeni army brought to power by the military coup that overthrew Yemen's quasimonarchical leader Imam Ahmed in 1962.[46] An article that appeared in *Hawwa'* in 1964, at the height of Egyptian involvement in the conflict, praises the Sallal government for bringing progress and enlightenment to Yemen's women. The Yemeni woman, the article asserts, is "living the sweetest days of her life. She has begun to see the light and ascend to a vast new awakening of development and progress." While she once suffered mutely under the "iron hand" of the monarchy, the Yemeni woman was now removing her veil and could take her rightful place in the perpetuation of the revolution and the building of her nation.[47] A separate article, which appeared in the women's pages of *Akhir sa'a*, purported to present "the true picture of the life led by women in post-revolutionary Yemeni society." The article's first page featured the heading "The Grip of the Imam has Been Lifted from around Her Neck."[48] A photo essay also included in *Akhir sa'a* juxtaposes a picture of a Yemeni woman with her entire body, including her face, obscured by a black burqa next to a picture of two unveiled young women in school uniforms. According to the caption, the two were learning math from one of the Egyptian women teachers who provided much of the staff for Yemen's system of female education.[49] Diplomatic propaganda thus went hand in hand with the politics of feminism being generated by these magazines.

Differences among Egyptian women also came to be constituted through articles on foreign women. The article discussed earlier, which accuses Pakistani women of backwardness, also repeatedly points to the similarities, in culture and situation, to peasant women in the Egyptian Sa'id (the South). Another piece describing the traditional nature of Yemeni rural society, wherein strict division between the sexes was enforced and girls' education was virtually nonexistent, declared that "The Yemeni peasant woman is a picture of the Egyptian peasant woman."[50] Through such narratives of progress and (under) development, representations of other women therefore constitute difference not only as a product of national politics and power, but also one of rural-urban division and the perceived temporal disjunctures they represent. In short, the journalists of the Egyptian women's press not only aimed a critical eye toward situations in other countries, but also tacitly remarked on the shortcomings found within Egypt itself. They manifest a self-consciousness about the limitations of Egypt as a role model for other Asian and African countries—to be a leader meant vigilance within its borders as well. Taken as one part of a wider discourse of modernity, such media narratives of progress were therefore neither fixed in terms of locations nor were they always wholly coherent in criteria. Far from showing a firm set of norms, attributes, and relationships, what is considered to be "modern" in these texts is fluid, indeterminate, and subject to multiple reinterpretations, contestation, and negotiation—a reflection of the time as well as the active role Egyptian women journalists had in defining it.

Negotiating Modernity

If depictions of other women were a consistent site for negotiations over what it meant to be "modern" in a general sense, it still left open to question what internal criteria there might be for "modern" Egyptian womanhood. What the "new woman" of Nasserist rhetoric was supposed to look like, how to reconcile the demands of development and progress with the preservation of Egyptian cultural authenticity, what constituted appropriate norms of masculinity and femininity—all of these subjects remained contentious issues. Representations of non-Egyptian women subsequently revealed the intrinsic tensions that the project of making Egypt "modern" was fraught with, in particular the anxieties about changing gender roles. But they also provided a way for readers to reconcile those tensions and imagine new possibilities for their lives, even as they foreclosed other possibilities.

To offer an example, in a 1958 article entitled "Equality, Does It Make Women Happy?" Amina Sa'id wrote about the life of women in the Soviet Union, pointing out that they had equal status to men in all areas of life. The Soviet woman worked in medicine, engineering, law, and industry, and the law guaranteed her equal salary and equal opportunity. At the same time, labor legislation offered her protection as a wife and mother, giving her generous maternity leave and the right to socialized day care for her children. Asserting that Soviet women enjoyed more rights than women in any other nation in the world, Sa'id wrote, "I believe that equality, in this depiction, expresses the hope of women among many peoples and I don't doubt that many deem the Soviet woman fortunate in what has come to her. [But] I say equality in this absolute meaning inflicts grave hardships on the Soviet woman and make her lose more than she gains." The picture of Soviet womanhood that Sa'id goes on to present is consequently a grim one. Her duties, to home and to nation, diminish her socially and physically. She is denied the validation which accrues to women as the pillar of home and family without being exempted from domestic duties. She works eight hours a day and, returning home in the evening, cooks, cleans, and cares for her husband and children for another five. She does nothing but work and sleep. She is too tired to care for her physical appearance, which begins to deteriorate at a young age. "Hard work," wrote Sa'id in summary, "crushes her femininity." In this narrative depiction of social progress and feminine decline, "modern" life and women's emancipation result in a process of desexualization and destruction of gender difference.[51]

Other articles that Sa'id wrote on her 1958 trip to the Soviet Union, however, provide an alternative story of Soviet womanhood. Of interest to Sa'id was the condition of women in the USSR's Asian republics, particularly those like Azerbaijan and Uzbekistan that had sizable Muslim populations. In an article subtitled "Eastern in Form and Content," she portrays Uzbek women as "fiercely" nationalistic and emphatic in their adherence to Uzbek cultural values. This strong sense of national identity is mirrored by their preference for traditional Uzbek clothing over Western fashion and their modesty in both dress and demeanor. Young Uzbek women, Sa'id wrote, were a picture of "innocent femininity . . . she is [of all people] most emphatic in defense of her honor and purity." Yet the preservation of cultural values did not mean that Uzbek women were "backward."[52] On the contrary, Sa'id argues in a second article that Uzbek women were not only economically and politically liberated like other Soviet women, they were socially liberated as well. At the same time, the Uzbek woman remained distinguished by "her dignity, refinement and modesty." She considered these a matter of propriety, just as she considered it a matter of propriety *(adab)* to serve her nation through working for national development.[53]

What is important about these varying depictions of the condition of Soviet women is not that they are contradictory. Rather, they draw our attention to the ways in which such contradictions described by Egyptian women journalists constituted removed, textual attempts to resolve the tensions within notions of modernity and authenticity that Egyptian women—their target audience—confronted on an everyday basis. In particular, such journalistic narratives represent the ways in which writers could help reconcile anxieties about the effect that changing gender roles would have on the boundaries between masculinity and femininity in Egyptian society and the health of Egypt's social order generally, which had been predicated on the strict regulation of such boundaries. As the case of Uzbek women demonstrated, through adherence to ostensibly "authentic" *national* cultural practices of gendered propriety and bodily discipline, the potential dangers of modern life could be averted, and women could take their place in the nation as fully enfranchised citizens and national subjects. Women did not necessarily have to choose between traditional roles and modern opportunities but could combine the two, thus safeguarding both their political and gender status. Representations of other women in the Egyptian women's press during the 1950s and 1960s, in sum, offered a textual resolution to those tensions and anxieties engendered by the Nasserist state-building project, which assumed the "emancipation" of Egyptian women as one precondition of the development of Egypt itself. This binding of the liberation of women with the liberation of the nation—both from colonial control and from "backwardness"— centered on the equating of *adab* with both women's participation in nation-building in the public sphere and gendered norms of modesty and refinement in the private sphere. The outcome was both emancipatory and disciplinary. It allowed women to make new claims for rights and to envision new sorts of freedoms and gender roles in the name of progress and modernity. However, it also placed such roles in the context of submission to the national/ist project. New or "nontraditional" roles for women could be justified in terms of service to the nation, but only if a sense of cultural authenticity was preserved through the policing of gendered boundaries.

A key test for this tension over "tradition" and "service to the nation" is found in a different set of articles describing the role women had in Third World revolutions. To offer one example, Hu Dum was an eighteen year old Vietnamese woman portrayed, in the pages of *Hawwa'*, who had left her village and family to fight with the North Vietnamese forces on the Ho Chi Min Trail. The article described her as "a symbol of bravery" in her nation's fight against colonialism. She became so well known and respected as a fighter and patriot that Ho Chi Min himself reportedly gave her a "fatherly kiss" when he met her for the first time. Yet she was also a potentially ambiguous figure who blurred the boundaries between masculinity and femininity. She is pictured in men's clothing carrying a rifle and is described as fighting alongside men in the field of battle. As a child, the author writes, she played with toy guns and airplanes instead of dolls. However, the possible conflict between ungendered national duty and the norms of proper female gendered subjectivity is ultimately resolved. With her long, silky black hair, gentle smile, and soft-spoken manner she is portrayed as the picture of modern Vietnamese womanhood: militant, determined, and self-sacrificing in the cause of national liberation, yet also demure, modest, and feminine, a dutiful daughter in the service of the Vietnamese national family.[54]

The "domestication" of revolution found in this particular case study was a common trope in depictions of fighting women. One of the most chronicled individual women in these articles was the Algerian freedom fighter Jamila Buhrid. Buhrid contributed to the armed resistance against French control that was waged in Algeria during the 1950s and early 1960s, and her arrest by colonial authorities made her a heroine across the Arab world. She was featured on the cover of a number of Egyptian magazines, including *al-Musawwar*, and her life story was made into a feature film by the internationally known Egyptian director Yusuf Chahine. An article about Buhrid, which appeared in *Hawwa'*, portrays the Algerian Revolution as a family affair. Jamila becomes politicized hearing her female schoolmates talk about their fathers and brothers fighting in the mountains. At home, she is pictured trying to answer the questions of her younger siblings about the conflict. Her uncle, a *mujahid* (freedom fighter), provides her an example of the worthiness of struggle. A faithful husband and a good father, he never shirked his family duties or duties toward the national struggle.[55] In another article, Algerian women's participation in armed struggle is similarly presented as a function of a woman's role within the family as the guardian and embodiment of national culture and the boundary marker of communal identity. "The lovely half (of society) has carried half the burden in national struggle and the gentle sex has traveled side by side with the other sex," the article argues. "[S]he knows how to kill and how to meet death." Yet at the same time, it was a "secret" that the same female freedom fighter was also culturally conservative in her home and with family. The author of the piece attributes this to the fact that fathers and grandfathers handed down customs and traditions along with patriotism and love for the *watan*, or nation. It was the gender-specific duty of Algerian women to retain and protect such customs from "corruption" by French colonialism.[56] Thus, even as she takes up arms at the side of her Algerian "brothers," she remains firmly located within the realm of cultural authenticity, represented and constituted by ties of kinship.[57]

In contrast to the women's press, articles in the mainstream press tended not to offer such resolutions over modernization and feminization to their readers. A comparison between two articles on women in China, which appeared within several years of each other in different publications, is instructive. A 1956 article in the more mainstream magazine *Ruz al-yusuf* stressed the defeminizing aspects of China's drive to modernize.[58] The author begins by declaring that although he had run across plenty of Chinese men who, ironically enough, looked like women and carried women's names, he had not seen even one female or, more specifically, one female that displayed any of the "distinguishing marks of femininity." In fact, with hair tightly braided or hidden under a cap and in the harsh, navy-blue pants and blouse that provided the ubiquitous national uniform in Maoist China, she is indistinguishable from a man, even to the point of possessing *rajula* (masculinity). The article marvels at the numbers of women in the workforce, but also blames production for the erasure of gender boundaries. After numerous descriptions of the hard, back-breaking labor undertaken by Chinese women in factories and fields, the author goes on to present a picture of women in China that is barely human. Chinese women, he writes, have no notion of love, either for husbands or children. In fact, he asserted, they feel oppressed by their duties as wives and mothers. Despite the presence of child-care facilities at factories and labor regulations that stipulated women had a right to take a break during the day to visit their children, few women exercised this right. "The madness of production in China is a sickness spread among the ranks of women," the article concludes, even if women were also the source of China's development. "The Chinese Woman, not the Chinese man is the sinew of the new renaissance and the pillar upon which the government is based. New China!"[59]

By contrast, a 1962 article in *Hawwa'*, which appeared a few years after the *Ruz al-yusuf* piece, offers a more complex view of Chinese women seeking to balance their multiple roles. Entitled "The Chinese Woman Has Ended the Battle of Construction and has Begun the Battle of Beauty and Elegance," the article begins in a way reminiscent of the *Ruz al-yusuf* article with the author recalling a previous visit to China when a female interpreter discussed the blurring of gender boundaries there.[60] "Listen. The Chinese woman is like every woman in the world. She is concerned about her clothes and elegance," she states. "But today we are building the nation. For the sake of this great goal we dedicate all the minutes of our lives." After the nation has been developed, she said "the Chinese woman will turn your gaze with her charms." Five years later, the author wrote, "Chinese women have returned to the world of femininity. . . . [T]he fashion of Chinese girls will come to rival that of American and European girls." The photo spread that accompanies the article underscores this conclusion.

One photo shows a woman shopping for fabric in a chic, Western-looking store. Another shows a mother with her fashionably dressed child with the caption: "Elegance extends to the small child in China. And this picture is evidence of the extent to which children here are given attention."[61] In sum, according to the *Hawwa'* article, the potentially destabilizing effects of development on gender boundaries are averted by the reinscription of those boundaries once the process of modernization is complete. By extension, the Egyptian women's press once again offered their female audience a model from their perceived global sisterhood to ponder and possibly emulate.

Conclusion

To summarize, representations of foreign women were a regular and recurring feature of the Egyptian women's press during the 1950s and 1960s. They were products of global and local struggles, reflecting a search for political community along gender lines both within and beyond the Egyptian nation-state. (On political community, see the introduction to this volume.) Enabled by a world order increasingly transformed by the political voices of colonial and postcolonial subjects, such media representations were bound up in Egyptian debates about transnational gender subjectivities, the cultural consequences of state and nation-building, and the gendered boundaries of citizenship and national identity. Although they can be read as contributing to new forms of transnational solidarity among colonized and formerly colonized women, they equally suggest how the liberating, emancipatory possibilities of postcolonial/anti-imperialist projects intrinsically limited their own possibility for realization. (For a different case study see the chapter by Brennan in this volume.) The vision of an anti-imperialist global sisterhood in these articles was undermined by recourse to a Western-influenced discourse of development and progress that not only objectified non-Egyptian women, but frequently positioned them as a locus of debate about gender and modernity in Egypt, thus echoing earlier imperial feminist practices.

Acknowledging the imperial genealogy of such discourses, however, should not prevent us from recognizing that they had complicated postcolonial trajectories as well. The representations through which Egyptian women authors attempted to make sense of their identities as national subjects—and to resolve the gender tensions that were part of that subjectivity—do not easily conform to a simple East-West binary. As discussed in this chapter, media depictions of "other women" elsewhere in Africa and Asia signal attempts by these writers and their audiences to address these issues, by extension reflecting broader conversations about what it meant to be a modern citizen across gender distinctions in a postcolonial society. The era of state feminism in Egypt—of which the Egyptian women's press was a crucial part—therefore challenges the idea that debates over modernity in the postcolonial world have entailed a one-dimensional embrace or rejection of Western ideas, knowledge, or technology. On the contrary, articles and images from the Egyptian women's press demonstrate that "modernity," if difficult to define, was nevertheless an idea claimed and debated by postcolonial women, offering a means of international solidarity as well as a measurement of advancement within national contexts during the early cold war period. If the definition and meaning of this expression ultimately proved elusive, the process of meeting, writing about, and imagining "other" women itself nonetheless provided a popular political means to envisioning other, possible futures.

Notes

1. "al-Zawaj, tanzim al-usra wa al-salam" ["Marriage and Family Planning and Peace"], *Hawwa'*, February 21, 1959.

2. Vijay Prashad, *The Darker Nations: A People's History of the Third World* (New York: New Press, 2007). I take the term "political imaginary" from Susan Buck-Morss, *Dreamworld and Catastrophe: The Passing of Utopia in East and West* (Cambridge: MIT Press, 2000), 12.

3. Odd Arne Westad, *The Global Cold War: Third World Interventions and the Making of Our Times* (Cambridge: Cambridge University Press, 2005), 98.

4. As quoted in Westad, *The Global Cold War*, 100.

5. James D. Le Sueur, "An Introduction: Reading Decolonization," in *The Decolonization Reader*, ed. James Le Sueur (New York: Routledge, 2003), 1–6.

6. The Nonaligned Movement, officially started in Belgrade in 1961 with 25 member states, was an outgrowth of the alliances made at Bandung. The Afro-Asian Peoples' Solidarity Committee, was founded in 1955 and in 1956 moved its headquarters to Cairo, where it remains to the present day.

7. The Egyptian Feminist Union was the first women's organization with an explicitly political program for women's emancipation. It grew out of the participation of elite women in the 1919 revolution against British rule as the women's wing of the nationalist Wafd (Delegation) Party, and was led by Hoda Sha'arawi, whose husband Ali was one of the leaders of the Wafd. For a complete history of the EFU, see Margot Badran, *Women, Islam and Nation* (Princeton: Princeton University Press, 1995).

8. It was on the return from the Rome 1923 IAW Congress that EFU president Hoda Sha'rawi and her young colleague Saiza Nabarawi made history by tearing off the light veils that covered their faces in the Cairo train station. The event has long figured in the narrative of nationalism and nationalist historiography as a "founding myth" of Egyptian modernity and liberation. The word *myth* is used here not because the event did not happen, but because it reflects the complex ways in which the actions of Sha'arawi and Nabarawi have been appropriated and fashioned as part of wider narratives of feminism, nationalism, and progress in Egypt.

9. This program dovetailed nicely with the newly expanded agenda of the EFU which, after Egyptian independence in 1922, broke away from the Wafd Party for failing to meet its demands for women's rights under the new constitution.

10. See Leila Rupp, *Worlds of Women* (Princeton: Princeton University Press, 1991), for an overview of the history of the IAW and other international feminist groups prior to 1945. Chapter 3 in particular offers discussion of European women's relations with non-Western women within these groups. Also see Antoinette Burton's excellent *Burdens of History: British Feminist, Indian Women and Imperial Culture, 1865–1915* (Chapel Hill: University of North Carolina Press, 1994). For an overview of the relationship between nationalism and the rise of women's movements in the non-Western world, see Kumari Jayawardena, *Feminism and Nationalism in the Third World* (London: Zed, 1986).

11. Burton, *Burdens of History*, 173.

12. Ibid., 191.

13. Ibid., 171.

14. Membership in the IAW was country-based. Although much of Asia and Africa remained under colonial control, the IAW deemed them countries

as opposed to colonial territories so that they would be eligible for IAW membership. Badran, *Women, Islam and Nation*, 108.

15. As quoted, ibid., 232.

16. The IAW continued to espouse a Western liberal feminist program.

17. Rupp, *Worlds of Women*, 3, 4.

18. Bahia Karam, "Introduction" in *Proceedings of the First Afro-Asian Women's Conference, Cairo, Jan. 14–23, 1961* (Cairo: Amalgamated Press of Egypt, 1961), 9.

19. Lakshmi Menon, "Closing Remarks" in *Report of the Proceedings of the First Asian-African Conference of Women, Held in Colombo, Ceylon, 15–24 of February, 1958* (Bombay: Mouj Printing Bureau, 1958), 293.

20. Chandra Mohanty, "Introduction: Cartographies of Struggle" in *Third World Women and the Politics of Feminism*, Chandra Mohanty, ed. (Bloomington: Indiana University Press, 1991), 4.

21. Daw Khin Hla, "Leader of the Burmese Delegation's Remarks at the Plenary Session," *Proceedings of the First Asian-African Conference of Women*, 15.

22. Karima Sa'id, "Opening Remarks" in *Proceedings of the First Afro-Asian Women's Conference*, 9. Karima Sa'id was the sister of *Hawwa'* editor Amina Sa'id and the Egyptian undersecretary of education.

23. Sabri Abu al-Majid, "Fi Viyitnam al-janubiyya: tuqadim al-ʾarus nusf al-mahr li-hamatha!" ["In South Vietnam, the groom pays half the dowry to his mother-in-law!"], *Hawwa'*, March 13, 1963, 43.

24. By "women's press," I mean not only magazines aimed at women, but the women's pages of various magazines aimed at a more general readership written by both men and women. I do this to get away from the idea that there is an underlying biological or essential cultural distinction that separates "women's writing" from other sorts of writing. What provides the coherence to the term *women's press* is a common politics of address, a common historical genealogy that was part of, yet also distinct from, the development of the press in Egypt as a whole through shared tropes, points of reference, and genres of writing.

25. For a basic account of the women's press in Egypt see Badran, *Women, Islam and Nation*; Beth Baron, *The Women's Awakening in Egypt: Culture, Society, and the Press* (New Haven: Yale University Press, 1994); Ijal Khalifa, "Al-Sihafa al-Nisa'iyya fi Misr, 1919–1939," MA thesis, Cairo University, 1966; and Ijal Khalifa, "Al-Sihafa al-nisa iyya fi Misr 1940–1965," PhD dissertation, Cairo University, 1969.

26. Marilyn Booth, *May Her Likes Be Multiplied: Biography and Gender Politics in Egypt* (Berkeley: University of California Press, 2001).

27. Booth hypothesizes that increases in female literacy and the spread of the novel displaced prescriptive biographies in magazines.

28. As early as 1954, the Nasser regime had begun to implement a systematic policy of control over the media. The journals of several of the opposition parties and various political organizations like the Muslim Brotherhood were closed, a trend that continued until 1960 when the press was nationalized. Control over the press was turned over to the National Union and later the Arab Socialist Union (the mass political organizations created by the regime as an alternative to a multiparty system), which was to supervise the publication of all newspapers and journals through five major publishing houses. The movie industry, which was the center of film-making for the Arabic-speaking world, was also nationalized in the early 1960s.

29. *Hawwa's* major competitor, *Bint al-nil (Daughter of the Nile)*, was closed in 1957 when its founder and editor, Duriyya Shafiq, was placed under house arrest for her criticism of the regime's increasing authoritarianism.

30. The largest weekly news magazine and most serious rival to *Akhir sa'a* and *al-Mussawar, Ruz al-yusuf* did not have a women's page after the early 1950s.

31. "Banat Iran" ["The girls of Iran"], *Hawwa'*, February 12, 1960.

32. "Ra'aytu al-mar'a al yamaniyya bila hijab" ["I saw the Yemmani woman without a veil"], *al-Musawwar*, March 18, 1958, 14, 15.

33. "Madha ta'rifina 'an al-mar'a fi Yughuslavia?" ["What do you know about the Yugoslavian woman?"], *Hawwa'*, December 12, 1958.

34. "Ihmdi rabina innaki Misiriyya" ["Thank God you are an Egyptian woman"], *Hawwa'*, August 27, 1966.

35. "Za'imat ifriqiyyat fil-mu'tamar al-kabir" ["African women leaders at the great conference"], *Hawwa'*, March 1, 1961.

36. "Ukhtik al-'iraqiyya" ["Your Iraqi sisters"], *Hawwa'*, October 25, 1958; "Ukhtik al-'iraqiyya fi maydan al-khidma al-ijtima'iyya" ["Your Iraqi sisters in the field of social service"], *Hawwa'*, December 23, 1961.

37. "al-Ma'ra al-Sudaniyya tuharib al-hijab" ["The Sudanese woman battles the veil"], *al-Mussawar*, March 8, 1957.

38. When she graduated in 1935, Amina Sa'id was the first woman to receive a degree in English from Faculty of Arts of Cairo University. Doria Shafik was one of the first Egyptian women in Egypt to gain a French *baccalaureate*.

39. These supranational visions of identity included Islamic, pan-Arab, and communist affiliations. Israel Gershoni and James Jankowski, *Redefining the Egyptian Nation, 1930–1945* (Cambridge: Cambridge University Press, 1995).

40. Amina Sa'id, "al-zawj al-alamani hakim bi amrihi" ["The German wife is ruled by his command"], *Hawwa'*, October 4, 1958.

41. Burton, *Burdens of History*, 101.

42. Amina Sa'id, "Nahnu muqassir fi haq ikhwatina al-'arabiyya" ["We are neglecting the rights of our Arab sisters"], *Hawwa'*, 12 February 1961.

43. Fumil Habib, "al-Mar'a fi Pakistan" ["The woman in Pakistan"], *Hawwa'*, July 9, 1960.

44. "Shaqiqatik al-sudaniyya fi tariqha ila al-tahrir" ["Your Sudanese sister in her path to liberation"], *Hawwa'*, December 12, 1959.

45. The Sudan was conquered by Mohammed Ali Pasha's troops, led by his son Isma'il, in 1824. In 1841 the Ottoman Sultan officially recognized the Mohammed Ali dynasty's claims over the area when it was added to the land grant that comprised "South Egypt." In 1899, the British and Egyptians signed the Anglo-Egyptian Condominium, outlining the administration of Sudan. Though under Egyptian sovereignty, it was run virtually as a British colony. Sudan did not achieve formal independence until 1956.

46. Yemen has been described as Egypt's Vietnam. In 1962, Yemen was ruled by Imam Ahmed in the North and the British, who retained their colonial control of Aden in the South. In September, a military coup brought Abdullah al-Sallal to power. Imam Ahmed's heir, Mohammed Badr, fled to the North where, with the support of affiliated tribesmen and the financial and material backing of Saudi Arabia, he mounted armed resistance to the Sallal government. Sallal requested aid from Egypt, which Nasser granted. Over the course of the next two years, Egypt's troop commitment grew from 8,000 to 70,000. Fighting became increasingly brutal as the conflict dragged on. Repeated negotiations between Saudi Arabia and Egypt failed to end the conflict until 1967.

47. "Ta'aysh al-mar'a al-yamaniyya ahla' ayyam hayatiha" ["The Yemeni woman is living the sweetest days of her life"], *Hawwa'*, March 11, 1964.

48. "Hakadha ta'aysh al-mar'a fil-Yemen" ["Thus lives the woman in Yemen"], *Akhir sa'a*, June 7, 1965.

49. "Hakadha Ta'aysh al-mar'a al-yamaniyya" ["This is how the Yemeni woman lives"], *Akhir sa'a*, June 7, 1965.

50. "Ra'aytu al-mar'a al-yamaniyya bila hijab!" ["I Saw the Yemeni Woman Without a Veil!"].

51. Amina Sa'id, "al-Musawa: hal tus'idu al-Mar'a?" ["Equality: Does it make women happy?"], *Hawwa'*, November 29, 1958.

52. Amina Sa'id, "al-Sufiyatiyya al-muslima ta'khud al-mahr" ["The Soviet Muslim woman takes a dowry"], *Hawwa'*, November 8, 1958.

53. Amina Sa'id, "al-Sufiyatiyya al-muslima kama ra'aytuha" ["The Soviet Muslim woman as I saw her"], *Hawwa'*, November 8, 1958.

54. Sabri Abdel Majid, "al-Ma'ra fi Viyitnam" ["The Woman in Vietnam"], *Hawwa'*, August 27, 1966.

55. "Batula fata Jamila Buhrid" ["Heroine Jamila Buhrid"], *Hawwa'*, March 15, 1958.

56. "al-Mar'a al-jaza'iriyya" ["The Algerian woman"], *Hawwa'*, June 14, 1960.

57. As Denise Kandiyoti argues, the identification of the (gendered) private with the inner sanctum of group identity has had serious implications for women's citizenship within the context of secular-nationalist projects. Denise Kandiyoti, "Identity and Its Discontents: Women and the Nation," *Millennium* 20, no. 3 (1991), 435. See Marnia Lazreg, *The Eloquence of Silence: Algerian Women in Question* (New York: Routledge, 1994) for the legacy that the dynamics and outcome of national struggle and the association of women with the inner sanctum of communal identity has had in Algeria.

58. "al-Mar'a fi Sin" ["The Woman in China"], *Ruz al-yusuf*, February 6, 1956.

59. Ibid.

60. "Intahat al-ma'ra al-siniyya min mu'araka al-bina' wa bada'at mu'araka al-jamal wa al-anaqa" ["The Chinese woman has finished with the battle of development and has begun the battle for beauty and elegance"], *Hawwa'*, February 3, 1962.

61. Ibid.

5

Radio Cairo and the Decolonization of East Africa, 1953–64

James R. Brennan

The radio weapon was perhaps the most important, for its influence was out of all proportion to the number of listeners, perhaps ten to each radio set. Its voice carried the stamp of authority and a reputation for veracity. Its emotional appeal, interspersed with popular music, had a special attraction for the still large numbers of illiterate people.
—Randal Sadleir, Information Officer, Tanganyika Public Relations Office, 1955-1961[1]

SHORTWAVE-RADIO BROADCASTING PROVIDED the most effective medium for spreading a generic anticolonial nationalism throughout Africa and Asia in the 1950s and 1960s. The radio battles for informational authority and editorial persuasion popularized cold war vocabularies and anticolonial bromides that satisfied colonial subjects' growing hunger for polemics. Of these shortwave broadcasts, the most politically important for Africa came from Cairo. Writing in 1957 about the influence of shortwave radio broadcasts in the Tanganyikan capital of Dar es Salaam, an astute colonial officer wrote:

Delhi, with its strong anti-colonial slant, has its listeners, but much the most popular of the foreign radios is that of Cairo: not only because it is anti-colonial and anti-British and anti-Western, but because its presentation is hard-hitting, unequivocal and makes no attempt to be fair.[2]

Between 1953 and 1960, the rhetoric of improvement fully yielded to that of confrontation to British colonial rule in East Africa. Radio broadcasts from Cairo offered a powerful vision of an emerging Afro-Asian world that would assist Britain's East African colonies to throw off the chains of Western colonialism. But this vision of Afro-Asian solidarity also raised into stark relief the political and economic disparities *among* the "Afro-Asians" residing in East Africa. Like the ideals espoused at Bandung, shortwave-radio propaganda claimed to erode political boundaries but paradoxically strengthened them. To the same extent that Gamal Abdel Nasser revealed his primary consideration to be Egypt's place in the Middle East rather than in an imagined "Afro-Asia," the primary considerations of East Africans proved to be an anti-colonialism that would first extinguish local racial hierarchies through victory of an African racial nationalism. Only after this initial process at the nation-state level could the region, if politically expedient, embrace a more broadly conceived "Afro-Asian" identity. Radio Cairo was located amid these local, regional, and intercontinental tensions. Its broadcasts popularized an effective anticolonial invective, but also accelerated regional conflicts, particularly in Zanzibar where violent rhetoric gave way to horrific violence. This chapter seeks to address the regional and global political opportunities provided by shortwave radio—as well as the constraints and tensions between various political movements and regional interests—raised by this rapidly spreading technology.

Nasser, Bandung, and Radio Cairo in East Africa

Although the political programming of Egyptian radio had grown anti-British in the late 1940s and early 1950s, the history of its regional and global ambitions began with the Egyptian Free Officers in the coup of July 1952. Nasser soon emerged as the new regime's leader, and had formed rough ideas about Africa and "Afro-Asian" liberation—most of which centered on expelling the British and Israelis from the Middle East and "restoring" the unity of the Nile Valley under Egyptian leadership.

Securing Egyptian influence over the Middle East was always Nasser's top foreign policy priority. It was only after efforts to form a pan-Arab defensive pact to oppose the Baghdad Pact had failed that Nasser opted to expand his political horizons by attending the Bandung Conference in April 1955. Bandung was Nasser's first major appearance on the international stage, and his anti-West inclinations were well-received and encouraged by China, India, and Indonesia. (See Bier's chapter in this volume for another case study of Egypt's role in early postcolonial politics.) In words of the state newspaper *Al-Goumhouryah*, Egypt's "inferiority complex disappeared at Bandung."[3] Nasser's foreign policy of "positive neutralism"—a term coined at Bandung—served as the malleable rubric for Egypt to fight colonialism on the grounds that deterrent wars could be necessary and passivity could not be justified.[4] Bandung inspired Nasser to turn toward Sub-Saharan Africa. Carrying the banner of "anti-imperialism," Nasser offered many African leaders diplomatic protection and support in Cairo. By 1962, no fewer than fifteen African countries had taken up the offer, with various bureau officers taking in an Egyptian government stipend of one-hundred pounds per month and free air travel, all supported by the African Section of the Egyptian Ministry of Information.[5]

After Bandung, Nasser launched a vigorous propaganda campaign for Africa, identifying Egypt as an ancient civilization African in its origin. Alleged racial difference between Africans north and south of the Sahara, Egyptian propagandists claimed, was merely an imperialist tool to create rifts and division. Nasser solidified his Afro-Asian credentials with the tremendous propaganda victory at Suez in November 1956.[6] Suez shook colonial administrators throughout East Africa. Randal Sadleir commented:

> I certainly felt at the time that things could never be quite the same again, and one could sense a definite change in the mood of people in Dar es Salaam. They had begun to realize that their erstwhile imperial masters had feet of clay.[7]

No less a figure than the Kenyan nationalist Oginga Odinga stated that "Africa was never the same after Suez and the coming into play on the continent and in the world of the forces of Pan-Africanism."[8]

Radio proved to be Nasser's most effective propaganda weapon. Voice of the Arabs, an Arabic-language broadcast that began on the first anniversary of the July Revolution in 1953, was the "pulpit for revolution" that enabled Egypt to "create a public opinion where none had existed before, among the illiterate and semiliterate masses of the Arab world."[9] Moreover, "Voice of the Arabs" ended Britain's postwar monopoly on propaganda in the Middle East.[10] From the beginning, these broadcasts reached East Africa, and had the effect of radicalizing demands of Arabs living on the Kenyan Coast. British military operations in Suez incensed Kenyan Arabs—funds were raised and special prayers were held for Egypt in mosques throughout the country.[11] British bombers destroyed Radio Cairo's transmitter in the early morning of November 2, but Voice of the Arabs listeners in East Africa picked up the signal again three days later.[12] Kenya's intelligence officers considered Arab hostility "unlikely to go beyond words," but that things could change if "a call for holy war is sent out by Egypt."[13] The colony's Intelligence Committee concluded:

> Cairo radio is listened to eagerly by Arabs and preferred to the B.B.C., Nairobi, and Mombasa (Sauti ya Mvita) radios. It is the most potent force for the encouragement of nationalism and subversive tendencies. The broadcasts from this station are sometimes virulent and nearly always anti-British in tone. It seizes on any local issue that might embarrass the British, or offers an opportunity to proclaim the cause of Arab nationalism; a recent example is the broadcasts on the sovereignty of the coastal strip following Mackawi's statements on the need for a revision of the 1895 Treaty.[14]

The treaty in question was a reference to the *mwambao* movement, which sought to exploit the legal fiction of the Sultan of Zanzibar's "ownership" of the ten-mile strip along Kenya's coastline, expressed in the 1895 treaty, to pursue demands for local autonomy from "mainland" Kenya. Ahmad Said, the principal Voice of the Arabs announcer, celebrated the cause as an appropriate anticolonial struggle. The following broadcast reveals the power as well as obvious limitations for such broadcasting in East Africa:

O! Arabs. News has reached us that an Arab Islamic Nation is being established in Zanzibar and the Coastal Strip of East Africa. . . . It is our duty then, to assist this blessed movement, so as to glorify it, support it and bring it up to join our Arab Procession. . . . Arab Nationalism is penetrating the East African Jungle and Central Africa. The Arab League of Nationals on the one hand, and the Arab Nations extending from the Atlantic to the Arabian Gulf, on the other hand should help our Brothers in Kenya and Zanzibar. . . . We shall help this Nationalism emitting from the heart of the African Continent.[15]

Subsequent political initiatives by Zanzibari politicians to reclaim the coastal strip for the Sultan were enthusiastically received by Arabs and, to a lesser extent, by Swahili inhabitants along the coast into the early 1960s.[16]

Yet only a small minority of East Africans understood Arabic. The seminal development of Egyptian propaganda for East Africa was the launch of the Swahili-language broadcast Sauti ya Cairo (Voice of Cairo) on July 3, 1954.[17] Initially thirty minutes in length, the program started at 19.00 local East African time with the Egyptian national anthem, followed by a five-minute recitation of the Koran, ten minutes of daily news, and either two weekly political commentaries or a cultural program that emphasized the history, culture, economics, and politics of Egypt. Each section was linked by short intervals of music.[18] In July 1955 the program was increased to forty-five minutes, in 1958 to a full hour, and in 1961 to an hour-and-a-half. Radio Cairo's first Swahili broadcast encapsulated the radicalism and paternalism of Egypt's African policy, announcing that "Egypt's geographical situation requires her to work for the liberation of the African continent, in which the Nile flows, from all forms of imperialism . . . [t]he transmission aims at linking the fighting peoples of Africa with the Arab peoples, who are also struggling for freedom, peace, and prosperity."[19] Generously funded by the state, Radio Cairo raided broadcast talent throughout East Africa, offering announcers and technicians larger salaries to tempt them away from colonial information service positions.[20] In addition to Sauti ya Cairo, Radio Cairo also launched a pseudo-clandestine station known as the Voice of Free Africa (Sauti ya Uhuru wa Africa) in April 1957, broadcasting in Swahili for East and Central Africa during the hour before

Sauti ya Cairo began, and on a frequency very close to that of Cairo's acknowledged broadcasts. Unlike Sauti ya Cairo, which began with qur'anic recitation, the Voice of Free Africa began with drumbeats and horn music, followed by political talk. The Voice of Free Africa claimed to be located "in the heart of Africa"—indeed at one point white Kenyan officials feared that its claims to be broadcasting from the White Highlands might be true. Despite Egyptian denials that the station was within their territory, British radio technicians eventually obtained a fix on the signal and confirmed that it was broadcasting from Cairo.[21]

Although Nasser played a central role in launching this full-scale propaganda campaign against European colonial powers in Sub-Saharan Africa, a remarkable feature of Radio Cairo broadcasts was the light editorial influence that Nasser or any other Egyptian official exercised over program content. Suleiman Malik, an announcer on Sauti ya Cairo and later Voice of Free Africa, remembered that Major Mohamed Faiq, Nasser's adviser on African affairs, had no influence over his activities at the Zanzibar National Party's (ZNP) Cairo office, and that people in the ZNP office enjoyed "complete independence."[22] Although this was certainly less true for Radio Cairo's central program, "Voice of the Arabs," it does seem that vernacular broadcasts to Sub-Saharan Africa were surprisingly independent of state controls, even despite the generous state salaries the announcers received. At times, the right hand of Egypt's vernacular propaganda did not know what the left hand was doing. Nasser appeared "surprised and sympathetic" in 1963 at the request of Kenyan Government officials to rein in Cairo's Somali broadcasts, which inflamed Somali irredentism toward Kenya's Northern Frontier District.[23] Free to choose their editorial content, Cairo's African radio announcers nonetheless borrowed liberally from Nasserite tradition of framing broadcasts around the identification of allies and enemies.

Art, Orthodoxy, and Zanzibari Politics in Radio Cairo's Anticolonial Invective

Zanzibar nationalists, who would identify themselves as "Zanzibaris" yet be identified by mainlanders as "Arabs," dominated the early years of Radio Cairo's Swahili-language broadcasts. Sharifa Lemke, the first broadcaster of Sauti ya Cairo, came from a prestigious Zanzibari family with close historical ties to the Sultan. She was also sister to Ahmed Lemke, who had studied in Egypt, joined a communist movement opposed to King Farouk, and later spent two years in an Egyptian prison. When he returned to Zanzibar in 1953, Lemke organized Zanzibari workers and students into a politically oriented multiracial club called the Zanzibari Association, which protested Britain's reliance on racial institutions.[24] Through these connections, the politics of the Zanzibari Association and later the ZNP informed the politics of Radio Cairo's early Swahili broadcasts—antiracialist, anticolonialist, and vaguely pan-Islamist. Sharifa Lemke was joined at Sauti ya Cairo in February 1955 by Ahmed Rashad Ali, before she finally left the job in November that year.[25]

Ahmed Rashad Ali became the major on-air personality of Sauti ya Cairo broadcasts during his long tenure from 1955 to 1964. Also from a family with close ties to the Sultan of Zanzibar, Rashad had been a sanitary inspector in Zanzibar town in the 1930s and then traveled to Oman in 1937. The following year he arrived in Bombay and remained there until 1947, where he became a professional football player and great admirer of Muhammad Ali Jinnah and the Muslim League. On his return to Zanzibar, he took up a job as an announcer with Sauti ya Unguja, the radio station of the government Information Office, as well as captain of the Malindi Sports Club football team. He joined Ahmed Said Kharusi, later editor of the radical newspaper *Mwongozi*, to produce anticolonial documents for the Zanzibar Human Rights Party, for which he was arrested, tried but not convicted for sedition, and ultimately dismissed from his government position. He was selected as a Radio Cairo announcer following an interview with Ali Muhsin al Barwani at the Arab Association premises in late 1954. Following a brief return visit to India as a broadcaster on All-India Radio, he began broadcasting from Cairo on February 27, 1955, reading news in Swahili as well as making a weekend political propaganda broadcast.[26]

Cairo broadcasts were particularly popular in Zanzibar, where an American diplomat reckoned there were more listeners "than in all the rest of East Africa combined."[27] A *Times* journalist visiting the island reported, "[i]n every other shop hang portraits of Nasser, and Arab radios seem permanently tuned in to Cairo."[28] Ali Sultan Issa, nephew to Ahmed Rashad, recalled that "[e]verybody in East Africa who spoke Swahili tuned in to that program, and in Zanzibar, we listened to [Ahmed Rashad's] programs in all the cafes. My uncle was a radical in those days, wanting to get rid of the sultan. His broadcasts infuriated the British, but they gave us inspiration."[29] Editorial connections between Zanzibar and Radio Cairo were tight in these early years—on the second anniversary of the Free Officers' Revolution, Zanzibar's Arab Association sent two telegrams to Cairo, the first praising Neguib and Nasser, the second to Radio Cairo informing them that Arab representatives had withdrawn from the Legislative Council in protest of the sedition case against editors of the radical newspaper *Al Falaq*.[30] Ahmad Rashad's "East African Newsletter," the broadcast's weekly political commentary, was part of a "machine for feeding material from Zanzibar to their compatriots in Cairo" that had developed, since late 1955, an "alarming effectiveness" to lay stinging attacks on the British in Zanzibar.[31] "It is clear," the acting British Resident in Zanzibar informed a visiting American diplomat, "from [Rashad's] news comments that he is being kept well-informed of local happenings by informants here."[32] The popularity of Sauti ya Cairo tended to fade as one moved away from the coast, in part because it employed a Zanzibari dialect (KiUnguja) not well understood "upcountry," as a Belgian survey of Congolese radio listeners discovered.[33]

British complaints centered on fears that Radio Cairo broadcasts might lead to violence in East Africa. The personal abuse of European officers in the Zanzibar government, as well as attacks on Zanzibari "traitors" who worked with the British, moved the British Resident to register a series of complaints.[34] Other broadcasts from Cairo already proved to be remarkably powerful in stirring people to action. In 1955, a Voice of the Arabs broadcast criticizing a British General's mission to Jordan led directly to riots in the streets of Amman.[35] Although there appears no analogous East African violence resulting directly from Sauti ya Cairo broadcasts, the program did usher in a new rhetorical era of sharp personal abuse on public figures. The broadcasts that most tightly grabbed British attention in East Africa concerned Mau Mau. Ahmad Rashad gave a wide range of anti-imperialist talks that labeled Mau Mau figures as "freedom fighters."[36] One broadcast explained that:

> There is no greater injustice than that which has been and still is endured by the people of Kenya. The fertile land of the people of the country is seized from them, and they are put in reserves, segregated from the settlers and without any reasonable relations with them. They are made to wear identity labels round their necks like dogs—and they are even forbidden to go to some places where dogs are allowed. If this is not injustice, what is it? Surely no one can call it democracy. Although the native of Kenya has no weapon but the panga which he uses to cut his way through the forest, he is labelled an enemy of freedom and security—while the imperialist troops, machine-guns in hands, are labelled soldiers of security and freedom! Whose security? Against whose security is the nationalist fighting? From whom are they afraid that he will steal his freedom?[37]

Radio Cairo's Swahili broadcast on New Year's Day 1956 wished, "God willing, may the remaining people of Kenya continue with their jihad for freedom, and we pray that He will grant them their freedom in the shortest possible time. Amen."[38]

Egypt's two Swahili-language programs, Sauti ya Cairo and Voice of Free Africa, collectively popularized a new political vocabulary that had an enormous impact in spreading anti-Western polemics throughout East Africa. The vivid language of invective directed against British colonial interests was the most striking aspect of Radio Cairo's Swahili broadcasts. The revelation of using the words "dogs" and "pigs" to describe British officials was the most powerful and memorable aspect of Radio Cairo invective. Resuscitating a tradition in Swahili poetry of the competitive insult,[39] this invective assimilated contemporary world events into a consistent and powerful anticolonial message. A broadcast from 'Voice of Free Africa' proclaimed:

> Africans, Indians and Arabs are brothers, as shown by the Bandung Conference. . . . Brothers, my African national compatriots, I appeal to you to work together with the Arabs and Indians, to

fight those white pigs side by side until freedom is attained. Disregard the venomous honeyed words of these white colonialist pigs— words which are intended to cause quarrels between you and to separate you and thus make you humble forever.[40]

Radio Cairo's early days were dominated by events and views concerning the Sultan's realm of Zanzibar and the Kenyan coast. In an early survey on the influence of Radio Cairo's Swahili broadcasting in January 1956, the governments of Uganda and Tanganyika stated that neither broadcast had much effect, but Zanzibar reported that it was "widely listened to" as the announcer was a Zanzibari, though there were as yet "no signs that public opinion has been much infected."[41] By August 1956, Radio Cairo broadcasts were reckoned to be "making a particular impact in Zanzibar and on the coastal region of Kenya where there are large Moslem communities," having the effect in Zanzibar of "intimidating the people who would otherwise be prepared to co-operate with the Government."[42]

The idea of a Zanzibari nationalism founded on allegiance to the Sultan and nonracialism—opposing both the colonial government's various racial laws on the one hand, and more significantly the African racial nationalism represented by the Afro-Shirazi Party (ASP) on the other—was the keystone of early Sauti ya Cairo broadcasts. Ahmad Rashad criticized the racial hiring and salary practices of new companies coming to Zanzibar, saying that "[t]he Zanzibaris cannot get accustomed to the subjugation of their famed 'Uzanzibari' (Zanzibarism)."[43] These early broadcasts reflected one side of the newspaper wars fought in Zanzibar between supporters of ZNP and ASP.[44] The ASP newspaper *Afrika Kwetu* attacked Sauti ya Cairo in early 1956 for not understanding who a real Zanzibari was. The announcer, presumably Ahmad Rashad, countered that "the difference between the words and birthright of the writer of 'Afrika Kwetu' and the announcer of the 'Voice of Cairo' is really a big one." He elaborated that "[t]he editor of 'Afrika Kwetu,' his ancestors and he himself are people of the mainland, whereas the speaker of the 'Voice of Cairo' and his ancestors before him were born in Zanzibar. Who is more a native of the country, the editor of 'Afrika Kwetu' or the announcer of the 'Voice of Cairo'?" The announcer finally concluded by comparing Egypt favorably to the East

African mindset of *Afrika Kwetu*, arguing that eleven different racial groups living in Egypt were "all working for their freedom and the freedom of their own country."[45] Both Sauti ya Cairo and Voice of Free Africa took free aim at ASP leader Abeid Karume. A Voice of Free Africa broadcast derisively referred to Karume as a "boatman" (he had earlier been a sailor) to emphasize his poor educational qualifications. Rather disingenuously, the broadcast asked:

> This boatman brother of ours who is President of the African Association of Zanzibar and an honourable member of the Legislative council must understand that times have changed and progress demands from us Africans to co-operate and be all united for the sake of the freedom of our countries. . . . Why does not our brother the boatman of Zanzibar, who leads a group of nationals, follow the example of Mr. Julius Nyerere, the leader of the nationals of Tanganyika, and of Mr. Tom Mboya, the leader of the nationals of Kenya? I have forgotten the name of this gentleman, but that is of no account.[46]

Tuning in to Radio Cairo thus also would broadcast one's political identity. As the public soundscape of coastal towns became increasingly fraught with racial tension, such declarations could lead to violence. In 1958, a riot broke out in Dar es Salaam after Arab shop owners refused African demands to change their publicly amplified radios from Cairo to Dar es Salaam to hear Nyerere speak in Legislative Council. Police arrested 120 people and "took action to control the volume of radios in all Dar es Salaam shops and streets and they removed some of the public address amplifiers in the Arab quarter of the city."[47] As late as January 1961, Sauti ya Cairo broadcasts supported ZNP in elections, attacking the ASP for not fighting for Zanzibar on the world stage at various solidarity conferences, as well as for advocating the continuation of British rule in Zanzibar.[48]

After this point, Egypt's Swahili-language radio broadcasts became remarkably agnostic on Zanzibari politics. Walking on eggshells following Zanzibar's election riots in June 1961, the Voice of Free Africa avoided assigning any partisan blame, and instead wished only that "the people of Zanzibar would soon be reconciled and would stop bloodshed."[49] Two weeks later, it hesitantly criticized the ASP for its historic "stubbornness."[50] Said Khalifah Muhammad, the second major personality after Ahmad Rashad on Sauti ya Cairo, lightly took up the ZNP cause by countering claims in the British "Intelligence Digest" that the ZNP was not party of the African people.[51] It was around this time that Ahmad Rashad Ali formally broke with ZNP and began to support, albeit tentatively, the Afro-Shirazi Party, but exactly when remains unclear—Ali Muhsin states was "[a] few years before the tragedy of 1964."[52] Direct commentaries on events in Zanzibar after June 1961 became sparse. As early as 1959, Sauti ya Cairo broadcasts had begun to stress pan-Africanism over Nasserite pan-Arabism—to the point where, according to Kenya Coast Provincial Commissioner, the program had "lost influence with the very size-able Arab community in Mombasa"[53]—but June 1961 seems to mark the real turning point. After Abdulrahman Babu's break with ZNP to form the socialist Umma Party in 1963, very few broadcasts from Radio Cairo openly supported ZNP activities.

Presumably to authenticate its popular African sensibilities, the Voice of Free Africa indulged itself in attacks on the South Asian communities of East and Central Africa for "covertly collaborating with the British against the Arabs and Africans."[54] But the gist of Egyptian radio broadcasts on race and racial mixing were, even on its more conscientiously "African" Voice of Free Africa program, over-whelmingly optimistic, and strikingly out of step with its allocation of support for political parties. One broadcast attempted to unravel the history of slavery to make sense of Afro-Asian relations. Here the broadcaster offers a Manichean overview, wherein the Afro-Asian world of Bandung on the one hand was one of true nonracialism, struggling against the hard racial categories of Western imperialism on the other. Responding to ASP and other African nationalist propaganda that emphasized the Arab role in the slave trade, and the often marginalized status of mixed-race children of Arab fathers,[55] the broadcaster states:

> In ancient times slavery prevailed all over the world, including Africa. Africans used to enslave other Africans and used to sell them to the Arabs, whom they used to transport to their own countries; even today Africans are selling Africans. In short, there are at

present Arab kings reigning in Arab countries who have in their veins African blood. Africans marry Arabs and Arabs marry Africans, and Indians marry Africans and Africans marry Indians, and their children are [word indistinct]. But in Britain and America there are several millions of Africans with White blood who are not accepted among the White people. . . . So, my traitorous and shameless brothers, hirelings of the white dogs, stop your dangerous game and adopt the spirit of the Bandung conference and let it bring the Africans, Asians and Arabs in East Africa together.[56]

This view of racial harmony was credible depending on the perspective of the listener. To ZNP supporters and its sympathizers, it confirmed the nonracial, anticolonial bona fides of a pan-Islamic nationalism.[57] To many African nationalists, it was a disingenuous description that attempted to obscure racial hierarchies and sexual exploitation that had long buttressed coastal social structures.

The Waning of Radio Cairo and Rise of National Broadcasting, 1961–64

In 1961, the United Arab Republic broke apart with the withdrawal of Syria from the union, and Egypt reappraised its foreign policy toward Sub-Saharan Africa. The country shifted away from its earlier explicit goal of political leadership and toward a new goal of cooperation, particularly within the economic sphere.[58] This followed severe setbacks in Egypt's African policy, most dramatically in Congo, where Egypt proved unable to influence events. Nasser found himself badly embarrassed after vainly sending arms and aid to support Patrice Lumumba; and again after recognizing Antoine Gizenga as head of state without support from other African states or the Soviet Union; and still again after supporting the failed Stanleyville government of Christophe Gbenye in 1964, until Egypt pulled out completely in April 1965.[59] The Congo issue polarized all pan-Africanists, and the subsequent formation of the UAR-friendly radical Casablanca group and the UAR-hostile conservative Monrovia group displayed the sharp limits to Egyptian leadership for all to see.

Generic anticolonialism was reaching its limits. Reflecting this shift in Egypt, as well as the political changes within East Africa, Radio Cairo propaganda had become somewhat stale by 1961. Swahili broadcasts were increasingly disinclined to discuss deeply polarizing issues such as race in Zanzibar or the future of the Kabaka and Bugandan exceptionalism in Uganda. Particularly problematic was Nyerere—his unchallenged leadership of PAFMECA and open support of ASP deeply frustrated ZNP supporters. Nyerere, who abandoned the ZNP to firmly support Abeid Karume's Afro-Shirazi Party in 1959, permitted the ASP to use the Tanganyika Broadcasting Corporation for political advertisements on its radio broadcasts in early 1963.[60] Kenya's white settlers and British colonial officials served evermore monotonously as the chief targets of propaganda after 1961, despite their increasing irrelevance. The politically unassailable demand to free the imprisoned martyr Jomo Kenyatta was pronounced over and over on both Cairo stations, with almost mind-numbing repetition. The creation of this new, careful, even apprehensive political orthodoxy was driven in part by the one unambiguous position taken by Radio Cairo on matters of significant internal division—the support for the Kenya African National Union and a strong central state over the objections of the Kenya African Democratic Union demands for regional autonomy. Unrelenting attacks on KADU and its leader Ronald Ngala dominated Sauti ya Cairo broadcasts after 1960.[61] Ngala was relentlessly portrayed as an imperialist stooge who sought to divide Kenya, making it "a second Congo," and its autonomous regions into "a second Katanga."[62] On Voice of Free Africa, the idea of *mwambao* separatism was already anathema by 1961.[63] Abdillahi Nasir, the unofficial "Swahili" leader of the *mwambao* movement, came in for torrential personal criticism from the Voice of Free Africa as someone conspiring to create "a second Katanga in Kenya by serving your masters the imperialists and the Boer dogs."[64]

After 1964, an angry sense of nationalist proprietorship over the airwaves had plainly asserted itself. An African observer admonished the radio-listening habits of Indians, Somalis, and Arabs in Dar es Salaam, demanding that they stop listening to shortwave broadcasts in other languages, and instead to listen only to the nation-building advice offered by Radio Tanganyika. He also observed that many who do happen to be tuned to Radio Tanganyika simply carry on with their business without understanding or even caring about the new orders of Tanzanian government officials.[65] The imperative of nation-building could ill-afford such indulgences as listening to external radio broadcasts.

Egypt retreated from its earlier role in East Africa as agent provocateur and political manipulator, and entered the business of religious proselytization. By 1964, Al-Azhar had placed over two-hundred religious scholars throughout the world, most concentrated in Africa including Tanzania and Zanzibar. These many missions from Al-Azhar sought to protect Islam "from the distortions of its enemies" and to fight Zionist propaganda. Arabic lessons for Swahili listeners of Radio Cairo began in 1962. Broadcasts paid significant attention to alleged Jewish spy rings in East African countries and devoted time to theological lessons that described Jewish treachery in the days of the Prophet.[66] Nasser himself gave the impression in a speech at the Addis Ababa Conference in May 1963 that he was more interested in strengthening pan-Arab and pan-Islamic ties than in staying atop African political events.[67]

In late 1964, Cairo launched the Voice of Islam, Al-Azhar's daily, thirteen-hour radio program of qur'anic recitation, on shortwave to Latin America, Africa, and the Middle East. The following year the Voice of Islam initiated vernacular broadcasts for sub-Saharan Africa.[68] Egypt's investment in radio programming continued to expand rapidly, keeping pace with the growing number of shortwave vernacular programs beamed to Africa by other world powers. By 1964, Egypt transmitted 766 hours per week, second in the world only to the United States, and in March 1965 opened the world's largest and most powerful broadcasting station.[69] But by then, Cairo had lost its monopoly of anticolonial, Afro-Asian nationalism in African vernacular languages. Propaganda investment shifted to pan-Islamic projects. As early as October 1960, ZNP officials had met with Major Saleh Salim of the UAR to discuss the relations between the Arab world and black nationalism. Salim stated that the Arab world could not at present interfere with African nationalism, but that this did not mean that "the Arab world should allow themselves to be placed in a position where they were completely subjugated, a particular danger as many of the African Leaders were Christians." Salim concluded that the only way to ensure Arab representation was "through the Muslim religion," and he urged the ZNP and all other Arab states to "secretly point out the possible dangers of African nationalism to followers of Islam, and to attempt to band all Muslims together into one single political unit capable of demanding safeguards." The ZNP delegation agreed to secretly contact East African Muslims to gain their cooperation.[70]

National radio policies of East Africa's newly independent states offered little support for the "Afro-Asian" ambitions of Radio Cairo. Tanganyika's vocal pan-Africanism represented the crest of a wave of xenophobia as hostile to Egyptian intrusion as it was to Western or communist propaganda encroachments. The new head of the Tanganyika Broadcasting Corporation (TBC) issued a staff memo insisting upon loyalty to African nationalist ideals, and rejecting "foreign" propaganda from the West, East, and Cairo. Staff members were instructed to approach all programming material with the following questions:

> Let us ask ourselves "What does this item mean in Tanganyika to an African? Is it African in thought, feeling and style? Or is it just a secondhand rehash of an alien idea?". . . . In short, we have all got to think as Africans, and if we are non-Africans, to make a conscious effort to do so. It is no part of the TBC's job to act directly or indirectly as a propaganda agent for any nation or organisation that is seeking, or will seek, to enter into our lives—and they are many.[71]

The disavowal of TBC's colonial past, both in the contemporary newspapers and later reflections, involved proposing a dualism between a colonial source of oppressive propaganda and a now-liberated source of "truth" propaganda to provide real development to the new nation.[72] In Kenya, the Kenya Broadcasting Corporation dramatically canceled its relay of the BBC news a few days after independence in December 1963, on grounds that the BBC had used the word *terrorists* instead of *fighters* to describe Mau Mau guerrillas—a fitting if sudden dismissal of a decade of British colonial propaganda and counterpropaganda.[73]

After independence, the inherited radio services first erected by colonial regimes jealously retained their local broadcasting monopolies. The Kenyan Government took over the Kenya Broadcasting Corporation in July 1964, and the Tanzanian Government took over the Tanganyika Broadcasting Services in July 1965, renaming it Radio Tanzania.[74] Thereafter, Radio Tanzania became famous as the regional home of ongoing liberation movements, which would use its facilities as their international voice. It served as the "one strong alternative voice" for Central and Southern Africa into the 1970s.[75] The logic of subsequent Radio Tanzania shortwave broadcasts to the colonized people of Africa was that, whereas Afro-Asian solidarity held esteem on a global stage, national liberation had to be achieved first. Indeed, the Organization of African States' Liberation Committee itself was headquartered in Dar es Salaam.

Conclusion

Radio Cairo's reputation was a casualty of the Six Days' War with Israel in 1967. Wildly optimistic reports of Egyptian victories on Voice of the Arabs broadcasts gave way to realization of a profound, humiliating defeat. Ahmed Said and the radio station were seen "not just as deceivers, but as the agents of Egyptian humiliation," and Said was imprisoned, kept under house arrest, and then condemned to lead "a furtive existence in a still hostile Cairo."[76] By this point, Radio Cairo transmissions to East Africa no longer played a significant role in East African politics. Afro-Asian ideals instead came to be realized increasingly through a series of bilateral relationships, in East African most notably between Tanzania and China (see chapters of Monson and Burgess in this volume). Particularly as an economic proposition, the promises of Bandung proved disappointing, and as a rule were largely superseded by such bilateral agreements.[77]

Bandung's ultimate significance for East Africa was the contingent form of ideological *communitas* (see the introduction), which it momentarily created, most forcefully in the generic anticolonialism that Egypt facilitated and amplified into the area's coastal regions. The nationalist orthodoxies that dominated the media of postcolonial East Africa had drunk deeply from the wells of anticolonial invective on offer from Radio Cairo during the 1950s. Transregional anticolonial propaganda of this period was domesticated and nationalized in the 1960s and 1970s as the defensive intellectual armaments of Africa's postcolonial states, whose very fragility fueled the aggressive assertion of nation-state sovereignty at the expense of transregional political movements. The initial thrust of intercontinental political solidarity as proposed at the Bandung meeting faded rapidly with the end of empire, and proved little match for the pressing needs to defend the fragile sovereignties of postcolonial Africa. Paradoxically, East Africa's postcolonial rhetoric of enemies, saboteurs, and parasites reflected both a quest for national independence from external interference in the hostile context of the cold war, as well as a heavy debt to one country's peculiar but powerful campaign of external interference in the name of Afro-Asian liberation.

Notes

1. Randal Sadleir, *Tanzania: Journey to Republic* (New York: St. Martin's Press, 1999), 215.

2. J.A.K. Leslie, *A Survey of Dar es Salaam* (London: Oxford University Press, 1963), 199.

3. Jacques Baulin, *The Arab Role in Africa* (Baltimore: Penguin Books, 1962), 69.

4. Said K. Aburish, *Nasser: The Last Arab* (New York: St. Martin's Press, 2004), 102; Baulin, *The Arab Role*, 73–75.

5. Tareq Y. Ismael, *The U.A.R. in Africa: Egypt's Policy under Nasser* (Evanston: Northwestern University Press, 1971), 36, 134; Baulin, *The Arab Role*, 46.

6. Ismael, *The U.A.R.*, 36, 103.

7. Sadleir, *Tanzania*, 185.

8. Ajuma Oginga Odinga, *Not Yet Uhuru: The Autobiography of Oginga Odinga* (New York: Hill and Wang, 1967), 175.

9. Winston Burdett, *Encounter with the Middle East* (New York: Atheneum, 1969), 23, quoted in Julian Hale, *Radio Power: Propaganda and International Broadcasting* (Philadelphia: Temple University Press, 1975), 72.

10. Aburish, *Nasser*, 80.

11. Baring to Lennox-Boyd, August 18, 1956, Colonial Office, UK National Archives, Kew [hereafter CO] 822/825/2; Governor's Deputy Kenya to Lennox-Boyd, November 12, 1956, CO 822/804/7.

12. See note on Foreign Office 371/11925/JE1433/93, UK National Archives, Kew [hereafter FO]. Swahili broadcasts resumed regular schedules by February 1957. Circular of Lennox-Boyd to Administering Officers, Africa, February 26, 1957, Dominions Office, UK National Archives, Kew [hereafter DO] 35/9645/15.

13. Governor's Deputy Kenya to Lennox-Boyd, November 12, 1956, CO 822/804/7.

14. Kenya Intelligence Committee: Appreciation of the Arab Situation at the Coast, October 1956, CO 822/804/2.

15. Saut el Arab broadcast, June 30, 1956, FO 371/119222/E1433/76.

16. On *mwambao*, see A. I. Salim, *Swahili-speaking Peoples of Kenya's Coast* (Nairobi: East African Publishing House, 1973), 220–46; idem, "The Movement for 'Mwambao' or Coast Autonomy in Kenya, 1956–1963," *Hadith* 2 (1970): 212–28; Richard Stren, *Housing the Urban Poor in Africa: Policy, Politics and Bureaucracy in Mombasa* (Berkeley: Institute of International Studies, University of California, 1978), 74–87; Hyder Kindy, *Life and Politics in Mombasa* (Nairobi: East African Publishing House, 1972), 184–91; and, more recently, James R. Brennan, "Lowering the Sultan's Flag: Sovereignty and Decolonization in Coastal Kenya," *Comparative Studies in Society and History* 50, no. 4 (2008): 831–61.

17. BBC Summary of World Broadcasts, part 4 (Middle East), First Series, Volume 687 [hereafter cited in the form BBC SWB I ME/687], July 6, 1956. Egypt also initiated a half-hour program in Amharic in December 1955, a broadcast in Somali in March 1957, and broadcasts in Lingala and Nyanji in 1961. Egypt initiated broadcasts to West Africa in English, French, and Hausa in December 1959, and broadcasts in Fulani in July 1961. Programs were assembled on the basis of requests received from listeners. See Ismael, *The U.A.R.*, 155–56.

18. Mathieson to Shepherd, July 3, 1956, FO 371/119222/E1433/73.

19. BBC SWB I ME/481, July 9, 1954.

20. British Embassy Khartoum to Africa Department, March 9, 1956, FO 371/119219/E1433/17.

21. Minute of Hopson, February 15, 1961, FO 1110/1370; Beith to Crowe, February 11, 1960, FO 1110/1347/PR136/1; Rothnie to Crowe, March 25, 1960, FO 1110/1347/PR136/1.

22. Sauda Barwani et al., eds., *Unser Leben vor der Revolution und danach* (Cologne: Rüdiger Köppe, 2003), 50–52. This was unlike the quid pro quo

arrangements of Russian contacts in Cairo, who offered Malik E£30 in exchange for publishing Russian-penned stories in the ZNP propaganda paper *Dawn in Zanzibar.*

23. Korry to Department of State [hereafter DOS], July 15, 1963, File 320, Dar es Salaam Embassy Classified General Records 1956–63, RG 84, United States National Archives and Records Administration, College Park, Maryland [hereafter NARA].

24. See Michael Lofchie, *Zanzibar: Background to Revolution* (Princeton: Princeton University Press, 1965), 140ff.

25. Trevelyan to Foreign Office, April 10, 1956, FO 371/119220/E1433/44; BBC SWB I ME/624/2, November 25, 1955; MacKinnon to DOS, January 7, 1956, File 350, Dar es Salaam General Records 1956–62, RG 84, NARA.

26. M. W. Kanyama Chiume, "Hii ni Sauti ya Cairo: The Story of Ahmed Rashaad Ali," *Sunday Observer* (Tanzania), July 8, 2001; author's interview with Ahmad Rashad Ali in Dar es Salaam, August 9, 1999; Evans to Stewart, February 9, 1956, FO 371/119219/E1433/5; Horgan to DOS, February 12, 1964, Pol 17 Zan-UAR, RG 59, NARA.

27. McKinnon to DOS, January 7, 1956, 745T.00/1-756, RG 59, NARA. A 1959 study stated 8,000 of Zanzibar's 34,000 Arab population listen to Cairo's Arabic broadcasts, whereas the "entire Arab population of Zanzibar and a large proportion of the Arabs in the coastal regions of Kenya and Tanganyika" listen to the Swahili broadcasts; it also estimates that some 17,500 Africans in Kenya listen to it, "plus about 50,000 by word of mouth." "UAR Activities—British East Africa," n.a., March 24, 1959, File RN-55-59, RG 306.

28. John Henderson, "Shadow of Nasser over Zanzibar," *Sunday Times* (London), June 23, 1957.

29. G. Thomas Burgess, *Race, Revolution, and the Struggle for Human Rights in Zanzibar* (Athens: Ohio University Press, 2009), 63.

30. Extract from Zanzibar Protectorate Intelligence report July 1954, CO 822/840/27.

31. Mathieson to Watson, February 25, 1956, FO 371/119219/E1433/7. See also Annex, "The Activities of Cairo Radio and Their Impact on Territories towards which They Are Directed," enclosed in Ellingworth to Waterfield, August 30, 1956, BBC Written Archives Collection, Caversham, Berkshire [hereafter BBC WAC] E1/1848/1.

32. Maddox to DOS, July 30, 1958, 745T.00/7-3058, RG 59, USNA.

33. "Belgian Study of Egyptian, Soviet and Indian Broadcasts Reaching the Congo," n a., n.d. [ca. September 1957], *Miscellaneous Domestic Correspondence Near East and Africa 1955–61,* Office of Research, RG 306, NARA.

34. Mathieson to Watson, February, 20, 1956, FO 371/119219/E1433/6.

35. Rais Ahmad Khan, "Radio Cairo and Egyptian Foreign Policy 1956–1959," PhD dissertation, University of Michigan, 1967, 32.

36. See BBC SWB I ME/690, July 17, 1956; O'Hagan to Governor [Kenya], September 29, 1956, CO 822/804/1/E2; Ali Muhsin Al Barwani, *Conflicts and Harmony in Zanzibar* (Dubai: self-published, 2000), 99; Mohamed Said, *The Life and Times of Abdulwahid Sykes (1924–1968): The Untold Story of the Muslim Struggle against British Colonialism in Tanganyika* (London: Minerva, 1998), 179–80; and Ismael, *The U.A.R.*, 155, 156.

37. "Cairo's Swahili Newsletter on East Africa," BBC SWB I ME/638, January 17, 1956.

38. "Cairo's Swahili Newsletter on East Africa," BBC SWB I ME/640, January 24, 1956.

39. See Ann Biersteker, *The Significance of the Swahili Literary Tradition to Interpretation of Early Twentieth Century Political Poetry*, African Humanities Discussion Paper 6 (Boston, 1990); for more recent developments, see Nathalie Arnold, "Placing the Shameless: Approaching Poetry and the Politics of Pemba-ness in Zanzibar, 1995–2001," *Research in African Literatures*, 33 (2002): 140–66.

40. BBC SWB I ME/365/L1, October 3, 1957.

41. Summary of replies to enquiry about effect of Cairo Broadcasts. Colonial Office, January 31, 1956, FO 371/119219/E1433/4.

42. Annex, "The Activities of Cairo Radio and Their Impact on Territories towards which They Are Directed," enclosed in Ellingworth to Waterfield, 30 August 1956, BBC WAC E1/1848/1.

43. Monitoring Report of Sauti ya Cairo talk given by Ahmad Rashad Ali, Sunday May 6, 1956, FO 371/119221/E1433/69.

44. See Jonathon Glassman, "Sorting out the Tribes: The Creation of Racial Identities in Colonial Zanzibar's Newspaper Wars," *Journal of African History*, 41 (2000): 395–428.

45. BBC SWB I ME/643/37, February 3, 1956.

46. BBC SWB I ME/607/M/3, July 22, 1958.

47. Duggan to DOS, October 27, 1958, 778.00/10-2758, RG 59, NARA.

48. BBC SWB II [i.e., second series] ME/546/B/2 January 23, 1961.

49. BBC SWB II ME/657/B/5 June 6, 1961; see also the pleas before the election in BBC SWB II ME/654/B/7 June 2, 1961.

50. BBC SWB II ME/768/B/5, October 14, 1961.

51. BBC SWB II ME/657/B/1-3 June 6, 1961; and BBC SWB ME/663/B/1, June 13, 1961. As early as March 1960, Ali Muhsin and others in ZNP were distancing themselves from the *mwambao* cause. See Extracts from "Zanzibar Intelligence Report" March 1960, CO 822/2134/6.

52. Barwani, *Conflicts and Harmony*, 110. As early as 1957, Ahmad Rashad turned down Ali Muhsin's request that he represent the ZNP at the first Afro-Asian Peoples' Solidarity Conference held in Cairo—Rashad having already begun to distance himself somewhat from the ZNP. Barwani et al., *Unser Leben*, 30. ASP held Rashad in sufficient esteem to appoint him head of the Zanzibar embassy in Cairo following the revolution. Horgan to DOS, February 12, 1964, Pol 17 Zan-UAR, RG 59, NARA. In the author's interviews with Ahmad Rashad Ali before his death, he refused to discuss this question or much of anything of detail relating to his years in Cairo.

53. LaMacchia to DOS, October 8, 1959, 745R.00/10-859, RG 59, NARA.

54. BBC SWB I ME/432/3 December 20, 1957.

55. For a discussion of this, see Glassman, op. cit., and James R. Brennan, "Realizing Civilization through Patrilineal Descent: African Intellectuals and the Making of an African Racial Nationalism in Tanzania, 1920–1950," *Social Identities*, 12, no. 4 (2006): 405–23.

56. BBC SWB ME/353/L/5, September 19, 1957.

57. The project of vindicating the history of Arab slavery from Christian-missionary attacks became a major part of Arab and pan-Islamic political activism in East Africa during the 1950s. For one such counterattack, used to justify the rights of Radio Cairo to criticize the British, see "Who Will Cast the First Stone?", *Mwongozi*, March 30, 1956.

58. Ismael, *The U.A.R.*, 72.

59. Ibid., 229.

60. Summary Intelligence Report for December, 1962, in Mooring to Maudling, January 3, 1963, CO 822/3058/1; Woods to Wool-Lewis, February 18, 1963, CO 822/3058/3; Wool-Lewis to Woods, March 11, 1963, CO 822/3058/5.

61. BBC SWB II ME/643/B/7 May 19, 1961.

62. BBC SWB II ME/786/B/3-4 October 14, 1961.

63. See, *inter alia*, BBC SWB II ME/82/B/1 December 23, 1961.

64. BBC SWB II ME/742/B/1 September 13, 1961.

65. Letter of M.J.D. Kwanoga, *Ngurumo* (Dar es Salaam), October 2, 1964.

66. BBC SWB II ME/913/B/6 April 5, 1962; BBC SWB II ME/822/B/6 December 16. 1961; BBC SWB II ME/1095/B/2 November 9, 1962; BBC SWB II ME 1112/B/2 November 23, 1962.

67. *The United Arab Republic's Policy in Africa* (LR 6/17), F.O.R.D., December 11, 1964, in DO 206/14/1.
BBC SWB I ME/618/A/9 August 4, 1958.

68. FBIS Station and Program Notes no. 397, August 4, 1964, BBC WAC E8/41; Ismael, *The U.A.R.*, 151, 152.

69. Ismael, *The U.A.R.*, 156.

70. Extract from Political Intelligence Report Zanzibar, October 24, 1960, in FO 371/150939/VG1051/210.

71. Tanganyika Broadcasting Internal Memorandum from Director General [M.B. Mdoe] to all program staff, February 12, 1962, BBC WAC E1/1510/1; emphases in the original.

72. See *Uhuru*, January 27, 1962, in BBC WAC E1/1510/2; and David Wakati, "Radio Tanzania Dar es Salaam," in *Making Broadcasting Useful: The African Experience*, ed. George Wedell (Manchester: Manchester University Press, 1986), 212.

73. "Notes on Cancellation of BBC News by KBC," n.a., December 14, 1963, BBC WAC E1/1448/1.

74. Wakati, "Radio Tanzania Dar es Salaam," 212; Dawson Marami, "Broadcasting in Kenya," in *Making Broadcasting Useful: The African Experience*, ed. George Wedell (Manchester: Manchester University Press, 1986), 187.

75. Hale, *Radio Power*, 85. See also Steve Davis, "Unomathotholo woGxotho: The African National Congress, Its Allies, Its Radio and Exile," MA thesis, University of Florida, 2005.

76. Hale, *Radio Power*, 75.

77. Odd Arne Westad, *The Global Cold War: Third World Interventions and the Making of Our Times* (Cambridge: Cambridge University Press, 2005), 104.

6

Mao in Zanzibar

Nationalism, Discipline, and the (De)Construction
of Afro-Asian Solidarities

G. Thomas Burgess

AFRICAN NATIONALISTS IN the mid-20th century gave considerable attention to the vexed question of how to project a unique
African personality and identity in a world in which the West's neocolonial influence appeared virtually unassailable. While seeking to
obtain the fruits of modernity, African intellectuals did not want to do
so entirely in conformity with Western thought and practices. As they
examined Africa's cultural heritage to find the basis for reinstituting
a sense of cultural independence, they disagreed over what "ancestral
practices" ought to be preserved.[1] While many shared a view of their
continent's precolonial past as "the ideal moment for Africa, when traditions existed in their purity, when human beings and gods obeyed
all the rules of nature and of the cosmos, when Africans were moral
and happy," they also developed new futurist discourses.[2] Activists in
the 1950s and 1960s sought to elaborate notions of a future Africa that
did not begin with the premise that it was necessary first and foremost to revitalize indigenous traditions or valorize the precolonial
past. Leela Gandhi, for example, refers to the "rhetoric of futurity"

in Frantz Fanon's essays, which emphasize "the struggle for creative autonomy from Europe." It was this emphasis on creativity in place of authenticity that differentiates Fanon and others from those who espouse "a nostalgic and uncritical return to the 'pre-colonial' past."[3] Recognizing these tensions in outlooks is crucial for complicating our understanding of the early postcolonial period in Africa and its possible outcomes.

Zanzibar was unique as it produced a variant of nationalism in which another nation—China—was widely regarded as *the* model for the islands' future. By the 1960s, a considerable portion of Zanzibar's emerging nationalist elite discovered China as a powerful idea, historical narrative, and set of nation-building precepts. More than anything else, China represented a series of compelling visual images for what sort of society nationalists in Zanzibar wanted to establish. If, as Sylvana Patriarca has observed, "all national identities are relational, [and] each one is relational in its own fashion," it is important to understand the material, discursive, and imagined relationships between China and Zanzibar.[4] These relationships began in the years following Bandung, in a series of encounters between Chinese officials and Zanzibari nationalists, when the view was consistently expressed that despite centuries of mutual historic isolation they should now regard one another as representatives of fraternal states and like-minded cultures. Although palpable cultural chasms existed, the Chinese were prepared to meet and engage Zanzibaris on the abstract level of memory and history, believing, as they did, that Africans were reenacting elements of their own recent past. The Chinese eventually succeeded in establishing themselves as Zanzibar's chief patron power, and in the 1970s gained a similar preeminent-aid relationship with the Tanzanian mainland. China hoped to use Tanzania as a "bridgehead" through which to spread the Maoist gospel throughout Africa.

This essay concentrates less on examining these Sino-Tanzanian aid relationships, with greater emphasis placed instead on exploring an element of nationalist thought in Africa frequently neglected by scholars: the search for a usable future. Futurist discourses were in no way equally present in all African nationalist movements, since they sometimes embodied a series of short-term aims simply to inherit and

"Africanize" control over national resources and the infrastructures of power to be left behind by the colonialists. Nevertheless, nationalists in Africa, as elsewhere in the developing world, embraced what Donald Donham refers to as the "meta-narrative of modernity."[5] They evolved elaborate ideas about Africa's future place in a world order in the 1960s that shunned stasis and sacralized "development." The power of the development ethos was such that it encouraged many African nationalists to adopt a critical view toward Africa's heritage and to regard the substance of "ancestral practices" as cultural forms to be molded and shaped in order to serve newly dominant agendas of development.

In Zanzibar, the search for a usable future resulted in the appropriation of China not only as an example of a nonwhite nation with solid anticolonial credentials, or an impoverished people that in a very short period of time appeared to have achieved miracles of nation building. China also attracted interest as a society consisting of millions of individuals fully mobilized for nationalist goals. Nationalists were deeply impressed by the appearance of labor and consumption discipline among ordinary Chinese citizens. They endlessly associated such discipline with development, as did Chinese officials who went to great efforts to provide their African guests with staged spectacles in which the correspondence between the two was unmistakable. Indeed, this essay demonstrates that for some Zanzibari nationalists the search for a usable future was an attempt to access the keys and mysteries of development, which they believed existed in habits of labor and consumption they had observed in China. They revered discipline as a necessary virtue for any society wishing to most effectively unleash its development capacities, and they examined their cultural ways in terms of the perceived presence or absence of this trait.

Whereas Frederick Cooper has noted that discipline, in its various forms, was part of the modernist package colonial regimes wanted to disseminate in Africa, along with a market economy, citizenship, industrialism, and achievement status systems, scholars have not fully engaged the notion that perhaps discipline was integral to both the colonial civilizing mission and the development project that followed, or that each possibly contained some of the same linear teleologies.[6]

With independence in Africa, the disciplinary project was neither repudiated nor abandoned. Nationalists in Africa counted progress, like the colonials, in the proliferation of the sort of disciplinary institutions examined by Foucault: the school, the army camp, the factory, and the hospital. They valued these institutions not only for their benefits in terms of health, education, and industry, but for the discipline they produced, and with discipline, the perception of added national power.

Many nationalists were convinced that, according to laws of development they considered to be universal, the principle of discipline was immutable. And to produce discipline, the state in Africa, similar to elsewhere, needed to assert itself as a pedagogue (see Chakrabarty in this volume). The lesson that Zanzibari nationalists took from the 20th century was that the state in other parts of the world no longer needed to rely on parents, elders, or religious authorities to impose social discipline. Nor did the state have to depend solely on schools and other disciplinary institutions observed by Foucault. The socialist world, for example, had evolved an array of techniques, rituals, and institutions that applied to the discipline of young people in particular. China had helped to pioneer a series of mass spectacles, where, in massive stadiums, thousands of citizens participated in marches, dramatizations, and synchronized flag demonstrations. One purpose of these festivals was to perform idealized visions of the future in which all poverty, greed, individualism, and backwardness had been abolished. In their search for a usable future, Zanzibari nationalists in the 1970s adopted such spectacles, known as *halaiki* in Swahili, and imported Chinese instructors to help impart a series of fantastic images of a society fully committed to nation building. Whereas nationalists in Zanzibar, as well as mainland Tanzania, welcomed Chinese development aid and expertise, they also wanted new techniques with which the state could assert itself as a pedagogue. As celebrations of an imagined future, *halaiki* performances spoke a transcendent visual language of forms and symbols.

By looking to China as their disciplinary model Zanzibari nationalists were consciously or not accomplishing a bit of theoretical derring-do: they were, at the same time, provincializing Europe *and* embracing universalist idioms.[7] Indeed, it can be argued that they and their Chinese patrons were constructing forms of Afro-Asian solidarity and South-East cooperation in the 1960s, that, at least on certain levels, embodied the Bandung spirit. Such construction, however, only came about through the deconstruction of much of Zanzibar's mixed African-Arab-South Asian cultural heritage. Those men responsible for the revolution in 1964—and the violence it engendered against Arabs and South Asians—rejected the claim made by those they overthrew, that Zanzibar's diverse Afro-Asian heritage was a positive historical force, despite the islands' traumatic history of slavery. Thus as they embraced a socialist, cosmopolitan, and future-oriented concept of development, Zanzibar's racial nationalists also initiated a reckoning with Zanzibar's once-privileged minority communities, a reckoning that was fundamentally parochial and past-oriented. As they appropriated Chinese knowledge and disciplinary techniques they also turned Arabs and South Asians in Zanzibar into exiles or second-class citizens—a simultaneous embrace and repudiation of Afro-Asian solidarities. (See, in this volume James Brennan's essay for a similar thematic conclusion on the limits of Afro-Asian unity.)

Cosmopolitanisms

A colonial guidebook from 1931 noted that Zanzibar is "one of the most cosmopolitan in the world and there are few races of which representatives may not be found in the two islands."[8] The islands were culturally as well as racially cosmopolitan. Ahmed Gurnah recalls that in Zanzibar Town, where he spent his childhood and youth, "several great cultures routinely mixed and exchanged goods and ways of living."[9] Cafés offered African, Arabic, Indian, and Chinese dishes, and cinemas packed in audiences to see everything from American Westerns to Egyptian dramas and Indian musicals. Congolese music competed with calypso, Latin bands, *taarab*, jazz, Bing Crosby, and rock 'n' roll. Kiswahili, Arabic, English, Hindi, and Urdu were commonly spoken in the streets, and read in over a dozen newspapers produced in the town. Secondary-school students read Mao, Frantz

Fanon, Kwame Nkrumah, and Che Guevara, as well as Islamic literature and theology. The town displayed a series of architectural styles,
from British-designed Anglo-Indian hybrids, Arabic townhouses,
Cubist-modernist apartments, to African bungalows.[10] These buildings were only the forms and facades of a larger truth, however: Zanzibar Town, as well as its rural hinterlands, was home for a remarkable
composition of individuals and communities from around the Indian
Ocean rim.

The 1950s were years of relative prosperity, sandwiched between
the rationing and shortages of World War II, and the depressed world
prices for cloves (Zanzibar's principal export) of the early 1960s. While
the days as the leading port city of East Africa were definitely over
(having been pushed aside by Mombasa and Dar es Salaam), Zanzibar
Town residents enjoyed urban amenities unavailable to earlier generations. Town shops displayed a wide array of commodities enticing to
tourists who increasingly passed through the streets, deposited on day
trips by the cruise liners making their way between Cape Town, Aden,
and Suez. For locals, such goods

> were tokens of the big world, which was always cleaner and brighter
> than the dark, familiar one of every day. This big world did not
> have to be European. It could be a Japanese calendar, with pictures
> of delicately-lit paper houses and miniature bushes of blazing aza-
> leas. Or it could be Lebanese grapes nestling in tissue-paper, in
> fruit boxes stamped with a silhouette of a cedar tree, or Iraqi dates
> in packets illustrated with a painting of an oasis. Nothing Indian,
> that was part of the odorous every day. European was best, though.
> The European world was remote and intimidating in a complicated
> way, and these tokens were like parts of its sprawling body, handled
> and consumed with some hunger.[11]

If there was anything distinct about Zanzibar Town in the 1950s,
it was its cosmopolitanism, still a matter of considerable nostalgia
for some who remember those times. While Western life provoked
considerable interest, the social and linguistic connections between
Zanzibar and Europe were not so "deep and all consuming" that
the "glitz of dominant [colonial] ideologies and lifestyles" excluded
everything else.[12] Whereas British expatriates dominated the higher

echelons of the civil service, they often withdrew to their own spaces and were many times known to lead lives several levels less than glamorous. Moreover the news from overseas, and from the islands themselves, was of colonial withdrawals and the end of Empire, which enhanced African self-confidence and "people's willingness and desire to explore other cultures themselves, and not just accidentally bump into them."[13]

Nationalist contests in Zanzibar in the 1950s and 1960s were a referendum on colonial power and cultural influence, but, on a much more visceral level, they were a debate over whether or not Zanzibaris would embrace, mediate, or reject their islands' cosmopolitan heritage. Some nationalists venerated this heritage as the very essence of island culture and civilization, and what distinguished Zanzibar from the allegedly less-civilized African mainland. In this formulation, Zanzibar was the conduit through which all progress and new ideas arrived in East Africa. Seif Sharif Hamad remembered that as a young man in the early 1960s

> I had a strong sense of Zanzibari nationalism, because we regarded ourselves in Zanzibar as more civilized than our brothers in the rest of East Africa. We thought we had a better culture, were more educated, and that we had better customs as a result of the intermingling of races and cultures here. We were unique, because as an island Zanzibar had a potpourri of influences and peoples from Africa, Asia, the Gulf, and Europe. . . . Zanzibaris were more exposed to the world. People came here from different parts of the world with their various experiences and traditions, and in their diversity formed a unique culture.[14]

The Zanzibar Nationalist Party (ZNP) in fact located the islands within a multicultural, polyglot, and predominantly Islamic western Indian Ocean world. The party advocated a kind of Afro-Asian solidarity, but on its own terms. While the party consistently deplored the use of racial categories, and even blamed such divisions in local society on reputed British divide-and-rule strategies, ZNP propagandists undermined their own appeals for unity and solidarity by basing them on an exclusive notion of the essence of Zanzibari culture that denigrated peoples and influences from the African interior as less civilized.[15] The ZNP regarded Islam as the basis for social unity in the islands; yet as the nationalist era progressed it became increasingly obvious that, at least in Zanzibar, Islam did not constitute a universal national culture capable of entirely trumping race or ethnicity. As Abdulrazak Gurnah writes in his novel *Admiring Silence*, politics "brought shocking things to the surface. We liked to think of ourselves as a moderate and mild people. . . . In reality we were nowhere *we*, but us in our separate yards, locked in our historical ghettoes, self-forgiving and seething with intolerances, with racisms, and with resentments." Africans had not forgotten or forgiven; they "wanted to glory in grievance, in promises of vengeance, in their past oppression, in their present poverty, and in the nobility of their darker skins."[16]

Nationalists of the Afro-Shirazi Party (ASP) cast Zanzibari political contests primarily as an African struggle for justice and freedom from Arab political, economic, and cultural hegemony. They rejected any notion of Afro-Asian solidarity; stigmatized Arabs as alien, former slave-owning oppressors; and defined the islands as extensions of the African mainland.[17] They claimed Africans needed to unify on the basis of race, not religion. Jamal Ramadhan Nasibu wrote in his newspaper *Agozi* in May 1959, "We are tired of being led by other people every day. Now we will lead ourselves because we already know that other people want to sit on Africans' heads forever. And rule them until doomsday."[18]

Both the ZNP and ASP produced rhetoric in the 1950s and 1960s that tended to divide Zanzibaris into mutually exclusive ethnic camps, and yet younger Zanzibaris throughout this period continued to be rather catholic in their cultural appropriations. They adopted Western clothing styles "to purchase extra excitement and power and maybe also like all other teenagers, to get up their parents' noses a little."[19] They listened to rock 'n' roll in part as a means of drawing distance from parents and teachers.[20] Such "gestures of *anti*-membership" were not taken lightly in an atmosphere already charged with political tension.[21] For some ZNP nationalists they were an affront to the Islamic, Afro-Asian cultural heritage of the islands, and evidence of an imperialist plot to subvert the young. In an editorial appearing in January 1963 in *Mwongozi*—an official organ of the ZNP—the editors claimed

that the new Twist dance craze was spreading through Zanzibari society "with the force of an epidemic." They argued British imperialists
used the Twist to seduce and corrupt island society in the same way
they used opium against the Chinese in the 19th century. "Imperialist
success" in this matter could be seen when

> a number of our young "politicians" who, for a limited number of
> minutes, are eloquent and vociferous in demanding the immedi-
> ate departure of the Imperialists and neo-colonialists spend many
> hours in 'twisting' them back to influence and authority. . . . Every
> minute devoted to exercises like the Twist is a minute lost to the
> individual, to his family and to the nation. The youth of a country
> cannot waste their time twisting and expect the same time to equip
> themselves for the task of nation building.[22]

The irony noted by the editors of *Mwongozi* is familiar to students
of nationalist movements in Africa, led as they often were by elites
who frequently possessed ambiguous attitudes and relationships
toward both the West and ancestral practices. At issue here was the
fate of the ZNP vision of Zanzibar as the "Islamic metropolis" of East
Africa.[23] At issue was what *kind* of cosmopolitanism the islands would
embrace. "The same people who read about Elvis later read about Mao
and Lenin," Gurnah would observe.[24] For some Zanzibaris fondness
for the Twist, Elvis, and Mao's quotations coincided. What the editors
of *Mwongozi* could not have predicted, however, was that very soon
those in the islands most open to new music from the West and new
ideas from Mao or Lenin would ally themselves with the racial nationalists of the ASP, and in so doing help to overthrow the ZNP and its
notion of Zanzibar becoming, after independence, a vibrant Afro-
Asian cultural synthesis under the guise of Islamic universalism.

Discovery

In 1955, almost no commercial ties or diplomatic relations existed
between China and African territories. Few Zanzibaris were even
aware of the Chinese Revolution. The Bandung Conference marked
the beginning of a new era, when Chinese officialdom looked upon

Africa as a key terrain in the anticapitalist crusade and a vast "storm center," in which the triumph of their model of revolutionary struggle was historically inevitable.[25] Chinese officials regarded the industrialized West as a capitalist "city" that could be surrounded by revolutions in "rural" Africa, Asia, and Latin America.[26] African nationalists were therefore a historic vanguard, privileged agents of the destruction of capitalism. The Chinese believed if only one or two African territories "would effect a real nationalist revolution their influence would be great and a revolutionary wave would roll up the African continent."[27] Aside from ideology, they also regarded Africa as a relatively open ground, between US and Soviet spheres of influence, for the extension of Chinese power overseas. Chinese propagandists encouraged African nationalists to project China's liberation from corruption, economic backwardness, and political powerlessness onto their own struggles against comparable foes. They did not hesitate to compare eruptions of Chinese history such as the Boxer Rebellion or the May Fourth movement to contemporary African events and conditions.[28] They spoke of tides, waves, and storms. During his diplomatic tour of Africa in 1965, Premier Zhou Enlai exclaimed "the national liberation movement in Africa . . . has become a mighty torrent pounding with great momentum at the foundation of the rule of imperialism." Quoting Mao, he added that, "the four seas are seething, clouds are lowering and waters raging, the five continents are rocked by storm and thunder."[29]

In 1957, the Chinese embassy in Egypt helped establish one of Bandung's organizational offspring, the Afro-Asian Peoples' Solidarity Organization (AAPSO), which attracted representatives from twenty-seven African territories and colonial territories. Chu Tu-nan expressed there what was to become a consistent theme in China's appeal to African nations: the "Chinese, Indians, Arabs and Negroes shared a heritage of ancient cultures that had been broken and ruined by the West's imperialism." The only answer, according to Chu, was tremendous effort by the world beyond the West to "build a new universal civilization, incorporating these lost traditions with the revolutionary elements of socialism." This new civilization would leave the West far behind.[30] In the years that followed, the Chinese launched an audio and visual assault on Africa. Radio Beijing broadcast to East Africa in English and Swahili, and the Chinese distributed glossy and well-illustrated monthly magazines showing scenes of "Chinese art, life, landscape, letters, and of course Chinese Communist society in gay and vivid colors."[31] In 1964, the Chinese Postal Ministry developed a new series of stamps that showed a Chinese man linking arms with an African.[32] Through their embassies in Africa, the Chinese distributed millions of copies of Mao's quotations. Through the AAPSO China funded liberation movements in Africa, offered scholarships to Africans to study at Chinese colleges and institutes, and arranged for visits of official African delegations to China, the number of which increased from 50 in 1959 to 105 in 1960.[33]

Abdulrahman Muhammed Babu (1927–96) was perhaps the first individual in East Africa to receive an official Chinese invitation. Babu was already by then a veteran politician and leading nationalist figure in Zanzibar. Arriving in London in 1951, he spent the next several years apprenticing with the British Labour Party, serving in various Pan-Africanist organizations and as joint editor of the radical anticolonial and socialist journal *African, Asian, and Latin American Revolution*.[34] Babu's organizational skills so matured in London that he was invited to return to Zanzibar in 1957 to assume the post of Secretary General of the ZNP. He sought not only to win elections in Zanzibar and achieve anticolonial objectives, but also to position the party within global confrontations between socialism and capitalism, and East and West. Thanks to his influence, the ZNP far surpassed the ASP in the breadth of its international connections and adopted anticolonial stands and organized demonstrations on a range of international issues, including the Algerian War and the Congo Crisis.

In a brief autobiographical sketch Babu described his first ecstatic encounter with China:

> In the 1950s, it was almost obligatory for young radicals to read as much as possible about the Chinese revolution and its success in 1949. . . . I studied China as a development model in contrast to the western model. China, in short, was a symbol of a poor, humiliated country emerging, through their own effort and against all odds, into a contender for world leadership. It evoked all the emotions of

joy and hope for the oppressed who were still struggling under very difficult circumstances. . . .

Thus, it is impossible to imagine the thrill with which I accepted the official invitation, in late-1959, to visit China. . . . The meetings with the Chinese leadership and the late night discussions with them on all questions of anti-imperialist struggle were most inspiring and helped to mould my world outlook. . . . Among the leaders I met included, of course, Chairman Mao, Chou en Lai, Marshal Chen Yi, Chu Ten, Deng Tsiao-Ping, and others. These were people of very strong character, well known for their resilience, perseverance and self-discipline who had liberated a quarter of the human race from repression and warlordism.[35]

Babu returned to Zanzibar in April 1960 and extolled at mass meetings what he had seen in China.[36] He likely influenced Ali Sultan Issa, a close friend since childhood, to later make the journey. Like Babu, Issa spent several years working and studying in London. In many respects, Issa typified the ambivalent image of a rebel Zanzibari youth that mastered the jitterbug, developed a taste for narrow trousers and Italian suits, read Lenin and Mao, and came to reject colonialism and capitalism. Like Babu, Issa embodied Zanzibari students' desires in the 1950s to travel beyond the traditional orbit of the islands within the western Indian Ocean and to access the cultural and intellectual capital of more secular lands beyond. In 1954, Issa became an active member of the British Communist Party, attending neighborhood lectures and cell meetings. He recalled, "All the intellectuals were there in Swiss Cottage: professionals, Jews, gentiles, lawyers, and doctors. I met so many fine people—it was like the Swahili saying, *udongo na waridi*, or clay and rose. I was the clay and I wanted the scent of a rose."[37]

Issa attended the Moscow Youth Festival in 1957, and the following year returned to Zanzibar where he quickly rose to prominence within the ZNP. Although in the 1960s he tapped a seemingly endless reserve of socialist patronage to make multiple trips to Eastern Europe, Cuba, and North Vietnam, he personally found China the most compelling. In 1960, he went on an official tour that retraced the steps of the Long March. From the viewpoint of the 21st century, he recalled:

The tour opened my outlook and broadened my horizons, to see the huge sacrifices of the Chinese, and how wherever they went they confiscated lands and gave them to the peasants. . . .

They took me to many cities. Poverty was not so visible there as in India; everyone had food and something to wear. . . . In general although I was already a member of the British Communist Party for four years and had visited Russia in 1957, I had not been as impressed by the greatness of the Russians as I was with the Chinese. Life is in a constant state of change, and I was free to develop and put all ideologies to the test, to see which was most viable and most suitable to our own conditions in Zanzibar. In China, I was deeply impressed by their vast and formidable country, by the people's sacrifice and their achievements, so that when I returned to Zanzibar I was in complete agreement with Babu about China, that this was the ideological line to follow.[38]

The Chinese were no doubt pleased by the effect of these visits, and increasingly singled the islands out for special attention. The number of Zanzibari delegations sent to China increased from two in 1960 to twelve in 1963, and their impact on shaping Zanzibari thought in the revolutionary era was profound.[39] Two delegations that arrived in 1960 were organized through the ZNP, and consisted of a total of thirty-seven islanders, some of them prominent journalists and trade-union officials. Their hosts introduced them to Mao and Zhou Enlai, took special care to demonstrate how Islam was "flourishing" in China, and gave tours of China's showpiece industrial projects and communal farms.[40] One trade-union leader and delegate recalled that his one-month visit to China in 1960 had far greater impact than the ten months he spent the previous year in East Germany, studying political economy. In China, he visited politically oriented museums and attended stage dramas conveying Maoist themes. He learned about the Long March, and any political discussions with his Chinese hosts lasted several hours.[41]

The experiences of the delegates were akin to the general portrait drawn by Philip Snow, who wrote that Africans arrived in China

in ones and twos and small delegations, to a welcome fit for heroes. They were carried shoulder-high, showered with flowers and confetti and bombarded with the din of traditional rejoicing, gongs and cymbals and fire-crackers. They were led before microphones to voice their demands for freedom to applauding crowds a half a million strong. They were borne round in limousines like ministers and seated beside the Chinese leaders at rallies and parades. ... Very humble Africans, unknown young men and women, were received with honour by the greatest personalities in the land.[42]

These visits served a crucial pedagogical purpose. As they visited museums, theaters, exhibitions, and showpiece development projects, African guests in China replicated something of the experience of Egyptians visiting Europe in the 19th century, who discovered "a place where one was continually pressed into service as a spectator by a world ordered so as to represent" some larger meaning.[43] On official, carefully stage-managed tours, Africans in China, even more so than in 19th century Europe, encountered a world in which everything was "collected and arranged to stand for something, to represent progress and history, human industry and empire; everything set up, and the whole set-up always evoking somehow some larger truth."[44] The habit of seeing the world as a permanent exhibition, to be assessed objectively, was especially seductive for traveling nationalists. It is difficult, in fact, to overestimate the importance of visiting and seeing as a distinct nationalist epistemology. Babu wrote that Africans visiting China in the late 1950s and early 1960s "saw the future being created under their very eyes; all sections of Chinese society were in one way or another involved in this creation."[45] China was "the perfect model for all African countries to emulate," because the Chinese taught that "we must learn to be frugal; to be collectively, a nation of savers and not of waste-makers and vulgar consumerism.... This requires exceptional discipline."[46] Snow reported that "African visitors were driven at the start of a day's excursion past a swarm of peasants building up a hillock of earth, then driven back in the evening to observe, to their astonishment, that the earth had already been shifted to the road or dam it was meant for and the hillock was gone."[47] Through such spectacles of labor discipline, Africans obtained "a picture of a society committed to its goals, willing to sacrifice short-term individual comforts for the common good of all.... China seemed to these Africans a beacon of morality . . . free of the greed and poverty which disfigured their new countries."[48]

The enthusiasm of these visitors stands in sharp contrast to that of Zanzibari students in China, whose treatment by the Chinese authorities cannot so easily be described as "red carpet." Haroub Othman recalled that Marxist and Maoist literature were widely available to students in his secondary school in Zanzibar, and that students like himself were literally "running away" when they got the chance to study overseas.[49] By 1961, about 118 students from 11 African territories attended the Languages Institute in Beijing.[50] Among these were eighteen students from Zanzibar, including four women, who had obtained scholarships through Babu and Issa. They were given modest living stipends and shared rooms with other African students. Yet their encounter with the Chinese Revolution, regardless of any initial impressions, was considerably more conflicted than African guests on VIP tours. Time was not on the side of Chinese authorities; providing for Africans' needs during extended periods of study, and managing their everyday mundane concerns with efficiency during a time of general rationing, lacked the inherent epistemological power of coordinating visits to a series of exhibitions and staged events.

Some African students, unsurprisingly, were deeply disappointed by the deprivations and relative squalor of Chinese cities in the early 1960s. Others found more irritating the constant monitoring of their movements and associations by government authorities. Contact with ordinary Chinese citizens was almost completely forbidden; what few acquaintances they had usually turned out to be government agents. The "spartan sexual regime" in China also proved deeply discouraging, in addition to language difficulties, low educational standards, and racial discrimination.[51] African students learned from Maoist textbooks how to say, "the people's communes like a newly risen sun, light up the path of progress for the Chinese people," rather than more practical phrases, like "a glass of water." Many feared their diplomas from Chinese institutions would prove worthless.[52] Relations between the African students and Chinese authorities deteriorated in 1961, notably over an incident that revealed the students' lack of consumer discipline, and their hosts' rigid enforcement of revolutionary norms. A Zanzibari student walked into a Chinese hotel lounge and demanded to be allowed to purchase a carton of cigarettes. When he was only offered a pack he attempted to use force, whereupon the hotel staff beat him, forcing his hospitalization. The African students countered with sit-ins and hunger strikes, and by mid-1962 only 22 of the original 118 remained.[53]

In contrast, Zanzibaris overwhelmingly preferred studying in Eastern Europe, where hundreds attended institutes and colleges in the USSR and East Germany in particular.[54] Their encounters with socialism in these countries were generally more positive than in China. Regardless of where they went, however, British intelligence agents in Zanzibar feared such youth would return to the islands as troublemakers and advocate Marxism as a solution.[55] These impressions were not completely unfounded. Referring to the number of students he and Babu were able to send overseas on scholarships, Issa recalled, "the main idea was to expose them . . . even though some students did not last very long in China and other places, most of them returned to Zanzibar and that was how we managed to politicize the whole island."[56] In the years prior to the revolution, then, socialism in Zanzibar was a movement born through the perpetual coming and going from the islands of youth aspiring to possess specialized knowledge, among whom Babu assumed a preeminent and inspirational role. "I Saw the Future and It Works" is not only the title given to a recent collection of Babu's essays and tributes by others to his memory, it is also a phrase that encapsulates the importance attached to Babu as an agent, exemplar, and interlocutor for his generation. It suggests a cosmopolitan relationship to history in which pasts and futures can be freely projected onto diverse cultures whose boundaries are porous and impermanent, especially according to the naked eye.

Seeing the future in practice meant obtaining a picture of society through a brief visit or longer period of residence elsewhere. For those Zanzibaris who were able to make such travel, these experiences underlined what they believed Zanzibar lacked and in the same stroke persuaded them of possible future alternatives. Such cosmopolitan visions at times closely resembled the world civilization spoken of by such personages as Chu Tu-nan. Supreme confidence in the human

will and socialist techniques for constructing knowledge, imposing discipline, and altering the motivational structure of individuals
meant that Babu and others could return from China and elsewhere
with various ideas for how Zanzibaris should exert themselves in a
national project of selective appropriation. They could privilege the
distant over the more familiar, and graft the historical narratives of
other nations onto their own, as either cautionary tales or authorita-
tive stories of the triumph of discipline and the human will over colonialism, exploitation, and underdevelopment. They could begin their
analysis of island history not from the moment Arabs first enslaved
or civilized Africans, but from an imaginary time in the future when
Zanzibar would fully realize its capacities for development. Zanzibar
was more than an Islamic enclave or an African island chain; it was
a showcase for socialism. What had taken place elsewhere, Babu and
his friends argued, had direct relevance on what was happening in
Zanzibar in the 1960s.

Nationalism

The Chinese were fortunate in Babu's considerable political skills.
Under the eclectic umbrella of the ZNP, Babu employed some of his
journalistic talents in propagating the Chinese view of world politics. With Chinese funding, he edited his own weekly broadsheet,
ZANEWS, which published anticolonial editorials and news articles
often taken directly from the New China News Agency. Babu was also
a skilled organizer; as secretary general of the ZNP, he received credit
for the party's remarkable comeback from defeat at the polls in 1957
to victory against the ASP in the June 1961 elections. For four years
Babu worked effectively with Ali Muhsin, an enormously popular
ZNP leader and spokesman of the more conservative mainstream of
the party, much of it based in rural Pemba. The two shared a sense
of Zanzibari nationalism and a common hostility toward the racial
politics espoused by the ASP. Both advocated forms of Afro-Asian
cooperation, yet the two men differed in the kind of cosmopolitan
order they wished to establish. Muhsin looked to Nasser and Islamic

principles rather than Mao or Lenin for guidance, and found Babu's Chinese connections increasingly problematic. Babu and his cohort of socialists, entrenched in the ZNP youth and trade union associations, rejected appeals to national unity on the basis of either religion or race, and in so doing were at odds with the vast majority of voters in either contending party. They were convinced the islands' primary contradictions were not between Arabs and Africans, or civilization and barbarism, but capital and labor. Their cast of cold war friends and enemies was also exceptional, and increasingly an issue in light of colonial desires to grant power to a moderate, pro-Western regime in the islands.

The colonial state imprisoned Babu for sedition in 1962; Issa accused Muhsin of conspiring with the British to remove Babu from politics, and resigned from the party. At a press conference, Issa read a statement entitled (with a nod to Fidel Castro), "Condemn Me Now but History Will Absolve Me," in which he castigated Muhsin. The statement also reflected socialists' universal claims, shared sense of secular time, and belief in the "science" of history:

> All students of history both contemporary and medieval will not fail to recall that what is taking place now in our country has taken place elsewhere on earth.
>
> What is taking place now in Zanzibar has not surprised me at all but confirms the belief I have always held since I have started to think and use my intelligence, to differentiate right and wrong, just and unjust.

Issa went on to describe the ZNP as a liberation movement that had temporarily united various classes, but which was led by Muhsin and other vacillating "parasites" unable to "march forward to a new system" that would erase all exploitation in the islands. Issa declared that new ideas always triumph over old ones, and that, depending on the contradictions within a society, old ideas fade peacefully or by force. When it came to Muhsin and other feudalistic, petit bourgeois "imperialist running dogs" in the ZNP, Issa was convinced they had become nothing more than local abstractions of malignant global forces. Issa declared: "We must be ruthless and wage a determined struggle against the enemies of the people, expose them for what they are." Thus, whereas socialism preached the brotherhood of man, it also created its own set of purge categories. Issa closed with an assertion of his faith in socialist historiography: "I am confident that we shall win in the end, and by we I mean the progressives not only in Zanzibar but throughout the world. VENCEREMOS, VENCEREMOS, VENCEREMOS [We Shall Conquer]."[57]

While such statements may have electrified local press audiences and either pleased or offended Issa's real or imaginary international audience, they failed to garner mass enthusiasm. Most islanders did not connect local incidents with a global struggle between progressive and reactionary historical forces. Founded on his belief in the serious-ness and relevance of faraway struggles in Cuba, Vietnam, Congo, and elsewhere, the urgency of Issa's appeal was lost on most of the voting population, for whom these places remained entirely abstract. Issa's analysis of the "objective realities" in Zanzibar, while conforming to the lessons socialists drew from their own historical experiences, did not cohere with the weight of local opinion that was either oblivious, indifferent, or in opposition to his characterization of the "contra-dictions" of Zanzibari society. His very nomenclature was problem-atic: relatively few in Zanzibar sought to explain human behavior by assigning certain class positions to political actors. For the less "exposed," race, ethnicity, and religion remained far more compelling identifiers. For only a relative few did his political references possess all the authority of a science. They were most appealing to members of his generation who were prepared to consider new analytical terms as they were ready also to listen to a new Frank Sinatra recording.

Revolution

When Babu was released from prison in early 1963 he saw that the political situation had changed during his detention. The ZNP was preparing without him, and in alliance with the smaller Zanzibar and Pemba Peoples Party, to contest a final round of elections before independence. Babu resigned from the ZNP, claiming the party had become too racialist. With his radical associates he formed the Umma Party, which had no impact on the outcome of the August elections, another win for the ZNP–ZPPP alliance. Peasants showed little to no interest in Umma but among the youth of Zanzibar Town the party gained a couple thousand members and considerable notoriety. Umma members allegedly abused alcohol, were sexually promiscuous, and did not pray or fast. Their non-Islamic lifestyles were as often the subject of controversy as their antigovernment pronouncements and public insistence on the relevance of the violent conflicts of distant lands. Umma hosted debates on Vietnam as well as more academic discussions on the meaning of such words as *imperialism*.[58] They sought a critical vocabulary suitable for what they considered a more-enlightened generation. Their repetitive invocations of the wisdom and development of secular "progressive" nations were unsubtle digs against the Islamic and Arab-centric cultural standards and mores of the older generation, which for years the ZNP had actively asserted and defended. Their hostility toward the ZNP pushed them toward a working alliance with ASP leaders like Abeid Karume, whom Babu had previously dismissed as unprogressive. If the comrades held Karume's racial politics in contempt, that contempt did not extend to his supporters' race or class origins, or their status as the downtrodden of the islands. The ASP enjoyed mass popularity among African workers and peasants, something that Umma lacked. The ASP also included elements that loathed Arabs, and were ready to instigate a revolution.

In January 1964 the ASP Youth League managed, only one month after independence and the departure of British security forces from the islands, to overthrow the elected ZNP–ZPPP government. What might have been a relatively bloodless regime change—accomplished in a matter of a couple days—quickly turned into an ethnic bloodbath, as Arabs and to a lesser extent South Asians were plundered, raped, massacred, detained, and forced into exile.[59] As the situation calmed, Babu and other leading Umma comrades quickly gained influence in the new regime as ministers, junior ministers, and army officers. ASP and Umma officially merged in March 1964, by which time Babu had emerged as by far the most able leader and spokesperson of a socialist faction within the Revolutionary Council that included ASP politicians like Kassim Hanga who had studied or traveled within the Eastern Bloc. Babu and his like-minded colleagues persuaded Karume to welcome dozens of experts and advisers from China, East Germany, and the Soviet Union. Whereas socialists assumed most cabinet-level positions in the new government, they were still required to maintain the trust and support of their less schooled and more moderate president, Abeid Karume. They were also compelled to maintain the approval of the Revolutionary Council, composed mostly of men who lacked overseas "exposure" or socialist convictions, were often illiterate, but who had taken leading roles in the actual seizure of power and the punishment of Arabs.[60]

Babu clearly recognized the ethnic nature of the violence. In his writings he repeatedly described the revolution as an anti-Arab, spontaneous "lumpen uprising," that Umma comrades needed to transform into an authentic revolution.[61] In an interview with the New China News Agency in 1964, Babu nevertheless faithfully inserted Zanzibar into the official Chinese master narrative: "The victory of the Zanzibar revolution was only a step in the revolution in Africa, Asia and Latin America," he asserted. "The Zanzibar people send greetings to Chairman Mao because they learned a lot from his works."[62] In June 1964 the Paris-based periodical *Revolution* published an interview of Babu in which he says:

> From the moment where the people take up arms, it is most difficult for a leader to moderate the ardor, the allure and the rhythm of the revolution. I believe that armed revolution itself compels a country to transform itself sooner or later into a socialist country. . . . An African revolution can transform itself into a socialist revolution. This is exactly the process that is going on in Zanzibar.[63]

The Zanzibari Revolution was a signal event in what Piero Gleijeses has characterized as "the season of the great illusion," when to many international observers in 1964–65 a continent-wide revolution seemed imminent in Africa.[64] In his introduction to Frantz Fanon's *A Dying Colonialism*, Argentine journalist Adolfo Gilly heralds the Zanzibari Revolution as further evidence that "Revolution is mankind's way of life today. . . . Capitalism is under siege, surrounded by a global tide of revolution."[65] Gilly could not have provided a clearer example of universalistic claims of socialism when he argued the French defeat in Vietnam inspired the Algerian liberation struggle, which in turn "unleashed the great tide of African revolution." Revolutionaries in Zanzibar "took advantage of this uninterrupted chain of revolutionary struggles to realize one of the greatest deeds of the epoch. . . . They took the road of socialist revolution, arms in hand, with no other support than the determination of the masses of Zanzibar—barefoot, poor, illiterate, armed as well as they could manage—and their own revolutionary courage."[66] Clearly, the power of socialism's master narrative was such that international observers might read local events anywhere in the world as part of an "uninterrupted chain." The "barefoot" revolutionaries did not, actually, have any other revolution in their minds so much as an opportunity to topple a government that intended in their eyes to exploit and oppress Africans. They created the conditions for the emergence of an African nationalist regime that was soon ready to experiment with socialist ideas and techniques from overseas.

Nation Building

Babu's growing power in early 1964 upset President Julius Nyerere of Tanganyika, who worried that Zanzibar, under Babu's influence, might serve as a regional base for the export of revolution. He didn't want Tanganyika and other states in East Africa to undergo ethnic violence comparable to that of the islands. Nor did he want cold war rivalries to influence regional politics. Speaking in 1963 at a conference of the AAPSO, Nyerere warned of a "second scramble for Africa," not between Western powers, but between the Chinese and Soviets eager to gain African allies.[67] In March 1964, he warned the American ambassador: "it is more important to me than to you that Zanzibar be nonaligned. The Chinese on Zanzibar threaten me more directly." The threat was not only Chinese "subversion," it was aid. Nyerere was convinced that the Chinese "could make a success for Zanzibar. Then what happens to what I stand for in Tanganyika and what happens to this country?"[68] In part out of his fear of cold war politics intruding into East Africa, Nyerere managed in late-April 1964 to personally persuade Karume to form a federation with Tanganyika, later entitled the United Republic of Tanzania.[69] Karume excluded Babu, his Foreign Minister, from these secret negotiations; he understood that one immediate benefit of the federation would be the safe transfer of Babu and his comrades to the mainland, where they would pose less of a threat to his power.[70]

Despite the union and the political exile of many former Umma members, wise socialist men from the East continued to arrive in Zanzibar, bearing gifts. The Umma comrades who remained in positions of power on the islands meanwhile set about revising the meaning and nature of the revolution. Their influence was immediately felt in the media and in education; as Minister of Education, Youth and Culture from 1965 to 1968, Issa introduced socialist teachings into the secondary-school curriculum. To pass their exams, students needed to be "politically minded" and demonstrate familiarity with the works of Mao, Marx, and Lenin. He also did his best, by sending thousands of youth to toil in work camps in the countryside, to instill labor discipline in the islands, and, inspired by Maoist models, to reduce the differences between urban and rural youth.[71] Also inspired by socialist precedent, Issa helped to orchestrate the confiscation of Arab and South Asian residences around Zanzibar Town. Issa and other comrades either downplayed or distanced themselves from the violence of the revolution, yet employed class categories in their speeches and writings that became ubiquitous in nationalist discourse of the 1960s and 1970s as general references to Africans, Arabs, and Asians. Whereas Karume's regime espoused revolutionary socialism, its understanding of nation building was very much based on the notion of racial uplift, which justified a decade-long assault on the wealth, exclusivity, and social status of formerly privileged non-African minority communities. What was left of the rapidly dwindling Arab and South Asian communities in the islands had their rights continually violated, either through socialist labels like *landlords* and *capitalists*, or actual ethnic markers. So much for Afro-Asian solidarity. Yet not according to revolutionary elites. When Karume, for example, encouraged members of the Revolutionary Council to take Arab and South Asian wives (regardless of whether the girls or women were willing or not), he certainly had in mind a society that was an Afro-Asian synthesis, just not the sort of one the ZNP had in mind.[72] If in 1948 there were over 15,000 South Asians in Zanzibar, that number had by 1972 been reduced to around 3,500.[73] Arabs, whose numbers were roughly triple that of the South Asians prior to the revolution, suffered a similar rate of attrition.

Life in the islands became increasingly isolated as the 1960s progressed, regardless of ethnic or racial status. The regime imposed rigid controls on citizens' travel outside the islands, discontinued most overseas scholarship programs, severely discouraged tourism, closed down all privately owned newspapers, banned Western dance, music, and selected clothing styles, burned Western books, and shut down all community associations not affiliated with the ruling party or that did not have a specific religious function. Its takeover of the wholesale and retail trades produced recurrent shortages, the closure of shops, and considerable deprivation. Old Stone Town's diverse neighborhoods were relentlessly drained of their people and vitality; only its three movie theaters retained something of their former popularity despite bouts of official censorship. Much of the old Stone Town was allowed to fall into ruin in favor of brand new East German-designed construction projects on the "African" side of town. Yet cosmopolitan ties endured and even flourished with the African mainland and the socialist fraternity of nations. In its first year of existence, the revolution attracted such notables as Malcolm X, Zhou Enlai, and Che Guevara. Guests from various African and socialist lands performed pilgrimages to Zanzibar's latest development projects: a modern state-owned apartment block, a new road, another school. Like the Chinese, Karume's regime arranged stage-managed tours to advertise the virtues of revolution, and to generate news for the official press. The story in *Kweupe* was always that these dignitaries were seeing the revolution, and were impressed.

China competed with East Germany and the Soviet Union for the status of chief patron power of the islands. Together, they provided enough aid, experts, and military hardware for the islands to earn the appellation of the "Cuba of East Africa." By 1970, the Chinese had expanded their aid program to include the construction of a new sports stadium and several small-scale factories. About 400 Chinese worked on the islands on these projects, in hospitals, state farms, and as trainers of Zanzibar's 3,000-person army. Successes in providing health services and clean water were matched by failed attempts to establish a viable state rice farm, shoe factory, and tractor repair service.[74] As the years passed, however, the Chinese gained favor with Karume, who appreciated their humble living standards, often no better than those of rural Zanzibaris.[75] By contrast, he became disillusioned with the high cost and/or poor success of Soviet and East German aid projects, so that by the 1970s China was clearly Zanzibar's leading foreign patron and development model. Issa recalled:

> There was no comparison. Here the Chinese were backward, they wanted to develop their country first, but still they helped. Here the Russians were advanced with Sputnik and everything, and yet they were meager. They were very mean and arrogant, I can say. That is my experience with the socialist superpowers. . . . Each helped in their own way but the Chinese in their own society were more akin to us: they lived in the fields, they planted with us, and they won the hearts of the people. So it was through our experience and contact with the Chinese that we looked for our solutions through the Chinese way.[76]

Issa's remarks would have pleased Zhou Enlai, since they reflected "The Eight Principles" of Chinese development assistance he articulated in the mid-1960s.[77] Chinese working overseas were instructed to embody the virtues of socialist discipline, and to be living advertisements for why China had accomplished so much in so little time. This was part of their pedagogical purpose. They became known for their work habits and modest lifestyles, in contrast to Soviet and East German experts, who were housed in hotels or well-appointed flats. An East German biology teacher in Zanzibar in the 1960s recalled that his students, after asking about the size of his salary, informed him that for that amount Zanzibar could support five to ten Chinese teachers, all of whom could live in the house he alone occupied.[78]

And yet China's actual social influence was limited by language barriers and the stringent demands imposed on Chinese overseas by their home government. Although meant to be living advertisements of the socialist New Man, they were forced to endure severe regimentation, and segregation from local society. Oral histories are full of recollections of Chinese workers moving in tight knots through the streets, in fear of denunciation by their peers and superiors. Any social influence they might have had was undermined by their justifiable fixation on questions of personal survival. Hamad remembered the Chinese "always moved around in groups. You never found a Chinese person alone . . . mostly we didn't bother ourselves about them because they kept to themselves. I heard about the wonderful Chairman Mao Tse Tung with his *Red Book*, which I never read. My image of China in those days was a country . . . that sent us commodities that were of poor quality."[79]

Chinese health professionals, farm laborers, and technicians also had less opportunity to exercise influence than Russian and East German secondary-school teachers for example. Zanzibaris relied on European instructors to fill the gaps left by departing British expatriates after the revolution; they also turned to the Soviet bloc for aid and advice in establishing an array of institutions intended to discipline the younger generation, including youth labor camps, and the Young Pioneers. Zanzibaris turned toward Asia, however, for inspiration and instruction in the art of mass spectacle; it was in the realm of the future that the Chinese probably exercised, through public ritual, their greatest pedagogical influence in revolutionary Zanzibar. Throughout the 1970s, Chinese and North Korean experts trained and organized *halaiki*—massive dramatizations and flag and calisthenics demonstrations involving thousands of participants.[80] Students and teachers prepared hours each school day for three months in advance for the annual January revolutionary festivals. So did the state. In 1965, for example, the president's office announced: "every citizen in this country is expected to participate in these celebrations," and ordered each government worker to donate a day's salary for the celebrations.[81] The annual commemorations took place in the massive Chinese-designed Amaani Stadium, on what was once the inland edge of Zanzibar Town, an enclosed and neutral space that permitted vast representations of the vigor and animation of the new state. It was a space without memory, easily appropriated for collective reckonings of the future.

The future needed festivals in its own image, ones of perfect order and symmetry, and so they were conducted according to a rigidly preconceived plan. Citizens acted out various scenes meant to dramatize the importance of development. Lines of people pretended to cultivate with hoes, with a mural in the background showing cloves and coconuts. To represent the workings of a factory, they formed a human pyramid.[82] Children held painted wooden boards; when they opened them and held them together a house would appear, symbolizing nation building.[83] To represent the past as an age of backwardness and humiliation, people pulled rickshaws through the football stadium, or they pretended to fish in old and outmoded dugout canoes.[84] The message was clear for all to see: the revolution had righted a century of wrongs and rescued Africans from misery and exploitation. Dramatizations of work in fishing, agriculture, and industry served as visual reminders of citizens' obligation to build the nation, and the essential dignity of labor. *Halaiki* was meant to advertise and celebrate discipline: the precision and tight economy of bodily gestures of a parade or a calisthenics display was meant as a persuasive sign of the emergence of an increasingly productive generation, for whom hard and efficient physical labor was a deeply felt need. Mass formations of uniformed young men and women moving in complete symmetry were meant to impress upon citizens the irresistible power of islanders fully mobilized for nation building.

Halaiki also served as a series of reassuring, highly synchronized dress rehearsals for a future that had abolished all poverty, vice, disorder, and privilege. In *halaiki*, the future intruded into the ordinary routines of the present, making the future for thousands a lived reality. For those who trained for three months, enacting the future was *the* routine of the present. *Halaiki* was also meant to be deeply satisfying as an exercise in inclusion. The festival displays temporarily abolished all social distinctions. *Halaiki* encouraged a sense of unity and egalitarianism by marching together students wearing the same style of uniform and executing thousands of equal and identical tasks. Each citizen's movements had meaning and significance only in relation to the whole. As a display of state power, *halaiki* was meant to remind citizens of the revolution, and to persuade them they were members of a collective much larger than themselves.

The festivals were also meant to be fun. Oral histories suggest the student performers, regardless of their politics, looked forward to the enthusiastic applause that awaited their performances. Despite enduring years of rationing, shortages, reduced salaries, and unemployment, citizens could find moments, through festival participation, of temporary fulfillment. David Apter observed that states in Africa and Asia in the 1960s employing comparable "mobilization systems" offered their citizens "purification in belongingness, comfort in comradeship, democracy in loyalty, brotherhood in membership."[85] Whether or not they always deciphered the visual codes, onlookers usually came away entertained, and frequently impressed. Zanzibari nationalists believed they had discovered a way in which to act upon the senses, to provide pleasure in order to encourage virtue. It was once a year at *halaiki* spectacles where, as in the festivals of the French Revolution, "desire and knowledge met, where the education of the masses gave way to joy."[86]

Conclusion

Babu was deeply disappointed by the formation of the United Republic of Tanzania in 1964, and his political exile from Zanzibar, which in later years he equated with the preemption of an imminent economic takeoff in the islands. In 1987 he wrote that Zanzibar "was the first country in Africa to try to emulate the Chinese experience." Unfortunately the union made it impossible for Zanzibaris "to take advantage of the Chinese development experience."[87] It "virtually killed the UJIMA spirit," in the islands, which Babu translated as "social power." This "communal spirit was about to shift" from violent revolution toward "enthusiasm for production." Instead of encouraging new attitudes toward labor and leisure, the union relationship led only to "disillusionment and ultimately cynicism."[88] Zanzibar's incipient economic takeoff was aborted when the regime failed to mobilize the people's energies for nation building. Karume's regime *did* impose heavy forced-labor requirements, however, and for over a decade continually harangued ordinary citizens to give up their leisure hours in order to build the nation.[89] Such intrusive assertions of state power are, in fact, one of the most repetitive features of oral histories of the 1960s and 1970s. Immediately after the revolution, islanders sometimes gathered in the thousands for "voluntary" labor assignments. Initially, there *was* "enthusiasm for production" in Zanzibari society; yet this spirit waned over time, not because of the union, but due to the coercion and incompetence of the revolutionary state.

Nor did the union prevent Babu, as a minister until 1972 in Tanzania's union government, from exercising important influence. One of the more significant ironies of Tanzanian history was his spectacular success in spreading the Sinophile gospel and engineering a cardinal shift in Nyerere's attitude toward China. Babu persuaded Nyerere in 1964 to see for himself what the Chinese had accomplished, and he traveled to Beijing to prepare for the president's official visit in February 1965.[90] The encounter had its intended, magical effect. Afterward, Nyerere effused to his new Chinese friends: "If it were possible for me to lift all the ten million Tanzanians and bring them to China to see what you have done since the liberation, I would do so." He added, "There is [a] lesson which we can learn from the Chinese revolution. It is that courage, enthusiasm, and endurance are not enough. There must also be discipline. . . . The single-mindedness with which the Chinese people are concentrating on development was the thing which most impressed me."[91] Instead of transporting millions of his countrymen to China, he supervised the establishment of a system of National Service that sent Tanzanian youth to rural-labor camps, where they were subjected to repetitive sermons on "the demand for dedicated exertion, the suspicion of certain forms of consumption, the eulogization of the virtues of frugality and self-denial."[92]

Nyerere cultivated a warm relationship with Beijing that lasted for two decades, and that involved considerable material aid. The TAZARA railway project, linking Tanzania's capital city, Dar es Salaam, with Lusaka, Zambia, became in the 1970s the largest Chinese-aid project anywhere in Africa. The thousands of Chinese workers it brought to Tanzania constituted the largest Chinese communist overseas presence anywhere in the world.[93] As Jamie Monson relates, in this volume, Chinese laborers worked alongside Tanzanians recruited to build the railway, serving while doing so as embodiments of labor discipline. Both the Chinese and the Tanzanians appreciated this pedagogical role, yet Tanzanian employees of the railway were both attracted and repulsed by the heavy labor demands of their Chinese "friends." Official media in Tanzania did not capture this ambivalence; in October 1970, Dar es Salaam's *Sunday News* welcomed the beginning of railway construction:

> Tanzania can take some pride in having . . . reintroduced the Chinese to Africa.
>
> We welcome the representatives of the People's Republic of China today, not just because of their timely assistance to our development efforts, but also because of the relevance which their experience has for us. . . .
>
> Some Western countries accuse Tanzania of being a bridgehead [of Chinese influence in Africa]. We reply that we would be proud, if by this is meant that the ideas of discipline, frugality, and self-reliance, of hostility to racism and imperialism, that have characterized the Chinese government since the revolution, were to spread through Tanzania into the rest of the great continent of Africa.[94]

Just as the railway construction was at its most intense, Nyerere arrested and detained Babu in 1972 for his leading role in the assassination of Karume in Zanzibar. After his release in 1978, Babu never made his home in Tanzania again. He eventually settled in London as a journalist and lecturer, and observed the decline of the Maoist gospel in Africa. By the 1980s, "the best-known Chinese in Africa was not Mao, but Bruce Lee. All over the continent cinemas celebrated the exploits of this deceased Hong Kong film star and exponent of martial arts."[95] Tanzania even came out with its own commemorative set of Bruce Lee stamps, in which the fighter was drawn in various costumes and poses.[96] In the more substantive realm of development, all the Chinese-built factories and state farms established in the islands with Chinese expertise were

6.1. Bruce Lee stamps, Tanzania

either by the 1980s defunct or operating at a net loss. In response to serious economic decline, Zanzibar opened itself to tourism, liberalized its trade policies, and enthusiastically embraced many principles of free market capitalism. By the 1990s, Western-donor agencies surpassed the Chinese in their development assistance to both the islands and mainland of Tanzania. In an island economy, where tourism was the only major growth sector, revolutionary "enthusiasm for production" was replaced by "enthusiasm for service." Always an exemplar of his times, Issa put politics aside to open, with Italian financing and a loan from a subsidiary of the World Bank, the first beach-resort hotel in Zanzibar. He can sometimes now be seen singing revolutionary songs in Chinese, Russian, and Spanish to his slightly disoriented hotel staff. The same man who once founded youth-labor camps in the countryside now takes equal pride in turning pristine beaches into playgrounds for well-heeled tourists. Tourist agencies organize tours to the palaces of the Arab sultans, or around the reviving neighborhoods of old Stone Town, and specifically ignore Karume's monumental apartment blocks built through "voluntary" labor.

Babu wrote a number of essays from London from the wistful viewpoint of "the Africa that might have been," in which his point of critical reference was often China. His sense of alienation resulted from African departure from what he perceived to be Chinese norms. Although in these passages Babu's ideological consistency appears somewhat strained, his geographical loyalties down through the decades are immaculate. His reverence for China as a place and as an idea suggests, once again, the role of visiting and seeing as a distinct nationalist epistemology. Thus Babu wrote in 1987 that even though Tanzania was for a time the world's leading recipient of Chinese aid, its leaders failed to learn from the wisdom of Mao's "Ten Major Relationships." These relationships included "Learn from Other Countries," in this case from China that "everything depended on people's own initiative and ingenuity," and "their enthusiasm for production."[97] What was missing from postcolonial Africa was "the ingenuity of the peasants, skilled manpower and mass enthusiasm for production."[98] African leaders failed to imitate Chinese experts working in Africa, who "adopted the same mode of life as their junior colleagues." They ignored the key ingredients of China's development: "a correct world outlook, scientific planning, frugality and a determined people." A cultural emphasis on frugality was "the essential ingredient for development, capitalist, socialist or any other type."[99]

Babu's exaltation of discipline as a value of universal relevance was not exceptional, but was in accord with the "single disciplinary model" presented by both the West and the East.[100] Michael Hardt and Antonio Negri have been wrong about many things, but they have cogently argued that despite the reality of cold war superpower confrontations:

The leaders of the socialist states agreed in substance on this disciplinary project. Lenin's renowned enthusiasm for Taylorism was later outdone by Mao's modernization projects. The official socialist recipe for decolonization also followed the essential logic dictated by the capitalist transnationals and the international agencies: each postcolonial government had to create a labor force adequate to the disciplinary regime.[101]

This essay demonstrates that in the 1960s the Chinese sought to break out of their historic isolation by offering not only material aid to nationalist movements in Africa, but also the enticing prospect of their collaboration in the creation of a new kind of civilization, the nature of which needed to be *seen* to be understood. The foundation of this civilization, of this usable future, would not only be African, or Afro-Asian, it would be founded on universal values like discipline that transcended all racial and cultural boundaries and ignored the autonomy of national-historical narratives. Some nationalists like Babu and Issa responded well to these ideas, perhaps as a function of their "exposure" to the world, or perhaps because of their generation's polyglot, cosmopolitan milieu, elements of which were prepared in the mid-20th century to follow a nation-building strategy that embraced the universal. In the 1960s, the idea of discipline was in fact so universal—and contested—that it would be *more* remarkable to imagine nationalists in Africa *not* actually engaging the concept.

Unlike Foucault, they did not regard disciplinary techniques as insidious, petty, or malicious. Nor did they distance themselves from discipline for its associations with the colonial civilizing mission. Rather, they looked to discipline as part of a strategy to access the means by which their societies might accumulate knowledge, power, and abundance. The phenomenon of nationalists searching for a new kind of national culture, no longer under colonial domination, and yet neither an uncritical return to the ways of the ancestors, is familiar now to scholars. Partha Chatterjee writes that nationalism "produced a discourse in which, even as it challenged the colonial claim to political domination, it also accepted the very intellectual premises of 'modernity' on which colonial domination was based."[102] In the case of Zanzibar, some nationalists adopted China rather than the capitalist West as their most immediate model and usable future. They believed the inculcation of socialist ideas of personal merit and prestige as applied to habits of work, leisure, and consumption would be an antidote to dependency and underdevelopment.

Zanzibari nationalists like Babu and Issa freely transposed the historical experiences of other societies onto their own, and adopted an imported future that clashed with Islamic universalism: the claim that a national culture that transcended race could be constructed in Zanzibar through a common embrace of Islam. The Afro-Asian solidarities asserted through such a vision did not appeal to revolutionaries, unless a radical rupture from the past could be realized: the end of Arab and South Asian economic hegemony in the islands. This was the project that superficially united the nationalists who seized power in 1964, whether they spoke the language of socialism, or of race. Racial nationalists looked more toward the past than the future glimpsed by their more socialist-minded colleagues, however—they sought to right a century of wrongs, and to erase all the humiliations of slavery and inequality. They were comfortable with the idea of a universal civilization that encompassed socialism and even the concept of discipline as a fundamental ordering principle of development schemes, in part because neither discipline nor development necessarily hinged on the defense of the human rights of ordinary islanders. The revolution, from the viewpoint of the 21st century, failed to deliver either development or discipline in Zanzibar, however. Such failings have allowed critics of the revolution to once again assert the concept of Islamic universalism as their rallying cry, to disparage the revolution on its own terms—the discourse of development—as well as in reference to the emergent cosmopolitan language of human rights. Unlike socialism, the spouse of African nationalism in Zanzibar for the entire revolutionary era, the language of human rights appears to be a more reluctant bride.

Notes

1. Toyin Falola, *Nationalism and African Intellectuals* (Rochester: University of Rochester Press, 2001), 47.

2. Ibid., 54.

3. Leela Gandhi, *Postcolonial Theory: A Critical Introduction* (New York: Columbia University Press, 1998), 19–20.

4. Sylvana Patriarca, "Indolence and Regeneration: Tropes and Tensions of Risorgimento Patriotism," *The American Historical Review,* 110, no. 2 (2005), 386.

5. Donald Donham, *Marxist Modern: An Ethnographic History of the Ethiopian Revolution* (Berkeley: University of California Press, 1999), 25.

6. Frederick Cooper, "Modernizing Bureaucrats, Backward Africans, and the Development Concept," in *International Development and the Social Sciences: Essays on the History and Politics of Knowledge*, eds. Frederick Cooper and Randall Packard (Berkeley: University of California Press, 1997), 81–82.

7. See Dilip Parameshwar Gaonkar, "On Alternative Modernities," in *Alternative Modernities*, ed. Dilip Parameshwar Gaonkar (Durham: Duke University Press, 2001).

8. Zanzibar National Archives (hereafter ZNA), Zanzibar Town, Tanzania, BA 109/6, *Guide to Zanzibar*, 1931.

9. Ahmed Gurnah, "Elvis in Zanzibar," in *The Limits of Globalization: Cases and Arguments*, ed. Alan Scott (London: Routledge, 1997), 117.

10. Ibid., 117–19.

11. Abdulrazak Gurnah, *Desertion* (New York: Pantheon Books, 2005), 127. Abdulrazak is the brother of Ahmed Gurnah.

12. Gurnah, "Elvis in Zanzibar," 123.

13. Ibid.

14. G. Thomas Burgess, *Race, Revolution, and the Struggle for Human Rights in Zanzibar: The Memoirs of Ali Sultan Issa and Seif Sharif Hamad* (Athens: Ohio University Press, 2009), 183.

15. Jonathon Glassman, "Sorting out the Tribes: The Creation of Racial Identities in Colonial Zanzibar's Newspaper Wars," *Journal of African History*, 41 (2000): 395–428; see also Michael Lofchie, *Zanzibar: Background to Revolution* (Princeton: Princeton University Press, 1965).

16. Abdulrazak Gurnah, *Admiring Silence* (New York: Free Press, 1996), 66–67.

17. Jonathon Glassman, "Slower than a Massacre: The Multiple Sources of Racial Thought in Colonial Africa," *The American Historical Review*, 109, no. 3 (2004): 720–54.

18. Agozi, 4 May 1959, as quoted in Lofchie, *Background to Revolution*, 193.

19. Gurnah, "Elvis in Zanzibar," 122.

20. Ibid., 131.

21. James Ferguson, *Expectations of Modernity: Myths and Meanings of Urban Life on the Zambian Copperbelt* (Berkeley: University of California Press, 1999), 212; italics original.

22. "Kuteka kwa Kufisidi," *Mwongozi*, January 25, 1963.

23. "Views and Comments: For Serious Consideration," *Mwongozi*, August 9, 1963.

24. Ahmed Gurnah, "Elvis in Zanzibar," 131.

25. John Cooley, *East Wind Over Africa: Red China's African Offensive* (New York: Walker, 1965), 211.

26. See, for example, George Yu, *China's Africa Policy: A Study of Tanzania* (New York: Praeger, 1975).

27. Cooley, *East Wind Over Africa*, 214.

28. Philip Snow, *The Star Raft: China's Encounter with Africa* (Ithaca: Cornell University Press, 1988), 71.

29. Cooley, *East Wind Over Africa*, 57.

30. Ibid., 16.

31. Ibid., 195, 197.

32. Ibid., 199.

33. Alaba Ogunsanyo, *China's Policy in Africa, 1958–71* (Cambridge: Cambridge University Press, 1974), 84.

34. See, for example, Tajudeen Abdul-Raheem, "Remembering A. M. Babu," in *Babu, I Saw the Future and It Works: Essays Celebrating the Life of Comrade Abdulrahman Mohamed Babu 1924–1996*, ed. Haroub Othman (Dar es Salaam: M and M Printers, 2001), 136–37.

35. A. M. Babu, "Memoirs: An Outline," in *Babu, I Saw the Future and It Works*, 15–16.

36. Haroub Othman, "Comrade Abdulrahman Babu: A Revolutionary Internationalist," in *Babu, I Saw the Future and It Works*, 115.

37. Burgess, *Race, Revolution, and the Struggle for Human Rights in Zanzibar*, 51.

38. Ibid., 60–61.

39. Cooley, *East Wind Over Africa*, 40.

40. *Adal Insaf*, "No One Starving or Jobless in China," September 13, 1960; American Consulate, DSM, to Secretary of State, 194, June 17, 1960, Central Decimal File 1960-3, Box 1709, National Archives, College Park, MD (hereafter NACP); Dispatch, King to Department of State, 51, September 19, 1960, Central Decimal File 1960-3, Box 1709, NACP; Ogunsanwo, *China's Policy*, 34–35.

41. Interview, Anonymous, Dar es Salaam, May 18, 1998.

42. Snow, *Star Raft*, 72–73.

43. Timothy Mitchell, *Colonising Egypt* (Berkeley: University of California Press, 1991), 12.

44. Ibid., 6.

45. A.M. Babu, "From China with Lessons for Africa," in *The Future that Works: Selected Writings of A. M. Babu*, eds. Salma Babu and Amrit Wilson (Trenton: Africa World Press, 2002), 33–34.

46. A. M. Babu, "The New World Disorder—Which Way Africa?" in *The Future that Works*, 319, 324.

47. Snow, *Star Raft*, 90.

48. Ibid., 91, 94.

49. Interview, Haroub Othman, Zanzibar Town, July 16, 2004.

50. Cooley, *East Wind Over Africa*, 202.

51. Alan Hutchison, *China's African Revolution* (Boulder: Westview, 1976), 186–88; Emmanuel Hevi, *An African Student in China* (New York: Praeger, 1963), 116, 119–43, 162–63.

52. Snow, *Star Raft*, 197; Cooley, *East Wind Over Africa*, 202–3.

53. Nearly the entire Zanzibari contingent left early. Snow, *The Star Raft*, 198–99; Ogunsanwo, *China's Policy*, 85; Bruce Larkin, *China and Africa, 1949–1970: The Foreign Policy of the People's Republic of China* (Berkeley: University of California Press, 1971), 142. Over the next few years the number of Zanzibari students in China rebounded, but was again seriously reduced by the onset of China's Cultural Revolution. Hutchison, *China's African Revolution*, 186–88.

54. In Eastern Europe, for example, they faced fewer social restrictions and issues of consumer deprivation. For a more general discussion of the Zanzibari student diaspora in the 1950s and 1960s, see Thomas Burgess, "An Imagined Generation: Umma Youth in Nationalist Zanzibar," in *In Search of a Nation: Histories of Authority and Dissidence from Tanzania: Essays in Honor of I. M. Kimambo*, eds. Greg Maddox, James Giblin, Y.Q. Lawi (London: James Currey, 2005); Thomas Burgess, "A Socialist Diaspora: Ali Sultan Issa, the Soviet Union, and the Zanzibari Revolution," in *Africa in Russia, Russia in Africa: 300 Years of Encounters*, ed. by Maxim Matusevich (Trenton: Africa World Press, 2006).

55. British National Archives, London CO 822, 2166, 26, British intelligence report, November 1960.

56. Burgess, *Race, Revolution, and the Struggle for Human Rights in Zanzibar*, 66.

57. Ali Sultan Issa, "Condemn Me Now but History Will Absolve Me," photocopied statement in author's possession.

58. Interview, Anonymous, Zanzibar Town, August 2, 2001.

59. The actual extent of the violence in January 1964 is a matter of hot dispute. Arabs of Unguja island suffered the most, yet more Arabs and South Asians went into immediate or eventual exile than were killed in the early days of the revolution. This excludes those who were raped, plundered, and detained.

60. For a lengthier recovery of the complicated political maneuverings within the new revolutionary regime, see Burgess, "A Socialist Diaspora."

61. A. M. Babu, "I was the First Third World Minister to Recognise the GDR," in *Babu, I Saw the Future and It Works*, 52–53. A. M. Babu, "The 1964 Revolution: Lumpen or Vanguard?" in *Zanzibar Under Colonial Rule*, eds. Abdul Sheriff and E. Ferguson (London: James Currey, 1991), 220–47.

62. As cited in Cooley, *East Wind Over Africa*, 41.

63. Ibid., 48.

64. Piero Gleijeses, *Conflicting Missions: Havana, Washington, and Africa, 1959–1976* (Chapel Hill: University of North Carolina Press, 2002), 7.

65. See Frantz Fanon, *A Dying Colonialism* (New York: Grove Press, 1967), 1.

66. Ibid., 3.

67. Hutchison, *China's African Revolution*, 43.

68. Donald Petterson, *Revolution in Zanzibar: An American's Cold War Tale* (Boulder: Westview, 2002), 154. Snow suggests Nyerere was also initially skeptical of the Chinese because of their official atheism, the doctrine of permanent revolutionary upheaval, and the Chinese reputation for regimentation. Snow, *Star Raft*, 88.

69. The federation agreement was not only the result of short-term political expediency, but also long-standing working ties between Nyerere and TANU and Karume and the ASP, and their shared African nationalism. The agreement took place in a period of intense discussions regarding the feasibility of establishing an East African federation also to include Kenya and Uganda.

70. For the union agreement see, for example, Issa Shivji, *Pan-Africanism or Pragmatism? Lessons of Tanganyika–Zanzibar Union* (Dar es Salaam: Mkuki na Nyota Publishers, 2008); Amrit Wilson, *US Foreign Policy and Revolution: The Creation of Tanzania* (London: Pluto, 1989).

71. Thomas Burgess, "To Differentiate Rice from Grass: Youth Labor Camps in Revolutionary Zanzibar," *The History of Youth in East Africa,* eds. Andrew Burton and Helene Charton (Athens: Ohio University Press, forthcoming).

72. For forced marriages in Zanzibar, see Esmond Martin, *Zanzibar: Tradition and Revolution* (Zanzibar: Gallery Publications, 2007), 69–71.

73. Lofchie, *Background to Revolution*, 71; Martin, *Tradition and Revolution*, 69.

74. Colin Legum, "Zanzibar: Another Papa Doc?" *Venture* 23, no. 6 (June 1971), 22–23; Alan Hutchison, "Clove Boom Helps Zanzibar in Diversification Drive," *African Development* February 1974, 49–57; Ogunsanwo, *China's Policy in Africa*, 136–37, 203; CIA Memorandum, December 2, 1968, United Republic of Tanzania vol. 2 Cables February 1965–December 1968, National Security File, Africa–Tanganyika, Box 100, Lyndon Baines Johnson Library, University of Texas, Austin TX.

75. Petterson, *Revolution in Zanzibar*, 167.

76. Burgess, *Race, Revolution, and the Struggle for Human Rights in Zanzibar*, 107.

77. Hutchison, *China's African Revolution*, 50–51.

78. Interview, Eckhart Schultz, July 22, 2004, Zanzibar Town.

79. Burgess, *Race, Revolution, and the Struggle for Human Rights in Zanzibar*, 227.

80. The popular Chinese term for *halaiki* translates roughly as "meeting of 10,000 people."

81. ZNA, AD 1/140 Kusherehekea Siku ya Mapinduzi, 10, Afisi ya Makamo wa Kwanza wa Rais, January 4, 1965.

82. Interview, Muhammed Idris Muhammed Saleh, Zanzibar Town, August 3, 2001.

83. Interview, Seif Juma Seif, Zanzibar Town, July 12, 2001.

84. Interview, Abdullah Suleiman Waziri, Makunduchi Kajengwa, July 11, 01.

85. David Apter, "Political Religion in the New Nations," in *Old Societies and New States: The Quest for Modernity in Asia and Africa*, ed. Clifford Geertz (New York: Free Press, 1963), 85.

86. Mona Ozouf, *Festivals and the French Revolution*, trans. Alan Sheridan (Cambridge: Harvard University Press, 1988), 9.

87. A. M. Babu, "China and Africa: Can We Learn from Each Other?" in *The Future that Works*, 168–69.

88. A. M. Babu, "Zanzibar and the Future," in *Babu, I Saw the Future and It Works*, 28.

89. Any perusal of *Kweupe*, the mouthpiece of the revolution from 1964 to 1972, illustrates the numbing repetitiveness of the nation-building rhetoric of the era.

90. Cooley, *East Wind Over Africa*, 41.

91. William Edgett Smith, *Nyerere of Tanzania* (London: Victor Gollancz, 1973), 160.

92. Ali Mazrui, *Cultural Engineering and Nation-building in East Africa* (Evanston: Northwestern University Press, 1972), 220.

93. Hutchison, *China's African Revolution*, 251, 259.

94. "Karibu," *Sunday News*, October 1970, as cited in Charles Swift, *Dar Days: The Early Years in Tanzania* (New York: University Press of America, 2002), 113.

95. Snow, *Star Raft*, 211.

96. The complete set is in the author's possession, though the date of their origin is unclear.

97. Babu, "China and Africa: Can We Learn from Each Other?" 170.

98. Ibid., 171.

99. Ibid., 173–74.

100. Michael Hardt and Antonio Negri, *Empire* (Cambridge: Harvard University Press, 2000), 250.

101. Ibid., 248.

102. Partha Chatterjee, *Nationalist Thought and the Colonial World: A Derivative Discourse?*, 2nd ed. (London: Zed, 1993), 30.

7

Working Ahead of Time

Labor and Modernization during the Construction of the TAZARA Railway, 1968–86

Jamie Monson

WHEN CONSTRUCTION OF the TAZARA railway was completed in 1975—one year ahead of schedule—its supporters announced triumphantly that Tanzanian and Zambian workers, with the cooperation of the Chinese people, had "smashed the imperialist slanders about the 'impossibility of a Tanzania–Zambia railway.'"[1] Five years earlier during the opening ceremonies that marked the start of railway construction, Tanzania's first president, Julius Nyerere, had witnessed African drivers handling earth-moving machinery and proudly declared, "We have our own industrial workers! We have our own industrial workers!"[2]

These public responses to the TAZARA project illustrate important threads in the discourse that accompanied Chinese development assistance to Africa during the periods of decolonization and postcolonial nation building. One thread was the emphasis on anti-imperialism: Chinese development assistance would succeed where the forces of imperialism and neocolonialism had predicted failure. The railway had been completed ahead of schedule, demonstrating to a world audience the transformative potential of Afro-Asian solidarity for achieving African independent modernization. President Nyerere's proud reference to Africa's new "industrial workers" introduced a related thread, by celebrating the technical knowledge acquired by the Tanzanian and Zambian laborers that worked on the project. For the TAZARA project represented not only the transfer of material technology in the form of the rails and the rolling stock, but also the transfer of technical skills from the thirty to forty-thousand Chinese railway "experts" that worked on the project to their African counterparts. In this way, Chinese development assistance was understood as a means to give confidence to new nations, by training a workforce and conveying life lessons to a newly independent generation of young Africans.

The construction of TAZARA can therefore be seen as embodying the integrated themes of anti-imperialism, modernization, and pedagogy that Dipesh Chakrabarty and Gary Burgess have referred to in this volume. Like other postcolonial nations that identified themselves as belong to the Third World at the time, Tanzania's approach to development after achieving independence in 1961 heavily emphasized modernization. The specific form of modernization had many features, one of which was acceleration. Modernizing at a rapid pace would enable Tanzania to "catch up" with Western countries, and to overcome the backwardness that was the legacy of colonialism.[3] Julius Nyerere was famously quoted as saying that "we must run while they walk," this phrase becoming the title of his biography in 1971.[4]

Tanzania's postcolonial modernization also emphasized the importance of developing independent industrial and agricultural technology as a foundation for self-reliance. Both the engineer and the skilled technical worker were idealized as modernizing figures, whose increased presence in Third World countries would not only bring about a transformation in economic productivity and in social development, but would also reduce political dependency. Indeed, the Chinese government reported in a confidential telegraph in 1965 that Southern Rhodesia was using the threat of withdrawal of its railway technicians from Zambia in an effort to apply political pressure on that country.[5]

Lastly, national modernization required instruction, or pedagogy in the larger sense as described by Chakrabarty. Instruction was necessary in order for Tanzanians to become modern in the technological ways described above, by developing their own engineers and technically skilled workers. Instruction was also important for the development of a modern public, members of which would not only hold political rights after independence but would also need to learn to act as good citizens through the guidance of state actors.[6]

The construction of the TAZARA railway promised to deliver on all three of these modernizing principles. It was the largest and most famous example of China's distinctive approach to development projects in Africa, as China "deliberately set out to be different" through the Eight Principles of Development Assistance to Africa circulated in 1963–64 by Zhou Enlai.[7] The project would be completed ahead of time, thereby achieving accelerated modernization. Chinese engineering technology would be transferred to African workers through training programs, thus helping to create a future labor force of skilled technicians. As they learned the discipline of hard work from their Chinese mentors, African workers would also develop the qualities of good citizenship. Tanzania's prime minister Rashidi Kawawa declared during the TAZARA inauguration ceremony in 1975 that the African workers had received "the best kind of training" from Chinese experts during the construction of TAZARA, and this expertise could now be applied to other development work.[8]

Meanwhile in China, during the 1960s and 1970s, the ideology of revolutionary modernization shared many of the same themes, as China declared itself to be part of the Third World. Like the newly decolonized African states, China had also emphasized rapid development and recovery from backwardness. China's socialist state after 1949 founded its political legitimacy on its potential not only to catch up with but surpass the West, particularly in the area of industrialization. This led to a combination of "revolutionary drives, developmentalist aspirations and nationalistic concerns," with an emphasis on industry and machine technology.[9] Yet China's experience with modernity was also deeply affected by its relationship with the Soviet Union. After following Soviet modernization models and receiving

Soviet technical assistance from 1953 to 1960, the abrupt withdrawal of the Soviet experts contributed to a shift in China's approach to technology and science toward domestic innovation and self-reliance. During China's Cultural Revolution, modernization ideology lifted up the revolutionary role to be played by ordinary workers and peasants in technology development, in direct confrontation with the previously dominant "elite technicians" and "productionists."[10]

These approaches to modernization during China's revolutionary period made the role of technology transfer during the construction of TAZARA more complex, and the challenges for the project's technical personnel more difficult. As historian Zhang Tieshan has said, TAZARA was a "unique project that took place at a unique time."[11] The multiple conjunctures of the Chinese Cultural Revolution, African independent nation building, and the politics of the cold war shaped the ways that political ideologies and practical lessons came together in the workplace. For the railway to succeed in technological terms and thereby to disprove the "slanders" of the neoimperialists, TAZARA would require the expertise of China's most highly trained and experienced railway engineers. At the same time, however, the approach to revolutionary modernization in China at this time idealized the role of everyday workers in solving technical problems and moving forward. At the same time, TAZARA planners wanted to complete the project ahead of schedule, a goal that came into conflict with the pedagogical function of the railway workplace as a site of technology transfer. During the TAZARA project, therefore, the intersections between rapid modernization, technology transfer, and pedagogy were complex and contradictory.

Brigades and Communes

African American writer and political activist Shirley Graham Du Bois traveled to China in 1967, in the same year that China, Tanzania, and Zambia signed the first formal agreement for TAZARA's construction.[12] As was common for foreign visitors to China at the time, Mrs. Du Bois was taken to visit model factories and rural communes, including the well-known Dazhai Production Brigade, "one of the famous red banners in China."[13] During her visit to a steel-pipe factory in Shanghai, the workers explained to Mrs. Du Bois what had happened to their factory's production after the Soviet experts withdrew their support in 1960. At first, the elite technicians of the factory had wrongly suggested that spare parts should be imported once again from an outside country, so that production quotas could be met. The factory workers had disagreed, they told Mrs. Du Bois, because they had embraced Chairman Mao's belief that the workers themselves should conduct their own experiments using existing materials. Within three months the workers had mastered the technical problems, they said, demonstrating their self-reliance. Workers succeeded in this revolutionary way because, following Mao's teaching, they had used their own creative power. In the end they produced even more goods than expected, and at an accelerated rate: "Today the factory . . . is repeatedly fulfilling its tasks ahead of schedule, continuing experiments."[14]

Shirley Graham Du Bois's description of her visit incorporated key elements of China's approach to revolutionary modernization in the 1960s, including self-reliance, acceleration of production, and the possibility that workers could learn technical skills through experimentation and practice. According to Chairman Mao the "masses" of ordinary workers had the potential, through labor, to become engineers or scientists.[15] Workers at a factory in Xi'an told Mrs. Du Bois that they had "lacked confidence" after the Soviet withdrawal. But once they began to investigate technical problems on their own, they were able to out-produce the original Soviet production targets.[16] On a return visit to China in 1974, Mrs. Du Bois was introduced to a model worker at the Northeast Machine Building Factory in Shenyang. The woman had started out as an ordinary worker, but through disciplined self-study she eventually became an engineer. She reportedly accomplished a year's production quota in twenty-one days, using creative experimentation to achieve success. This model worker, Mrs. Du Bois wrote in her diary, was "a woman who runs ahead of time," reflecting the imperative of overcoming backwardness through acceleration.[17]

Many of these same themes were repeated for the visiting delegations from Africa that came to China during the 1960s and 1970s. China's positive experiences, as a so-called Third World country undergoing revolutionary modernization, were demonstrated to visiting youth leagues, women's groups, economic delegations, and health-care workers. During a visit to China with a public-health delegation in 1973, Tanzania's Minister of Public Health (later to become Tanzania's second president), Ali Hassan Mwinyi, said, "Both Tanzania and China are homes of revolutions. But you moved faster than us. You must have numerous experiences for us to learn."[18] These themes were also present in the Chinese approach to development assistance in Africa, including those ideas that had been shaped by the Sino-Soviet split. The young nations of Tanzania and Zambia were seen as lacking in self-confidence after years of colonial dependency, while neoimperialist aid projects threatened to reinforce their reliance upon outside experts and imported materials. The experience of building a large-scale, technically complex infrastructure project under Chinese tutelage was therefore viewed as a critical step toward the development of African workers and their new nations. TAZARA's project planners had anticipated from the start that the railway could be completed "ahead of schedule." Through acceleration, they would amplify their message that Africans, working side by side with their Chinese friends, could accomplish the very things that imperialists had claimed were impossible.[19] Through the experience of work, African youths would learn both the discipline of labor and the technology of modernization—they would become Africa's new industrial workers.

When he returned to China after working on the TAZARA project, internal-combustion engineer Ma Luhua published a poem he had written about his experiences in Africa. He titled it, "The Wooden Molds Workshop Is Quiet," and began by describing the thoughts of a solitary Chinese technician as he sat smoking his pipe on a quiet East African evening. A year earlier, on a bright sunny morning, African youths had first arrived at the workshop to report for work. The poet–engineer had made up his mind to teach them technology in such a way that the imperialists would open their eyes wide with amazement. In the process of work at the factory, he wrote in his poem, the workers' clothes became soaked with sweat, hundreds and thousands of clothes. They labored diligently for three-hundred days and three-hundred nights, until they had fully mastered the skills of cutting and drilling. Each piece of wood was stained red from the abrasions on their hands. The sweating bodies of the African workers were physically located at the wooden-molds factory, yet Ma described their gaze as directed outward toward the future. From their vantage point at the workplace, they envisioned the African people marching forward along the path toward self-reliance (*zi li geng sheng* 自力更生).[20]

Ma Luhua's poem was published together with others written by Chinese technicians and engineers that had worked on TAZARA, in a volume titled *Rainbow of Friendship*. The poems provided living evidence, wrote the book's editors in the introduction, that poetry in China was not the domain of elites but could be authored by ordinary people. The editors described the poems as "a new flowering branch in the poetry creation of amateur worker and peasant poets."[21] Several poems in the *Rainbow of Friendship* collection described the ways that the experience of work on the railway could be pedagogical. A poem about "Workplace Lessons" describes the teaching of technical drawing in the following stanzas:

"Drawing"
Instructing carefully over and over again,
Teaching hand-in-hand,
Even when asked three or five times I do not find it bothersome,
I am willing to show my heart of red.

I hope you will learn the technical skills of drawing as soon as possible,
For the burden of independent national industry is waiting
for you to shoulder it.
Your passion is flowing freely from the tip of your drafting pen,
Let us together vigorously draft the blueprint for a beautiful life.[22]

In this poem, the drawing of the blueprint represents mastery of a highly technical design skill. It was also a metaphor for the planning expertise urgently needed by African civilizations so that they could plan for an independent future. Thus the African worker, once he had received training from his Chinese mentor, would be able both to creatively imagine and to technically plan for a future of independence and self-reliance. And the Chinese technician in turn, by teaching his African worker–student, would gain a "heart of red." This redness of the heart (like the redness that stained the wooden molds) was a reference to the positive qualities of a "politically correct comrade," one that possessed a strong heart (for courage), a strong mind (for ideology), and strong skills (for technical proficiency).[23]

In practice, ideology and work experience came together in complex ways during the construction of TAZARA. Ideology could get in the way of construction goals, as Zhou Enlai recognized when he suggested at the start of the project that excessive propaganda would be counterproductive. He urged the Chinese workers to set aside leftist formalism and to focus their attention on their work, assuring them that "completing one's own job well is equivalent to completing a political job."[24] Thus, work on the railway in itself would be a liberating act. The engineering experts who were asked to train the African labor force struggled to find the right balance between competing political and technical mandates. As Chinese and African workers toiled side by side, the experience of hard work and work discipline could feel like drudgery rather than liberation, causing many African workers to leave the project. Interviews with retired workers, documentary evidence, poetry, and other forms of expression allow us to explore the ways that ideology came together with—and also departed from—practice in the transnational railway construction workplace of TAZARA.

The TAZARA Railway

The TAZARA railway was designed and constructed between 1968 and 1975. The 1,060-mile-long project was built with financial and technical assistance from China amounting to over $400 million, in the form of a long-term interest-free loan.[25] China agreed to support the railway project after several requests for assistance from Western donors and from the Soviet Union had been rejected. TAZARA became China's largest international development project and the third largest infrastructure development project in Africa (after the Aswan and Volta Dam projects). Like most railways in the world, this one was built with both political and economic objectives. Known as the Freedom Railway, TAZARA was conceived to provide the critical outlet to the sea that landlocked Zambia needed in order to break from its dependency on Rhodesian, Angolan, and South African rails and ports. TAZARA was therefore an antiapartheid as well as a pan-African project, intended to serve as a symbol of revolutionary Third World solidarity and resistance to the forces of colonialism, neocolonialism, and imperialism.

The Chinese railway experts and technicians who came to East Africa to work on the TAZARA construction project were recruited from throughout China through the regionally based railway bureaus of the Chinese Ministry of Railways. Most were between twenty-five and forty years of age, with prior railway experience and varying levels of expertise. There were three primary conditions for recruitment, according to retired workers: membership in the Chinese Communist Party, expertise in railway-construction technology, and a personal character of courage and resilience in order to persevere in difficult working conditions.[26] The majority of the workers recruited for the TAZARA project were among the most qualified in China at the time, in part because of the high visibility of the project and also because China's own industrial production was in disarray as a result of the Cultural Revolution.

Workers from China's Second and Third Railway Bureaus were especially valued for recruitment. Those from the Second Railway Bureau had just completed building the Chengdu-Kunming railway through the rugged mountains of Sichuan and Yunnan in 1970, and were respected for their skills and perseverance in difficult terrain.[27] The Second Railway Bureau's training school for technicians in Chengdu was specialized in teaching the construction of tunnels and bridges.[28] Mr. Rao Xue De remembers that 204 workers from his department in the Second Railway Bureau were recruited to work on TAZARA, after which he was posted as their team leader. Other members of his team also served as instructors. Workers from the

Third Railway Bureau, meanwhile, had taken part in the Korean War and were known for their strong wills, toughness under pressure, and high level of discipline.[29]

One retired TAZARA worker composed a poem to describe the years of traveling far from home, which had characterized his life's work in the Third Railway Bureau:

> We constructed roads both within and outside the Great
> Wall
> We built bridges both above and below the rivers.
> We went to Korea, Vietnam and Tanzania for foreign
> assistance
> Our footprints are all over the Xing'anling Mountain range.
>
> Four decades have flown by as fast as one second
> Suddenly, the hair has grown gray.
> We were never able to take care of our older generations,
> Leaving wives and children to stay home.
> We age alone eventually with all sorts of illness and
> disability.
> However, if you ask me who I am
> I am a Communist Party member.[30]

Being far away from China during the years of the Cultural Revolution was not easy for some recruited workers. Leaving loved ones behind without their husbands and fathers caused anxiety when there was chaos and violence at home. For others, working on the TAZARA project could be an opportunity to leave their troubles behind, or to rehabilitate a damaged reputation.[31] There were material advantages to serving in Africa, for Chinese TAZARA workers received a supplemental field allowance equivalent to the forty-yuan salary that continued to be paid to their families back in China. These funds could be saved and used to purchase a luxury item (Omega watches were popular) or even food to be taken home, where such commodities were in short supply. Many described feeling a sense of honor (荣誉, *rong yu*) while working on the project, and signed up feeling that it was a form of service to their country (国家观念, *guojia guannian*) and to the party.[32]

In contrast to their Chinese counterparts, the Tanzanian and Zambian workers were younger men who had no previous background in railway work. Most were recent graduates or members of the national service, for worker recruitment had focused on finding dedicated and disciplined youths rather than workers with prior railway experience or technical knowledge. Trainees were expected to be in good health, to have good work habits, and good discipline. The minimum education was Standard 7 or 8 (primary level), but this could be waived in case of workers who were of good character. [33]

The labor-intensive approach to TAZARA construction meant that the majority of workers would be engaged in strenuous manual labor in challenging environmental conditions. For this reason, physical fitness was a primary requirement for those seeking to work on the railway. Rogatus Nyumayo remembers that young men in Iringa had to submit to a physical examination, to ensure that they were fit for the demanding labor of railway work. "They measured us up like we were soldiers," he recalled. Those who did not measure up were left behind. Rogatus had been living in Iringa in 1971 when he responded to an announcement posted at the TANU office there. "They took 800 people from Iringa in one day," he remembers, "in about five buses from Iringa town. They took us straight to camp at Mkela Base Camp, to work on the tunnels. After about three days they divided us up into work teams."[34]

For Tanzania and Zambia, recruitment criteria reflected the importance of building national identity and pride in TAZARA for both countries, although in the end the project hired more Tanzanian than Zambian workers.[35] It was a political priority to recruit a workforce that represented not only both countries but also diverse regional origins. In Tanzania, recruitment was carried out under the auspices of the national party, TANU, and announcements were sent out throughout the country where they were posted at the local TANU offices.[36] At the time there were few employment opportunities for young men, particularly those with minimal education and skills. Andrew Mangile learned of TAZARA through the TANU Labor Office in Dar es Salaam where he had been checking every two or three weeks for news of a job. He was hired by the project on October 31, 1969, and assigned to the Kurasini base camp where he was in charge of the storehouse of water pipes.[37]

Workers were also recruited through the Tanzanian National Service or JKT (*Jeshi la Kujenga Taifa*). A group of seven-thousand Tanzanian youths were recruited from the National Service in 1970, given a two-week training program including military drill, and then sent out to construction camps between Dar es Salaam and Mlimba.[38] Most of the recruits who responded to this national campaign were young men aged sixteen to twenty-five (this was in contrast to the Chinese workers, who tended to be in their thirties and forties), and few had much education beyond the primary level.[39]

Technical Training: Workshops

Training of the African workers was approached in three ways. A carefully selected group of around 1,700 workers were given formal education in TAZARA workshops, particularly as the construction phase of the project neared completion and the operations phase began. Railway training schools were opened at Mang'ula (1971), Mgulani (1972), and Mbeya (1974) in Tanzania, and at Mpika in Zambia (1974). Mang'ula offered courses on four topics: construction and maintenance of the permanent way and bridges; telecommunications; signaling; and locomotive driving. A smaller number of workers were sent to China for further studies; some two-hundred Tanzanians and Zambians were sent to Beijing Jiaotong University in 1972 for a two-year training course, and some of these graduates returned later for further study.[40]

The teaching staff at Beijing Jiaotong University was responsible for establishing the curriculum, textbooks, and instruction for the training of African railway workers, both at the African workshops and also in China. They faced several difficult challenges as they carried out this responsibility, challenges that were directly related to the political and economic circumstances of the time. When they were first asked to pull together a foreign assistance training team in 1970 and 1971, the needed teaching staff was no longer at their Beijing university campus but had been relocated to the countryside, where they were working as manual laborers on railway construction sites. Once the selected teachers had been identified and located, they were then reviewed by party leaders and evaluated according to their technical skills as well as their character and background.

For the workshops in Africa, meanwhile, a suitable curriculum, including English-language teaching materials, had to be developed. Here, the training staff faced additional challenges. Their desire to carry out construction work at a fast pace led some project leaders to encourage implementation of short-term training sessions for the technicians and technical workers in Africa; some even proposed workshops of only one or two weeks. This was hardly an adequate timeframe for preparing inexperienced African recruits. At the same time, there was an expectation in some quarters that teaching should reflect the innovations of China's revolutionary period, including an emphasis on enduring bitterness, working hard under pressure, and maintaining revolutionary optimism. For those charged with designing courses and training the African workforce, these were conflicting imperatives and caused a great deal of confusion. In interviews for a CCTV documentary series on China–Africa foreign assistance, Beijing Jiaotong University professors recalled that even producing a textbook during this time involved lengthy considerations of how to combine ideological and technical content, and in what proportions.[41]

At Beijing Jiaotong University the normal course of study for training Chinese railway technicians had lasted four years before the Cultural Revolution. When they were asked to train the African workers for TAZARA, however, project leaders stressed the urgency of developing personnel in a short period of time, so the course was reduced in length to two-and-a-half years. The first six months of this study period was devoted to an intensive language course, because technical instruction was carried out in Chinese. Special teaching materials also had to be developed by the university staff members, to accommodate the language barrier as well as the specific requirements of the TAZARA project. Thus the instructional methodology that the instructors developed stressed the importance of learning skills in a short period of time, both in the classroom and through practice.

The African trainees were taken out for practical internships on the Chinese railway system between 1972 and 1974, where they not only worked in factories, but also practiced working as conductors, carrying out such tasks as ticket collecting and accounting. Passengers were notified in advance that a group of African railway students would be checking their tickets, so that they would not be startled by their presence.[42]

Technical Training: Teaching by Example

Teaching through practice was also at the core of training methodology for the majority of the Africans who worked on the project. For most of these TAZARA workers, technology transfer took place on the job, not through formal training but through the Chinese practice at this time of "teaching by example." The managers of Chinese projects in Africa approached worker mobilization through a combination of rhetoric and exhortation, teaching and demonstration. According to this model, young African workers would learn new skills through practical work as they labored alongside their Chinese counterparts, supplemented with occasional theoretical lectures.[43] They would be exposed to the work culture of industriousness and hard work, including the organization of the workday into hourly shifts and other forms of discipline. During the construction of TAZARA, these work values were conveyed in regular meetings, wherein workers were encouraged to ensure smooth transport in the sections that had already been completed, to do away with complacency and retain a revolutionary spirit, and to implement the guiding policy of hard struggle and self-reliance.[44] Teaching by example, according to a 1967 report on China–Tanzania technical cooperation, was "characteristic of the classless international proletariat anti-imperialist ideology," an ideology that would best be transmitted by "helping them learn to operate the machinery."[45]

This 1967 report on technology transfer during China's technical cooperation with Tanzania emphasized the simultaneous deployment of mechanical skills, revolutionary ideology, and practical lessons. In

7.1. Learning surveying techniques on the job.

its description of progress made at the Chinese-built Urafiki textile mill in Dar es Salaam, the report began by stressing the importance of sustaining Mao's ideology and revolution, moved on to emphasize the benefits of worker solidarity and practical cooperation, and then switched to technical specifications for certain types of dye and the width of cotton cloth. The last section of the report stressed the interconnectedness of ideology and practice through hands-on mentoring.

In oral interviews carried out in 2007–8, retired railway-construction workers in China and East Africa recalled in rich detail the ways that these work values and directives were experienced in everyday practice during construction. In response to a survey conducted in the mid-1980s, former TAZARA construction workers in Tanzania remembered that their Chinese supervisors had helped them the most by actually working together alongside them, "not just standing aside, hand-in-pocket, directing workers by finger-pointing."[46] African workers emphasized that the most positive aspect of their association with their Chinese counterparts was the educational instruction. "It was a true friendship," said John Gilbert of his relationship with Chinese technicians, "even if you did not understand something, they explained it to you until you understood it." Another worker stated, "The Chinese [expert] taught us with honesty. He left you knowing that you had learned your job well."[47]

Mr. Rao Xue De remembers his role as a teacher this way:

> In terms of construction we usually took the African workers with us and we taught them techniques hand-in-hand [手把手, *shou ba shou*, literally, "my hands hold your hands"]. For example, without payment we nurtured [培养, *pei yang*] the local people's ability to drive the small bulldozers and vehicles. We used body language if we couldn't communicate in [spoken] languages, and eventually all black workers were able to manage [those skills]. We nurtured a large number of technical workers; many of these men later became the core technicians of TAZARA and they participated in management.[48]

One retired Tanzanian worker remembers that, as a young man, he was discouraged after sustaining a minor injury at a construction site. His Chinese mentor tirelessly exhorted him to continue working despite the setback, and he went on to learn Chinese and become a highly placed railway engineer. Another Tanzanian worker remembers that after completing secondary school, he began working on the railway with the back-breaking job of splitting stones in a quarry in the forest. Because he was seen to be hard-working and to have good character, his Chinese mentors promoted him until he was finally selected to join the railway-operations staff. "We kept working with the Chinese for a long time," he remembered, "and then the Chinese left us on our own. Indeed, until today we are caring for the railway, we had grown experienced ourselves by that time."[49] The experiences of these two workers illustrate the way that worker-skills training at the most menial level on the TAZARA project could form the basis for promotion to a higher level of technical accomplishment and responsibility.

In practice, however, the emphasis on acceleration created a grueling pace of construction labor that led to dissatisfaction among many workers. The Chinese management was willing to push the workforce night and day to show what could be achieved—and to build African confidence—at a time when the world was watching. The teams that built tunnels between Mlimba and Makambako used electric lighting to allow work to continue twenty-four hours a day. John Gilbert remembers working at Kisaki building bridges as part of a twenty-four-hour crew. In the tunnels-section, workers put in successive eight-hour shifts around the clock: "You worked for eight hours, you then rested eight hours, then you started again," recalled Beatus Lihawa.[50] During resting shifts, the workers retreated to their temporary shelters in the worker camps. Electricity generated at the Base Camps allowed for day and night activity. At Mang'ula Base Camp, engineers who worked in the factories and workshops also put in twenty-four-hour shifts with rotating rest breaks. Retired Chinese technicians from the fifth group of the tunnels team remember that they began work at

7.2. Presidents Kaunda and Nyerere (center) inspecting a tunnel at Kisarawe Village with leaders Jin Hui and Pu Ke (from left), October 1, 1970. [Caption information from TAZARA archives photo gallery.]

four in the afternoon and continued throughout the night, working for sixteen-hour shifts and then resting for one eight-hour shift. They had to work quickly in order to complete their tasks before the onset of the rainy season. Retirees from this group remember that they were the most highly qualified and efficient of the tunnels-working groups; thus, even though their equipment was inferior to that of the others, they were able to lay two kilometers of rail bed per day.[51] While some of the other teams stopped working when the rainy season started, they remember, the fifth group persevered.

Tanzanians and Zambians had a mixed response to this approach to labor. Although many joined in and respected the Chinese enthusiasm for hard work, they were not always willing to endure such a strenuous timetable. Many Africans left the project, according to both Chinese and African accounts.[52] Conflicts took place, for example, when African workers completed their assigned duties before the end of the work shift. The workers felt that they had finished for the day and were entitled to rest. Their supervisors insisted that they take on additional work until the end of their shift. These conflicts over the definition of work and the workday were exacerbated by language difficulties.[53]

Many found the work to be so difficult and conditions so demanding that they abandoned their jobs. Desertion consequently became a problem.[54] Those who stayed with the project only managed to survive the suffering they endured in the difficult sections, according to John Gilbert, through their own fortitude: "We persevered here with the Chinese."[55] Rogatus Nyumayo used the same term when remembering the tunnels construction, saying that the work was challenging "but we ourselves just persevered."[56]

One retired Chinese supervisor explained the way that religion also got in the way of the labor regime. The Chinese were not religious and their construction schedule did not allow time to observe the Sabbath, he recalled, "because we simply could not stop halfway for weekend rest during our construction." This caused some opposition from Catholic missionaries who told their congregations that "workers should not go to work for the Chinese people on Sundays; otherwise God will not bless you."[57] There were also stories that circulated about missionaries who attempted to give copies of the Bible to Chinese workers, and these efforts to interfere put them in the camp of "imperialists, revisionists, and counterrevolutionaries" who were enemies of the project. The late Hashim Mdemu explained in an interview that as a Muslim, he was also frustrated that the work schedule did not allow time for him to conduct his prayers. This factor, along with the difficult working conditions he experienced at the Namawala subcamp, digging culverts, caused Mr. Mdemu to leave the project.[58]

The workplace experiences and resulting levels of expertise of the African workers differed depending upon the jobs to which they were assigned. Most began at the most menial level carrying out rudimentary and unskilled tasks, for example crushing rock in the quarry or digging out ditches and culverts. From the ranks of these workers the Chinese supervisors sought out the brightest pupils and those with special aptitude, for example the ability to learn Chinese, and then trained them for promotion to more technically advanced work. Liu Liyuan was in charge of handling the track-laying machine, which required an unusually high level of skill. He worked together with a small team of eight-to-twelve African workers who alternated in shifts of four. As the machine lifted up the heavy steel rails and then lowered them down onto the concrete sleepers, the workers were responsible for the delicate task of making sure that the rails were placed in exactly the right position. This required precise communication and "working together very harmoniously in a careful way," according to Mr. Liu, and the workers that he trained were very capable and bright. They started work at such a young age that he literally watched them grow up during the project, Mr. Liu recalled. "Within six months, one young man grew one foot in height."[59] These technical workers who were trained through close relationships with their Chinese mentors went on to become the core technicians and managers of the railway, and came to be recognized as the TAZARA "construction generation."

During TAZARA's construction there was a contradiction in the intention of railway authorities to accomplish their task ahead of schedule, on the one hand, and the Chinese development principle of conveying technical knowledge and skills to the African workforce.

7.3. Placing the concrete sleepers onto the railbed.

As Philip Snow put it, "Speed was a trademark of the construction teams, and training slowed them down."[60] It remained difficult for the Chinese to both mobilize and supervise a vast workforce with varying levels of experience, while simultaneously training that workforce to do the required tasks and to sustain the railway's operations into the future. These multiple goals were often contradictory in practice: the Chinese were both boss and teacher; the Africans both laborer and student.

In the end, the imperative of acceleration—of completing the railway successfully and ahead of time—prevailed over the ideal of workplace pedagogy. The number of workers that had received specialized training and promotion remained a small percentage of the overall workforce at the time of handing over in 1975, in particular in the areas of railway operations and maintenance. The Chinese government therefore agreed to provide additional assistance and training during a period of technical cooperation that lasted for ten years, from 1976 to 1986. During the first two years of cooperation some one-thousand Chinese railway experts continued to assist the railway with operations management, maintenance and repairs, and financial management. At the same time they provided instruction in the field and training in the technical workshops. For the first two years, from 1976 to 1978, each station had an African stationmaster that worked side by side with a Chinese partner, learning station-management skills through their daily activities. The African foremen who supervised the work gangs responsible for track inspection and maintenance also worked with Chinese partners in a similar way, learning on the job.[61] In subsequent years, the Chinese gradually withdrew from an active role and served primarily as advisers, reducing the number of personnel to 750 after 1978, down to 150 in the 1980s. Chinese instructors continued to teach courses at the training workshops, especially at Mpika training workshop in Zambia.[62]

Professor Peng Pingpan was one of the teachers who traveled to Zambia in 1975 along with two others from the technical institute of the Chengdu Second Railway Bureau. Professor Peng taught railway operations while his colleagues taught transportation and construction. Others who taught at the Mpika workshop were sent from diverse railway institutes throughout China, where they specialized in electronics and communications signals. Professor Peng recalled that the teaching methods used at Mpika included both classroom lessons and field practice, with a focus on practical rather than theoretical lessons. Professor Peng also participated with others from the Second Railway Bureau in writing a textbook on building bridge supports for use in Tanzania and Zambia between 1977 and 1979.[63]

Modernization and Development

Mr. Liu Yiyuan described witnessing the physical growth of the young Africans on his track-laying team, as their bodies grew and they matured into adults. Professors at Beijing Jiaotong University also watched the young African recruits in their charge develop discipline, maturity, and professionalism. The experience of railway work was one of growing up in other ways as well. Most of the African workers were from rural areas and had limited experience with machine technology beyond what they may have learned in primary school. For many of them it was their first time to be employed for a wage and to follow a structured and regimented work schedule. The African workers themselves describe their experiences during construction as a process of coming of age. They remember joining the workforce as young men, unmarried, many having served only briefly in the National Service. They recall that the experience of construction was demanding and difficult for them. At the same time, they developed skills and in some cases a viable trade that gave them a new position in society. The experience of building the railroad, wrote D. E. Stambuli after TAZARA's completion, had lifted workers and their families out of their deteriorated condition into "a modern civilized type of life."[64]

Themes of modernization and development were part of the ideology that shaped the railway construction project. These ideals were conveyed in worker meetings and circulated through the use of slogans and exhortation in the workplace. Yet just as work skills were most often transferred through hands-on experience and example, ideals of modernization were also passed on through person-to-person mentoring. This kind of mentoring relationship was made easier due to the age difference between the two groups. Retired African workers described their relationship with their Chinese counterparts as one of juniors and elders. They learned practical skills such as shoe repair, and were given advice on how to save their salaries and practice thrift. In some cases, the Chinese technicians helped the African workers by keeping their cash salaries for them in a safe place.[65] Thus the workplace pedagogy of modernization included not only labor practices but also life lessons.

At Beijing Jiaotong University, peer mentoring was used intentionally as a teaching method to help the African students learn more quickly. A group of around 30 recent graduates from the university was called back to the campus in 1971 and asked to accompany the African students in their classroom activities. They were also given English lessons so that they could facilitate communication and comprehension. The Chinese peer mentors accompanied their African classmates both on campus and off, visiting them in their dormitories and studying together with them, and also joining them on off-campus excursions and outings.[66]

The experience of working on TAZARA could also be a transformative one for the Chinese workers who spent two-to-four years of their lives far from home. In interviews, workers described becoming more knowledgeable about the world during a time when China was isolated and had few friends. During the journey by sea from Guangzhou, Chinese railway workers witnessed the bright lights of Hong Kong as well as the military conflict in Vietnam. Their ships were overflown by American fighter jets when they entered the South China Sea, and in Singapore Mr. Rao recalls the tensions that ensued after his ship docked next to a Soviet vessel. He was moved when he witnessed the gap in living conditions between China and two of the four "Asian tigers" (Hong Kong and Singapore), and felt the tensions of diplomatic relations with other countries firsthand, as "every aspect of life was tightly watched and controlled" during his twenty-one-day journey at sea.[67]

The Chinese workers also described their railway work in Africa as a liberating experience since they were exposed to new technical and management challenges. Mr. Wang Huimin described how he learned to repair British Land Rover engines and Japanese earth-moving machinery, technologies that were not available to him in China.[68] In this and other ways, he said, work on TAZARA opened his mind to new ways of thinking that benefited him greatly after the project was completed. Chinese railway technicians also described their exposure to local technologies used in rural African communities. The structures they built for housing and other purposes in the work camps used local materials, and they relied upon the help and knowledge of the African workers to construct them. They witnessed the grass-burning techniques that local farmers used on their fields, then adapted this knowledge to clear the way for surveying long distances in the grasslands.[69] Mr. Wang Huimin described experimenting with the use of sticky anthill clay as a way to stabilize soils in marshy areas, allowing them to build up stronger structures of wooden supports.[70]

The TAZARA railway technicians had to experiment in other ways to solve technical problems. They made adjustments to the steel used in the rails so that it could more easily withstand tropical temperatures as well as the corrosive effect of being stored next to the Indian Ocean for long periods of time.[71] A method for joining the rails using copper helped to avoid swelling of the seams during the hot weather.[72]

Most significantly, a special braking system had to be developed for the TAZARA rolling stock since the Tanzanian railways used air brakes whereas the Zambian railways used an older vacuum system. The adoption of this dual-braking system was described by retired technicians in Taiyuan:

> Tanzania used the air brake while Zambia used the vacuum brake. They were completely different, and neither agreed to make a compromise on this difference. Thus, there were arguments between the two countries, and the arguments were later promoted to a national level and finally had to be discussed during government negotiations. At last, Premier Zhou put forward a solution. Any problems that technicians do not understand should be handed over to the masses for resolution, because the masses may come up with better ideas. Hence, this issue was handed over to the February 7 Machine Factory. Several workers were selected to work on this problem. They came up with two sets of brakes. When entering Zambia, the air brake would be closed, and when entering Tanzania the vacuum brake would be switched off thereby solving this problem.[73]

This description of the way that workers from the February 7 Machine Factory solved the problem—a technical challenge that had been taken up to the national level—resonates with the themes of self-reliance and worker self-confidence that characterized Chinese domestic and international approaches to modernization at the time. In this version of events, it was Zhou Enlai who reminded the railway specialists that the masses had "better ideas" and therefore should take over the task of designing braking technology. Like the workers in the factories that Shirley Graham Du Bois visited, in this account workers used their creativity to develop a solution to a problem that had seemed intractable.

Conclusion

Dipesh Chakrabarty reminds us that Richard Wright asked about postcolonial Indonesia, "Where is the engineer who can build a project out of eighty million human lives, a project that can nourish them, sustain them, and yet have their voluntary loyalty?"[74] The real and symbolic role of the engineer during the TAZARA railway construction project could be transformative in some of the ways that Wright had imagined. For technology transfer in China-African development assistance at this time was expected not only to be material in form, but also to fulfill the ideological and pedagogical functions of modernization. Working on the railway project under the mentorship of Chinese engineering experts would make African youths into disciplined workers and good citizens, equipped with a larger vision of progress that enabled them to imagine the African people "marching on the path of self-reliance" and to plan the future of their civilizations.

From the beginning, the railway's planners had anticipated that the railway project would be completed ahead of schedule, to showcase the possibilities for Chinese development assistance through a highly visible project that had been rejected by Western donors. Chinese railway experts with skills and experience were recruited for the project, and those who were sent to Tanzania and Zambia included both high-level engineering experts and a large number of mid-level railway technicians.[75] At the same time, what was needed to make the project both sustainable and self-reliant was a trained and competent African workforce that could take on the railway management and operations after its completion. It was the mentoring that took place between these "experts" and the African "youth" that was most celebrated in public statements about construction—and most positively remembered by those who took part in the project.

Yet it can be difficult to distinguish between the figures of the Chinese engineer, the technician, and the worker during TAZARA's construction. This is due in part to the multiple roles that they played in official statements about the project, in practice in the workplace, and in worker memories. Chinese workers from the February 7 Machine Factory who had been trained as skilled machinists ended up doing completely different tasks during the TAZARA project, for example provisioning goods.[76] In Africa, the terminology used for different participants in the project could also be confusing. All of the Chinese participants were referred to as "experts" or *wataalamu* in Tanzania whether they were high-level engineers or mid-level technicians. Tanzanian participants during construction were referred to in Chinese sources as "friends" while in the Tanzanian press they were most often referred to not as workers at all but as youths or *vijana* in Kiswahili, emphasizing their role in nation building.

Although the role of the engineer could be viewed as a central one in decolonization in the case of TAZARA, at the same time the ideology of the Cultural Revolution emphasized the role of the "masses"—the ordinary workers—in solving technical problems, as the quotation above from the February 7 Machine Factory illustrates. There are therefore, two related contradictions in the TAZARA project's modernization and development model. On the one hand, the project required the sustained contribution of China's trained and experienced engineers in order to succeed. On the other hand, during the project the role of everyday workers in solving technical problems—the self-reliance of the masses through their own creativity and innovation—was still foregrounded in the language of development. At the same time, the goal of completing the project ahead of time, along with other political imperatives, could be in direct conflict with the implementation of teaching methodologies that were required for a sustainable future. Thus the intersections between modernization, pedagogy, and anti-imperialism during the project were complex and contradictory. It was only during the ten-year commitment to technical cooperation after TAZARA's completion (during the post-Mao era of reform) that railway technology transfer had the most potential to fulfill the project's pedagogical goals, in particular for those African technicians who returned to China for further study.

Acknowledgments

It would not have been possible to collect the materials presented here without the collaboration and friendship of Li Baoping and Liu Haifang. Research assistance from Wayne Soon, Claire Yanjing Du, Ru Sheng, and Alan Goodyear was also indispensable. Others whose generosity contributed to this chapter include Shen Xipeng, Peng Tao, and Lu Duanfang.

Notes

1. "Tanzania, Zambia celebrate railway completion," *North China News Agency,* October 24, 1975.

2. Zhang Tieshan, *Youyi Zhilu: Yuanjian Tanzan Tielu Jishi* 友谊之路：援建坦赞铁路纪实 [The road of friendship: the memoirs of the development assistance of the Tanzania–Zambia railroad] (Beijing: Zhongguo Duiwai Jingji Maoyi Chuban She, 1999), 220; Interview with Zhang Tieshan, Tianjin, August 2, 2008.

3. Homi Bhabha developed the concept of the "post-colonial time lag," drawing on Frantz Fanon's idea of "belatedness," in Homi Bhabha, *The Location of Culture* (London: Routledge, 1994).

4. William Edgett Smith, *We Must Run While They Walk: A Portrait of Africa's Julius Nyerere* (New York: Random House, 1971).

5. "Kaunda's Attitude towards Building TAZARA, Telegraph from Chinese Embassy in Zambia, 1965, August 17," 2. Chinese Ministry of Foreign Affairs Archives 108-00649-02.

6. See Gary Burgess's essay in this volume for more on citizenship, nation-building, and modernization in Zanzibar and the Tanzanian mainland during this period.

7. Deborah Bräutigam, *Chinese Aid and African Development: Exporting Green Revolution* (London: Macmillan, 1998), 23; see also Law Yu Fai, *Chinese Foreign Aid: A Study of Its Nature and Goals, 1950-1982* (Fort Lauderdale, FL: Verlag Breitenbach, 1984).

8. "Tanzania, Zambia celebrate railway completion," *North China News Agency,* October 24, 1975.

9. Lu Duanfang, *Remaking Chinese Urban Form: Modernity, Scarcity and Space, 1949–2005* (New York: Routledge, 2006), 6.

10. Sigrid Schmalzer, "On the Appropriate Use of Rose-colored Glasses: Reflections on Science in Socialist China," *Isis* 98, no. 3 (2007): 571–83; Sigrid Schmalzer, "Labor Created Humanity: Cultural Revolution Science on Its Own Terms," in *The Chinese Revolution as History*, eds. Joseph Esherick, Paul Pickowicz, and Andrew Walder (Stanford: Stanford University Press, 2006), 185–210.

11. Interview with Zhang Tieshan, Tianjin, August 2, 2008.

12. For more background on Shirley Graham Du Bois' life, see Gerald Horne, *Race Woman: The Lives of Shirley Graham Du Bois* (New York: New York University Press, 2000).

13. Shirley Graham Du Bois, "Travel Diary, China 1967," entry for June 16, 1967. MC476-4.20v, Schlesinger Library, Radcliffe Institute, Harvard University.

14. Shirley Graham Du Bois, "China Visit, 1967: Travel Diary Transcript," 2–4. MC476-4, Schlesinger Library, Radcliffe Institute, Harvard University.

15. Schmalzer, "Labor Created Humanity," 186–89.

16. Du Bois, "Travel Diary, China 1967," entry for June 16, 1967.

17. Du Bois, "Travel Diary, China 1974," MC476-5.1v. Schlesinger Library, Radcliffe Institute, Harvard University. For a description of the ideal of the worker–scientist during the Cultural Revolution, see Schmalzer, "On the Appropriate Use of Rose-colored Glasses." For a discussion of postcolonial time and "catching up" in China, see Duanfang, *Remaking Chinese Urban Form*. On postcolonial time, space, and ideas of "backwardness," see also Akhil Gupta, *Postcolonial Developments: Agriculture in the Making of Modern India* (Durham: Duke University Press, 1998).

18. "Plans for hosting Tanzanian Health Delegation," Shanghai Municipal Archives B242-3-398, 44.

19. When TAZARA crossed the border into Zambia in 1973, the headline in the *Times of Zambia* announced TAZARA BEATS SCHEDULE BY TWO YEARS, foregrounding the theme of acceleration for African readers. *Times of Zambia,* August 25, 1973. In fact this was an exaggeration; Tanzania's TANU party reported that the crossing took place one year and one month earlier than anticipated. "Utekelezaji wa Maazimio ya Mkutano Mkuu wa 15 Kichama," Tanganyika African National Union, Dar es Salaam, 1973.

20. Ma Luhua, "Mu Mofang Li Jing Qiaoqiao" 木模房里静悄悄 [Silence in the wooden mold workshop], in *Youyi De Caihong* 友谊的彩虹 [Rainbow of friendship], compiled by Youyi De Caihong Bianji Xiaozu 友谊的彩虹编辑小组 [Rainbow of friendship editing team], (Peking: Renmin Wenxue Chuban She, 1975). Translation by Claire Yanjing Du.

21. These poems were part of a larger genre of poetry published during the Cultural Revolution penned by the "masses" of workers and peasants. Duanfang, *Remaking Chinese Urban Form*, 108–9.

22. Unknown Poet, "Gongdi Ketang Jiancai," 工地课堂剪彩 [Science in field classrooms], in *Youyi De Caihong* 友谊的彩虹 [Rainbow of friendship], compiled by Youyi De Caihong Bianji Xiaozu 友谊的彩虹编辑小组 [Rainbow of friendship editing team].

23. Interview with Jin Hui, Beijing, July 5, 2007.

24. Zhang, *The Road of Friendship*, 135–37. Translation by Claire Yanjing Du.

25. George T. Yu, *China's Africa Policy: A Study of Tanzania* (New York: Praeger, 1975), 132. See also George T. Yu, "Working on the Railroad: China and the Tanzania–Zambia Railway," *Asian Survey,* 11, no. 11 (1971): 1101–17.

26. Some retired Chinese railway workers also recalled a fourth recruitment criterion, that workers have wives and children at home, which would help ensure their return to China.

27. Interview with Rao Xue De, Chengdu, September 2, 2008. Interview by Ye Xiaolin, translation by Claire Yanjing Du.

28. Interview with Peng Pingpan, Chengdu, September 3, 2008. Interview by Ye Xiaolin, translation by Claire Yanjing Du.

29. Interview with Zhang Deshun, Taiyuan, October 20, 2008.

30. Interview with retired workers in Taiyuan, October 20, 2008. Translation by Claire Yanjing Du.

31. Interviews with retired workers in Sichuan, Taiyuan, and Tianjin, August–October 2008.

32. Interview with Guo Bao Jun, Guangzhou, November 2, 2008. Translation by Claire Yanjing Du.

33. "Local Workers' Participation in the Railway Construction," TAZARA Brief Progress Report, March 3, 1970, National Archives of Zambia (NAZ) MFA 1/286/144, 4.

34. Interview with Rogatus Nyumayo, Mlimba, July 26, 2000.

35. Between 1969 and the end of 1972 the majority of the workers were from Tanzania. After railway construction crossed the border in 1973 the emphasis shifted to Zambian workers, but overall the project hired more Tanzanians than Zambians. *TAZARA Annual Report and Accounts for 1973/74*, 12.

36. Interview with Benedict Mkanyago, Mchombe, July 7, 2000.

37. Interview with Andrew John Mangile, "Aboard Kipisi Train," July 26, 2000.

38. Sendaro, Ali Mohammed, "Workers' Efficiency, Motivation and Management: The Case of the Tanzania–Zambia Railway Construction," PhD dissertation, University of Dar es Salaam, 1987, 199-205; D. D. S. M. Momello, "Final Report on Tunnels Construction, Mkela Base Camp," 1972, 13; *Standard*, February 19, 1970.

39. Momello, "Final Report."

40. TAZARA "Annual Report," 1973/4, 6.

41. CCTV documentary film, *Passions Dedicated to Africa*, 2006; Personal communication with Ru Sheng, August 2009.

42. Ibid.

43. "Minutes of Talks between the Railway Delegation of the Government of the People's Republic of China and the Railway Delegations of the Governments of the United Republic of Tanzania and the Republic of Zambia Concerning the Preparatory Work for the Construction of the Tanzania/Zambia Railway," NAZ MFA 1/286/115.

44. Zhang, *The Road of Friendship*.

45. "China's Aid to Tanzania's Textile Mills Unit: Final Report on Technical

Cooperation, July 1968–June 1969," Shanghai Municipal Archives, B124-3-240-1, 6–15. Translation by Hu Lingque.

46. Sendaro, "Workers' Efficiency," 239.

47. Interview with Rogatus Nyumayo, Mlimba, July 26, 2000.

48. Interview with Rao Xue De, Chengdu, Sichuan, September 2, 2008. Interview by Ye Xiaolin, translation by Claire Yanjing Du.

49. Interview with Hosea Mngata, Mlimba, 2000.

50. Interview with Beatus Lihawa, Mlimba, July 20, 2000; Momello, "Final Report," 9.

51. Interview with retired railway workers in Zhaoqing, November 3, 2008.

52. There are no data currently available to show actual numbers of African workers who joined and left the project over its duration. Project leader Jin Hui stated that because African workers would come and go, it was difficult to maintain a stable labor force. Interview with Jin Hui, Beijing, July 5, 2007.

53. Sendaro, "Workers' Efficiency," 187. Philip Snow, *The Star Raft: China's Encounter with Africa* (London: Weidenfeld and Nicolson, 1988), 173. These conflicts are similar to those experienced in colonial work settings. See, for example, Keletso Atkins, *The Moon Is Dead, Give Us Our Money! The Cultural Origins of a Zulu Work Ethic* (Portsmouth, NH: Heinemann, 1993); Frederick Cooper, "Colonizing Time: Work Rhythms and Labor Conflict in Colonial Mombasa," in *Colonialism and Culture,* ed. Nicholas B. Dirks (Ann Arbor: University of Michigan Press, 1992): 209–46.

54. Interviews with Rogatus Nyumayo, Mlimba, July 26, 2000; Salum Mwasenga, Mang'ula, July 30, 2000; Hashim Mdemu, Ifakara, June 2000. Richard Hall and Hugh Peyman, *The Great Uhuru Railway: China's Showpiece in Africa* (London: Gollancz, 1976), 128.

55. Interview with John Gilbert and Hosea Mngata, Ifakara, April 20, 2000.

56. Interview with Rogatus Nyumayo, Mlimba, July 26, 2000.

57. Interview with retired workers in Taiyuan, October 2008.

58. Interview with Hashim Mdemu, Ifakara, 2000.

59. Interview with Liu Liyuan, Tianjin, August 2, 2008. Translation by Liu Haifang.

60. Snow, *The Star Raft,* 164.

61. Interview with Du Jian, Beijing, August 2008.

62. Zhang, *The Road of Friendship.* Translation by Claire Yanjing Du.

63. Interview with Peng Pingpan, Chengdu, September 3, 2008. Interview by Ye Xiaolin, translation by Claire Yanjing Du.

64. D. E. Stambuli, "Staff Commentary," appendix 9 in "Final Report," Momello, 1972. These experiences were similar to those described by participants in colonial-railway projects. See Lisa Lindsay, "Money, Marriage and

Masculinity on the Colonial Nigerian Railway," in *Men and Masculinities in Modern Africa,* eds. Lisa Lindsay and Stephan Miescher (Portsmouth, NH: Heinemann, 2003), 150.

65. Interview with Du Jian, Beijing, August 2008.

66. CCTV documentary film, *Passions Dedicated to Africa,* 2006; Personal communication with Ru Sheng, August 2009.

67. Interview with Rao Xue De, Chengdu, Sichuan, September 2, 2008. Interview by Ye Xiaolin, translation by Claire Yanjing Du.

68. Interview with Wang Huimin, Tianjin, July 6, 2007. Translation by Wayne Soon.

69. Zhang, *The Road of Friendship,* 178-80.

70. Interview with Wang Huimin, Tianjin, July 6, 2007. Translation by Wayne Soon.

71. According to workers interviewed in Taiyuan, copper and manganese were added to the steel in the factory in China. Interview with retired workers in Taiyuan, October 2008.

72. Interview with Liu Liyuan, Tianjin, August 2, 2008. Translation by Liu Haifang.

73. Interview with retired workers in Taiyuan, October, 2008.

74. Richard Wright, *The Color Curtain: A Report on the Bandung Conference* (London: D. Dobson, 1956), 132, as cited in Chakrabarty in this volume.

75. The question of Chinese participation in the project is in part the result of the lack of reliable data on the numbers of workers who went to Africa, their background qualifications, and experience. New research being carried out by Shen Xipeng of East China Normal University should help make this question more clear.

76. Interview with retired factory workers at February 7 Machine Factory, Beijing, April 10, 2009.

8

Tricontinentalism in Question

The Cold War Politics of Alex La Guma and
the African National Congress

Christopher J. Lee

IN JANUARY 1971, Oliver Tambo in his capacity as president of the
exiled African National Congress (ANC) delivered an address to a
meeting of the Afro-Asian Peoples' Solidarity Organization (AAPSO)
held in Tripoli, Libya. Citing the accomplishments and setbacks since
the historic 1957 founding of AAPSO in Cairo, he remarked that "we
see not only the new flags of freedom flying where once colonialism
ruled supreme," but the fact that "the strongholds of imperialism, colonialism, neo-colonialism and racism are being challenged, harassed
and attacked in a global anti-imperialist offensive which, even in the
short space of time since the last meeting of the Council, has assumed
a new intensity and a new ferocity."[1] Among the struggles that Tambo
listed as part of this global effort included the Vietnam War, the
Arab–Israeli conflict, the African American civil rights movement,
the anticolonial struggle in Guinea-Bissau, and the regional effort
found in southern Africa against "an imperialist-backed alliance of
Portuguese colonialists, Rhodesia racists and South African fascists."[2]
In sum, Tambo remarked that the "Afro-Asian revolution" remained

"an unfinished revolution," even though there was "clear evidence that imperialism is losing ground."[3] He recommended that more funding and material support be secured to aid the struggles he identified and that AAPSO "initiate a new and powerful campaign to sink all differences and forge a solid united front of all anti-imperialist forces."[4]

This chapter is concerned with the placement of South Africa's antiapartheid struggle within a context of Afro-Asian revolution as described by Tambo. By extension, it questions the position of South Africa within broader histories of decolonization during the latter half of the 20th century. Comparing the antiapartheid cause to other movements, Rob Nixon has written that no "other post–World War II struggle for decolonization has been so fully globalized; no other has magnetized so many people across such national divides, or imbued them with such a resilient sense of common cause."[5] Although Nixon is entirely correct about the global support that eventually ensued, the South African struggle has not always fit easily into a paradigm of decolonization. Robert Thornton, for example, has made the basic point that South Africa's achievement of self-governing status within the British Commonwealth in 1910 marked its transition to postcolonial status.[6] This view consequently suggests that the antiapartheid movement approximated civil-rights struggles found elsewhere, a paradigm further reinforced by a number of comparative histories, particularly with the United States.[7] In contrast, Mahmood Mamdani has argued for the colonial structure of apartheid rule and that the South African situation must not be seen as exceptional, but part of a broader political pattern found in sub-Saharan Africa. From this vantage point, the antiapartheid movement can be seen as fundamentally anticolonial in character.[8]

This academic question of definition equally engaged South African activist–intellectuals at the time. Given the longevity of 20th-century activism that spanned both segregation (1910–48) and apartheid (1948–94) eras, this essay does not intend to decide definitively which of these two paradigms is more useful or accurate. Rather, it explores how these competing views evolved on the ground, particularly in relation to the shift from activism internal to South Africa to activism positioned in the global public sphere that occurred during the

1960s. Although organizations had cultivated transnational conversations prior to the 1960s and political activism continued inside its borders—particularly through the rise of the Black Consciousness Movement, military activities of the Umkhonto we Sizwe (MK), and later the United Democratic Front (UDF) during the late 1960s, 1970s, and 1980s—it is this transition to exile and its intersection with contemporary conflicts in Southeast Asia, the Middle East, and southern Africa that more completely defined the antiapartheid struggle as anticolonial in character. The anti-imperial politics of Afro-Asian solidarity played a crucial role in this transformation. Working within this context of late decolonization, South African activist–intellectuals utilized an evolving political language and rhetoric to make sense of their situation and how it approximated political conditions found elsewhere. In sum, a diplomatic politics of recognition took hold, distinguished by a set of comparative political practices that employed categories such as "colonialism," "imperialism," and "anti-imperialism" to create transnational political alignments and initiate new forms of political community during the cold war era. Although South Africa was not a formal participant at the 1955 Bandung conference, the ANC did take active part in the organizations and meetings it inspired in the decades that followed. Indeed, Tambo's 1971 speech on the importance of Afro-Asian solidarity reflected a broader strategic shift following the 1969 Morogoro Conference in Tanzania that sought to reassert the political prominence of the ANC after the setbacks of the early 1960s. The 1963–64 Rivonia Trial and its repercussions of exile and imprisonment for a number of activists—Nelson Mandela being one among many—forced the ANC to escalate its approach of revolutionary armed struggle via its military branch, the MK, thus approximating the approach of other anticolonial movements found in southern Africa and elsewhere. Under Tambo's leadership, the ANC went on to establish and maintain a number of local missions throughout postcolonial Africa and Asia, including Egypt, Ghana, Nigeria, and India.

To advance these diplomatic efforts required personnel on the ground, who could interpret the South African cause and explain why it should garner support across the postcolonial world. This essay focuses on Alex La Guma as one of these figures. La Guma is better known today as a writer who produced a sequence of novels centered on Cape Town during the apartheid period. However, his career as an exiled representative for the ANC in London and Havana and as a prominent member of the Permanent Bureau of Afro-Asian Writers, a cultural branch of AAPSO, speak to the complex set of international politics that he and many other South African activists entered during the cold war period. His life helps to answer the basic question regarding the meaning of tricontinentalism, with its sweeping politics and diverse locales, for individual people. La Guma is particularly well-poised as an example of South African engagement with tricontinental politics, given his status as an author and his consequent abilities as a political and social observer, a skill seen in his fiction and non-fiction writing alike. But he was not alone. Figures such as him, Tambo, Ruth First, and others helped generate transnational conversations and the comparative recognition mentioned previously through correspondence, travel,

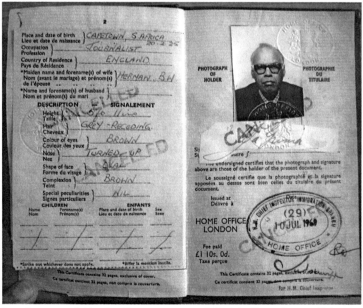

8.1. Passport of Alex La Guma, courtesy of the Mayibuye Centre, University of the Western Cape.

and exile. In sum, this chapter uses the life of La Guma as a lens for examining this complex political period and, by doing so, to demonstrate how the antiapartheid struggle intersected with a broader pattern of late decolonization that appeared in the post-Bandung era—a situation that extended, and complicated, that meeting's legacies.[9]

Origins, Careers, Politics

Biography is a genre that has tentatively emerged within postcolonial scholarship. Although biographies and autobiographies of political leaders are common, the recent aim of this approach has been to examine more personal angles to anticolonial political struggles and expansive postcolonial situations that defy easy narration. Antoinette Burton, for example, has explored the life of Santha Rama Rau—a South Asian writer and intellectual who garnered acclaim in the United States after World War II—to understand how individual lives intersected with and interpreted broader patterns of social change, in her case British decolonization and the rise of American power in its place during the cold war period. Individual lives provide unique "ways of seeing and knowing" that evince the political and personal dilemmas that people face, beyond chronological labels of *postcolonial* or *cold war* that can subsume such details.[10] Indeed, Burton argues for the expression *career* over *biography* to emphasize the need to understand how lives are influenced by certain relations of power—situations that often fragmented lives—rather than being a mere compilation or consolidation of facts.[11] The interaction between private and public life often rendered such senses of wholeness as figments of the historical imagination rather than an accurate reflection of one's self-conscious subjectivity. Diana Wylie has addressed similar issues in her biography of Thami Mnyele, an activist and artist for the ANC, who lived in exile in Botswana during the late 1970s and 1980s. With limited written documentation, Wylie's study works on several levels, providing a life history of an artist–activist who remained marginalized, despite his talent, but also a portrait of how such people negotiated extreme political circumstances beyond their control. The antiapartheid struggle both mitigated and enhanced his artistic career, defining his public and private life to the point that his involvement ultimately led to his premature death in 1985, through a cross-border raid against ANC activists by the South African military.[12]

The life of Alex La Guma fits into a similar framework. Like Mnyele and others who went into exile, little written documentation is left, reflecting the instability of living under conditions of near-constant uncertainty. Perusing his personal papers, which are archived at the University of the Western Cape's Mayibuye Centre, scrapbook newspaper clippings and occasional correspondence, much of it official rather than personal, are all that remain. However, several items stand out—namely, his passports and a map of his travel destinations while in exile, which include places scattered across Latin America, Europe, Africa, the Middle East, and Asia. This visual evidence not only points to the limits of labeling him as simply a "South African writer," but equally underscores the cold war internationalism of his political work. In a number of ways, the tricontinentalism of the last two decades of his life summarize a career that had deep roots.

Born in 1925 in the District Six neighborhood of Cape Town, La Guma grew up in a household that fundamentally influenced his social and political views. His father, James La Guma, was involved with the Industrial and Commercial Workers' Union (ICU) as Assistant General Secretary under Clements Kadalie during the early 1920s, and by 1925 he had joined the Communist Party of South Africa (CPSA). In 1927, the senior La Guma participated in the historic meeting of the League Against Imperialism held in Brussels, one of the key issues being the right to self-determination among colonized peoples. Following his father's political path, Alex joined the Young Communist League in 1947, the South African Coloured Peoples' Organization (SACPO) in 1954, and later the ANC. In December 1956, Alex La Guma was arrested along with 155 other activists as part of the infamous Treason Trial that lasted until 1961. He went into exile in 1966.

Alex died in 1985 while living in Cuba, then serving as the ANC representative for the Caribbean and Latin America. By the end of his life, he had published four novels, a collection of stories, an edited book on apartheid, and a memoir of his travels in the Soviet Union.[13]

8.2. Passport of Alex La Guma, courtesy of Mayibuye Centre, University of the Western Cape.

Not only had he achieved the respect of African writers such as Wole Soyinka and Ngũgĩ wa Thiong'o, but he had also drawn wider international attention through the receipt of a Chevalier des Arts et Lettres from the French government and a Soviet Order of Friendship of the Peoples, both in 1985. His work has since received increasing posthumous critical attention, with particular focus on the connections between his political life and his fiction. Kathleen Balutansky, in an early and prevailing assessment, has argued that these two aspects are inseparable, comprising an aesthetics that underscore the dissolution of the individual in favor of the political collective.[14] Abdul Jan-Mohamed has similarly placed La Guma's work within a theory of Manichean aesthetics, where a dialectical opposition exists between the "assumption that each individual has the right to live a decent life and his depiction of the actual deprivation of that right."[15] La Guma's fictive portrayals and factual experiences of marginalization and exile therefore represent "a more dramatic version of the *generic* exclusion experienced by all nonwhite South Africans."[16] Through the inseparability of his politics and aesthetics, Alex La Guma has consequently come to symbolize the archetype of the writer-as-activist.[17]

However, the critical focus on his fiction, particularly his Cape Town–centered novels, has left aside aspects of his political career that speak to the tricontinental politics that he came to embrace personally and as an ANC representative. Although his fiction and political life continued to address South Africa, his activity as a member of the Permanent Bureau of Afro-Asian Writers based in Cairo—which awarded him its Lotus Prize for Literature in 1969—introduced him to a wider literary and political audience, taking him throughout sub-Saharan Africa, Latin America, and Asia. His short stories "Come Back to Tashkent" (1968) and "Thang's Bicycle" (1976) reflect on these travels, to Soviet Central Asia and Vietnam respectively. Their publication in the literary journal *Lotus: Afro-Asian Writings*, which was the key periodical of the Bureau, further asserted La Guma's sense of literary and political solidarity with writers from across Africa, Asia, and the Middle East. In his essay "Literature and Life" (1970) published

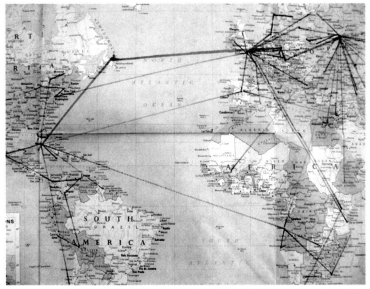

8.3. Detail of personal map, courtesy of Mayibuye Centre, University of the Western Cape.

in *Lotus*, he cited not only the role of writers in revolutionary struggle, but noted the anti-imperial affinities between movements found in Southeast Asia and southern Africa. "The people of Vietnam, the people of Portuguese colonies, of Namibia, Zimbabwe[, and] South Africa who are today waging an armed struggle for national liberation and independence simultaneously struggle for the rebirth of their national cultures," he insisted.[18]

Beyond contributing to *Lotus*, La Guma worked as an active member of its editorial board and eventually became the Acting Secretary General of the Permanent Bureau during the late 1970s and early 1980s. His political and literary commitments therefore not only became more closely intertwined, but evolved as his life in exile became more expansive, linking the antiapartheid struggle to social movements found in other parts of the world. Through over a dozen pieces that appeared in *Lotus* as well as contributions to such journals as *Présence Africaine*, *Moscow News*, and the *Moscow Literary Gazette*, La Guma's writing spoke for the South African cause to an international Afro-Asian audience, helping build tricontinental connections that had developed through the 1955 Bandung conference, the 1961 establishment of the Non-Aligned Movement, and the 1966 founding of the Organization of Solidarity with the People of Asia, Africa, and Latin America, or OSPAAAL. Similar to other intellectuals of his generation, La Guma faced a changing set of questions over political ideas, strategy, and party affiliation during the course of his life. The longevity of white-minority rule ensured this predicament of change and progression. Yet his career as both a writer and activist offer a firsthand view as to how activist–intellectuals confronted difficult issues of translating global political ideas to the South African context, as well as presenting the antiapartheid cause to sympathetic supporters beyond its borders. Resolving these aims posed a distinct challenge of reconciling ideology with ground-level facts through the strengths and limitations of political rhetoric. But as an exiled ANC activist based in London and Havana, La Guma was, by constrained circumstance and political need, forced to.

It is important here to situate James La Guma as an influence in Alex's internationalist sensibility.[19] As mentioned previously, the elder

La Guma had attended the 1927 League Against Imperialism meeting—an important precursor to the 1955 Bandung conference, given its focus on the colonial-world future—as part of the South African delegation, which also included J. T. Gumede of the ANC and Daniel Colrane of the South African Trade Union Congress. They went on to meet with Soviet officials in the USSR, including Nikolai Bukharin, with whom they developed the once-controversial "Native Republic" thesis. Drawing upon the resolutions of the League Against Imperialism meeting, this political program had two main components that essentially hinged on the central question, described at the start of this chapter, as to whether South Africa could be defined as a colonial situation. It answered this in the affirmative. Arguing for national self-determination as the initial step toward socialist revolution in South Africa, it interpreted South Africa as a colony, despite the Union's self-governing status since 1910. Second, it located the origin of revolutionary change not to urban workers but to the rural peasantry. Unifying these principles was the perspective that the concerns of black South Africans should take precedent, that political sovereignty on the basis of majority interest established the needed premise for socialist revolution to take place. This directive from the Comintern and the decisive shift it constituted generated enormous internal debate about its viability, particular among white leaders and workers who held key positions within the CPSA. As Allison Drew has written, the notion of a "Native Republic" was seen as an anticolonial parallel to the nationalist "Black Republic" and "Africa for the Africans" slogans of Marcus Garvey and other pan-Africanists that the CPSA had previously criticized.[20]

However, a shift in strategy was deemed necessary. An increasingly competitive relationship with the ICU, an uncertain relationship with the Comintern, and unavoidable questions in the socialist world as to how to address colonialism and Wilsonian nationalism elevated the necessity of developing a cohesive program of action.[21] James La Guma played a crucial part in the eventual acceptance of this proto-anticolonial policy, a role Alex describes in a biography of his father that went unpublished during both of their lifetimes.[22] Although the Comintern was perceived as correct from a long-term strategic standpoint, S. P. Bunting, the CPSA leader, believed the thesis weakened unity in the short-term and posed the specter of a "race war."[23] It appeared less threatening to La Guma, who began to commit much of his energy to the ANC. When invited to return to the Soviet Union later in the year for the tenth anniversary of the October Revolution, Bunting was reluctant to have La Guma reprise his role as an intermediary for the CPSA. Not only did he prefer someone less involved with the ANC, but Bunting also expressed trepidation at any "new tasks" that would be "drawn up by people with insufficient knowledge of South African affairs."[24] James La Guma did go, however, and he submitted to the Comintern a paper entitled "Report on the South African Situation in the Party" detailing the dissent the thesis had generated.

A more thorough debate took place upon his return. It was not entirely along racial lines, yet the division between Bunting and La Guma—between "equating all whites with imperialism" versus educating "white workers that their future lay in unity with blacks," as depicted by Alex—was largely defined by such implications.[25] A set of irreconcilable tensions took hold, and in April 1928, La Guma moved on to become general secretary of the Federation of Non-European Trade Unions. Meanwhile, Bunting and other CPSA members traveled in July and August to the USSR to attend the Sixth Congress of the Comintern with the hope of presenting their contrary position. Eddie Roux, for example, argued for the revolutionary potential of white workers and against the racial dynamic intrinsic to the Native Republic thesis. Bunting's final speech at the conference extended this position. A "native republic" slogan would simply exacerbate tensions between white and black workers and white and black South Africans generally.[26] Yet the outcome of this Moscow visit resulted in a greater sense of clarity regarding the differences between the theory and policy of the Comintern and the local circumstances of the CPSA. It consequently demanded resolution. As Roux wrote shortly thereafter, "it is time the CPSA put its theoretical house in order."[27] Overcoming this impasse, the CPSA leadership recognized the salience of the Native Republic thesis and the ultimate authority of the Comintern in guiding policy shortly thereafter.

What is important about this moment in South African political history is that it set the stage for conceptualizing the antiapartheid cause, which was still two decades ahead in the future, as anticolonial in nature. Moreover, for the purposes of this chapter, it provides a vital backdrop to the political and intellectual sensibilities that Alex La Guma cultivated during the cold war, demonstrating the personal pathways of political influence that could develop across generations, as Alex's exercise in biography tacitly suggests. Comparing the anti-apartheid struggle to other anticolonial efforts as Alex did through his writing and travel while in exile was therefore not a stretch, but in fact had a deep history, personally as well as within the broader South African political scene. Although the intervening decades would witness the inclusion of pan-Africanism, black nationalism, and forms of civic disobedience—like the 1952 Defiance Campaign, which resembled civil-rights struggles elsewhere—this perspective would reemerge when it proved politically useful, particularly during the era of late decolonization. In sum, Alex's tricontinental political view can be seen as a later fruition of the trajectory established by his father decades earlier. Of particular interest is the continued role the Soviet Union had in their political careers. The Soviet Union continued to provide a source of political support for the South African cause, as Alex's memoirs of his travels there demonstrate.

Soviet Journeys—Alex La Guma in the USSR

Despite the critical attention his fiction has received, little has been granted to his nonfiction account of traveling through the USSR, entitled *A Soviet Journey* (1978). This condition is reflective of his stature as a writer of fiction, though it overlooks a text that situates La Guma beyond South Africa, specifically within a cold war context of tricontinentalism. According to Eugene La Guma, Alex's son, his agreement to write about his travels was "his way of saying thank you" for the audience he and the ANC found there during the struggle against apartheid.[28] *A Soviet Journey* can consequently be read as both a travel memoir and a work of political propaganda. Indeed, the expression *journey* refers to not only La Guma's personal travels, but equally the political and economic journey that the Soviet Union itself had undertaken over the course of the 20th century. Given these elements,

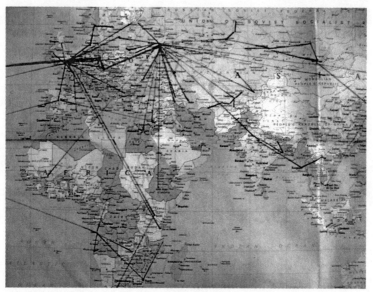

8.4. Detail of personal map with attention to travels in the Soviet Union, courtesy of Mayibuye Centre, University of the Western Cape.

it is largely a political memoir, both of Alex and the USSR itself, with such a viewpoint seen from the start. In the opening paragraphs to the prologue, Alex describes his "childhood impressions of one-sixth of the world's surface" as amounting to both a romantic, cinematic take on the Soviet Union—through films like *Resurrection* (1931), based on a story by Leo Tolstoy—but also a politically driven view, based on "the stories of Gorky," his father's "reminiscences of two brief trips to Moscow in the 1920s," and occasions when "the Friends of the Soviet Union in South Africa showed *The Battleship Potemkin* and *The Stone Flower*."[29] These elements not only describe La Guma's childhood memories, but they also offer cultural reference points from the early Soviet era. They set a political chronology in motion both for Alex and the Soviet Union alike.

In many ways, *A Soviet Journey* is a straightforward account of his experiences and encounters while traveling in the USSR over several trips, exemplifying what some critics have remarked as his skill as a naturalist.[30] Alex traveled throughout much of it—from Moscow and

Leningrad, to Kazakhstan and Central Asia, to Siberia. Moreover, he traveled there often, approximately once a year from 1967 until the end of his life, in both his capacity as an ANC official and through his involvement with the Bureau of Afro-Asian Writers.[31] His story "Come Back to Tashkent" (1968) drew from this experience, with the Bureau itself holding several meetings in Central Asia as well as publishing Soviet writers on occasion and on topics like Leninism in the pages of *Lotus*. In 1975, Alex was formally invited by the Writers' Union of the USSR to travel for a period of six weeks and to write his impressions for a book. The details of this particular trip were therefore combined with reflections on previous ones to constitute the narrative as a whole.[32] This technique is seen in the section entitled "Flashbacks," where he describes, for example, how in November 1967 during celebrations for the fiftieth anniversary of the Bolshevik Revolution he met a man named Maximov, who knocked on his door to announce that he had photographed and interviewed his father in 1927.[33] Such personal anecdotes are interwoven with his literary interests—musings on Pushkin and Dostoyevsky while in Leningrad, for instance— as well as his political ones.

The latter commentary in particular illuminates a theme of political relevance to La Guma and other activists and political leaders who sought a vision of a "usable future." (See the essay by G. Thomas Burgess in this volume.) The majority of *A Soviet Journey* is committed to his experiences in the Soviet republics of Central Asia and Siberia, where La Guma spends a considerable amount of time describing what he sees as the political, social, and economic advances that the Soviet system has provided. In contrast to his father's experience, *A Soviet Journey* therefore provides an African perspective on the USSR, not a Soviet perspective on South Africa. His travel narrative subsequently underlines what he perceives as similarities between South Africa and these Asian republics and, in turn, the imagined political possibilities at hand for a postapartheid South Africa. In his second chapter, "The Footsteps of Alexander," La Guma describes, for example, that prior to 1917 "the peoples of Russia were dispersed in widely different levels of economic, political and cultural development, and outside European Russia, few formed real nations—many lived a nomadic life, their economy, social relations and culture dominated by a patriarchal–feudal system."[34] Despite these conditions, socialism had "enabled once backward peoples to catch up quickly with the advanced."[35] This language of development intersects with frequent, and in retrospect troubling, comparisons—of Siberia once being the "'Darkest Africa' of the Northern Hemisphere" and the Bolshevik Revolution leading it "out of tribalism," for example—which serve to articulate a broader vision, a political similarity, and possibility.[36] Key symbols of modernity like railways, irrigation projects, and electricity production become important features of his narrative.[37] From a cultural angle, he comments that Muslim women in these regions had achieved "the same rights as men in all spheres of economic, cultural and socio-economic life."[38] Overall, in his eyes the Soviet system had successfully addressed questions of economic underdevelopment and cultural difference, thus superseding the failings of, what he termed, the "tsarist colonial regime."[39]

This memoir of Central Asia is not necessarily unique. Kate Baldwin has examined similar travel experiences and accounts of the Soviet Union by African American intellectuals—specifically Claude McKay, Langston Hughes, W. E. B. Du Bois, and Paul Robeson. In this regard, it is fascinating to note the similarities between La Guma's experiences and these activist–intellectuals, not least the fact that all viewed the Soviet Union at one time as an ally in the struggle against global racial oppression. In particular, Langston Hughes—who traveled to the Soviet Union from June 1932 to June 1933 and described his visit in the Soviet-published *A Negro Looks at Soviet Central Asia* (1934) and later in his memoir *I Wonder as I Wander* (1956)—depicts the transformation of Central Asia in terms very similar to La Guma. Baldwin observes that Hughes compared "going South" in Central Asia to "going South" in the US, with these travels providing him "an opportunity to rethink racial topographies in terms familiar to him."[40] Like La Guma, he was aware of "Russification" and its critics, though he too saw such trends as progressive and modern, not necessarily colonial in character. In Baldwin's words, Hughes left his readers through his analogies to speculate on what a postsegregation United States might appear like, subsuming temporarily "the complex contours of Soviet colonization in the positive, forward-moving machine of industrialization."[41] Such textual similarities possessed by both Hughes and La Guma's books undoubtedly stress political affinities on the surface, but they also elide the negative consequences of Soviet power as well.[42]

Such willful positions and sympathetic perspectives are certainly linked to their own subjectivity and past experiences of racial discrimination and political oppression. What is counterintuitive and worthy of mention, however, is that their memoirs also mirror and at times reproduce Eurocentric cultural biases toward Soviet Asia. These Western preconceptions are inscribed not only in tropes of economic modernization as cited before, but also in more intimate cultural and gendered realms as Baldwin points out. Their mutual fixation on the plight of Muslim women, for example, manages to essentialize the condition of these women at the same time that Hughes and La Guma seek to highlight their political status. However, it is difficult to categorize such narratives as either Western-biased or politically radical without oversimplifying them. Indeed, La Guma's memoir is at once experimental, politically and aesthetically, through its exercises in comparison and similitude, as well as holding to certain conventions, namely East–West and premodern–modern binaries that render Soviet Asia legible to Eurocentric frames of reference. (See also Laura Bier's essay in this volume.) In short, La Guma's text manages to valorize preexisting political and cultural sentiments for his readers, if in contrasting ways. Such textual paradoxes and inconsistencies over affirming progress politics through problematic predispositions must be situated and read in light of the general social contexts and political anxieties that La Guma, like Hughes and other intellectuals, undoubtedly encountered.

These observations about perspective and partiality reemphasize how travel constitutes transitory sites or "contact zones," to borrow the classic expression used by Mary Louise Pratt, for negotiating the complex space between received knowledge and firsthand experience.[43] Held ideas could be reinstated, take new form, or be reinvented completely, with the individual traveler being an intersection for such political and cultural processes of reimagining. In this sense, *A Soviet Journey* fits into La Guma's sequence of novels by mobilizing a political perspective through the means of descriptive narrative.

Yet the key difference between this memoir and his longer fiction is that his memoir consists of material completely beyond South Africa, even if La Guma signals his own self-consciousness about this departure by comparing what he sees to how it relates to the South African situation.[44] Although he had experimented with stories beyond South Africa in his short fiction, as mentioned before, it is clear that this work, his longest work of nonfiction, pushed his limits as a writer. Yet it fits into the tricontinental politics that had preoccupied him through his activities with *Lotus* and the Bureau of Afro-Asian Writers. It presents a committed engagement of comparison between two continents, in addition to offering a political appraisal of the possibilities that a postapartheid South Africa might have achieved.

Conclusions

To conclude, this essay has examined the career of Alex La Guma within the context of tricontinentalism during the cold war, first as a means of locating the transformation of the antiapartheid struggle into an anticolonial movement and second as a way of understanding how individual activist–intellectuals negotiated broader sets of transnational politics that took hold during this period. Moreover, for the purposes of this volume, it points to the different parts of Asia that influenced the political imagination of African activists (in contrast see the preceding essays by Burgess and Monson). Individuals like La Guma were positioned as contingent political and cultural brokers, translating their own experience as intermediaries into reflective and usable political insights through the act of writing. (On translation, see Laura Bier's essay in this volume.) This type of interpretation at the individual level therefore points to the ways in which activist–intellectuals negotiated difficult political presents and surmised possible futures, thus addressing and frequently redefining the meanings of such expressions as *colonial* and *postcolonial.* La Guma's contributions to *Lotus: Afro-Asian Writings* and his memoir *A Soviet Journey* constitute attempts at making sense of certain political conditions, to ask questions of commensurability—but they equally reflect upon the origins and personal meanings of political

life. *A Soviet Journey* in particular demonstrates that travel writing—
Mary Louise Pratt again—is a normalizing discourse. Yet in this case
not one entirely of difference as frequently found in European portrayals, but also one of connection and similitude, in the present and in an
imagined political future.[45]

The tricontinental politics of La Guma's later work also explain the
lack of critical attention it has received. A striking absence in *A Soviet
Journey* is that of the Soviet gulags that had received worldwide recognition by the 1970s, in large part through the work of the writer
Aleksandr Solzhenitsyn. This denial of recognition—indeed the cel-
ebratory conclusion—within his narrative raises crucial questions
that are difficult to answer as to whether his manuscript was censored,
given its publication by Soviet authorities, or whether this was an ethical oversight of La Guma himself. Eugene La Guma, Alex's son, has
relayed in an interview that his father held "orthodox Soviet thoughts"
and that he did not question the position of Soviet authorities.[46] What
can be assumed, then, is that La Guma wrote under constrained conditions, and through his ongoing political commitments an avoidance
of certain issues was strategic on his part. Still, these fundamental
questions complicate our understanding of the text, his politics, and
those of others on the South African Left during the last two decades
of the antiapartheid struggle. Abdul JanMohamed has written that
the popularity of political writers like Solzhenitsyn is in part due to
their revalorization of certain preexisting Manichean dialectics. On
the other hand, the fiction of writers like La Guma has been marginalized due to their critical engagement and reconfiguration of these
conventionally accepted dialogues.[47] This perspective appears to hold
true here. The tricontinental politics of La Guma, which pushed his
writing beyond the nation-state context of South Africa, has left that
work with less attention than it deserves.

This predicament of marginalization speaks to larger issues as
well. Modern South African politics has posed a distinct challenge to
chronologies of anticolonial nationalism, decolonization, and postcolonial politics through its unique political formation and timeframe
and its complex interaction with global political trends such as communism, pan-Africanism, and later forms of tricontinentalism. South

African activist–intellectuals made fundamental contributions to this global public sphere of ideological ferment and politics that persisted throughout the 20th century, at times across familial generations. Indeed, this essay suggests that the shared problems of translation and commensurability can be read generationally as well as geographically, thereby underscoring the importance of life histories and careers, as Antoinette Burton argues, in defining resistance chronologies of anticolonialism, decolonization, and postcoloniality. The global conversations initiated and sustained by figures like the La Gumas point to the reassurances and anxieties of influence between states and activists, theory and practice, and—at times—fathers and sons.

Notes

1. Oliver Tambo, "Afro-Asian Solidarity," in *Preparing for Power: Oliver Tambo Speaks*, comp. Adelaide Tambo (London: Heinemann, 1987), 89.

2. Ibid., 90

3. Ibid.

4. Ibid.

5. Rob Nixon, *Homelands, Harlem and Hollywood: South African Culture and the World Beyond* (New York: Routledge, 1994), 1.

6. Robert Thornton, "The Potential Boundaries: Steps toward a Theory of the Social Edge," in *Postcolonial Identities in Africa,* ed. R. Werbner and T. Ranger (London: Zed Books, 1996).

7. See, for example, George M. Fredrickson, *Black Liberation: A Comparative History of Black Ideologies in the United States and South Africa* (New York: Oxford University Press, 1995).

8. Mahmood Mamdani, *Citizen and Subject: Contemporary Africa and the Legacy of Late Colonialism* (Princeton: Princeton University Press, 1996).

9. Ruth First's work on African politics is an example of this transnational engagement beyond the antiapartheid struggle. See Ruth First, *The Barrel of a Gun: Political Power in Africa and the Coup d'État* (London: Allen Lane, 1970).

10. Antoinette Burton, *The Postcolonial Careers of Santha Rama Rau* (Durham: Duke University Press, 2007), 20, 26.

11. Ibid., 24. For other biographies that might be viewed as postcolonial, see Charles van Onselen, *The Seed Is Mine: The Life of Kas Maine, a South African Sharecropper, 1894–1985* (New York: Hill and Wang, 1996); Clifton C. Crais and

Pamela Scully, *Sara Baartman and the Hottentot Venus: A Ghost Story and a Biography* (Princeton: Princeton University Press, 2009).

12. Diana Wylie, *Art and Revolution: The Life and Death of Thami Mnyele, South African Artist* (Charlottesville: University of Virginia Press, 2008).

13. These books include Alex La Guma, *A Walk in the Night and Other Stories* (London: Heinemann, 1967); Alex La Guma, *And a Threefold Cord* (Berlin: Seven Seas, 1964); Alex La Guma, *The Stone Country* (London: Heinemann, 1974); Alex La Guma, *In the Fog of the Season's End* (London: Heinemann, 1972); Alex La Guma, *Time of the Butcherbird* (London: Heinemann, 1979); Alex La Guma, ed., *Apartheid* (London: Lawrence and Wishart, 1971); Alex La Guma, *A Soviet Journey* (Moscow: Progress Books, 1978).

14. Kathleen M. Balutansky, *The Novels of Alex La Guma: The Representation of a Political Conflict* (Washington, DC: Three Continents Press, 1990), 7-10.

15. Abdul R. JanMohamed, *Manichean Aesthetics: The Politics of Literature in Colonial Africa* (Amherst: University of Massachusetts Press, 1983), 227.

16. Ibid.

17. For other critical work on La Guma, see, for example, S. O. Asein, *Alex La Guma: The Man and His Work* (Ibadan: Heinemann Educational Books (Nigeria), 1987); Cecil A. Abrahams, *Alex La Guma* (Boston: Twayne, 1985); J. M. Coetzee, "Man's Fate in the Novels of Alex La Guma (1974)," in *Doubling the Point: Essays and Interviews*, ed. David Atwell (Cambridge: Harvard University Press, 1992): 344–67; Andre Odendaal and Roger Field, eds., *Liberation Chabalala: The World of Alex La Guma* (Bellville: Mayibuye Books, 1993); Fritz H. Pointer, *A Passion to Liberate: La Guma's South Africa—Images of District Six* (Trenton: Africa World Press, 2001).

18. Alex La Guma, "Literature and Life," *Lotus: Afro-Asian Writings* 1, no. 4 (1970): 239.

19. Blanche La Guma, interview by the author, September 4, 2004.

20. Allison Drew, *Discordant Comrades: Identities and Loyalties on the South African Left* (Aldershot : Ashgate, 2000), 97.

21. For an overview, see Drew, *Discordant Comrades*, ch. 4.

22. Mohamed Adhikari, ed., *Jimmy La Guma: A Biography by Alex La Guma* (Cape Town: Friends of the South African Library, 1997).

23. Ibid., 39. For more on Bunting, see Allison Drew, *Between Empire and Revolution: A Life of Sidney Bunting, 1873–1936* (London: Pickering and Chatto, 2007).

24. Adhikari, *Jimmy La Guma*, 43.

25. Ibid., 45.

26. "Document 26: S. P. Bunting, Statement on the Kuusinen Thesis,

presented at the Sixth Comintern Congress, August 20, 1928," in Allison Drew, ed., *South Africa's Radical Tradition, A Documentary History: Volume 1, 1907–1950* (Cape Town: UCT Press, 1996), 86, 91, 93.

27. "Document 27: Letter from E. R. Roux to Douglas Wolton, September 5, 1928," in Allison Drew, ed., *South Africa's Radical Tradition*, 93.

28. Eugene La Guma, interview by the author, July 30, 2004.

29. La Guma, *Soviet Journey*, 11.

30. Nahem Yousaf, *Alex La Guma: Politics and Resistance* (Portsmouth: Heinemann, 2001), 25.

31. Eugene La Guma, interview by the author, July 30, 2004.

32. Abrahams, *Alex La Guma*, 19.

33. La Guma, *Soviet Journey*, 25.

34. Ibid., 34.

35. Ibid.

36. Ibid., 163, 179.

37. Ibid., 50, 159.

38. Ibid., 39.

39. Ibid., 133.

40. Kate A. Baldwin, *Beyond the Color Line and the Iron Curtain: Reading Encounters between Black and Red, 1922–1963* (Durham: Duke University Press, 2002), 109.

41. Ibid.

42. For further discussion on Langston Hughes, see David Chioni Moore, "Local Color, Global 'Color': Langston Hughes, the Black Atlantic, and Soviet Central Asia, 1932," *Research in African Literatures*, 27, 4 (Winter 1996): 49-70; David Chioni Moore, "Colored Dispatches from the Uzbek Border: Langston Hughes' Relevance, 1933-2002," *Callaloo*, 25, 4 (2002): 1115-1135. For a related, fascinating assessment of the post-Soviet condition also by Moore, see David Chioni Moore, "Is the Post in Postcolonial the Post in Post-Soviet? Notes Toward a Global Postcolonial Critique," *PMLA*, 116, 1 (2001): 111-128.

43. Mary Louise Pratt, *Imperial Eyes: Travel Writing and Transculturation* (London: Routledge, 1992), 6, 7.

44. La Guma himself was persistently aware of his outsider position, as his comparisons attest to, though also through passing comments on his inability to speak Russian fluently or even conversationally.

45. Mary Louise Pratt, "Scratches on the Face of the Country; or, What Mr. Barrow Saw in the Land of the Bushmen," in *"Race," Writing, and Difference*, ed. Henry Louis Gates Jr. (Chicago: University of Chicago Press, 1985), 139.

46. Eugene La Guma, interview by the author, July 30, 2004.

47. JanMohamed, *Manichean Dialectics*, 262.

Part 3

The Present

Predicaments, Practices, Speculation

9

China's Engagement with Africa

Scope, Significance, and Consequences

Denis M. Tull

THE PERIOD SINCE the end of the cold war, when observers would invariably name the US, France, and the UK as the only foreign powers to have substantial interests in Sub-Saharan Africa, is drawing to a close. Over the course of roughly the past ten years, the People's Republic of China has established itself as an increasingly influential player across the continent. Given the impressive scale and scope of its renewed engagement, Chinese forays into Africa may turn out as one of the most significant developments for the region in recent years. For one thing, the return of China may single-handedly invalidate the conventional wisdom on Africa's international marginalization; even more so since other states of the global south, notably India and Brazil, are also forging closer ties with Africa. For another, China's political and economic involvement in Africa has a palpable impact on the domestic scene in many African states, which will further augment should China continue to pursue a more globally oriented foreign policy, particularly toward non-Western regions.

Taking the general transformation of Chinese foreign policy as a starting point, this essay analyzes China's foreign policy toward Africa since the early 1990s. The first half of the paper reviews the scale of

China's political and economic involvement, and examines the objectives and strategies underlying Chinese foreign policy toward Sub-Saharan Africa. Although by no means Beijing's only objective, oil interests will receive particular emphasis. The second part of the paper looks at the impact that China's renewed engagement has on the countries of the region by considering its economic and political repercussions. It is argued that China's economic impact may prove to be a mixed blessing whereas the political consequences of its return are likely to prove deleterious.

China's Shifting Foreign Policy

China's increasing involvement on the African continent is a manifestation of the remarkable transformation of the country's foreign policy over the past twenty years. Although China watchers are still debating the nature and scope of that change, they mostly agree that China has been seeking a more-active role in the international system in recent years. Beijing has expanded and intensified its bilateral relations throughout the world, has joined regional bodies dealing with security and economic issues, and has extended its involvement in multilateral organizations. As a result, China's foreign policy as a whole is by and large considered to be more dynamic, constructive, flexible, and self-confident than was the case during the preceding decades.[1] As veteran diplomat Zbigniew Brzezinski asserts: "China is clearly assimilating into the international system."[2]

Chinese efforts to conduct a more-active foreign policy beyond its Asian neighborhood set in as early as 1989.[3] The fierce reactions of Western states to the massacre in Tiananmen Square (June 1989), including an arms embargo imposed by the US and the European Union (EU), and the persistent Western criticism of China's human-rights record ever since, induced Beijing to seek closer ties to non-Western countries. Developing countries were effectively elevated to a "cornerstone" of Chinese foreign policy in an effort to build coalitions to shield Beijing from Western criticism. Given their numerical weight in international organizations, African states played an important role in the Chinese stratagem. Since many African leaders were themselves at the time under growing domestic and external pressure to liberalize their political systems, they were more than willing to go along with Chinese claims that Western demands for democracy and the respect for human rights amounted to thinly veiled imperialistic maneuvers intent on interfering in the domestic politics of developing states and undermining their stability and progress at large. Gauging the relations between developing and developed states in terms of a North-South conflict, this discourse served as a powerful glue whereby China sought to construct a common identity with African states vis-à-vis the paternalistic West. With these considerations in mind, China moved swiftly to increase its assistance to developing countries substantially, most of which were African nations.[4]

A second factor that led the Chinese leadership to steer a more-active foreign policy course in the post-1989 period was the expected emergence of an uncontested international hegemony of the US which, it was feared, would hold back China's ascendancy as a global political power.[5] To address the problem, Beijing advanced the concept of *multipolarity*, defined as the construction of more or less flexible alliances to contain every form of hegemony and to build a new and just international order. Since China obviously conceived of itself as one indispensable pole in the international system, the government reached out to non-Western states to bolster its international position with regard to the US, particularly its room for maneuver within the UN Security Council and other international bodies. The coming into office of the administration of G. W. Bush, which conceptualized China as a "strategic competitor"—President Clinton had referred to China as a "strategic partner"—probably reinforced Beijing's belief in the necessity of a multipolar world and the need for new allies.[6]

At the end of the same decade, a third factor corroborated Beijing's view that a global foreign policy had become a sheer necessity. While the strength of China's economy was to no small degree based on its dynamic integration into the world economy, the financial crisis in Asia in 1997 alerted the Chinese leadership to the risks of economic interdependence as it exposed the vulnerability of the country's outward-oriented economy to external shocks. By implication, regional and international stability, mainly but not exclusively in economic terms, turned into strategic objectives.[7] Therefore, Beijing moved to modify and broaden the conceptualization of its (inter) national interests. For if outside events could imperil the continued economic growth, China's precarious domestic situation, including increased social tensions, would no doubt pose a serious challenge to the political monopoly of the Communist Party. Consequently, the Chinese leadership regarded a more-active foreign policy as the best strategy to defend and assert its national interests. The need to expand and strengthen China's bilateral relations, including those with the states in Africa south of the Sahara, was part of this strategy. Accordingly, China's rapidly increasing engagement in Africa is not so much reflecting a singular or specific policy toward the continent. Instead, it is part and parcel of a wider policy thrust that manifests itself equally in Chinese relations toward other regions of the world such as Latin America and the Middle East.[8]

Taking Stock of China's Involvement in Africa

Western responses to the Tiananmen massacre in 1989 provided the initial trigger which compelled the Chinese government to seek closer ties to Africa after a lengthy period of reduced activity.[9] In the three years following the carnage, Foreign Minister Qian Qichan visited no less than fourteen African countries and thus laid the foundation for an intense diplomacy that continues unabated until today.[10] During the past decade, for example, more than one-hundred high-level meetings have taken place between Chinese and African diplomats and envoys.[11] In addition, and at a time when Western states are generally inclined to roll back their diplomatic presence in Africa, China maintains embassies in every African country—except for the six states entertaining diplomatic relations with Taiwan.[12] By the same token, the number of Chinese commercial representations is growing fast.

Although an emerging economic superpower, China continues to portray itself, at least to African audiences, as a developing nation to underline the quasinatural convergence of interests between China, "the biggest developing country and Africa, the continent with the largest number of developing countries" (Jiang Zemin). At the same time, Beijing acknowledges its superior international standing and uses its permanent seat in the UN Security Council to position itself as a mentor of African countries. This includes claims to support fairer global trade and Africa's various reform-oriented institutions such as the New Partnership for Africa's Development (NEPAD) and the African Union (AU) as well as an enlarged UN Security Council. Although most of these pledges have remained extremely vague, China's increasing involvement in UN peacekeeping missions in Africa has been substantial. In 2004, some 1,400 Chinese participated in 9 UN missions on the continent. The biggest contingent (558 troops) was sent to war-torn Liberia after the incoming Liberian government (2003) ended diplomatic relations with Taiwan.[13]

As another signal of its commitment to Africa, Beijing points to its support for debt cancellation in favor of African countries. Over the past decade, China has canceled the bilateral debts of 31 African countries totalling some $1.27 billion.[14] Similarly, President Hu Jintao's promise to provide development assistance "within our power" is part of Beijing's repertoire to underline its support for Africa.[15] In 2002 some 44 percent of China's widely spread overall assistance to developing countries of $1.8 billion went to Africa.[16] Although this represents a large amount when measured against China's GDP per capita (2002: $911), the country clearly lags behind the volumes disbursed by major Western nations.[17] As a result, it is far from clear whether China is prepared to become a dedicated donor nation, with the obligations and commitments this may entail, or whether it will continue to emphasize its own status as a developing country, defining whatever it deems to be "within its power" and thus foregoing international agreements among donors.

However, the limited financial value of China's aid is considerably enhanced by political considerations. The Chinese government and its African counterparts frequently stress that Beijing's aid comes with few political strings attached. Contrary to Western donors, China's cooperation with or support of African governments does not hinge on conditionalities pertaining to specific political objectives or standards (that is, human rights, democracy). Of course, the notable exception from China's purported rejection of political demands is the issue of Taiwan; that is, Beijing's insistence that it is the only legitimate representative of China. The "One China" principle therefore remains an important objective, even though the race for recognition between both countries is no longer as important as it was in the past, partly because in recent years Beijing was considerably more successful than Taipei in its attempts to persuade African countries to shift recognition away from its rival.[18]

Out of the wide range of Chinese activities in Africa, economic transactions provide the most powerful evidence of China's increasing interests in the continent. The skyrocketing of Chinese-African trade deserves particular emphasis. Between 1989 and 1997 the bilateral-trade volume grew by 430 percent and since then has more than quintupled. It reached $24 billion in 2004, amounting to 6.3 percent of the extraregional trade of the states south of the Sahara.[19] In the first ten months of 2005 Chinese-African trade grew by 39 percent to $32.17 billion.[20] As a result, China has overtaken the UK as Africa's third most important trading partner in 2005 (after the US and France). However, the African share of Chinese external trade is only about two percent and the Chinese-African trade represents a mere 40 percent of the US-African trade volume.

Beijing's active promotion of economic interaction with Africa has significantly contributed to the impressive growth rates of bilateral trade. In institutional terms, this has been flanked by the creation of the Forum on China-Africa Cooperation in 2000.[21] Furthermore, a Chinese-African Chamber of Commerce was opened in Beijing in March 2005, which aims at promoting trade and economic relations with initially five African countries.[22] That institution is only the latest among a fast-growing number of initiatives and agreements between China and Africa. As of 2005, China has bilateral trade and investment agreements with 75 percent of Africa's states. Of the 40 bilateral investment agreements China entered between 1995 and 2003, 18 were established with African countries.[23] Enhanced Chinese economic interest in Africa is also reflected by the fact that some 700 Chinese enterprises with a total investment of about $1.5 billion are currently operating in Africa.[24] Finally, the Chinese have signaled willingness to negotiate the establishment of a free-trade zone with southern African states.[25]

What are the factors behind the Chinese-African trade boom? The massive export of goods to Africa is part of the story. Due first to its large and cheap labor force and second to the acute poverty in vast parts of Africa, China offers low-price export goods such as textiles and clothing, electronic devices and machines, which find a huge and soaring demand. In 2003, China was the second-biggest exporter of goods (eleven percent) to the member states of the Economic Community of West African States (ECOWAS). Given its burgeoning exports to Nigeria, West Africa's largest economy, China has since then almost certainly narrowed the gap with the ECOWAS leading supplier, that is, France. After Nigeria's imports from China had multiplied by a factor of ten in the period between 1994 and 2002, Nigerian imports from China climbed from $1.76 billion in 2003 to $2.28 billion in 2004.[26]

Chinese imports from Africa have grown even faster. In comparison to the primarily *commercial* objectives of its export trade with Africa, the *strategic* value of China's imports from the continent stands out. It is driven by Beijing's need to secure natural resources to sustain its economic boom at home.[27] For instance, China's share in the increase in global demand for some mineral resources such as aluminum, nickel, and copper varies between 76 and 100 percent.[28] Similarly, China's oil consumption will increase dramatically over the next three decades; and so will its reliance on oil imports, which accounted for 37 percent of its oil consumption in 2003.[29]

Africa's resource-rich countries are in a position to provide an ample percentage of China's requirements. There is little doubt that natural resources are at the core of China's economic interests in Africa—or perhaps even its overall interest in the continent. In terms of China's imports from Africa, nine out of its ten most important trading partners are resource-rich countries. Remarkably, the list even includes emerging oil-producer Chad, one of the few African countries to recognize Taiwan.

Table 2. Most-important African trading partners in 2004 (imports)

Imports from Africa	Million US-Dollar	Percent
Angola	3422.63	27.4
South Africa	2567.96	20.6
Sudan	1678.60	13.4
Republic of Congo	1224.74	9.8
Equatorial-Guinea	787.96	6.3
Gabon	415.39	3.3
Nigeria	372.91	3.0
Algeria	216.11	1.7
Morocco	208.69	1.7
Chad	148.73	1.2
Total	11043.72	88.4

Source: International Monetary Fund, Direction of Trade Statistics (May 2005).

It is probably no coincidence that Beijing's rising interest in Africa comes at a time when sizable new discoveries of oil have been made on the continent, particularly in the Gulf of Guinea. Africa's largest producers, Angola and Nigeria, are set to at least double their production within the next decade. Important oil fields have also been explored in Equatorial-Guinea, São Tomé e Principe, and Chad whereas minor reserves are located in Mauritania and Côte d'Ivoire.[30] Together with long-standing producers Congo-Brazzaville and Gabon, these new discoveries could bring African oil output to seven-million barrels a day within the next ten-to-fifteen years.[31] Bolstered by a massive infusion of investments of $360 billion (2001–30) that transnational companies have announced to make, production could reach thirteen-million barrels per day in 2020.[32]

Regardless of these projections, Africa's contribution to China's overall oil imports is already significant. In 2004, Africa's share of Chinese overall oil imports reached 28.7 percent, up from 25.2 percent in 2003.[33] Angola, Beijing's most important African oil supplier, exported 117 million barrels to China in 2004, a 60 percent increase from the previous year.[34] With a share of about 13 percent of Chinese

oil imports, Angola came close to the level provided by China's leading oil supplier, that is, Saudi Arabia (125 million barrels).

Strategic Elements of China's Policy Toward Africa

The extent to which China appears to be welcomed with open arms by
many African leaders is perhaps the most striking element of recent
Sino-African relations. By offering their African counterparts a mix
of political and economic incentives, the Chinese government is successfully driving home the message that increased Sino-African cooperation will inevitably result in a "win-win situation" for both sides.
The power of this argument is enhanced by a subtle discourse that
posits China not only as an appealing alternative partner to the West,
but also as a better choice for Africa. Although this is certainly debat-
able with respect to Africa and its ordinary citizens as a whole, there
can be little doubt that sizable benefits of China's return will accrue to
state elites.

Most obviously, an important appeal stems from the fact that China
stubbornly sticks to the dogma of national sovereignty. It fiercely
continues to repudiate the increasingly powerful notion that outside
interference into the domestic affairs of a state can be legitimate. China's donor policies reflect this state-centred orthodoxy to the degree
that, the issue of Taiwan aside, no political conditions are attached
to its development assistance. Western donors, in contrast, have pro-
gressively undermined the sovereignty of African states by imposing
reform agendas on them: first in the guise of Structural Adjustment
Programs (SAPs) in the 1980s, followed in the 1990s by demands for
democratic reform. In light of the persistent stress that economic and
political conditionalities have forced on African governments, it is
hardly surprising that the Chinese stance on the issue of sovereignty
is gratefully acknowledged by African governments. In a barely con-
cealed complaint against the intrusive attitudes of Western donors, a
spokesman of the Kenyan government no doubt echoed a widespread
sentiment on the continent when he noted: "You never hear the Chinese saying that they will not finish a project because the government

has not done enough to tackle corruption. If they are going to build a road, then it will be built."[35] Such observations underline that nonintrusive China presents an attractive partner of African governments; that is, not only for plainly authoritarian leaders, but also for the great many among African governments presiding over hybrid regimes for which the distribution of patronage remains an exigency of political survival.[36]

That a number of African regimes have been unable to manage the political economy of reform over the past two decades, sometimes with disastrous consequences like outbreaks of violent conflict, was not lost on the Chinese government. In conjunction with the wholesale failure of economic reforms (SAPs), these setbacks, in Beijing's view, have but confirmed its analysis that the patchy record of Western-driven reform efforts in Africa will inadvertently facilitate Chinese advances on the continent. As Renmin Ribao, the official newspaper of the Communist Party, notes:

> owing to the general failure in the West's political and economic behaviour in Africa, African nations, which were only suspicious at first, are now negating Western-style democracy and have reinitiated "Afro-Asianism" and proposed "going towards the Orient." This has opened up new opportunities for further enriching the content and elevating the quality of China-Africa cooperation.[37]

Furthermore, Chinese aid tends to benefit the governments of receiving countries more directly than the policies of Western donors, who are preoccupied with the reduction of poverty. The Chinese, unlike Western countries, do finance grandiose and prestigious buildings (presidential palaces, football stadiums) that African leaders highly appreciate for their very own political reasons.

In return, Beijing can count on valuable diplomatic support by African governments to defend its interests on the international level, particularly in multilateral organizations with "one country—one vote" arrangements. In the United Nations Commission on Human Rights, for instance, African countries have frequently played a prominent role in frustrating Western efforts to bring about a formal condemnation of China's human-rights record.[38] More recently, intense courting led to China's recognition as a market-economy by a fair number of African states. This is a crucial status in the wake of China's WTO accession, helping to shield it from accusations of dumping.[39] Finally, diplomatic backing by African states pertains to the recognition of the principle of "One China" and the pursuit of the concept of a multipolar world.

Although noninterference remains an article of faith for the Chinese leadership, it is but one factor explaining China's growing influence in Africa. Particularly in the economic realm, it has only limited explanatory power. What matters more are the strategies that Chinese companies pursue in their conquest of Africa's markets. Firstly, Chinese firms appear to be significantly less risk-averse than their Western counterparts, especially in war-torn states such as Angola, DR Congo, and Sierra Leone, where a "first mover advantage" plays out in favor of risk-taking entrepreneurs.[40] This is also true in a more general sense insofar as Chinese businesses seem to consider the challenging political and economic environment in many African states as an economic opportunity. Thanks to their willingness to take significant risks, Chinese firms are able to derive huge profits from rates of return on Foreign Direct Investment said to be much higher in politically volatile Sub-Saharan Africa than in other parts of the developing world.[41]

Secondly, the success of Chinese businesses in Africa may also relate to their focus on specific sectors. In no small part due to the feeble presence of Western rivals, China has become a major player in the field of infrastructure (roads, railways, barrages, power plants, and so forth). Strictly speaking, though, many of these projects are not commercial. Some are financed through "tied" Chinese aid. Others are not profitable since the Chinese tend to set costs below market rates. And yet, the lack of short-term commercial profits does not preclude that investments will yield significant returns in the long term. Since most infrastructure projects are public-sector works, China conceives its investments as goodwill projects to woo the sympathies of African state leaders. This enables China to gain political influence, which often opens the doors for commercially or strategically more attractive businesses in other sectors, that is, to win tenders for oil and mining concessions.[42] A third advantage is noticeable in instances wherein China is targeting African states suffering from Western-imposed sanctions. Since Western states are still by far the most important trading partners of African states, Western sanctions de facto turn these countries into niche markets. Having no legal or political obligation to abide by Western-imposed sanctions, China can position itself as an alternative partner of "pariah-states."[43] China has adopted this free-riding strategy in Sudan and Zimbabwe.

China's Oil Interests

Since 1998, when a White Paper of the Chinese Ministry of Defense proclaimed energy security as an integral part of China's overall security, the country's global-economic, foreign, and security policies have become closely intertwined.[44] In the process, Beijing stepped up its efforts both to expand its oil imports and to diversify its oil suppliers. In line with this policy, China has increased its oil imports from Africa and has augmented the number of its African suppliers. In 2004 the country was reported to have oil stakes in as many as eleven African states.[45] In January 2006, China's top offshore oil producer, CNOOC, agreed to pay \$2.3 billion for a 45 percent stake in a Nigerian oil and gas field, its largest-ever overseas acquisition.[46] For the time being, however, the vast bulk of Chinese oil imports from Africa is provided by two countries: Angola and Sudan. Beijing's involvement in both countries is somewhat emblematic of the approach sketched above. First, it underscores the interconnectedness of political, diplomatic, and economic strategies to secure oil supplies. Second, it points to the fact that China's efforts often focus on what may be called *niche markets.*

From a Chinese point of view, niche countries and their oil sectors are characterized by limited competition: either because Western multinational companies have no or only limited access for political reasons like embargos (for instance, Sudan, Iran) and/or because the countries are relatively new or emerging oil producers offering significant opportunities. Given the inadequate financial and technological competitiveness of Chinese oil companies,[47] the targeting of niche countries forms a strategic decision to secure oil stakes. China's widening demand for African oil thus corresponds to its overall energy security policy insofar as Sudan and many of West Africa's oil-producing countries in the Gulf of Guinea can be subsumed under the first and second category of niche countries respectively.

A well-considered combination of diplomacy and economic incentives forms Beijing's key instrument to lock up African oil supplies. China's major oil companies are owned by the state and act as an extended arm of the Chinese government, which supports the overseas activities of its oil companies through a variety of instruments.[48] As such, strategic objectives to secure oil supplies often override commercial concerns.[49] By dispensing soft loans and credit lines, development assistance, gifts and other incentives, arms deliveries and diplomatic backing, Beijing seeks to cultivate the favor of governments in oil-producing states and, by extension, obtain privileged access and opportunities for its companies.[50] Thus, oil interests and bilateral relations between China and African countries go hand in hand.

Somewhat reminiscent of a mercantilist approach, this *petro-diplomacy* can be seen in Angola where Chinese imports have grown by 400 percent since 2001. Recently, the state-owned China Exim-bank released a $2 billion loan package to Angola in exchange for ten-thousand barrels a day of oil.[51] The deal was of mutual benefit. While it enabled the Angolan regime to circumvent donor pressure for increased fiscal transparency, it will strengthen the Chinese foothold in the Angolan oil economy.

The strategic elements of China's energy-security policy in Africa are brought into its sharpest relief in Sudan. Having acquired a 40 percent stake in the Greater Nile Petroleum Operating Company (GNPOC) in 1996, American sanctions against Khartoum and the incremental withdrawal of other Western oil companies enabled China's state-owned CNPC to become the largest foreign investor in Sudan's nascent oil production.[52] When, in 2004, the full extent of Khartoum's genocidal campaign in the Darfur provinces came to daylight, the US and other Western states sought action against Sudan in the UN Security Council. There, however, attempts to bring Khartoum to book were repeatedly frustrated by China.[53] It either abstained from casting its vote or threatened to make use of its veto right.[54]

Notwithstanding its reference to state sovereignty and the concomitant appraisal of Darfur as a "domestic issue," Beijing's intransigency in the Security Council was essentially linked to its oil interests. First, Sudan is a nonnegligible provider of China's oil imports (6.9 percent). Second, the GNPOC joint venture is the largest overseas oil investment of the Chinese CNPC. Over the years an estimated $5 billion have been invested in the acquisition of exploration and drilling licenses, the construction of pipelines, refineries and other essential infrastructure. The scale of these investments highlights China's long-term strategic interests in Sudan, which is expected to increase its production of 340,000 barrels a day to 500,000 barrels a day in 2005, and 750,000 barrels a day by 2006.

It comes as no surprise therefore that Beijing opposed UN sanctions, which could have jeopardized its Sudanese investments and oil supplies for many years to come.[55] In fact, Beijing perpetuated a highly advantageous status quo. Chinese companies can continue to operate without the competition of financially and technologically superior Western firms whose return to Sudan could pose a severe threat to their dominance of the Sudanese oil economy. Interestingly, the peace agreement between Khartoum and the rebels of the Sudan People's Liberation Army (SPLA) of January 2005 contains an explicit guarantee for all oil concessions, which the Sudanese government has granted during the war.[56] The clause undoubtedly presented a reward for China's steadfast diplomatic support for Khartoum during the diplomatic height of the Darfur crisis.

China's Economic Impact

China's undeniable appeal to African states, notably as a trading partner, is the flipside of their fading economic importance to the West. Partly as a result, a good number of African elites and intellectuals appear to regard China as both an appealing economic model worth emulating and a potential catalyst for socioeconomic development.

No less important, they conceptualize emergent South-South relations as a historical opportunity for African states to escape the neocolonial ties to the West. And yet, it is not evident that Chinese-African trade differs significantly from Western-African trade patterns; nor is it clear that China's engagement will substantially improve African prospects for development. Judging from its most important trading partners (imports), Beijing's economic interests in Africa do not vary from those of Western states.[57] This seems to suggest that rapidly growing economic exchanges between Africa and China will neither fundamentally alter Africa's asymmetrical integration into global markets, nor will they reduce Africa's dependency on a few price-volatile primary goods that account for 73 percent of its overall export revenues.[58] Even outside the extractive sector, there is some reason to doubt that China's economic engagement will encourage sustainable economic growth in Africa. The evidence from an examination of textile industries, one of the few African economic success stories in recent years, is ambivalent indeed.

When the US-sponsored African Growth and Opportunity Act (AGOA) came into effect in 2000, a fair number of Chinese textile companies established themselves in Africa. The move had two closely related objectives: first, to exploit the preferential access to the US market that AGOA had conceded to certain African products, including clothing and textile.[59] Second, shifting parts of the production to Africa enabled Chinese firms to circumvent the trade barriers the Agreement on Textiles and Clothing of the so-called Uruguay Round had imposed on them to protect markets in Europe and the US from cheap Asian imports. The combined effect of the AGOA agreement and the flexible strategies of Chinese companies contributed to the rise of textile industries, notably in southern and eastern Africa. When the Agreement on Textiles and Clothing expired on January 1, 2005, and access restrictions for Asian textiles to Western markets were removed, Africa's intermittent textile boom witnessed a meltdown. American demand for African textiles plunged in favor of even cheaper garments made in China, and Africa-based Chinese companies were already relocating their production back to China.[60] In the process, tens of thousands of workers have lost their jobs or risk doing so in the near future, for example in South Africa, Zimbabwe, Lesotho, and Kenya.[61] Thus African textile producers will be hit by losses of global-market shares whereas the efforts of African countries to diversify their economies and exports will endure a severe setback. Even South Africa, the continent's most sophisticated economy, is negatively affected. To begin with, manufactured goods as a share of exports to China fell from fifty percent in 1993 to eight percent in 2003. The structure of South African trade relations with China thus mirrors the wider problem of Africa's unbalanced-trade relations insofar as some ninety percent of its exports to China consist of raw materials (for example, ore, platinum, and diamonds). In 2004 South Africa incurred a trade deficit with China of $1.9 billion. Were it not for Beijing's imports of oil and other raw materials, the aggregated African trade with China would show a huge deficit.[62]

To make matters worse, most African producers are simply not in a position to compete with Chinese companies even in Africa's domestic markets, as they are unable to undercut Chinese production costs and prices.[63] Local retailers, too, are faced with the rapidly increasing business competition from expatriate Chinese traders.[64] Although there is some evidence that the economic activities of Chinese entrepreneurs can make a positive contribution to local development,[65] a cursory perusal of local press reports indicates that their remarkable presence also stirs significant local resentments.[66]

Although the diversification of trading partners is an encouraging sign, African countries have to recognize that China will not per se have a positive impact on their economies. China's foreign-trade policies are not driven by altruistic motives.[67] Chinese and African businesses are first and foremost economic contenders for investments and markets, in particular in the field of labor-intensive and export-oriented manufacturing like textile and clothing.[68] To date, however, nothing indicates that Africa will be able to compete successfully with China, a result of which is that its exports to China are by and large limited to capital-intensive commodities. If anything, this imbalance may have had the effect of Africa creating jobs in China while Chinese imports have undermined job markets in

Africa. Although this is the result of legitimate market competition, it nonetheless contravenes Chinese statements that enhanced Chinese-African interaction always results in win-win situations. The least one can say is that Beijing's high-flying rhetoric often pales in the face of stark realities. So far, for example, the relative sparseness of Chinese long-term investments in Africa outside of the extractive sector certainly belies what official Beijing likes to cast as its economic commitment to Africa. Therefore African governments would be naive to take Beijing's rhetoric of South-South solidarity at face value. The harsh reality is that China is no less self-serving than any other state. If any proof was needed, the recent episode in Chinese-Zimbabwean relations provided it.[69]

The Zimbabwean regime of Robert Mugabe has in recent years turned to China to soften the impact of US and EU sanctions. But when Mugabe traveled to China to secure a bailout from the Beijing government he returned almost empty-handed, reportedly receiving a mere $6 million for grain imports.[70] According to one report, "the platinum concessions offered by Zimbabwe were not a sufficient incentive for China to grant funds on the scale requested by Mugabe."[71] That China's interests supersede vague discourses on South-South solidarity is also a lesson learned by South Africa. Complaining that cheap Chinese textile imports threaten to annihilate local industries, South African trade unions exhorted the Pretoria government to take recourse to the WTO to protect textile industries. Reacting to these concerns, a Chinese official dryly noted that "any move by the South African government to restrict textile imports from China would violate the WTO free trade agreement."[72]

China's hard-nosed economic interests are also reflected in Angola, where some 2,500 Chinese workers have arrived to work for Chinese companies whose work will be financed by the oil-backed loan that Beijing granted to the Angolan government. According to one source, a total of 30,000 Chinese workers are expected eventually in Angola for the same purpose.[73] The least one can say is that China's massive transfer of personnel is doubtful to have a positive impact on African job markets, the building of local capacities, and the transfer of technologies.[74]

Political Consequences

To assess the political impact of China's growing involvement on the continent, it may be useful to differentiate three groups of African countries. First, China's manifest return to Africa occurs at a time when many countries of the region continue to undergo difficult political transitions from authoritarian to democratic political systems (*democratizing/transition countries*). The assumption that China will make a constructive contribution to support transitions to democracy in Africa's fragile states appears somewhat farfetched. In contrast to all other major donors in the region, except Libya, the promotion of democracy is not an objective of China's foreign policy. Such a policy appears inconceivable to the extent that it does not square with Beijing's relativistic conception of individual human and political rights. In addition, the self-interest of the political elite of the one-party state does contravene the notion of democracy support abroad. Doing so would logically imply that China's communist leaders would dent their domestic political legitimacy. This is one of the reasons why Beijing doggedly clings to the dogma of noninterference. Its defense of sovereignty, often to the benefit of unsavory regimes, is likely to undermine existing efforts at political liberalization at large. For revenues from trade (and taxes), development assistance and other means of support widen the margins of maneuver of Africa's autocrats, and help them to rein in domestic demands for democracy and the respect for human rights.[75] These mutually advantageous interactions are at the core of China's attractiveness to African state leaders and they are likely to go to the detriment of ordinary Africans.[76]

Second, China's impact on *mineral-rich countries* is also a source of concern. Chinese interest in African resources comes at a time when Western nongovernmental organizations, recently supported by governments, have initiated an evermore prominent debate on the relationship between mineral wealth on the one hand and its detrimental effects on developing countries on the other. It revolves around possible options and regulatory frameworks to transform mineral wealth from a "curse" into a vector of socioeconomic development. In light of its rapidly growing reliance on imports, it seems implausible that

China will join these efforts, let alone subordinate its economic interests to international attempts to solve the structural problems of richly endowed countries, as these are likely to hold back its access to resources.[77]

What is more, Beijing has no economic incentive to fall in line with Western views on issues such as fiscal transparency and accountability. By rejecting regulation efforts on the grounds of noninterference, China can position itself as a free-rider and is prone to win the political favor of and, by extension, economic benefits from sovereign-conscious governments (for instance, Angola). In that regard, the case of Darfur/Sudan is illuminating insofar as it underscores the extent to which China is prepared to defend its economic interests. If Sudan provides any clue for the future, it seems inconceivable that Beijing, unencumbered by the humanitarian tragedy in Darfur, will compromise its interests for the sake of "minor" (domestic) issues such as transparency.

A third group of countries where China's forays may be particularly perceptible are *postconflict states*. On the one hand, China's increasing involvement in UN peacekeeping in those states is certainly a positive development, even more so since only a small minority of Western industrialized states has shown the political willingness to make troops available for peacekeeping on the continent. On the other, however, one has to question the coherence and credibility of Chinese peacekeeping efforts if the country otherwise pursues strategies that may contribute to the eruption or prolongation of violent conflicts. For example, while China is currently an important troop-contributing country to the UN Mission in Liberia, its economic interests helped President Charles Taylor to maintain himself in power. China imported almost half of Liberia's timber in 2000 and thus provided Taylor with considerable wherewithal. It was only in July 2003 that China and France, likewise an important buyer of Liberian timber, brought themselves to reluctantly nod through UN sanctions against Liberia's timber exports, which both had previously opposed on the devious grounds of "increased unemployment" in Liberia.[78] The plummeting of revenues from timber exports and rebel groups forced Taylor to leave the country in August 2003 and the peace process finally began.

Conclusion

Will China's powerful return to the continent and the concomitant diversification of Africa's external relations change in any meaningful way the position of African states in the international system? In political terms, this may well be the case in the future, but it appears that this question will not be decided upon in Africa, but in Beijing and Washington. Should Brzezinski's contention be correct that China is assimilating into the international system, the answer, at least in the long run, will probably be *no*. For if China's integration in global markets is socializing the country's foreign policy and if in turn Beijing's interests, notably energy security, will be accommodated by nonconfrontational Western behavior, the Chinese needs for allies in Africa and other parts of the non-Western world are likely to diminish. In economic terms, China's impact on Africa's place in the global economy is equally uncertain. To begin with, the diversification of Africa's external economic ties is a potentially promising development. However, the big picture so far is one in which Chinese-African economic relations are widely unbalanced and tend to replicate Africa's asymmetrical relationships with the West—a West from which Beijing so vividly claims to differ. As a result, Africa's marginal place in the global system, defined by its limited value as a provider of mineral resources, may in effect be perpetuated by the fact that Chinese economic interests in Africa do not differ substantially from those of Western states. As the case of textile industries demonstrates, initial economic impulses from Chinese investments may not be sustainable insofar as Chinese companies pursue cool-headed strategies in the hunt for comparative advantages in an era of economic globalization. As for development assistance, China's aid may have a marginal socioeconomic impact. Not only is much of its aid tied, it also helps to underpin the political economies of narrow state elites. Judging from its increasing influence, however, China's elite-centered modes of assistance have proved extremely effective. They help to cultivate the goodwill of African leaders that provide Beijing with diplomatic support and valuable contracts as a matter of reciprocity. In this sense, state elites are probably the economic and, by extension, the political winners of China's growing involvement in Africa.

That aspect hints at the political repercussions of China's engagement with African states. Beijing uses the pillars of its foreign policy, notably unconditional respect for state sovereignty and its corollary, noninterference, in the pursuit of its interests, be it energy security, multipolarity, or the "One China" principle. To achieve these goals, Beijing is prepared to recklessly defend autocratic regimes that commit human-rights abuses and forestall democratic reforms for narrow ends of regime survival. Finally, China's increasingly prominent role as a supplier of arms to Africa is also a source of concern.

In summary, there is virtually no way around the conclusion that China's massive return to Africa presents a negative political development that "almost certainly does not contribute to the promotion of peace, prosperity and democracy on the continent."[79] Despite this, Western decision makers have little reason to claim the moral high ground vis-à-vis China. A fair number of flaws and criticisms that need to be leveled against Beijing's politics in Africa do equally apply, though to a lesser extent, to Western policies toward Africa.[80] And yet, it also needs to be borne in mind that the policies of Western governments toward Africa have come to reflect a more-normative and reform-oriented edge in recent years and, despite pervasive ambiguities, have broadly sought to promote democracy, human rights, and conflict prevention.

More importantly, however, will prove the nature of the relationship between Africa's international organizations (that is, AU, NEPAD, and ECOWAS) and an increasingly influential China. Beijing's support for AU and NEPAD has so far proved little more than rhetoric and is ambivalent at best. For instance, China is insisting that its support for NEPAD be channeled through the framework of the China-Africa Cooperation Forum, thereby enabling it to avoid "the potentially awkward position of having to support the key structural elements that are ultimately necessary for NEPAD's success: transparency, democracy, free press."[81] Similar ambiguities surround China's support for the AU, which seems to be limited to warm words and smaller ad hoc payments. That the Chinese government donated $400 thousand in support of the AU's mediation efforts to resolve the Darfur crisis in early 2005, a move it hailed as a contribution to peace-building in Africa, appears disconcertingly cynical.[82] This raises important questions as to the relationship between China and Africa's reform-minded bodies exactly because AU, ECOWAS, and NEPAD have recently espoused procedures and principles that clearly contravene the cornerstones of Chinese statecraft (that is, sovereignty, noninterference). The progressive pathway taken by the African Union and ECOWAS in regard to the prevention and resolution of violent conflicts is particularly at odds with Beijing's political concepts, for both organizations claim far-reaching prerogatives, including military intervention, in order to prevent or terminate large-scale human-rights abuses and crimes against humanity. One may also recount that NEPAD's so-called African Peer Review Mechanism is, at least in theory, an instrument of political interference in the domestic affairs of states, which aims at promoting development and democracy in Africa. In the final analysis, it is not obvious how these competing conceptions can be squared—provided that Africa's regional bodies are determined to put their pledges for democracy and human rights into practice.

Notes

1. E. S. Medeiros and M. Taylor Fravel, "China's New Diplomacy," *Foreign Affairs*, 82, no. 6 (2003): 22–35; R. Sutter, "Asia in the Balance: America and China's 'Peaceful Rise,'" *Current History*, 103, no. 674 (2004): 284–89.

2. Z. Brzezinski and J. Mearsheimer, "Clash of the Titans," *Foreign Policy*, 146 (2005), 46.

3. This section is based on I. Taylor, "China's Foreign Policy towards Africa in the 1990s," *Journal of Modern African Studies* 36, no. 3 (1998): 443–60.

4. Ibid., 450.

5. D. J. Muekalia, "Africa and China's Strategic Partnership," *African Security Review*, 13, no. 1 (2004), 10.

6. E. Economy, "Changing Course on China," *Current History*, 102, no. 665 (2003): 243–49.

7. M. A. Weinstein, "China's Geostrategy: Playing a Waiting Game," January 9, 2005, <http://www.pinr.com>.

8. Note, however, that Beijing recently issued an official paper on its policy toward Africa. The paper ("China's Africa Policy") is available on the website of the Chinese Ministry of Foreign Affairs, <http://www.fmprc.gov.cn/eng/zxxx/t230615.htm>.

9. For the historical background, see P. Snow, *The Star Raft: China's Encounter with Africa* (Ithaca: Cornell University Press, 1989).

10. I. Taylor, "The 'All-weather Friend'? Sino-African Interaction in the Twenty-First Century," in *Africa in International Politics: External Involvement on the Continent*, eds. I. Taylor and P. Williams (London: Routledge, 2004), 87; R. Marchal, "Comment être semblable tout en étant différent? Les relations entre la Chine et l'Afrique," in *Afrique-Asie: Échanges inégaux et mondialisation subalterne*, ed. R. Marchal. Forthcoming.

11. See *BBC Monitoring Newsletter*, 2005.

12. These are Burkina Faso, Chad, Gambia, Malawi, São Tomé e Principe, and Swaziland. In October 2005, Senegal (once more) established relations with Beijing instead of Taiwan.

13. However, China also provided 125 police officers in the UN mission in Haiti, which recognizes Taiwan.

14. *BBC Monitoring Newsletter*, 2005.

15. *Christian Science Monitor*, January 6, 2005.

16. *The Economist*, February 7, 2004; *L'humanité*, February 4, 2004.

17. For example, Germany's bilateral assistance to Sub-Saharan Africa was $1.34 billion in 2002.

18. I. Taylor, "Taiwan's Foreign Policy and Africa: The Limitations of Dollar Diplomacy," *Journal of Contemporary China*, 11, no. 30 (2002): 125–40.

19. Source: International Monetary Fund, *Direction of Trade Statistics*. The United Nations Development Programme (UNDP) puts the figure much higher, that is, $29.64 billion. See <http://www.undp.org.cn>.

20. *BBC Online*, January 6, 2006.

21. See *IRIN News*, December 17, 2003; Muekalia, "Africa and China's Strategic Partnership," *African Security Review*, 8–10; Taylor, "The 'All-weather Friend'?" 89–91.

22. The creation of the institution was supported by UNDP. See UNDP press release, "New Public–Private Partnership to Promote Sino-African Ties," March 18, 2005.

23. United Nations Conference on Trade and Development (UNCTAD), *World Investment Report 2004* (Geneva: UNCTAD, 2004).

24. *Beijing Time*, December 16, 2003.

25. *China Daily*, November 26, 2004.

26. *Mail and Guardian*, May 23, 2005.

27. D. Zweig and Bi Janhai, "China's Global Hunt for Energy," *Foreign Affairs*, 84, no. 5 (2005): 25–38.

28. R. Kaplinsky, "The Sun Rises in the East," Commission for Africa Report Response, Institute of Development Studies, London, 2005, <http://www.ids.ac.uk/ids/news/CFA%20Response/Kaplinsky Response.pdf>.

29. See "China Struggles to Fulfill Spiraling Energy Demands," *Jane's Intelligence Review*, 16, no. 7 (2004), 56.

30. S. Ellis, "Briefing: West Africa and Its Oil," *African Affairs*, 102, no. 406 (2003), 135.

31. *International Herald Tribune*, July 31, 2004.

32. See International Energy Agency, *World Energy Investment Outlook* (Paris: IEA, 2003), 167; *Africa Confidential*, March 28, 2004.

33. For 2004, see *Dow Jones Newswire*, January 21, 2005. For 2003: Institute of Energy Economics, January 2004, Japan <http://eneken.ieej.or.jp>.

34. See Energy Information Administration 2005 <http://www.eia.doe.gov/emeu/ipsr/t11b.xls>.

35. Cited in *USA Today*, June 21, 2005.

36. On the political economy of reform and nonreform see N. Van de Walle, *African Economies and the Politics of Permanent Crisis, 1979–1999* (Cambridge: Cambridge University Press, 2001).

37. BBC Monitoring Newsletter, January 8, 2004.

38. See, for example, *International Herald Tribune*, May 15, 2002.

39. See *Inter Press Service*, June 13, 2004; T. Rumbaugh and N. Blancher, "China: International Trade and WTO Accession," IMF Working Paper (04/36), Washington, DC, 2004, 12.

40. See, for instance, *SouthScan*, June 30, 2005; *Financial Times*, March 15, 2005.

41. See United Nations Office on Drugs and Crime (UNODC), *Why Fighting Crime Can Assist Development in Africa* (Vienna: UNODC, 2005), 78.

42. For the example of Ethiopia, see *Wall Street Journal*, March 29, 2005; on Cameroon, see *Cameroon Tribune*, May 30, 2005.

43. C. Alden, "China in Africa," *Survival*, 47, 3 (2005), 155.

44. See "China Struggles to Fulfill Spiraling Energy Demands," *Jane's Intelligence Review*, 16, no. 7 (2004): 56.

45. *Africa Energy* 77 (August 2004) 12, 19; *Africa Confidential*, May 28, 2004.

46. *Wall Street Journal*, January 9, 2006.

47. *New York Times*, December 14, 2004.

48. E. S. Downs, "The Chinese Energy Security Debate," *The China Quarterly*, 177 (2004), 25, 30.

49. See "NOCs 1—IOCs 0," *Petroleum Economist*, April 2005, 4–9; see also *International Herald Tribune*, March 2, 2005.

50. China ranked second in arms transfers agreements with African states from 2000 to 2003. See R. F. Grimmett, "Conventional Arms Transfers to Developing Nations, 1996–2003" (Washington, DC: Congressional Research Service, 2004), 27. See also Taylor, "The 'All-weather Friend,'?" 94–97.

51. *Africa Confidential*, December 17, 2004.

52. American sanctions and the pull out of Western companies were related to Sudan's support of terrorism and human-rights violations in the oil-producing South. See D. H. Johnson, *The Root Causes of Sudan's Civil War* (Oxford: James Currey, 2003), 162–64; Human Rights Watch, *Sudan, Oil and Human Rights* (New York: Human Rights Watch, 2003).

53. See *Reuters*, September 15, 2004; *The Independent*, October 15, 2004.

54. Needless to say, China does not bear the sole responsibility for the international failure in Darfur. One has also to take into account the inconsistent positions of the US government and the ambiguous role of France. See M. Clough, "Darfur: Whose Responsibility to Protect?" in *World Report 2005* (New York: Human Rights Watch, 2005): 24–39.

55. Oil fields in Darfur may be another reason for Beijing's position. See *New York Times*, August 8, 2004.

56. F. Berrigan, "Peace Accord in Sudan: Good News for People or Oil Companies?," *Foreign Policy in Focus*, January 14, 2005, <http://www.fpif.org/fpiftxt/985>.

57. See table. The pattern is also evident in regard to investments since the extractive sector attracts 50-to-80 percent of all foreign-direct investments to Africa. See "FDI—Oil Be Back," *EIU Business Africa*, October 1, 2004.

58. *EIU Business Africa*, November 16, 2004.

59. As of 2005, thirty-seven African states are participating in AGOA.

60. International Monetary Fund, *Regional Economic Outlook Sub-Saharan Africa* (Washington, DC: IMF, 2005), 15–20.

61. *Business Report*, May 20, 2005.

62. Taylor, "The 'All-weather Friend,'?" 98.

63. *Independent*, April 25, 2005; *The Reporter* (Gaborone), May 27, 2005.

64. For example, some 5,000 Chinese live in Lesotho, some 3,000 in Cameroon, that is, the country hosts by now more Chinese than French citizens. Nigeria has a population of some 50,000 Chinese. See *BBC Monitoring*, August 7, 2005; Author's interview, Yaoundé, Western diplomat, May 2005.

65. D. Bräutigam, "Close Encounters: Chinese Business Networks as Industrial Catalysts in Sub-Sahara Africa," *African Affairs*, 102, no. 408 (2003): 447–67.

66. Alden, "China in Africa," 157. The titles of some articles are highly indicative: "Zimbabwe's New Colonialists," *Weekly Standard*, May 25, 2005; "Mixed

Reaction to Chinese Invasion," *The Reporter*, May 24, 2005; "Uganda Should Invite 'Real' Chinese Investors," *New Vision*, May 10, 2005; "Mozambique Invaded by China, Claims Renamo," *AIM*, May 10, 2005.

67. M. Mbeki, "China and SA Must Lessen Dependence on the West," *Sunday Times* (Johannesburg), October 24, 2004.

68. R. Jenkins and C. Edwards, *How Does China's Growth Affect Poverty Reduction in Asia, Africa, and Latin America?* (Norwich: University of East Anglia, 2004).

69. For an assessment of Zimbabwe's relations with China, see Friedrich-Ebert-Foundation (FES), *The "Look East Policy" of Zimbabwe Now Focuses on China* (Harare: FES, 2004).

70. *Zimbabwe Independent*, July 29, 2005. In the same week, however, China opposed discussion at the UN Security Council of a UN report into Zimbabwe's demolition campaign that left some 700,000 persons homeless.

71. *BBC Online*, August 1, 2005.

72. *IRIN News*, June 29, 2005.

73. *Le Monde*, July 6, 2005.

74. C. Alden, "Leveraging the Dragon: Toward 'An Africa that Can Say No,'" March 1, 2005, <http://yaleglobal.yale.edu/display.article?id=5336>.

75. For the case of Zimbabwe, see *Christian Science Monitor*, May 30, 2005.

76. Alden, "China in Africa," 153.

77. For a useful overview over the menu of options in resource-rich countries, see I. Bannon and P. Collier, eds., *Natural Resources and Violent Conflict: Options and Actions* (Washington, DC: World Bank, 2003).

78. P. Johnston, "Timber Booms, State Busts: The Political Economy of Liberian Timber," *Review of African Political Economy*, 31, no. 101 (2004), 447.

79. Taylor, "The 'All-weather Friend,'?" 99.

80. See various contributions on Western policies toward Africa in I. Taylor and P. Williams, eds., *Africa in International Politics: External Involvement on the Continent* (London: Routledge, 2004).

81. D. Thompson, "China's Soft Power in Africa: From the 'Beijing Consensus' to Health Diplomacy," *China Brief*, 5, no. 21 (2005), 2.

82. People's Republic of China, Ministry of Foreign Affairs, press release, January 6, 2005.

10

Superpower Osama

Symbolic Discourse in the Indian Ocean Region
after the Cold War

Jeremy Prestholdt

"THERE ARE TWO superpowers in the world," a man in Mombasa, Kenya explained in 2002: "the United States and Osama bin Laden." "At the moment," he added, "Osama is the one with the upper hand."[1] To appreciate the logic of this equation, and thus the symbolic potency of bin Laden, we should recognize that much of the world saw 9/11 as an unprecedented symbolic blow to the United States. Some embraced the actions of the hijackers as a figurative victory over a hegemon that they believe bears great responsibility for global inequities. In a world increasingly defined by shared imagery, from brand logos to twenty-four-hour television news, 9/11's planners strategically harnessed the dramaturgy of visual simultaneity. They not only targeted icons of America's financial and military prowess, but there was just enough time between attacks for news cameras, which fed thousands of media outlets worldwide, to be trained on the World Trade Center at the moment the second plane struck.[2] Unable to mount a significant military offensive against America, the hijackers delivered a resounding blow to the superpower both by striking its prominent national symbols and capturing the spotlight of the international media.

Jean Baudrillard was among the first to reflect on 9/11 as more than an act of violence but also, and perhaps more importantly, a symbolic assault on the United States.[3] Baudrillard's analysis of the global repercussions of the event stressed the extraordinary humiliation of 9/11.[4] This humiliation of the superpower inflicted by individuals, not a state, was a primary catalyst for the proliferation of Osama bin Laden iconography—from murals to T-shirts—after the attacks, particularly in Africa, South Asia, and Southeast Asia. The profound humiliation dealt the US also helps to explain the seemingly contradictory response of some in the global South: sympathy for the victims of the attacks counterbalanced by a sense of vindication. In the horror and humiliation of 9/11 a *symbolic exchange*, to use Baudrillard's expression, was struck. The humiliation felt by a sizable portion of the world's population, who see their interests as marginal to the desires of US multinational corporations and foreign policy-makers, was repaid, at least in the eyes of many, by the humiliation of America on its own soil. To a great extent this is why the event, or more precisely the *media event*, of 9/11 engendered excitement across the global South.[5]

Genuinely surprised by this mixed response to 9/11, the American press turned its attention to voices articulating the psychological traumas of humiliation in the global South. The crude "Why do they hate us?" question that occupied the US media for months after 9/11 offered fleeting consideration of such voices. Though moored in overly simplistic terms and absent of insight into the motivations of the hijackers, the ensuing debates about perceptions of America and American foreign policy revealed a cacophony of voices articulating similar sentiments. A *Dateline NBC* interview with unnamed Pakistani men in December 2001 captured visceral reactions that revealed a dual sense of historical humiliation and vindication:

> HODA KOTB, *DATELINE* CORRESPONDENT IN PAKISTAN: What was your reaction when you learned about the World Trade Center bombing?
>
> UNIDENTIFIED MAN 2: I was kind of a bit happy that someone at least had done something to America.

KOTB: Was there any satisfaction in the World Trade Center bombings?

UNIDENTIFIED MAN 3: Not really satisfaction, but a certain sense that you have brought the world's greatest power to their [sic] knees for a minute, because they're devastated, and they don't know what to do.

KOTB: And that felt good?

MAN 3: Good in a way, yes. Because you do that to us all the time, and then you don't expect us to do anything in return.[6]

Almost two years after the attacks, twenty-seven-year-old Nigerian shoe salesman Sanusi Ibrahim was more direct. Wearing a bin Laden T-shirt, he explained that he considered Osama a hero because, "he will continue to shame America."[7] It is this perception of the 9/11 attacks as a response to historic humiliation that registered so profoundly in many parts of the world.[8] And since all of the perpetrators died, the symbolic capital of the attacks went to the event's coordinator, making Osama bin Laden a common symbol of discontent for many people around the world. In his orchestration of such an extreme act of hostility toward the superpower, Osama came to be seen among some, according to Khalid Mahmud, as a "restorer of pride to so much of the Third World."[9] Osama bin Laden became the singular icon of an event that symbolically brought, in the eyes of the unnamed Pakistani man, "the world's greatest power to [its] knees."

This essay is an attempt to account for the popularity of Osama bin Laden imagery and its relation to deeper social and political frustrations. It traces both how Osama bin Laden became one of the most celebrated folk heroes in recent history and, just as importantly, how his symbolic manifestations became references for a great variety of grievances, ones often incommensurate with his agenda. Osama became a powerful icon both because of the symbolic exchange of 9/11 and because people interpolated the imagery of his actions into a diversity of national and transnational rhetorics of discontent. His image has appeared on everything from protest posters in Surabaya to mobile-phone screens in Amsterdam and graffiti in Rio de Janeiro. Osama T-shirts in Cape Town were captioned, LONG LIVE. In Peshawar and Niamey similar T-shirts labeled Osama, WORLD HEAD and

My Hero. In Caracas, a popular shirt bearing Osama's image simply read, The Best. This objectification of Osama suggests that in many parts of the world bin Laden imagery is far less contingent on his message than his mutability as an icon, or the ease with which his symbolic acts wrought an iconography that can be integrated into individual worldviews, local political discourses, and consumer desire.

After 9/11, Osama became a symbol of political sensibilities, popular sentiment, and, in many places, current style. For a small few, bin Laden's popularity derived from his narrow political vision. For others, bin Laden was an object of fashion. Osama T-shirts, posters, and perfume (sold in Pakistan and India) came into vogue as a means of personal reference to events of great significance. Yet others perceived Osama as an ideal hook on which to hang their particular frustrations. For instance, many who celebrated his attacks on the United States decried the killing of civilians. Others saw Osama as a defender of morality in the face of American cultural imperialism. Many more agreed with his critiques of American interventionism but did not share his interest in a global caliphate. It is this symbolic pliability of Osama that concerns me here. More specifically, I am interested in how the icon Osama, much like other icons, has acted as a focal point, symbolically linking people in many parts of the world in a "community of feeling" based on shared sentiments, often beyond the boundaries of region and religion. (See the introduction to this volume.) Indeed, the reasons why bin Laden gained emblematic importance in disparate locales after 9/11 differed, in some cases dramatically, according to the grievances he was imagined to address. The extent to which people saw their interests as according with the actions of bin Laden suggests that as a floating icon Osama has become an important reference in post–cold war symbolic discourse.

I will begin by exploring the ways in which the icon Osama has been integrated into articulations of particular grievances. I will then address the conflation of local dissatisfaction and global consciousness that has, since the end of the cold war, fostered intense resentment of the West, ensured the attractiveness of overarching icons of dissent, and made the Osama icon resonant with a variety of experiences. By way of example, I will focus on one locale where young people were

10.1. Osama Bin Laden T-Shirt, 2008. Photograph by the author.

attracted to Osama iconography immediately after 9/11: Mombasa, Kenya. To appreciate the conceptual links young Mombasan Muslims (particularly those who self-identify as "Swahili") made with Osama's actions, I will highlight the experiences of middle- and lower-class urban Muslim men, from the 1980s to the present, and the repercussions for them of al Qaeda operations in Kenya as well as 9/11. Through this strategy I wish to demonstrate how, in the immediate aftermath of 9/11, people in one locale fused their particular frustrations with a potent symbol. In Mombasa, references to Osama implied neither an adherence to his ideological positions nor a desire to mimic his actions, but instead hinged on perceptions of Osama as embodying a range of desirable qualities, almost superhuman abilities—perceptions shared by many around the world. Osama iconography mirrored that of other global icons in Mombasa: symbols used to articulate rhetorics of dissent that are simultaneously domestic and transnational.

Symbolic Calculus in the Post–Cold War World

Icons of dissent are not new. Lenin, Mao, Malcolm X, Che, Mandela, Subcomandante Marcos, and many others have been appropriated around the world as symbols of fashion and personal political persuasion. By the turn of the 21st century many of these earlier icons retained little of their once-subversive veneers. In contrast, Osama's actions made him a highly controversial, and therefore extremely potent, iconic reference. In fact, many saw Osama as filling the post–cold war void of opposition to the West's liberal-democratic project.[10] In the absence of a superpower alternative to the United States, Osama offered a screen onto which the grievances of diverse populations could be projected. Though not the leader of a state or national political movement, Osama gave a face to what Anna Lowenhaupt Tsing calls the "dream space" of global possibility.[11] The US government's rhetoric only enhanced this position. Presidents Bill Clinton and George W. Bush both referred to Osama as "America's public enemy number one." Giving him such a title only validated perceptions of Osama's power. To be so feared, many concluded, Osama must be extraordinarily powerful. As posters depicting Osama locked in battle with American fighter jets or juxtaposed with President Bush suggest, the elevation of Osama to public enemy number one had the effect of confirming the perceived equivalence of Osama with a superpower.

For Osama to be imagined as a superpower, historical timing was critical; only after the cold war was such equivalency plausible.[12] The North Vietnamese and Afghan mujahedeen, for instance, challenged and defeated the US and USSR without the world's presumption that they were the equivalents of superpowers. The dissolution of the Communist Bloc, however, spurred a rethinking of the notion of superpower and how to challenge it. It is no coincidence that bin Laden, a player in the defeat of one superpower, gained insights into the global challenge of another, adding to his meek arsenal one of the most powerful weapons of the post–cold war world: the global media.[13] The Afghan mujahedeen defeated the Soviets by finding ingenious ways to produce psychologically injurious effects. For instance, they took great pains to ensure that the Soviets never saw them, dead or alive. Soviet soldiers came to fear the opponents they referred to as *dukhi*, or ghosts.[14] A decade after the Afghan war, Osama orchestrated the use of American airliners and the global media to similar effect. The logic was clear. Since an al Qaeda military defeat of the US was impossible, the attackers turned to the symbolic realm. There, a handful of individuals could have dramatic effect as real military power can be obscured in an equation of symbols: humiliation met by humiliation on TV. It is this confrontation—the play of real-time images that graphically demonstrated American humiliation, what Mark Danner has called the *Spectacular*—which captivated the world.[15] Possessing limited military resources, al Qaeda used this simple logic of symbolic confrontation to its advantage.

The incessant reproduction of Osama's image by the global media has been critical to his popularity. The visuality of information in the post–cold war world, combined with local frustrations and similarities of grievance, has allowed for a linking of particular concerns with geopolitics in new and abstract ways. The familiarity many people now have with other parts of the world as a result of the visual media has not necessarily been accompanied by proportionally enriched material realities. Indeed, the visible prosperity of parts of the post–cold war world has done little to dampen the frustrations of many that do not enjoy such wealth. As Yahia Said explained in the days after 9/11, "The level of wealth [elsewhere] is so much more visible in poor countries now, through television [and] movies," that this has created a "profound sense of being left out."[16] Comparisons serve to heighten both the frustration and humiliation of people who see themselves as having little and see others as benefiting from their dispossession. This inseparability of shifts in self-perception and global consciousness has had profound effects on dissent.[17] New media made Osama accessible across the globe, and the visuality of inequality made him all the more attractive.

The popularity of Osama imagery after 9/11 was an important barometer of post–cold war disillusionment. It was also a dramatic indicator of the enduring commonalities of grievance across the global South, echoing sentiments expressed nearly fifty years earlier at the Bandung meeting. The underlying dissatisfaction and sense of marginality that drew Kenyans, Pakistanis, and Indonesians to the Osama icon after 9/11 are rooted in shared histories of colonialization, postcolonial repression, and inequality, common experiences that constitute what Christopher J. Lee refers to as certain "communities of fate." (See the introduction to this volume.) With an eye to such common grievances, and in a bid to garner sympathy, Osama has largely limited his message to critique. He has presented himself not as a leader but as a populist instigator. He has produced no political manifesto nor has he articulated a detailed political vision beyond references to a global Islamic state. Instead of mapping a clear political course for Muslim societies, he condemns US interventionism and state repression throughout the Muslim world.[18]

By leveling broad and vague critiques, Osama has left his image open to extraordinary interpretation. This has allowed for his appeal in places such as Lanzhou, China, where Ma Wenke has explained that, "Bin Laden fights to defend freedom, equality and justice for all the Muslims who are oppressed throughout the world."[19] Likewise, in Southeastern Nigeria, Commander Dokubo Asari, leader of a predominantly Christian, ethnically Ijaw militia (the Niger Delta People's Volunteer Force), told reporters that he drew inspiration from Osama because of his, "stand against western imperialism and the corruption of the minds of the people of the world." "This should appeal to any discerning mind," Asari concluded, "and that of any person who stands against evil."[20] More generally, the high esteem in which many held Osama after 9/11 made him a reference for general attributes, such as bravery and fearlessness, to which many young people aspire. Because he is a particularly intimidating symbol, many have used Osama to project images of themselves as fearless or dangerous. In the Eastern Democratic Republic of Congo as well as Côte d'Ivoire (non-

Muslim) combatants painted the word "Osama" on their vehicles and used bin Laden T-shirts as fatigues.[21] Even Thailand's Hell's Angels, a group that certainly has no affiliation with al Qaeda, emblazoned their motorcycles and helmets with images of Osama.[22] Despite his role in the horrific 1998 bombing of the American Embassy, a cross-section of young Nairobians evoke the Osama icon in similar ways. In 2008, among buses *(matatu)* emblazoned with images of 50 Cent and Barack Obama, one *matatu* in the majority-Christian capital sported an Osama portrait with the menacing caption DESTROYER.

Al Qaeda's attack on the United States allowed the world to make Osama a symbol not just of the grievances he expresses, but also of more general frustrations, principles, and desirable traits. Whereas some Muslims are, no doubt, attracted to bin Laden due to his visions of a global Islamic state, the popularity of Osama beyond those sharing his political vision demonstrates his utility as a hook on which to hang individual and collective worldviews. To a degree, Osama shapes these diverse readings by presenting himself through a material vocabulary that combines the pious with the insurgent. In the most frequently reproduced images of Osama, he wears a starched *dishdash* and white turban to signify devoutness under even the harshest conditions. He juxtaposes these symbols of piety with a camouflage field jacket and a Kalashnikov at the ready. The symbolism he wishes the world to grasp is easily readable: he is a pious guerrilla, "traditional" and revolutionary. By signifying both the religious and the rebel—a man who is willing to risk his life for his values—he directs a play of symbols that resonates with Muslim and non-Muslim audiences.[23]

One striking example of this image of Osama as both a man of principles and counterweight to the excesses of American hegemony was a 2003 Calcutta street-theater production *(jatra)* that featured a Hindu cast and attracted mixed Hindu and Muslim audiences. The *jatra*, which drew large crowds in the wake of the American invasion of Iraq, portrayed Osama as a solitary heroic figure facing a White House filled with bloodthirsty killers intent on carrying forth their agenda regardless of its cost in innocent lives. With melodramatic color the *jatra* painted America as acting in total disregard for basic human values whereas Osama seems a devout Robin Hood, striving to protect the innocents America heartlessly attacks. Though the government threatened to shut down the production for fear that it might exacerbate tensions between Hindus and Muslims, the jatra had the opposite effect. It accorded well with public condemnations of American military intervention in Afghanistan and Iraq, and it highlighted critiques of American foreign policy shared by Hindus and Muslims.[24] In their dramatization of 9/11 and its aftermath the jatra's Hindu producers confirmed America as the global villain and made Osama a sympathetic hero.

As complex as the rationales for Osama's popularity in some non-Muslim communities have been, the reasons for his popularity among Muslims have been even more multifaceted. Mombasa provides an interesting case study of the reasons why Osama was interpolated into the symbolic discourse of some Muslim communities after 9/11. Although bin Laden's pronouncements diverge from the general interests of Mombasan Muslims, the symbolic potency of one man attacking a superpower—particularly one that claims to be acting for the benefit of all Muslims—is compelling.[25] To gain better perspective on Osama imagery in Mombasa after 9/11, we should see him as part of a broader continuum of fashionable icons that embody desirable attributes. Bollywood, Hollywood, and East Asian film stars, particularly action-film stars, have long been symbols of virility, desirability, courage, and power. Since the 1980s, Bob Marley has been a constant reference for young Mombasans who find in him an empathetic voice whose critiques of inequality resonate with and shape their own. In the 1990s, Malcolm X and American rapper Tupac Shakur became common references for defiance among young men.

In the more recent past, young Muslim (and non-Muslim) Mombasans have celebrated Che Guevara and 50 Cent, the former because he embodies a fashionable challenge to the status quo and the latter a spirit of fearlessness. The diversity of this pantheon not only illustrates Mombasans' familiarity with transnational popular culture but also offers insight into the way that young people evoke symbolic aspects of an icon without reference to the ideology of the actual historic figure. For instance, the popularity of Bob Marley among Muslim youth has led many young men to grow dreadlocks; yet, hardly any espouse

10.2. Tupac Shakur on a *matatu*, 2005. Photograph by the author.

Rastafarianism. By the same token, many young Mombasans admired Osama after 9/11, but they did not emulate him. Young men who downloaded Osama images for their mobile screens were no more jihadists than Mombasans who wear Che shirts are socialist revolutionaries.

In the days after 9/11, Osama became part of a Mombasan iconic pantheon that traversed the boundaries of religion, politics, and entertainment. The fact that Osama bridged these arenas—he is a self-proclaimed representative of Muslim political interests who has captured the media limelight—made him a likely symbol. What propelled bin Laden to "superpower" status among some young men was that he came to symbolize not only an irreverence for the US and general critique of injustice, but he also appealed directly to many Muslims' sense of marginalization and common cause with other Muslims globally.

For the remainder of this essay, I will consider the confluence of global consciousness and local grievance that made Osama a symbol of dissent among some young people in Mombasa's predominantly Muslim Old Town and adjacent Swahili neighborhoods. For a time immediately after 9/11, Osama bin Laden was a celebrated folk hero among many middle- and lower-class urban Muslims, those who felt socially and politically marginalized by both the Kenyan central government and the local political elite. In the days following the 2001 attacks on the World Trade Center and the Pentagon, Old Town Mombasa was spattered with Osama graffiti: VOTE FOR OSAMA, SUPER POWER OSAMA, OSAMA IS OUR HERO.[26] Some even tagged one of the Old Town's thoroughfares "Osama bin Laden Street."[27] Osama's image appeared on T-shirts, mobile phones, and the walls of shops. Later, it appeared on posters at demonstrations against government repression and the American occupations in Afghanistan and Iraq. A banner at a 2001 protest of the American invasion of Afghanistan read: BIN LADEN IS OUR HERO.[28]

Mombasans rejected bin Laden's calls to violence. Yet Osama imagery led government authorities and analysts of the Kenyan coast to conclude that Osama references were a clear indication of local collusion with international terrorism.[29] Such a superficial interpretation of Osama imagery is not only dangerous, given the deeper suspicion of Muslims in Kenya (a point to which I will return below), but it also misses the symbolic poignancy of Osama's actions. More distressingly, it obscures the political grievances that many young, urban coastal Muslims used Osama imagery to represent.

In the sections that follow, I will provide context to Osama iconography by outlining specific histories of repression, cosmopolitanism, and translation that made Osama a powerful symbol for the grievances articulated by some young Mombasan Muslims. An examination of the popularity of Osama imagery in Mombasa demonstrates the points of slippage between Osama's message and his image, and challenges the presumption that Osama references evidenced material support for terrorism. By focusing on the view-points of young Muslims who neither subscribed to bin Laden's political agenda nor shared his commitment to violence, but who gravitated to the Osama icon as a symbol for their personal and collective experiences, we can better appreciate the deeper angst that has given Osama imagery as well as other iconography transnational appeal in the absence of shared ideology.

Cosmopolitanism and Marginality

Few have addressed the profound sense of political and social marginalization felt by middle- and lower-class Mombasan Muslims since the 1980s or the forms of global consciousness that have affected their perceptions of national and international events. The intersections of national alienation and cosmopolitanism have been instrumental in the shaping of local political imaginations, and these acted as a principal catalyst in the appeal of Osama imagery to some Mombasan youth. A distinct religious and cultural minority, many coastal Muslims faced eroding political representation and, consequently, diminishing educational and economic opportunities in the 1980s. But even while many young Mombasan Muslims suffer from discrimination and lack of access to educational opportunities within Kenya, they, in contrast to their rural Muslim neighbors, are one of the most cosmopolitan segments of Kenya's population.[30]

For centuries, the coast of Kenya absorbed immigrants from across Eastern Africa, Arabia, the Persian Gulf, and South Asia. This ensured significant cultural and religious diversity. In the limited space of Old Town Mombasa, Sunni, Shia, and Ibadhi Muslims live alongside Hindus and Christians. In surrounding suburbs, Muslims and Christians of multiple ethnic backgrounds, both from the coastal region and other parts of Kenya, live in close proximity. The great diversity of Mombasa's population has seeded an ideological, religious, and cultural dynamism. This dynamism is further compounded by class differences within sociocultural communities as well as the constant flow of people, goods, and ideas, particularly through urban Mombasa.

In the recent past, increased short-term employment opportunities for wealthy and middle-class Muslim Mombasans in Saudi Arabia, the Persian Gulf, Western Europe, and North America have further broadened Mombasa's networks of exchange. Thus, the anger sometimes directed toward the US overlays a relationship to the West that runs much deeper than relationships to any Islamist organizations.[31] Finally, a history of cosmopolitanism has shaped Mombasan desires for information from abroad. Since the late 1980s, rooftop satellite dishes on the coast have pointed away from Nairobi toward the Indian Ocean, bringing Arab, Asian, and Western news into coastal homes. Because even those who do not own satellite dishes regularly congregate at neighbors' homes to watch television—a phenomenon reminiscent of what James Brennan describes for radio listeners in the late colonial period (see Brennan in this volume)—most Mombasans in Old Town and its suburbs have long been exposed to programming that offers different viewpoints from those presented by Kenyan broadcasters.

The mobility and ever-expanding global consciousness of both middle- and lower-class Muslim Mombasans has been encouraged, in part, by increasing alienation. After independence in 1963, the Kenyan government pursued a pointedly inward-looking national-developmentalist agenda. The geopolitical and domestic pressures of the new state contributed to highly undemocratic power structures that bore many similarities to their colonial predecessors. This condition produced significant political disillusionment by the 1980s, and resulting political dissent across Kenya was met with repression by President Daniel arap Moi (1978–2002). Few segments of Kenya's population saw as significant a decline of fortunes by twenty-four years of Moi policy as middle- and lower-class coastal Muslims. Systematically passed over for political favors and represented in national politics by only a handful of fellow Muslims, many Muslims saw increasingly constricted economic and education opportunities in the 1980s. While the most politically well-connected in the Muslim community benefited from Moi's presidency, the economic opportunities and political voice of many young Muslims were severely limited by state distribution of coastal resources and the systematic harassment of Moi's critics.

The strategic importance of Mombasa as Eastern Africa's most valuable deep-water port also contributed to the alienation of those who claimed the historic city as their home. The port is critical to the Kenyan economy, and so its control has been a paramount concern of the colonial and postcolonial governments. Yet at independence, the legal status of the coastal region posed something of a historical conundrum. Though long administered by Nairobi, a ten-mile strip of the coast, which included the Port of Mombasa, was technically leased from the Sultan of Zanzibar and so was under British "protection." Practically speaking, this made little difference in the governing of the coastal region, but the drive toward independence raised the question of the coast's right to postindependence autonomy. (See Brennan in this volume.) Recognizing the economic necessity of the Port of Mombasa for postcolonial Kenya, the colonial government swiftly quashed separatist dreams of coastal autonomy, a move that drew—and still draws—the ire of many Mombasans.[32]

At independence, the coast was folded into a patrimonial state that systematically rewarded its clients with resources and political power. Soon, many less politically well-connected coastal residents were dispossessed of what economic opportunities they maintained during colonialism.[33] By the early 1990s, very little of the profits from, or opportunities offered by, regional mineral extraction, the tourist industry, or the Port of Mombasa were seen by any but the wealthiest Arab, Asian, and "upcountry" businessmen.[34] By the late 1990s, no Muslim had ever headed any of the government's more than two-hundred corporations. Only one, MP Sharif Nassir, had been appointed to the President's Cabinet.[35] Moreover, Muslim elected officials, both by choice and by constraint, did little to address the wellbeing of their constituents.

This political marginalization had multiple repercussions for middle- and lower-class Mombasan Muslims. For instance, many suffered acutely from a deteriorating state-educational system and found discrimination when applying to national universities. Lack of access to higher education had follow-on effects for employment. By the late 1990s, unemployment on the coast was twice that of the national average. Though the poor, both urban and rural, were most profoundly affected by the lack of opportunities, during research in Kenya in the 1990s I met no middle-class Mombasan Muslim who attended a Kenyan university, and knew few young people who had steady jobs. Thus, while not suffering in the same way as their poorer, rural neighbors, by the early 1990s middle-class Mombasan Muslims felt incredibly marginalized.

The 1990s would prove a watershed decade in the political consciousness of many young Mombasan Muslims. The national groundswell for constitutional reform that forced multiparty elections in 1992 also led to the creation of a national opposition party with deep roots in Mombasa: the Islamic Party of Kenya, or IPK. As many of its early leaders explained, the IPK was conceived as a transcultural party that sought a collective voice for the grievances of Muslims at the coast and beyond. But as party supporters were primarily young, urban, and many were "mixed race" Swahili, detractors claimed that the IPK was the party of wealthy, urban "Arabs."[36] Though the IPK was not ideologically "fundamentalist," it used Muslim identity as an instrument to draw support in the predominantly Muslim coastal region. This strategy largely alienated Christians and Muslim leaders, but it succeeded in galvanizing a cross-section of young Muslims in Mombasa.

Though Muslimness was not a political organizational frame strong enough to bridge the ethnic, class, and economic divisions of Coast Province, the IPK was a grassroots movement that offered an alternative to the Christian-dominated leadership of the other major parties. The IPK also had a knack for mobilizing young people. As a result, the Moi administration saw the party as a serious threat to its own Kenyan African National Union (KANU) victory in Coast Province. Ahead of the 1992 elections, President Moi denied the IPK registration on the dubious grounds that no political party could claim religious affiliation.[37] To complicate matters, in May of 1992 police arrested several religious leaders who supported the IPK. Among them was the influential preacher Sheikh Khalid Balala, an unofficial but self-proclaimed spokesman for the party, against whom the government brought charges of treason. This move stoked rising flames of discontent, not only bringing more young people to the IPK cause but also driving thousands of young Mombasans to the streets.[38] So incensed were some Mombasans that Mombasa's most-renowned intellectual, Ali Mazrui, warned the government that it faced a "Muslim uprising" if it chose to ignore continuing discrimination against coastal Muslims.[39] The trial and later exile of Khalid Balala further energized young urban Muslims, though none more than Mombasa's Swahili population. Over the next three years, increasing police harassment of IPK supporters provoked several violent clashes between youth in Mombasa and the authorities, while the IPK faced additional opposition from the United Muslims of Africa, a group widely believed to have received significant support from KANU to act as a political counterweight to the IPK.[40]

In the mid-1990s increasing poverty, minimal representation at the national level, political violence on the outskirts of Mombasa instigated by KANU officials, and a series of human-rights infringements added to Mombasan Muslims' sense of alienation.[41] But perhaps no events had as dramatic immediate effects on coastal Muslims as the 1998 bombings of the American embassies in Nairobi and Dar es Salaam, 9/11, and the 2002 al Qaeda attacks on Israeli targets near Mombasa. The bomb in Nairobi killed over two hundred Kenyans, and despite their sympathy for the victims Mombasan Muslims braced for an assault. In the days following the blast it became clear that young Swahili and Arab Mombasans would be the primary targets of the ensuing investigations. The presumption that the bombers must have been of, or found shelter in, the Mombasan Muslim community led to raids of Old Town by Kenyan security forces and FBI investigators. These raids, much like the detention of IPK leaders five years earlier, incited young Muslims against the federal government—and now the United States as well. The indiscriminate targeting of Muslims by joint Kenyan–US investigative forces gave Mombasans their first taste of American heavy-handedness. Though none were charged in relation to the attack, scores of Mombasans were detained. The seemingly free reign given the Americans by the Moi administration infuriated many Kenyans.[42]

Three years later 9/11 would spur further government harassment of the Mombasan Muslim community and inflame tensions smoldering since the early 1990s. The FBI generated lists of up to two-hundred Kenyans suspected of having links to al Qaeda and circulated these lists among Kenyan authorities. By November 2001, the Moi administration had ordered the arrest of more than fifty Muslims. A handful of those swept up were soon released, but most detainees were held for weeks without charge and interrogated.[43] The pretext for the arrests had been that the suspects received money from suspicious Middle Eastern sources. The reality was that most of the transactions were remittances from relatives working in Southern Arabia and the Gulf. The arrests, which included well-known businessmen and politicians—Rishad Amana, Chairman of the Democratic Party's National Youth Congress and the Muslim Youth of Kenya among them—seemed a political-intimidation tactic under the guise of fighting terrorism.[44]

Adding insult to injury, the Moi administration complied with other US requests in the weeks after 9/11. The most dramatic was a series of new passport regulations for citizens of Asian and Arab descent, which challenged some Muslims' rights to citizenship. The new regulations stipulated that Kenyans of Asian and Arab decent, including Swahili who can trace their African ancestry back indefinitely, had to produce either their grandfather's birth certificate or passport before they could qualify for a passport or even renew their current one.[45] Few Kenyans of any religious or ethnic background can produce their grandfather's birth certificate, and this clear affront to many in the Muslim community at the behest of the US caused outrage in Mombasa.

The eagerly awaited inauguration of President Mwai Kibaki in 2002 offered hope to Muslims who overwhelmingly supported the new president's National Rainbow Coalition (NARC) Party. These hopes were quickly dashed. Soon after Kibaki's swearing in, Sheikh Khalifa, a former IPK activist, explained to reporters in Mombasa, "If there is a community that has got a raw deal from the NARC government . . . it is the Muslim community. We featured nowhere in the appointments."[46] Things would only get worse for Muslims in the wake of the November 2002 bombing of the Israeli-owned Paradise Hotel and attempted downing of an Israeli airliner departing Mombasa. The

Kibaki administration beefed up the Antiterrorist Police Unit and ordered the liquidation of several Muslim NGOs thought to have colluded with terrorists. Though the surviving attackers were never captured, in August 2003 the police uncovered two al Qaeda operatives holed up in suburban Mombasa. "Now, Mombasa appears like a town under siege," Kenya's *Daily Nation* reported immediately after the discovery, and in the following days hundreds of Muslims were arrested.[47]

Though it may never be clear precisely how many were detained, somewhere between five-hundred and twelve-hundred coastal residents, mostly young Swahili and Arab men, were brought in for interrogation. Some of those swept up in the operation were interrogated by foreign agents while others were tortured.[48] Even the more benign interrogations demonstrated contempt for Kenyan Muslims. Those questioned at Mombasa Central Police Station were routinely called *Walqaeda,* or members of al Qaeda, and asked equally menacing and rhetorical questions such as, "Why are you a Muslim?" or "Why do you have a Muslim name?" At the same time, the state sharpened its investigative apparatuses by creating a vetting committee to identify foreigners "of Arab extraction" living in Mombasa's Old Town, an area now designated, despite the fact that the two operatives were living in a distant suburb, as a "hide-out for suspected terrorists."[49] To make matters worse, these measures came against the backdrop of an issue gaining national attention: an antiterrorism bill reminiscent of the American Patriot Act.

From its inception, the Antiterrorism Bill raised suspicions. It matched similar bills passed in Uganda and Tanzania, and was presented in June of 2003, soon after President Kibaki returned from a visit to Washington. Touted as part of the Global War on Terrorism, it gave Kenyan authorities unprecedented freedoms.[50] As an Amnesty International analysis of the bill suggested, it defined terrorism so vaguely that virtually any act of political dissent qualified. It allowed for incommunicado detention—a tactic that was often already employed in cases of suspected terrorists—and the denial of the right to legal representation during interrogation. At the same time it offered state officials immunity from prosecution. It proposed to severely curtail freedoms of association and expression while easing national restrictions on extradition.[51] The legislation seemed draconian and many in Kenya saw it as a thinly veiled US agenda. Not only did the American ambassador urge the parliament to quickly pass the bill but soon after the bill appeared President Bush announced a $100 million initiative to fight terrorism in Eastern Africa, part of the President's East African Counterterrorism Initiative (EACTI), with at least $35 million earmarked for Kenya.[52] Despite National Security Minister Chris Murungaru's proclamation that it was parliament's "moral duty" to support the measure, the Antiterrorism Bill faced overwhelming opposition.[53] The sound of voices critical of the legislation was deafening, and the bill foundered.[54]

Political marginalization and diminishing opportunities since the early 1990s, as well as police aggression and government suspicion of Mombasan Muslims, has created a generation of young people particularly resentful of Kenyan civil authorities. What is perhaps worse is that the abuses that followed each al Qaeda attack in Kenya threatened to take away Muslims' basic rights of citizenship. The deep suspicion with which many Kenyans regard coastal Muslims was reflected in a rhetorical question posed to Muslims in the *Daily Nation* after 9/11: "Are you Kenyans or were you just granted visas into a peaceful East African country?"[55] Despite coastal residents' genealogies, many non-Muslim Kenyans equate Swahiliness with foreignness. Their very right to be Kenyan seeming to hang in the balance, young Mombasan Muslims turned to alternative forms of political identity that linked myriad local grievances with more cosmopolitan concerns. It is this consciousness that Osama imagery would symbolize after 9/11.

Cultural Politics and Symbolic Discourse

During the 1990s Mombasa saw a profound conflation of religio-cultural identity and transnational political sensibility. Nowhere is this more evident than in the rhetoric of protest. In 1993, demonstrators taking to the streets in reaction to the arrest of the IPK's Sheikh Balala chanted *"Takbir, Takbir!* ["Praise" (to God)]."[56] In 2003, several protest chants resounded with, "Osama bin Laden!" As we have seen, the decade-and-a-half since the end of the cold war was marked by political repression, disillusionment, and a sense of abjection among many Mombasan Muslims. At the same time, mobility and increasing access to diverse media drew young Mombasans' attention to the plights of other Muslims across the globe. In 1997, for instance, an anti-Israel protest in Mombasa brought more people to the streets than any demonstration in recent memory.[57] Antipathy toward the US and its allies has largely been organic, seeded in the experiences of Mombasans as well as their exposure to a diversity of news media. It has also grown out of the tangible threads that bind local and national politics, the interests of American foreign policy, and the policies of the Israeli state.

To address the multiple dimensions of Mombasan youth critique, and thus the logic of Osama as an attractive icon, I wish to consider in this section two interrelated themes: the strengthening of Muslim identity as a political catalyst for action as well as Mombasan Muslims' resentment of American intervention, in Kenya and globally. A multiethnic and multiracial community, cross-sections of Mombasan Muslims have drawn on their common religious background and shared sense of marginality to consolidate their political voice. This was particularly evident with the popularity of the IPK, a party that attracted marginal and previously apolitical youth. As many former IPK supporters explained to me, the IPK gave streetwise young men direction and even helped some to become better Muslims.[58] Though Muslim identity was not sufficient to overcome social differences, as the harassment of IPK activists worsened in 1992 and 1993 the catalytic role of Islam was strengthened; that is, as those who supported the IPK were increasingly targeted, their Muslimness became more important to their social and political identities. This coincided with widening global circuits of pan-Islamism.

As Thomas Burgess and James Brennan argue in this volume, Muslim communities in East Africa have regularly sought to link local circumstances to larger political continuums. Echoing the communities of political sentiment of the 1950s and 1960s that Burgess and Brennan describe, in the 1990s many Mombasan Muslims began to see the condition of Muslims worldwide as cause for local political concern. This was, in part, a response to a global Islamic "awakening." By the end of the cold war, as Mahmood Mamdani and others have argued, the successes of the Afghan and "Afghan-Arab" mujahedeen against the Soviets demonstrated the potential of a transnational Muslim effort.[59] In the early 1990s the founders of the IPK drew inspiration from predominantly Muslim political movements abroad—particularly those in the UK and Sudan—even though the IPK agenda was far more secular than many of its models.

The condition of Muslims worldwide became intertwined with local political consciousness and political vision in 1990s' Mombasa. For instance, the plight of Bosnians and Palestinians sparked several demonstrations in the early 1990s. Likewise, American interventions in the Islamic world, such as the first Gulf War and the American presence in Somalia, drew condemnation from many Mombasans. Such interventions fed suspicions about the intentions of American foreign-policy makers toward Muslims. Sympathy for Iraqis during the Gulf War even led many Mombasans (as well as other East Africans) to cast Saddam Hussein as a defiant hero. After 9/11, the extralegal detention of Muslims at Guantanamo Bay and the abuse of Iraqi prisoners at Abu Ghraib became focal points of attention, particularly since many in Mombasa perceived these practices as congruent with American and Kenyan security forces' actions against Mombasan Muslims. From the mid-1990s, television played a particularly important role in shaping perceptions of shared Muslim suffering. Perhaps more than any other medium, TV reinforced Mombasans' sense of community with Palestinians, Afghans, and Iraqis. For example, diverse imagery offered by satellite TV gave Mombasans a daily window on American responses to 9/11. The dramatic scenes of the Afghan and Iraq occupations broadcast by al-Jazeera and other networks have shaped and confirmed Mombasan critiques of US hostility toward Muslim populations.[60]

The sense of shared grievances with Muslims across the globe was everywhere evident in Mombasa by 2001. In early September of 2001, a poster at a rally in solidarity with Palestinians read THE INTIFADA IS INTERNATIONAL. Soon after 9/11, graffiti on the wall of the Mombasa

Central Post Office proclaimed, SUPER POWER BIN LADEN. AMERICA IS FINISHED. ISRAEL IS NEXT. A few months later, one young Mombasan explained that, "[i]t is our duty as Muslims to stand with fellow Muslims anywhere in the world. That is what the Holy Koran tells us to do."[61] By 9/11, Mombasans had tapped into a deep politico-religious rhetorical vein that offered a wellspring of discursive sustenance to dissent without binding it to the vision of a global caliphate propounded by Osama bin Laden. This sense of common cause with Muslims in other world regions was only given greater urgency by American actions as well as the actions of governments aligned with American interests, such as those of Kenya and Israel. Though few Mombasans necessarily see American foreign policy as a vast conspiracy against Muslims, in 2001 N. S. Bakari wrote from Mombasa, "[t]he question Muslims in Kenya are asking is this: Why is the world

10.3. Osama graffiti, 2005. Photograph by the author.

so indifferent to the brutal killings of Muslims in Palestine, Iraq, the Philippines, Somalia and other places by Western forces?"[62] It is this seeming indifference on the part of the West—an unwillingness to acknowledge the suffering of Muslims in particular—which made Osama bin Laden's assault on American insularity so symbolically poignant to many young Mombasan Muslims.

As much as America is seen to stand for injustices worldwide, some young Mombasans appropriated Osama imagery in response to the specific actions of American investigators in Kenya as well as US support for counterterrorism operations in Kenya. For instance, the free hand given to FBI investigators in Mombasa after the embassy bombing and the 2002 attacks is seen by many Mombasans as a microcosmic illustration of American interventions globally. As prominent community leader Sheikh Ali Shee explained, the US and Israeli governments send their intelligence agents to Kenya to "punish Muslims for siding with Palestinians in the Middle East, at the behest of fighting terrorism."[63] Although American investigators may not see their work as retribution, presumed Mombasan connections with Islamist movements are a great concern of foreign investigators and counterterrorism agencies in Kenya. Thus, to link local Muslim support for the Palestinian cause with American investigations in Mombasa is not an illogical step. In early 2000, the alignment of local grievances with global injustices came to a public head when Muslim leaders boycotted functions by the American Ambassador Johnnie Carson during his visit to Mombasa. In response to the Ambassador's request for a meeting, Muslim leaders outlined a simple condition for their attendance: that the US government cease "exploiting Muslims globally."[64] A few months later, for the first time, chants of "Osama bin Laden" rose from a crowd demonstrating against American and Israeli actions.[65] Osama had become a powerful symbol of some Mombasans' grievances, in no small part because those grievances were simultaneously local and transnational.

Mombasans' linking of their interests with those of other Muslims has grown out of a desire for transnational political communion, but it has also been fed by perceptions of America's long-term influence in Kenya. Multiple Kenyan regimes have cultivated a close relationship with the United States, and, to a lesser extent, Israel. Though representatives of the United States were critical of Moi's heavy-handed efforts to limit the effectiveness of opposition parties in the early 1990s, Kenya enjoyed a very close relationship with America throughout the cold war. The US Embassy in Nairobi has been central to American monitoring of the Eastern Africa region, and the US has long maintained access to Kenyan military facilities, including the Port of Mombasa and airbases across central Kenya. Moreover, the intermittent presence of American servicemen in search of alcohol, drugs, and prostitutes has done little to gain America the sympathies of Mombasans who have since independence seen a dramatic increase in prostitution both in the city and at the beach hotels on the outskirts of town.[66]

The relationship between the US and Kenyan governments has taken on new life with America's Global War on Terrorism. American forces have vigorously employed Kenyan military facilities at the coast as part of an international counterterrorism coalition that after 9/11 included British and German forces. Kenyan military facilities are now stations—benignly referred to in US military discourse as *lily pads*—used to stage attacks on suspected al Qaeda operatives in Somalia.[67] Since 2002, US Marines (later Army and Navy as well) have been stationed at the Kenyan Navy base near Lamu on the Northern coast. Joint US-Kenya military training exercises, codenamed Operation Edged Mallet, have become an annual event in the Lamu Archipelago. These training exercises have included the patrol of the interisland waterways and major roadways of the Northern Kenyan coast.[68] After 9/11, a German Naval Air Wing detachment based in Mombasa even began monitoring ships plying the Gulf of Aden and the Somali coast.[69] The Kenyan government's hosting of military forces actively engaged in surveillance of the Kenyan coast and much of the Western Indian Ocean region has served to expand the rift between coastal Muslims and Nairobi.

The mutuality of the relationship between the Kenyan and US governments since 9/11, as I suggested with the Antiterrorism Bill, has been a particular concern of Kenyan Muslims. In 2002–03 alone the United States trained more than five-hundred Kenyan security officials in the US and provided direct funding to the Antiterrorism

Police Unit in Kenya.[70] Unfortunately, the majority of those detained or arrested by the new Antiterrorism Police Unit seemed to have been Swahili or Arab Kenyans. Though the extent to which American authorities have been involved in counterterrorist investigations has remained unclear, stories of Kenyans detained by Americans are so common that they have deeply affected Muslim perceptions of the US and its interests. Finally, as I suggest above, President Bush's $100 million aid package to assist counterterrorism efforts in East Africa, and the Kibaki administration's eager acceptance of it, seemed to offer further evidence of the largely harmonious desires of the Kenyan and US governments.[71]

Since 1998, many young Swahili Mombasans have felt that American and Kenyan counterterrorism investigations have been unduly focused on them. This concentration on urban Muslims by both American and Kenyan investigators further international-ized critiques of counterterrorist tactics and made the transnational signifying qualities of Osama all the more attractive. Yet, counter-terrorism efforts in Kenya have also made the act of referencing Osama a dangerous practice. Regardless of individual and collective rationales for evoking Osama, Mombasans had largely dispensed with his iconography by 2005. No doubt one of the reasons for this was that the Kenyan police saw Osama, quite apart from icons such as 50 Cent or Che Guevara, as a powerfully subversive symbol. Per-haps the most dramatic example of authorities' suspicion of Osama references came in the trial of several Swahili suspects accused of assisting the al Qaeda operatives who carried out the 2002 attacks near Mombasa. The only pieces of evidence submitted by the pros-ecution to substantiate charges of conspiracy were multiple news-paper cuttings of Osama found in one of the defendant's possession and a picture of the defendant pasted back-to-back with a photo of Osama.[72] These were insufficient proof of collusion, yet the use of Osama images as evidence demonstrated both the general suspicion of Kenyan Muslims and the ease with which investigators drew a relationship between iconography and material support for terror-ism. All of the suspects in the trial were acquitted in 2005, but by then few in Mombasa still risked evoking Osama. Additionally, by

2005 Osama, like so many icons before him, was falling out of fashion in Mombasa and around the world.

Conclusion: Seeing Traces before the Eye

Though much literature in the fields of globalization studies and transnational history emphasizes mobility, the way in which humanity has become interfaced, how we incessantly *see* each other, has contributed to equally profound social and cultural shifts.[73] Images are critical components of recent forms of global integration not simply because seeing is our primary desire, as perhaps it always has been, but also because of the proliferation of shared symbols. Yet, if seeing has become the guiding epistemology of the post–cold war era, the world we see is increasingly complicated because we see more than we can comprehend. It has been the necessary translation that follows from the complications of sight, one in which language and the printed word do not always take a primary role, that serves the Osama icon so well. It is continually translated into local discourses in ways that transcend bin Laden's words. The ways in which the global media references bin Laden has insured this condition. Osama's image can be found on magazine covers, in newspapers, and on TV screens, while his words are far less accessible. Western news agencies often quote only his most bombastic statements, and more than a decade-and-a-half after the first World Trade Center bombing few news outlets anywhere regularly release full transcripts of his communiqués.[74] Thus, in most parts of the world, Osama remains visible but largely mute. By shedding the ghost skin of the mujahedeen for the ubiquity of the global media, posters, and T-shirts, Osama has become a malleable sign.

Once, in a discussion with Tayseer Allouni, bin Laden explained that the Soviet Union has become little more than "traces before the eye" *(athran ba`da `ayn)*, a figment of the imagination.[75] He could have just as easily been referring to himself since his perceived power now emanates not from what he does, but from the imaginations of others. Whereas the USSR is only remembered, Osama is continuously evoked. It is this unceasing reference, the perpetual act of *seeing* him that allowed Osama the symbolic resonance of a superpower. Seeing, as much as reading or hearing, is a powerful mode of perception because of its arbitrary nature, its abstract enframing. Seeing allows us to make our own sense of things, interpreting the received images in ways that may or may not be consonant with the translations of others. And translation has significant political import. For instance, in 2002 Sheikh Juma Ngao, head of the Mombasa branch of the Supreme Council of Kenyan Muslims, explained Kenyan Muslims' frustrations with a simple declaration: "Muslims here see what is happening in Palestine and Afghanistan."[76] A fellow Mombasan interviewed by the Associated Press explained the political repercussions of seeing in more specific terms. "My children sit all day and watch TV, and they see Palestinian people being killed by Jews, Afghans killed by Americans, and they have no context."[77] In Mombasa, television and the internet provide myriad and dramatic images that enrage as much as they placate. There, as elsewhere, it is translation that matters.

Collecting and translating information, visually above all else, is a reciprocal practice. While Mombasans surf the Web or watch TV, antiterrorism police monitor cyber cafés in Muslim neighborhoods, and an American command ship collects information on terrorist suspects in seven Eastern African countries.[78] German spotter planes fly above, carefully studying ships passing along the coast. The crews photograph each vessel and forward the images to the US Navy, which integrates these into an American intelligence database in service of the Global War on Terrorism. Though little can be determined about a ship from high above, in 2002 the commander of the German team in Mombasa explained that, "[i]f you see tiny boats 40 to 50 miles off the coast with a bunch of people on them, you have to wonder." A pilot of one of the patrol planes was more candid: "If Al Qaeda is going to cross here, they'll at least know that someone is looking at them."[79] So they drift, watcher and suspect, across sky, sea, and land looking at each other, each knowing that the other is watching, each concerned about how the other perceives them, each divining meaning from the others' gaze, each compelled to continue watching, deeply suspicious of the other.

The hunger to see does not ensure the integrity of images, and thus seeing offers only relative understanding. Yet, even though seeing ships on the high seas or watching satellite TV are exercises in abstraction, the conclusions drawn, accurate or not, become concrete. If, following Marshall McLuhan, the user of the media is inherently its content, symbolic discourse is a significant mode of engagement since it allows for dramatically contrasting translations that yield actionable meaning. In the symbolic discourse of the post–cold war world some see America as "finished" because the battle lines are no longer evident and many watching the War on Terrorism do not measure power simply by "boots on the ground." Symbolic power afforded by the spectacle of Osama's actions, combined with an indifference to his words, permit him to serve as a powerful icon for many around the world. As shorthand, Osama became an iconic projection of the grievances and desires of many, whether proponents of a global caliphate, critics of Western interventionism, frustrated by domestic conditions, or simply impressed by the audacity of bin Laden's actions. Evoking Osama, much like denouncing America, at once globalizes local grievances and gives them the weight, real or imagined, of transnational consensus—the semblance of a critical, existential *communitas*. (See the introduction to this volume.)

"We have no idea anymore of what is such a symbolic calculation, as in poker or potlatch," Baudrillard wrote of post–cold war symbolic discourse, "with minimal stakes and maximal result." Yet maximal result, he argues, is what al Qaeda achieved in the media event of 9/11: "an initial shock, provoking incalculable consequences, while American gigantic deployment . . . obtained only derisory effects— the storm ending so to speak in the flutter of butterfly wings."[80] Here in the limelight of desire is the icon Osama, constantly replicated on television, never more than a click away on the internet. It flutters about in incalculable ways, a constant reminder of the humiliation of a superpower uncertain as to how to destroy a symbol. The icon appeals because it is appropriated as an intangible sign for positions of marginality, an abstract component of a symbolic vocabulary used as a counterweight to America's liberal democratic project. After 9/11 many saw the Osama icon as an attractive retort to the anonymity of humiliation because they perceived the extreme actions of al Qaeda as a reflection of their own frustrations. Iconography has its own power, and with the symbolic exchange of 9/11 some began to imagine that the storm might, too, become traces before the eye.

Notes

1. Manoah Esipisu, "Mombasa Bombings," *The Independent*, November 22, 2002.

2. The symbolic importance of the image of the planes hitting the towers was evident in popular T-shirts. A T-shirt for sale in Mombasa depicted the first tower on fire and the second plane heading toward the World Trade Center. The caption read: 09:03 BOEING 757 CRASHES INTO SOUTH TOWER. After 9/11 mobile phone screens depicting the second plane hitting the tower were also popular in many parts of the world, including Kenya.

3. Jean Baudrillard, *The Spirit of Terrorism, and Requiem for the Twin Towers* (New York: W. W. Norton, 2003); Elemer Hankiss, "Symbols of Destruction," *After September 11*, <www.ssrc.org/sept11/essays/hankiss.htm>; Retort (Iain Boal, T. J. Clark, Joseph Matthews, and Michael Watts), *Afflicted Powers: Capital and Spectacle in a New Age of War* (New York: Verso, 2005), 24–37.

4. Jean Baudrillard, "The Violence of the Global," *CTheory*, May 20, 2003, <www.ctheory.net/text_file? pick=385> (reprinted in *The Spirit of Terrorism*, 2003 edition). Baudrillard describes the event as "acts of humiliation responding to another humiliation."

5. In addition to celebrating on September 11, some Argentines openly defied the world minute of silence. Tariq Ali, "The Clash of Fundamentalisms," (paper presented at the Weatherhead Center for International Affairs, Harvard University, February 12, 2004). Hisham Aidi also makes this point in relation to his linking Spanish-speakers' critiques of US imperialism with a newfound interest in Islam. See Hisham Aidi, "Let Us Be Moors: Islam, Race and 'Connected Histories,'" *Middle East Report*, 229 (2003): 1–18.

6. *Dateline NBC*, December 7, 2001.

7. Aminu Abubakar, "Bin Laden Still Dear to Nigerian Muslims on Eve of Bush Visit," *Agence France-Presse*, July 10, 2003 (reporting from Kano, Nigeria). Another Kano resident, Sadiq Ahmed, describes Osama's success as "exposing America to shame despite its claim of being the strongest nation on earth." "Osama Baby Craze Hits Nigeria," *BBC News Online*, January 3, 2002. <news.bbc.co.uk/low/ english/world/africa/newsid_1741000 /1741171.stm>.

8. Jeffrey N. Wasserstrom, "Anti-Americanisms, Thick Description, and Collective Action," *After September 11*, <www.ssrc.org/sept11/essays/wasserstrom.htm>; Achin Vanaik, "The Ethics and Efficacy of Political Terrorism," in

Critical Views of September 11: Analyses from around the World, eds. Eric Hershberg and Kevin W. Moore (New York: W. W. Norton, 2002).

9. Quoted in Colin Nickerson, "Assessing Bin Laden: Some in Region See a Robin Hood Story," *Boston Globe*, September 24, 2001.

10. After the cold war, Che Guevara reemerged as a similarly unmoored icon. It should be remembered, however, that Che's personal trajectory was somewhat different from previous revolutionaries. He was never a head of state and he was involved in revolutionary causes for years after his departure from Cuba. Killed in an attempt to foment a pan-Latin American revolution, he was transformed into a figure much larger than the Cuban Revolution.

11. Anna Lowenhaupt Tsing, *Friction: An Ethnography of Global Connection* (Princeton: Princeton University Press, 2005).

12. Thomas Friedman argues that "super-empowered men" (a direct reference to bin Laden), those who use integrative technology to affect desired ends, are a unique phenomenon of contemporary globalization. But it is misleading to think of bin Laden himself as super-empowered. It was his actions and iconic associations, not his actual capacities, that found traction across the global South. See Thomas L. Friedman, *The Lexus and the Olive Tree: Understanding Globalization* (New York: Anchor Books, 2000).

13. Mark Danner argues that the hijackers used television to attack America "at its point of greatest vulnerability: at the level of spectacle." See Mark Danner, "Is He Winning? Taking Stock of the Forever War," *New York Times Magazine*. September 11, 2005, 50; Melani McAlister, *Epic Encounters: Culture, Media, and U.S. Interests in the Middle East, 1945–2000* (Berkeley: University of California Press, 2001); and Melani McAlister, "Television, Terrorism, and the Making of Incomprehension," *Chronicle of Higher Education*, December 7, 2001, 13.

14. Artyom Borovik, *The Hidden War* (New York: Atlantic Monthly Press, 1990).

15. Mark Danner, "The Battlefield in the American Mind," *New York Times*, October 16, 2001. Marc Howard Ross makes a similar point in "The Political Psychology of Competing Narratives: September 11 and Beyond," *After September 11*, <www.ssrc.org/sept11/essays/ross.htm>; Retort, *Afflicted Powers*.

16. Quoted in Ellen Hale and Vivienne Walt, "Extremists' Hatred of U.S. Has Varied Roots," *USA Today*, September 19, 2001.

17. This is a now-familiar factor in moments of radicalism, evident in many epochs of quickening global integration. Eric Hobsbawm, *Revolutionaries* (New York: New Press, 2001).

18. See, for example, Osama bin Laden's, "Letter to America," *Observer*, November 24, 2002. Martin Walker, "Brand Osama has widespread appeal,"

United Press International, September 21, 2001; Anonymous, *Through Our Enemies' Eyes: Osama bin Laden, Radical Islam, and the Future of America* (Washington, DC: Brassey's, 2003); Faisal Devji, *Landscapes of the Jihad* (Ithaca: Cornell University Press, 2005).

19. "Since September 11 (2001)," Wenke added, "Muslims have lifted up their heads." Boris Cambreleng, "Young Chinese Muslims Look up to 'Hero' bin Laden," *Agence France-Presse*, February 25, 2003.

20. "Our Links with Biafra," *The News* (Nigeria), September 20, 2004. This sentiment was shared in the Pollsmoor maximum-security prison in Cape Town soon after 9/11. A prisoner named Junaid explained to journalist Jonny Steinberg: "People misunderstand what [Osama] has done. . . . In the US, they make male prostitution legal. They have gambling and alcohol. They make abortion legal. . . . And they are trying to force western doctrine on Afghanistan." Jonny Steinberg, "Walls of mental prisons soar ever higher in wake of polarising 9/11," *Business Day* (South Africa), June 12, 2004.

21. George Packer, "Gangsta War: Young Fighters Take Their Lead from American Pop Culture," *New Yorker*, November 3, 2003, 76, 77.

22. Jason Burke, *Al-Qaeda: The True Story of Radical Islam* (London: Penguin, 2004), 39.

23. Begoña Aretxaga, "Terror as Thrill: First Thoughts on the 'War on Terrorism,'" *Anthropological Quarterly*, 75, no. 1 (Winter 2002): 143–44.

24. "Starring Osama bin Laden," Arun Rath reporting for *Frontline World*, <www.pbs.org/frontlineworld/stories/india205/thestory.html> (posted June 2003); "Interview with Arun Rath," <www.pbs.org/frontlineworld/stories/india205/rath.html> (posted June 2003).

25. Cabinet member, MP, and former mayor of Mombasa Najib Balala explained the popularity of Osama in Mombasa in terms that might also apply to Che or Malcolm X: "Anyone who is an underdog, who fights against authority, is a hero [in Mombasa], especially for the young people, many of whom are unemployed." Declan Walsh, "Imam warns of 'undeclared war' between US, Israel," *Independent on Sunday*, December 1, 2002.

26. "Muslims Stormed the Streets Over Military Actions," *The Nation*, October 13, 2001.

27. "Ferry Company Orders Removal of bin Laden Portrait," *Agence France-Presse*, November 8, 2001.

28. "Muslims Protest in Kenya, Police Involved in Mombasa," *Agence France-Presse*, October 12, 2001; "Kenya's Muslims Debate bin Laden's Role," Associated Press, December 3, 2002.

29. "Investigators Probe Pro-bin Laden Graffiti in Kenyan City," *Agence-France Presse*, September 25, 2001.

30. Kai Kresse, *Philosophising in Mombasa: Knowledge, Islam and Intellectual Practice on the Swahili Coast* (Edinburgh: Edinburgh University Press for the International African Institute, 2007). This phenomenon is not unique to Mombasa. See Jean and John L. Comaroff, "Reflexions sur la jeunesse, du passé a la postcolonie," *Politique Africaine,* 80 (2000): 90–110; Mamadou Diouf, "Engaging Postcolonial Culture: African Youth and Public Space," *African Studies Review,* 46, no. 2 (2003): 1–12.

31. Ali Mazrui, "Stages of Globalization in the African Context: Mombasa," in *Hybrid Urbanism: On the Identity Discourse and the Built Environment,* ed. Nezar Al Sayyad (Westport, CT: Praeger, 2001), 111–30.

32. James R. Brennan, "Lowering the Sultan's Flag: Sovereignty and Decolonization in Coastal Kenya," *Comparative Studies in Society and History,* 50, no. 4 (2008): 831–61; Seif Mohamed Seif, "Letter: New Attempt to Register IPK Sign of the Times," *Coast Express,* May 30, 2003.

33. Carole Rakodi et al., "Poverty and Political Conflict in Mombasa," *Environment and Urbanization* 12, no. 1 (2000): 153–70.

34. Coast Express Writer, "Upcountry People Also Have Vast Interests," *Coast Express,* November 14, 2003.

35. Chege Mbitiru, "Radicalization of Islam Feared as Muslim Activism Increases," Associated Press Wire Service, September 17, 1993.

36. Alamin Mazrui and Ibrahim Noor Shariff argued that the IPK, while inspired by global Islamist movements, was an "Islamic expression of Swahili ethno-nationalism." See Alamin Mazrui and Ibrahim Noor Shariff, *The Swahili: Idiom and Identity of an African People* (Trenton: Africa World Press, 1994), 153.

37. Thomas P. Wolf, "Contemporary Politics," in *Kenya Coast Handbook: Culture, Resources and Development in the East African Littoral,* eds. Jan Hoorweg, Dick Foeken, and R. A. Obudho (New Brunswick, NJ: Transaction Publishers, 2000); US Department of State, "Kenya Human Rights Practices, 1994," February 1995.

38. Human Rights Watch, *Kenya: Human Rights Developments, 1992,* <www.hrw.org/reports/ 1993/WR93/Afw-02.htm>.

39. "Kenya Warned of Muslim Uprising," *Xinhua General Overseas News Service,* June 6, 1992. Ali Mazrui has elsewhere suggested that in the early 1990s, the coast seemed poised for a "Black *Intifadah.*" See Ali A. Mazrui, preface, *Kenya Coast Handbook,* xxvi.

40. Wolf, "Contemporary Politics," 142.

41. Human Rights Watch, *Violence as a Political Weapon,* <www.hrw.org/reports/2002/kenya/ Kenya0502-04.htm> (2002).

42. "FBI Interrogations Incur Muslim Wrath," *Independent Online* (South

Africa), June 19, 2000, <www.iol.co.za/news/africa_newsview.php3?clickid=
68&art_id=qw 95968626210B251&set_id=1> Katy Salmon, "Muslims Say FBI
Targets Them," *Inter Press Service*, March 6, 2003.

43. Francis Thoya, "Suspects Go to Court to Halt FBI Extradition Bid," *Daily
Nation*, November 13, 2001.

44. "Dismay at Police Roundup of Muslims," *Indian Ocean Newsletter*,
November 17, 2001; Hervé Maupeu, "East African Muslims and the 11 September Crisis," *Mambo!*, 2 (1) 2002: 5.

45. Timothy Kalyegira, "Kenya's Muslims Protest New Passport Laws,"
United Press International, September 26, 2001; "Split Over Coast Muslim
Demo," *Daily Nation*, June 7, 2001. Khelef Abdulrahman Khalifa El-Busaidy,
executive director of Muslims for Human Rights, eventually sued the Attorney
General and the Immigration Department for their refusal to grant his son a
passport without a copy of his grandparents' birth certificate.

46. Karim Rajan, Mwakera Mwajefa, and Jonathan Manyindo, "Imams
Criticise Anti-terror Drive," *Coast Express*, April 11, 2003.

47. Ngumbao Kithi, "Threat Hovering Over Coastal Region's Security Forces
Step Up Surveillance," *Sunday Nation*, August 31, 2003.

48. Amnesty International found that at least one of the detainees inter-
rogated by foreign agents was threatened with internment at Guantánamo Bay.
Another was tortured with electric shocks. Amnesty International, "Kenya: The
Impact of 'Anti-terrorism' Operations on Human Rights," March 23, 2005, <web.
amnesty.org/library/Index/ENGAFR320022005?open&of=ENG-2AF>; "Sixth
Suspect Charged Over Deadly Kenya Blasts," *Agence France-Presse*, September
18, 2003; "500 imigrantes ilegais são detidos no Quênia," *Agence France-Presse*,
August 31, 2003.

49. Stephen Mbogo, "Arrests May Have Prevented Attack on Anniversary of
US Embassy Bombing," CNSNews.com, August 6, 2003.

50. Francis Thoya, "Imam's Fury Over New Anti-terror Bill," *Coast Express*,
June 20, 2003.

51. Amnesty International, "Memorandum to the Kenyan Government on
the Suppression of Terrorism Bill 2003," <http://web.amnesty.org/library/print/
ENGAFR320032004>; Harrison Kinyanjui, "Opinion: Anti-terror Law Will
Roll Back Kenya's Civil Liberties," *East African*, June 30, 2003.

52. Sandra T. Barnes, "Global Flows: Terror, Oil, and Strategic Philanthropy,"
African Studies Review, 48, no. 1 (2005): 1-22; "Letter: Terrorism: Ambassador
Spelled Out US Demands," *Daily Nation*, June 19, 2003.

53. Nation Team, "Suspected Terrorist, 24, Is Arrested," *Daily Nation*, June
30, 2003.

54. Muslim Civic Education Trust (Kenya), *Toleo 213: Suppression of Human*

Rights Bill?, January 9, 2004; Samwell Siringi, "Threats of Mass Action Over Bill on Terrorism," *Daily Nation*, July 16, 2003; Issa Hussein, David Mugonyi, Adan Mohamed, Patrick Mathangani, and Onesmus Kilonzo, "Suspected Terrorist, 24, Is Arrested," *Daily Nation*, June 30, 2003.

55. "Letter," *Daily Nation*, October 18, 2001.

56. "Kenya: Balala Charged with 'Intent to Kill'; Supporters Demonstrate in Mombasa," BBC News On-line, May 24, 1993.

57. Quoted in Shabbir Versi, "Mombasa Throbs with Anti-blasphemy Rally," Muslim Media.com, August 16–31, 1997, <www.muslimedia.com/archives/world98/blasphem.htm>.

58. Anonymous, Mombasa, May 30, 2005; Anonymous, Mombasa, July 26, 2008.

59. Mahmood Mamdani, *Good Muslim, Bad Muslim: America, the Cold War, and the Roots of Terror* (New York: Pantheon, 2004).

60. Nahdi, "A Cocktail of Grievances in Paradise," 24.

61. Tom Osanjo, "The Kenyan Town Where Arafat Is a Hero," Panafrican News Agency Daily Newswire, April 14, 2002.

62. N. S. Bakari, "Letters: Shed No Tear for Osama Friends," *Daily Nation*, October 27, 2001.

63. Bogonko Bosire, "Kenyan Muslims Claim Harassment Over Blast Probe," *Agence France-Presse*, March 5, 2003.

64. Nation Correspondent, "Imams Warn the US Over 'Misuse,'" *Daily Nation*, February 29, 2000.

65. "Anti-Israel Protests Rock Mombasa," *Times of India*, October 21, 2000.

66. Nahdi, "A Cocktail of Grievances in Paradise," 24.

67. On the "lily pad" as a less-visible method of extending American military agendas, see Chalmers Johnson, *The Sorrows of Empire: Militarism, Secrecy, and the End of the Republic* (New York: Metropolitan Books, 2004), and Sandra Barnes, "Global Flows."

68. "Kenya Army, US Marines Conduct Joint Military Drill," BBC Worldwide Monitoring, text of report by Kenyan KTN-Y TV, March 8, 2007.

69. Patrick Mayoyo, "US Warns of Missile Attacks in Nairobi," *East African*, March 17, 2003.

70. Emily Wax, "Fearing Attack, Kenya Searches for Al Qaeda Suspect," *Washington Post*, May 16, 2003.

71. "Suspected Terrorist, 24, Is Arrested," *Daily Nation*, June 30, 2003.

72. Jillo Kadida, "Lawyer Calls Case 'Ploy to Get Cash for Terror Squad,'" *The Nation*, April 26, 2005; "Bomb Suspect 'Had Osama Cuttings'" *East African Standard,* July 28, 2004.

73. Marshall McLuhan with Louis Forsdale, "Technology and the Human

Dimension," in *Marshall McLuhan, the Man and His Message*, eds. George Sanderson and Frank Macdonald. (Golden, CO: Fulcrum, 1989), 24. For McLuhan, TV seemed the catalyst for making the world not just a "global village," but more a global theater: a condensed visual space through which we translate experience.

74. Three recent publications offer greater access to Osama's words: Brad K. Berner, *Jihad: Bin Laden in His Own Words, Declarations, Interviews and Speeches* (BookSurge: 2006); Osama bin Laden, Bruce Lawrence, ed., James Howarth, trans., *Messages to the World: The Statements of Osama bin Laden* (London: Verso, 2005); Randall B. Hamud, ed., *Osama Bin Laden: America's Enemy in His Own Words* (San Diego: Nadeem Publishing, 2005).

75. Tayseer Allouni with Osama bin Laden, "A Discussion on the New Crusader Wars," <www.islamicawakening.com>. Many thanks to Matt Hopper and Ilham Makdisi for their translations of this phrase.

76. Dexter Filkins, "Amid Pain, Muslims in Kenya Feel Deep Anger," *New York Times*, December 2, 2002.

77. "Kenya's Muslims Debate bin Laden's Role," Associated Press Wire Service, December 3, 2002.

78. Frank Gardner, "War on Terror Africa-style," BBC On-line, February 21, 2003, <news.bbc.co.uk/2/hi/africa/27837 17stm>.

79. "Hunting for Elusive Terrorists off Somalia's Coast," April 2, 2002, <www.hamarey.com/ index.php/article/article view/220/1/4/>; Patrick Mayoyo, "US Warns of Missile Attacks in Nairobi," *East African*, March 17, 2003.

80. Baudrillard, *Spirit of Terrorism*.

Epilogue

The Sodalities of Bandung:
Toward a Critical 21st-Century History

Antoinette Burton

Several years ago when I proposed a panel on nationalism in the age of Bandung for the annual meeting of the American Historical Association—the largest general professional organization for historians in the United States—I was told that no one on the program committee, save the South Asianist, knew what Bandung was. This strikes me as paradigmatic of the fate of Bandung in 20th century memory and history in the West. Our panel, which was accepted, took place in the fiftieth anniversary year of Bandung, an occasion that was marked by a few commemorative meetings and volumes but that was hardly met with the brouhaha produced by "the first intercontinental gathering of colored peoples in the history of mankind," as President Sukarno of Indonesia proclaimed it in the opening session in April of 1955.[1] If North Americans know about Bandung at all, they most often apprehend it through the lens of histories of racial solidarity and cross-racial possibility of the kind that Richard Wright captured in his eyewitness account of the conference, *The Color Curtain*:

> We drove past the conference building and saw the flags of the twenty-nine participating nations of Asia and Africa billowing lazily in the weak wind; already the streets were packed with crowds

and their black and yellow and brown faces looked eagerly at each passing car . . . to catch sight of some prime minister, a U Nu, a Chou En-lai, a Nehru . . . it was the first time in their downtrodden lives that they'd seen so many of their color, race and nationality arrayed in such aspects of power, their men keeping order, their Asia and their Africa in control of their destinies. Imperialism was dead here, and as long as they could maintain their unity, organize and conduct international conferences, there would be no return of imperialism.[2]

Even if we allow for the possibility of its ironic posture—articulated via its ambiguous declarative about the end of empire–Wright's narrative participates in the romance of overcoming that David Scott has identified as generically predictive of anticolonial histories that have flourished under the sign of postcoloniality in the wake of Bandung.[3] As such, stories like Wright's have helped to shape apprehensions of Bandung mainly among Leftist academics and activists, who tend to view it as the inaugural moment not just of Third World alliance-making but of racial brotherhood—as evidenced both by the way Bandung is typically conflated with "Afro-Asian solidarity" and by the way that nexus is presumed to rest on a combination of shared outrage at the racial violence of European imperialism and the shared racial community that apparently ensued. When it's not comparatively invisible to mainstream historians west of Suez, then, Bandung bears the burden of representing the bittersweet promise of postcolonial modernity, the ultimate dream deferred: a beacon of what global anticolonial politics was, might have been, and could be again in a "new" post-9/11 age of racialized empire. Indeed, as older imperial forms have dissolved and been reconsolidated under the pressures of globalization and Western military aggression, the stakes of understanding Bandung as the embodiment of postcolonial cold war history—what Vijay Prashad calls "the story of the darker nations"—are arguably higher than they have ever been in the half-century and more since the conference took place.[4]

This collection categorically rejects the romance of racialism that haunts many accounts of Bandung and its aftermath in favor of going to ground, through a purposeful return to the complex and uneven geographies of the postcolonial cold war world as seen from outside the US and to its fitful, uneven, and aspirationally global temporalities as well.[5] Acknowledging that "Bandung contained both the residual romance of revolution" and the *"realpolitik* of a new world order in the making," the essays collected here advocate for a more empirically grounded approach to historicizing the kinds of political community that emerged in a wide range of sites and spaces across the intercontinental world invoked by "Afro-Asia"—a conceit that was more and less than the sum of its parts and which, then, and now, evokes a broad range of events determined largely by postcolonial elites and big-ticket cold war crises. This is, of course, to say nothing of the "limited value of Asia" itself as "an ideal of communitarian togetherness," or of the fraught designations of Asia East and West within it.[6] The case studies in this volume bring difference sites of political practice into view—from the Cairo women's press to the TAZARA Railway to the South African memoir–travelogue—and in so doing, make available multiple frames of analysis and an equally diverse set of geographical parallelograms that capture the (re)territorializations of political community "beyond the archetype of the nation-state" in the so-called age of Bandung. Tacking between the Scylla of imagined communities and the Charybdis of a transnationalist impulse most often routed through the naturalized nationalism of a US-imperial universal, the preceding chapters aim to rethink Third World postcolonial community as a contingent, fugitive set of formations that arose around the collision of technological, legal, and discursive forces with movements of people, ideas, and labor/capital in ways that were predictable and, in some cases, utterly unanticipated from the vantage point of Bandung. What results from this "constellation" is nothing less than a realignment of the postcolonial cold war political map—one that requires a narrative more nuanced than histories of either superpower competition or atomized Third World struggle can provide, and that these essays point us toward new and innovative ways. As Prashad has said of the Third World more generally, Bandung was not so much a place as it was a geopolitical project, one whose cross-hatchings, outcroppings, and tendrils are made accessible for the first time by the histories on offer here.[7]

And yet what of the presumption of Afro-Asian solidarity—as the foundation of post-imperial political community and as a guarantor of Third World non/alignment—which was at once feared and maligned in the West and so perpetually invoked by people of color and others as the aspirational standard-bearer of radical postcolonial politics? State Department anxieties about the convergence of so many colonial and recently excolonial leaders and about the transnational racial solidarities potentially set in motion by a historically unprecedented global gathering of "coloured peoples" notwithstanding, Bandung circulated in cold war discourse as a carrier of the promise of *interracial* solidarity. If, as Jason Parker has suggested, attention to race obliges us to embrace "a different picture and periodization" of the global cold war order than we have historically grasped, the jagged and underexamined hyphen between Afro and Asian was and is replete with ambiguity when it comes to the question of race as well.[8] Its geographical parameters are vague and are predicated on histories of European map-making and subimperial fantasy that predate the 1955 conference by decades (at least). Was India part of Afro-Asia, and if so, what part? Nehru believed it was *prima inter pares* in civilizational terms, and he arguably viewed a decolonizing Africa as a set of successor states to the Raj over which independent India would seek market advantage and to which it would offer geopolitical tutelage. This was, perhaps, a different register of the pedagogy of development that Dipesh Chakrabarty cites above, but it remains historically significant nonetheless for Bandung history—not least because of the ways the Nehruvian postcolonial imaginary carried racial hierarchies of brown over black into diplomacy and global strategy during the first quarter of the cold war. How and where China fits into this schema is the subject of some of the most energetic recent scholarship, as essays by Jamie Monson and Thomas Burgess here illustrate. In a powerful piece called "Black like Mao" (in a recent collection entitled, notably for our purposes, *Afro Asia: Revolutionary Political and Cultural Connections between African Americans and Asian Americans*), Robin D. G. Kelley and Betsy Esch illustrate how black and white were interrupted and remade by yellow and red via the phenomenon of a pan-African black Maoism. Their approach not only registers the color of ideological affinity and disaffection alike but indexes the links between US civil-rights struggles to the problem of global class struggle as the articulation of a shared *cultural-cum-political* community as well.[9] Taken together, their work and this volume prompt us to ask: Where exactly does the cold war civil-rights movement in the US belong in truly global histories of Bandung? And what, to borrow from David Luis-Brown, were the "chronotypes of decolonization"?[10] For blacks of Wright's generation (and for many before), the "Afro" in Afro-Asian solidarity was refracted through the Harlem Renaissance as much as it was through Moscow's communist experiments, as Christopher Lee notes in his essay on Alex La Guma. Identifying these multinodal points of connectivity—and historicizing how they were shot through by promiscuous histories of race admittedly yet to be written—is critical to appreciating the full range of meanings ascribed to Bandung as a culmination of a half-century of such links *and* as a vehicle for the dissemination of an ideal of cross-racial affinity into the contemporary moment, still.

The intercontinental and area-studies emphasis of this collection grows in part, of course, out of wariness about the overburdening of Bandung by americo-centric racialist/multiculturalist approaches to Afro-Asian solidarity—approaches that have been partly responsible for the kind of utopian, teleogizing tendencies of Bandung history produced in the West. That chauvinist framework has left its imprint even and perhaps especially on postcolonial critics whose work has not been immune to the impact of US race relations, in ways that are only just beginning to be appreciated.[11] The arms-length approach to the sentimentalization of solidarity characteristic of this book project is part of a broader attempt on the part of all the contributors, then, to interrupt the facile equation of "Afro-Asian" with self-evident (read *Americanized)* racial categories: to map the complex and fraught relationships of racial identity with the overlapping material realities of class, caste, and linguistic identity: to wit, the cry of the "Voice of Free Africa" in James Brennan's essay, which invokes the racial brotherhood of "Africans, Indians, *and Arabs*" in a direct citation of the spirit of Bandung (italics mine). Whereas its racial solidarities were dependent on the dialectic of (in this case) the white colonialist "pig" and his anticolonial enemies, "Afro-Asia" here was also absorptive, drawing "Arab" into the mix and, as Brennan shows, revealing rifts and fissures among comrades that were hardly exclusively about race, if at all. Here as elsewhere across the newly postcolonial world, the question of where legacies of imperial racism stop and new racialized politics begin remains an open question, one with critical significance for the histories of transregional/transnational community formations of the kind that these authors aim to materialize. This book thus does a much-needed service to the historiography of postcoloniality by opening the door to histories grounded in a variety of contingent examples that fail, in the best sense, to add up to anything like a triumphalist, linear metanarrative about racially harmonious cooperation or even race-based structures of community feeling.

Critical histories of Bandung can and should operate from this framework of skepticism about the emplotment of racial solidarity *tout court* on the post-1955 landscape. Yet we still need, it seems to me, histories that expressly engage a persistent nostalgia for Bandung, which appears to have aided an almost continual consolidation of narratives about the value of interracial solidarity even while on the ground, the ties were, in Ann Stoler's terms, *tense and tender*—if not mostly tense.[12] Needless to say, such tension-filled histories were not new to Bandung, as Ho Chi Minh's interwar "intercoloniale" experiences in Paris testify.[13] The romance of racialism that this collection seeks to counter was, like all romances, also a melodrama, resting not just on the fragmented connectivities that the authors have unearthed but on the convulsive violence of emotional/psychic conflict and of embodied subjectivity-in-the-making.[14] And, I would contend, its melodramatic energies derived not simply from Bandung's promise of interracial solidarity but from the ideal of interracial *brotherhood* it continuously deployed. So we profit enormously from work like Laura Bier's in this collection, which underscores the critical role that women played in pushing postcolonial agendas forward and, significantly, in generating internal hierarchies that structured for the domain of "Third World Woman" as well. Indeed, among the most urgent agendas for Bandung history is more research on women's roles, both organizational and otherwise, in the making of the postwar postcolonial community outside the West. Writing in the long shadow of Chandra Mohanty, the best of this new research is, like Bier's, skeptical of triumphalist narratives and invested in recovering the disputed categories and unhappy experiences that often underlay colonial and postcolonial feminist politics.[15] Feminist accounts of the postcolonial world must continue to press against their own limits. As Jean Allman has suggested, they must do so by addressing not just the "disappearance" of non-Western women from the narrative but the "significant disjuncture between women's often high profile roles as nation builders and their very limited roles in the consolidation of the postcolonial state"—and, I would add, in the consolidation of post-Bandung histories as well.[16]

But as urgently needed is an interpretive framework that enables us to appreciate how and why Afro-Asian solidarity was coded through racial confraternity, and how and under what conditions its cultures—including its cultures of historiography—have continued to be grounded in its masculinist and heteronormative ideals. How, one is tempted to ask, if global sisterhood as a modus operandi and a category of analysis is long since dead, can that of Third World Brotherhood persist uninterrogated? We know, of course, that for all its false universalism and anachronism, international solidarity between women has had, and continues to have, a formidable affective power and so it must be reckoned with as a historical phenomenon rather than discarded as if it exerted no dialectical pull on the present. Much the same approach is needed to understand the nostalgia for an Afro-Asian brotherhood that was always imperfectly manifest, before, during, and after the conference of Bandung. There is undoubtedly a host of homosocial histories of interracial solidarity—of struggle through conflict and violence, through affective connection and *disidentification* at the site of race and ethnicity and sexuality—still to be written. Those images, whether textual or visual, which circulate from Bandung proper, suggest handshaking, public displays of affection and aversion, and all manner of pas de deux between world leaders and presumably between delegates at all levels, in all kinds of spaces, public and private.[17]

What, indeed, of Bandung's embodied histories? How did the men who attended meet, live, eat, drink, keep their social and political distance and hook up (and with whom) during the lived experience of that April of 1955? What of the specter of interracial intercourse between brown and black, between yellow and mixed, between colored and "other," which could be found wherever local, regional, intraregional, and global flowed from and into "difference" in the pre- and postcolonial world that the conference purported to give voice to? What histories of suspicion and diffidence, of push and pull, were made wherein women and men of different communities labored together, wherein men of different caste and color bought and sold from each other, wherein competing pollution complexes, shaped by political economies of race and residence, language, and religion, existed cheek by jowl?[18] Why do histories of Bandung, whether elegiac or antielegiac, occlude these compelling questions even as they nod to the importance of gender and the category of culture as objects of enquiry and procedural tools? This is all the more intriguing when one considers how critical "racial reproductivity" is to nationalist and anti-imperialist discourses in the context of what we might call pan-Afro-Asianism: a decolonizing iteration, one might say, of the patriarchal bargain long struck between colonizer and colonized in the masculinist sodalities wherein official power most often operated in the pre-postcolonial world.[19] Yet as Mrinalini Sinha has so effectively shown, even event-based history (like her revisionist account of the 1929 Mother India scandal) can embed cultural analysis and explain the ideological and material work of gender and sexuality in constituting and reconstituting global orders in tension with and against the grain of the nation-state and its sovereign subjects.[20] We need histories that refuse all of Bandung's pieties and romances and break, finally, from its presumptively fraternal narratives, if not its epistemological grasp, as this collection so effectively begins to do.

The point here is not simply to linger in the tensions of Afro-Asian encounter and politics in all their intercontinentality and incommensurability. Such tensions ran afoul of a variety of hyphens, as Wright's dis-ease with what he saw of African traditions on his pre-Bandung trip to Ghana famously testifies—and as Saidiya Hartman's remarkable memoir of her own trip to Western Africa echoes and refracts some fifty years later.[21] Nor is it just to argue for the recovery of the connective tissue of Afro-Asian relationships as political community via recourse to gender and race and sexuality as analytical categories. The latter are not essential/ized identities or locative positions so much as they are instruments in the political struggle for and against the historiography we have of postcoloniality. To insist on this is to call for a recognition of the possibility that they can leverage *the historicity*—the indexical trace—of domains such as culture and the social—and make the *agency* of those territorializing forces in shaping specific iterations of political community qua political, qua community, more appreciable than they otherwise might be. The real challenge that this book throws down is the problem of how Bandung might be positioned as a threshold moment for postcolonial history and what that reorientation might mean for narrating accounts of 20th century racial and sexualized global orders in the process. If, as Arjun Appadurai claims, Bandung was "key in the formation of our life," histories of Bandung, as event, as age, as culture, as paradigm, must provoke questions about who that *we* is, questions about how—and whether—our collective lives have been conscripted by the species of postcolonial history it apparently set in motion.[22]

Notes

1. Quoted in Jamie Mackie, *Bandung 1955: Non-alignment and Afro-Asian Solidarity* (Singapore: Didier Millet, 2005), 14.

2. Richard Wright, *The Color Curtain: A Report on the Bandung Conference* (Jackson: University Press of Mississippi, 1995 [1956]).

3. David Scott, *Conscripts of Modernity: The Tragedy of Colonial Enlightenment* (Durham: Duke University Press, 2004).

4. Vijay Prashad, *The Darker Nations: A People's History of the Third World* (New York: New Press, 2007).

5. Here I am indebted to David Luis-Brown, *Waves of Decolonization: Discourses on Race and Hemispheric Citizenship in Cuba, Mexico and the United States* (Durham: Duke University Press, 2008), 39 ff.

6. Here I draw on Sridevi Menon, "Where Is West Asia in Asian America?

'Asia' and the Politics of Space in Asian America," *Social Text,* 86, no. 24 (Spring 2006), 61.

7. Prashad, *The Darker Nations,* xv.

8. Jason Parker, "Cold War II: The Eisenhower Administration, the Bandung Conference and the Reperiodization of the Postwar Era," *Diplomatic History,* 30, no. 5 (2006), 870.

9. Robin D. G. Kelley and Betsy Esch, "Black like Mao: Red China and Black Revolution," in *Afro Asia: Revolutionary Political and Cultural Connections between African Americans and Asian Americans,* eds. Fred Ho and Bill V. Mullen (Durham: Duke University Press, 2008): 97–154.

10. Luis-Brown, *Waves of Decolonization,* 17.

11. Malini Johar Schueller, "Articulations of African-Americanisms in South Asian Postcolonial Theory: Globalism, Localism and the Question of Race," *Cultural Critique,* 55 (Fall 2003): 35–62; Inderpal Grewal, *Transnational America: Feminisms, Diasporas, Neoliberalisms* (Durham: Duke University Press, 2005).

12. See Ann Laura Stoler, ed., *Haunted by Empire: Geographies of Intimacy in North America* (Durham: Duke University Press, 2006).

13. William J. Duiker, *Ho Chi Minh* (New York: Hyperion, 2000), 79–85, 594, fn55. See also Brent Hayes Edwards, "The Shadow of Shadows," *positions,* 11, no. 1 (2003): 11–49.

14. Luis-Brown, *Waves of Decolonization,* 39 ff.

15. Chandra Mohanty, Ann Russo, and Lordes Torres. eds., *Third World Women and the Politics of Feminism* (Bloomington: Indiana University Press, 1991). For an example of this new work see Charlotte Weber, "Unveiling Scheherazade: Feminist Orientalism in the International Alliance of Women," *Feminist Studies,* 27, no. 1 (2007): 125–57.

16. Jean Allman, "The Disappearing of Hannah Kudjoe: Nationalism, Feminism, and the Tyrannies of History," *Journal of Women's History,* 21, 3 (Fall 2009): 15–35. Special issue entitled "Critical Feminist Biography."

17. Augusto Espiritu gestures toward Nehru's uneasiness with Carlos P. Romulo and Richard Wright's sense of connection to him in "'To Carry Water on Both Shoulders': Carlos P. Romulo, American Empire, and the Meanings of Bandung," *Radical History Review,* 95 (2006): 173–90. Parker's "Cold War II" offers an equally intriguing image of the journalist Norman Cousins kneeling by Romulo, an image in which Romulo has his arm around Cousin's shoulder in what looks like a tight, fraternal-paternal embrace. See Parker, "Cold War II," 880.

18. See, for example, Anjali Gera Roy, "Bhangra Remixes," in *India in Africa, Africa in India: Indian Ocean Cosmopolitanisms,* ed. John C. Hawley (Bloomington: Indiana University Press, 2008): 95–116.

19. For racial reproductivity see Alys Eve Weinbaum, *Wayward Reproductions: Genealogies of Race and Nation in Transatlantic Modern Thought* (Durham: Duke University Press, 2004). For patriarchal bargain, see Deniz Kandiyoti, "Bargaining with Patriarchy," *Gender and Society,* 2, no. 3 (1988): 274–90. Thanks to Ken Cuno for the precision of the latter reference.

20. Mrinalini Sinha, *Specters of Mother India: The Global Restructuring of an Empire* (Durham: Duke University Press, 2006).

21. Kevin Gaines, "Rethinking Richard Wright in Ghana: Black Radicalism and the Dialectics of Diaspora," *Social Text,* 19, no. 2 (2001): 75–101; Saidiya Hartman, *Lose Your Mother: A Journey along the Atlantic Slave Route* (New York: Farrar, Straus and Giroux, 2007).

22. Arjun Appadurai, quoted in Revathi Krishnaswamy and John C. Hawley, eds., *The Postcolonial and the Global* (Minneapolis: University of Minnesota Press, 2008), 290.

Select Bibliography

Abdulgani, Roeslan. *The Bandung Connection: The Asia-Africa Conference in Bandung in 1955*. Translated by Molly Bondan. Singapore: Gunung Agung, 1981.

Aburish, Said K. *Nasser: The Last Arab*. New York: St. Martin's, 2004.

Adas, Michael. *Machines as the Measure of Men: Science, Technology and Ideologies of Western Dominance*. Ithaca: Cornell University Press, 1989.

Adhikari, Mohamed, ed. *Jimmy La Guma: A Biography by Alex La Guma*. Cape Town: Friends of the South African Library, 1997.

Ahmed, Leila. *Women and Gender in Islam*. New Haven: Yale University Press, 1992.

Aidi, Hisham. "Let Us Be Moors: Islam, Race and 'Connected Histories.'" *Middle East Report*, 229 (2003): 1–18.

Alden, Christopher. "China in Africa." *Survival* 47, no. 3 (2005): 147–64.

———. *China in Africa*. London: Zed, 2007.

———, Daniel Large, and Ricardo Soares de Oliveira, eds. *China Returns to Africa: A Rising Power and a Continent Embrace*. New York: Columbia University Press, 2008.

———. "Red Star, Black Gold." *Review of African Political Economy*, nos. 104/5 (2005): 415–19.

Allison, Roy. *The Soviet Union and the Strategy of Non-Alignment in the Third World*. Cambridge: Cambridge University Press, 1988.

Allman, Jean Marie. *The Quills of the Porcupine: Asante Nationalism in an Emergent Ghana* (Madison: University of Wisconsin Press, 1993).

Alpers, Edward, Gwyn Campbell, and Michael Salman, eds. *Resisting Bondage in Indian Ocean Africa and Asia*. New York: Routledge, 2007.

———, Gwyn Campbell, and Michael Salman, eds. *Slavery and Resistance in Africa and Asia*. New York: Routledge, 2005.

Amin, Samir. *Re-reading the Postwar Period: An Intellectual Itinerary*. New York: Monthly Review Press, 1994.

Anderson, Benedict. *Imagined Communities: Reflections on the Origin and Spread of Nationalism*. London: Verso, 1983.

Andrew, Christopher M. and A. S. Kanya-Forstner, *France Overseas: The Great*

War and the Climax of French Imperialism. London: Thames and Hudson, 1981.

Anonymous. *Through Our Enemies' Eyes: Osama bin Laden, Radical Islam, and the Future of America*. Washington, DC: Brassey's, 2003.

Appadorai, A. *The Bandung Conference*. New Delhi: Indian Council of World Affairs, 1955.

Appadurai, Arjun. *Modernity at Large: Cultural Aspects of Globalization*. Minneapolis: University of Minnesota Press, 1996.

Apter, Andrew. *Beyond Words: Discourse and Critical Agency in Africa*. Chicago: University of Chicago Press, 2007.

Archibugi, Daniele, David Held, and Martin Köhler, eds. *Re-imagining Political Community: Studies in Cosmopolitan Democracy*. Stanford: Stanford University Press, 1998.

Arendt, Hannah. *The Origins of Totalitarianism*. New York: Harcourt Brace, 1951.

Aretxaga, Begoña. "Terror as Thrill: First Thoughts on the 'War on Terrorism.'" *Anthropological Quarterly* 75, no. 1 (Winter 2002): 143–44.

Arjomand, Said Amir, ed. *The Political Dimensions of Religion*. Albany: State University of New York Press, 1993.

Arnold, Nathalie. "Placing the Shameless: Approaching Poetry and the Politics of Pemba-ness in Zanzibar, 1995-2001." *Research in African Literatures* 33 (2002): 140–66.

Arrighi, Giovanni. *Chaos and Governance in the Modern World System*. Minneapolis: University of Minnesota Press, 1999.

Asad, Talal. "Two European Images of Non-European Rule." In *Anthropology and the Colonial Encounter*, ed. Talal Asad, 103–18. New York: Humanities Press, 1973.

Asian-African Conference, *Asia-Africa Speaks from Bandung*. Jakarta: Ministry of Foreign Affairs, Republic of Indonesia, 1955.

Asian Relations: Report of the Proceedings and Documentation of the First Asian Relations Conference, New Delhi, March–April, 1947. Introduced by D. Gopal. Delhi: Authorspress, 2003.

Atieno Odhiambo, E. S. and John Lonsdale, eds. *Mau Mau and Nationhood: Arms, Authority, and Narration*. Athens: Ohio University Press, 2003.

Atkins, Keletso. *The Moon Is Dead, Give Us Our Money! The Cultural Origins of a Zulu Work Ethic*. Portsmouth, NH: Heinemann, 1993.

August, Thomas. *The Selling of Empire: British and French Imperialist Propaganda, 1890-1940*. Westport, CT: Greenwood, 1985.

Aydin, Cemil. *The Politics of Anti-Westernism in Asia: Visions of World Order in Pan-Islamic and Pan-Asian Thought*. New York: Columbia University Press, 2007.

Babu, A. M. "The 1964 Revolution: Lumpen or Vanguard?" In *Zanzibar Under*

Colonial Rule, ed. Abdul Sheriff and E. Ferguson, 220–47. London: James Currey, 1991.

Babu, Salma and Amrit Wilson, eds. *The Future that Works: Selected Writings of A. M. Babu*. Trenton: Africa World Press, 2002.

Badran, Margot. *Women, Islam and Nation*. Princeton: Princeton University Press, 1995.

Bailey, Martin. *Freedom Railway: China and the Tanzania-Zambia Link*. London: Collings, 1976.

———. "Tanzania and China." *African Affairs* 74, no. 294 (1975): 39–50.

Baines, Gary and Peter Vale, eds. *Beyond the Border War: New Perspectives on Southern Africa's Late-Cold War Conflicts*. Pretoria: UNISA Press, 2008.

Balutansky, Kathleen M. *The Novels of Alex La Guma: The Representation of a Political Conflict*. Washington, DC: Three Continents, 1990.

Barnes, Sandra T. "Global Flows: Terror, Oil, and Strategic Philanthropy." *African Studies Review* 48, no. 1 (2005): 1–22.

Baron, Beth. *The Women's Awakening in Egypt: Culture, Society, and the Press*. New Haven: Yale University Press, 1994.

Barron, Thomas J., Owen Dudley Edwards, and Patricia J. Storey, eds. *Constitutions and National Identity*. Edinburgh: Quadriga, 1993.

Baudrillard, Jean. *The Spirit of Terrorism and Requiem for the Twin Towers*. New York: W. W. Norton, 2003.

Baulin, Jacques. *The Arab Role in Africa*. Baltimore: Penguin, 1962.

Beer, Lawrence W., ed. *Constitutional Systems in Late Twentieth Century Asia*. Seattle: University of Washington Press, 1992.

———, ed. *Constitutionalism in Asia: Asian Views of the American Influence*. Berkeley: University of California Press, 1979.

Berner, Brad K. *Jihad: Bin Laden in His Own Words, Declarations, Interviews and Speeches*. N.a.: BookSurge, 2006.

Betts, Raymond F. *Decolonization*. New York: Routledge, 2004.

Bhabha, Homi K. *The Location of Culture*. London: Routledge, 1994.

bin Laden, Osama and Bruce Lawrence, eds. *Messages to the World: The Statements of Osama bin Laden*, trans. James Howarth. London: Verso, 2005.

Blair, Dorothy S. *African Literature in French*. Cambridge: Cambridge University Press, 1976.

Blaustein, Albert P. *The Influence of the United States Constitution Abroad*. Washington, DC: Washington Institute for Values in Public Policy, 1986.

——— and Gisbert H. Flanz, eds. *Constitutions of the Countries of the World*. New York: Dobbs Ferry, 1971–94.

Bonakdarian, Mansour. "Negotiating Universal Values and Cultural and National Parameters at the First Universal Races Congress." *Radical History Review*, issue 92 (2005): 118–32.

Booth, Marilyn. *May Her Likes Be Multiplied: Biography and Gender Politics in Egypt.* Berkeley: University of California Press, 2001.

Borovik, Artyom. *The Hidden War.* New York: Atlantic Monthly Press, 1990.

Bose, Sugata. *A Hundred Horizons: The Indian Ocean in the Age of Global Empire.* Cambridge: Harvard University Press, 2006.

Boserup, Ester. *Women's Role in Economic Development.* New York: St. Martin's, 1979.

Brausch, G. E. J. "African Ethnocracies: Some Sociological Implications of Constitutional Change in Emergent Territories of Africa." *Civilisations* 13, nos. 1–2 (1963): 82–94.

Bräutigam, Deborah. *Chinese Aid and African Development: Exporting Green Revolution.* London: Macmillan, 1998.

——. "Close Encounters: Chinese Business Networks as Industrial Catalysts in Sub-Sahara Africa." *African Affairs* 102, no. 408 (2003): 447–67.

Brennan, James R. "Lowering the Sultan's Flag: Sovereignty and Decolonization in Coastal Kenya." *Comparative Studies in Society and History* 50, no. 4 (2008): 831–61.

——. "Realizing Civilization through Patrilineal Descent: African Intellectuals and the Making of an African Racial Nationalism in Tanzania, 1920–1950." *Social Identities* 12, no. 4 (2006): 405–23.

Brzezinski, Z. and J. Mearsheimer. "Clash of the Titans." *Foreign Policy*, 146 (2005): 46–49.

Buck-Morss, Susan. *Dreamworld and Catastrophe: The Passing of Utopia in East and West.* Cambridge: MIT Press, 2000.

Burgess, Thomas. "An Imagined Generation: Umma Youth in Nationalist Zanzibar." In *In Search of a Nation: Histories of Authority and Dissidence from Tanzania: Essays in Honor of I. M. Kimambo*, ed. Gregory H. Maddox and James L. Giblin, 216–49. London: James Currey, 2005.

——. *Race, Revolution, and the Struggle for Human Rights in Zanzibar: The Memoirs of Ali Sultan Issa and Seif Sharif Hamad.* Athens: Ohio University Press, 2009.

——. "A Socialist Diaspora: Ali Sultan Issa, the Soviet Union, and the Zanzibari Revolution." In *Africa in Russia, Russia in Africa: 300 Years of Encounters*, ed. Maxim Matusevich, 263–91. Trenton: Africa World Press, 2006.

Burke, Jason. *Al-Qaeda: The True Story of Radical Islam.* London: Penguin, 2004.

Burton, Antoinette, ed. *After the Imperial Turn: Thinking with and through the Nation.* Durham: Duke University Press, 2003.

——. *Burdens of History: British Feminists, Indian Women and Imperial Culture, 1865–1915.* Chapel Hill: University of North Carolina Press, 1994.

——. *The Postcolonial Careers of Santha Rama Rau.* Durham: Duke University Press, 2007.

Burton, J. W., ed., *Nonalignment.* London: Andre Deutsch, 1966.

Callaway, Helen. *Gender, Culture and Empire: European Women in Colonial Nigeria*. Urbana: University of Illinois Press, 1987.

Castro-Klarén, Sara and John Charles Chasteen, eds. *Beyond Imagined Communities: Reading and Writing the Nation in Nineteenth-Century Latin America*. Baltimore: Johns Hopkins University Press, 2003.

Césaire, Aimé. *Discourse on Colonialism*, trans. Joan Pinkham. New York: Monthly Review, 2000 [1955].

Chakrabarty, Dipesh. "Globalization, Democratization, and the Evacuation of History." In *At Home in the Diaspora: South Asian Scholars in the West*, ed. Veronique Benei and Jackie Assayag, 127–47. Bloomington: Indiana University Press, 2003.

———. *Provincializing Europe: Postcolonial Thought and Historical Difference*. Princeton: Princeton University Press, 2000.

Chamberlain, M. E. *Decolonization: The Fall of the European Empires*. Oxford: Blackwell, 1999.

Chandler, David P. *The Tragedy of Cambodian History*. New Haven: Yale University Press, 1991.

Chatterjee, Partha. *The Nation and Its Fragments: Colonial and Postcolonial Histories*. Princeton: Princeton University Press, 1994.

———. *Nationalist Thought and the Colonial World: A Derivative Discourse?* 2nd edition. London: Zed, 1993.

Chaudhuri, K. N. *Trade and Civilization in the Indian Ocean: An Economic History from the Rise of Islam to 1750*. Cambridge: Cambridge University Press, 1985.

Chomsky, Noam. *Hegemony or Survival: America's Quest for Global Dominance*. Boston: Metropolitan Books, 2003.

Comaroff, Jean and John L. "Reflexions sur la jeunesse, du passé a la postcolonie." *Politique Africaine* 80 (2000): 90–110.

Connelly, Matthew. *A Diplomatic Revolution: Algeria's Fight for Independence and the Origins of the Post–Cold War Era*. Oxford: Oxford University Press, 2002.

Cooley, John. *East Wind Over Africa: Red China's African Offensive*. New York: Walker, 1965.

Cooper, Frederick. *Africa Since 1940: The Past of the Present*. Cambridge: Cambridge University Press, 2002.

———. *Colonialism in Question: Theory, Knowledge, History*. Berkeley: University of California Press, 2005.

———. "Colonizing Time: Work Rhythms and Labor Conflict in Colonial Mombasa." In *Colonialism and Culture*, ed. Nicholas B. Dirks, 209–46. Ann Arbor: University of Michigan Press, 1992.

———. "Conflict and Connection: Rethinking Colonial African History." *American Historical Review* 99, no. 5 (1994): 1516–45.

———, Allen F. Isaacman, Florencia Mallon, William Roseberry, and Steve J. Stern, eds. *Confronting Historical Paradigms: Peasants, Labor, and the Capitalist World System in Africa and Latin America*. Madison: University of Wisconsin Press, 1993.

———. *Decolonization and African Society: The Labor Question in British and French Africa*. Cambridge: Cambridge University Press, 1996.

———. "Empire Multiplied." *Comparative Studies in Society and History*, 46, no. 2 (2004): 247–72.

——— and Randall Packard, eds. *International Development and the Social Sciences: Essays on the History and Politics of Knowledge*. Berkeley: University of California Press, 1997.

———. "Possibility and Constraint: African Independence in Historical Perspective." *Journal of African History* 49, no. 2 (2008): 167–96.

——— and Ann Laura Stoler, eds. *Tensions of Empire: Colonial Cultures in a Bourgeois World*. Berkeley: University of California Press, 1997.

Cooray, Joseph. *Constitutional and Administrative Law of Sri Lanka*. Colombo: Hansa Publishers, 1973.

Crabb, Jr., Cecil V. *The Elephants and the Grass: A Study of Nonalignment*. New York: Praeger, 1965.

Crais, Clifton C. and Pamela Scully. *Sara Baartman and the Hottentot Venus: A Ghost Story and a Biography*. Princeton: Princeton University Press, 2009.

Crawfurd, John. "On the Physical and Mental Characteristics of the European and Asiatic Races." *Transactions of the Ethnological Society of London* 5 (1867): 58–81.

Crowder, Michael. *Senegal: A Study in French Assimilationist Policy*. London: Methuen, 1967.

Damas, Léon-Gontran. *Pigments*. Paris: Présence Africaine, 1962.

Darwin, John. *Britain and Decolonisation: The Retreat from Empire in the Post-War World*. Basingstoke: Macmillan, 1988.

———. *The British in the Middle East 1918–1922*. London: Macmillan, 1981.

Delavignette, Robert. *Freedom and Authority in French West Africa*. London: Oxford University Press, 1950.

Diouf, Mamadou. "Engaging Postcolonial Culture: African Youth and Public Space." *African Studies Review* 46, no. 2 (2003): 1–12.

Dirks, Nicholas B., ed. *Colonialism and Culture*. Ann Arbor: University of Michigan Press, 1992.

Dirlik, Arif, Vinay Bahl, and Peter Gran, eds. *History after the Three Worlds: Post-Eurocentric Historiographies*. New York: Rowman and Littlefield, 2000.

Dirlik, Arif. *The Postcolonial Aura: Third World Criticism in the Age of Global Capitalism*. Boulder: Westview, 1997.

Donham, Donald. *Marxist Modern: An Ethnographic History of the Ethiopian Revolution*. Berkeley: University of California Press, 1999.

Dotson, Floyd and Lillian. *The Indian Minority of Zambia, Rhodesia, and Malawi*. New Haven: Yale University Press, 1968.

Downs, E. S. "The Chinese Energy Security Debate." *China Quarterly* 177 (2004): 21–41.

Doyle, Michael W. *Empires*. Ithaca: Cornell University Press, 1986.

Drew Allison. *Between Empire and Revolution: A Life of Sidney Bunting, 1873–1936*. London: Pickering and Chatto, 2007.

———. *Discordant Comrades: Identities and Loyalties on the South African Left*. Aldershot: Ashgate, 2000.

———, ed. *South Africa's Radical Tradition, A Documentary History: Volume One, 1907–1950*. Cape Town: UCT Press, 1996.

Duara, Prasenjit, ed. *Decolonization: Perspectives from Now and Then*. New York: Routledge, 2004.

———. "The Discourse of Civilization and Pan-Asianism." *Journal of World History* 12, no. 1 (2001): 99–130.

———. *Rescuing History from the Nation: Questioning Narratives of Modern China*. Chicago: University of Chicago Press, 1995.

Duchacek, Ivo D. *Power Maps: Comparative Politics of Constitutions*. Santa Barbara: American Bibliographical Center–Clio Press, Inc., 1973.

Duiker, William J. *Ho Chi Minh*. New York: Hyperion, 2000.

During, Simon. "Introduction." In *The Cultural Studies Reader*, ed. Simon During, 2nd edition, 1–28. London and New York: Routledge, 2000.

Economy, E. "Changing Course on China." *Current History* 102, no. 665 (2003): 243–49.

Edwards, Brent Hayes. *The Practice of Diaspora: Literature, Translation, and the Rise of Black Internationalism*. Cambridge: Harvard University Press, 2003.

———. "The Shadow of Shadows." *Positions* 11, no. 1 (2003): 11–49.

Eley, Geoff, ed. *Becoming National: A Reader*. New York: Oxford University Press, 1996.

Elias, T. O. *Ghana and Sierra Leone: The Development of Their Laws and Constitutions*. London: Steven and Sons, 1962.

———. *Nigeria: The Development of Its Laws and Constitution*. London: Stevens and Sons, 1967.

Elkins, Caroline and Susan Pedersen, eds. *Settler Colonialism in the Twentieth Century: Projects, Practices, Legacies*. New York: Routledge, 2005.

Ellis, Stephen. "Writing Histories of Contemporary Africa." *Journal of African History*, 43, no. 1 (2002): 1–26.

Escobar, Arturo. *Encountering Development: The Making and Unmaking of the Third World*. Princeton: Princeton University Press, 1995.

Espiritu, Augusto. "'To Carry Water on Both Shoulders': Carlos P. Romulo,

American Empire, and the Meanings of Bandung." *Radical History Review* 95 (2006): 173–90.

Esposito, Roberto. *Bíos: Biopolitics and Philosophy,* trans.Timothy Campbell. Minneapolis: University of Minnesota Press, 2008.

Falola, Toyin. *Nationalism and African Intellectuals.* Rochester, NY: University of Rochester Press, 2001.

Fanon, Frantz. *A Dying Colonialism,* trans. Haakon Chevalier. New York: Grove, 1967.

———. *The Wretched of the Earth,* trans. Constance Farrington. New York: Grove, 1963.

Federation of Malaya. *Federation of Malaya Constitutional Proposals.* Kuala Lumpur: Government Press, 1957.

Ferguson, James. *The Anti-politics Machine: "Development," Depoliticization, and Bureaucratic Power in Lesotho.* Cambridge: Cambridge University Press, 1990.

———. *Expectations of Modernity: Myths and Meanings of Urban Life on the Zambian Copperbelt.* Berkeley: University of California Press, 1999.

Ferguson, Niall. *Empire: The Rise and Demise of the British World Order and the Lessons for Global Power.* New York: Basic, 2003.

First, Ruth. *The Barrel of a Gun: Political Power in Africa and the Coup d'État.* London: Allen Lane, 1970.

Fischer, Louis. *The Life of Mahatma Gandhi.* New York: Collier, 1962.

Frank, Andre Gunder. *Crisis in the World Economy.* London: Heinemann, 1980.

Friedman, Thomas L. *The Lexus and the Olive Tree: Understanding Globalization.* New York: Anchor, 2000.

Friedrich, Carl J. *Transcendent Justice. The Religious Dimensions of Constitutionalism.* Durham: Duke University Press, 1964.

Gaines, Kevin. "Rethinking Richard Wright in Ghana: Black Radicalism and the Dialectics of Diaspora." *Social Text,* 19, no. 2 (2001): 75–101.

Gandhi, Leela. *Postcolonial Theory: A Critical Introduction.* New York: Columbia University Press, 1998.

Gandhi, Mahatma. *The Story of My Experiments with Truth: The Autobiography of Mahatma Gandhi.* Boston: Beacon, 1957.

Gao Jinyuan. "China and Africa: The Development of Relations Over Many Centuries." *African Affairs* 83, no. 331 (1984): 241–50.

Gaonkar, Dilip Parameshwar, ed. *Alternative Modernities.* Durham: Duke University Press, 2001.

Gates, Jr., Henry Louis, ed. *"Race," Writing, and Difference.* Chicago: University of Chicago Press, 1985.

Geiger, Susan. *TANU Women: Gender and Culture in the Making of Tanganyikan Nationalism, 1955–1965.* Portsmouth, NH: Heinemann, 1997.

Gershoni, Israel and James Jankowski. *Redefining the Egyptian Nation, 1930–1945*. Cambridge: Cambridge University Press, 1995.

Ghai, Yash P. *Constitutions and the Political Order in East Africa*. Dar es Salaam: University College Dar es Salaam, 1970.

Gifford, Prosser and William Roger Louis, eds. *The Transfer of Power in Africa: Decolonization 1940–1960*. New Haven: Yale University Press, 1982.

———, eds. *Decolonization and African Independence: The Transfers of Power, 1960–1980*. New Haven: Yale University Press, 1988.

Gilroy, Paul. *The Black Atlantic: Modernity and Double Consciousness*. Cambridge: Harvard University Press, 1993.

Giradet, Raoul. *L'idée coloniale en France, 1871–1962*. Paris: La Table Ronde, 1972.

Girault, Arthur. *Principes de Colonisation et de Legislation Coloniale*. Paris: Larose, 1895.

Glassman, Jonathon. "Slower than a Massacre: The Multiple Sources of Racial Thought in Colonial Africa." *American Historical Review*, 109, no. 3 (2004): 720–54.

———. "Sorting out the Tribes: The Creation of Racial Identities in Colonial Zanzibar's Newspaper Wars." *Journal of African History*, 41 (2000): 395–428.

Gleijeses, Piero. *Conflicting Missions: Havana, Washington, and Africa, 1959–1976*. Chapel Hill: University of North Carolina Press, 2002.

Goldwin, Robert A. and Art Kaufman, eds. *Constitution Makers on Constitution Making*. Washington, DC: American Enterprise Institute for Public Policy Research, 1983.

Goswami, Manu. "From *Swadeshi* to *Swaraj*: Nation, Economy, Territory in Colonial South Asia, 1870 to 1907." *Comparative Studies in Society and History*, 40, no. 4 (1998): 609–36.

———. *Producing India: From Colonial Economy to National Space*. Chicago: University of Chicago Press, 2004.

———. "Rethinking the Modular Nation Form: Toward a Sociohistorical Conception of Nationalism." *Comparative Studies in Society and History*, 44, no. 4 (2002): 770–99.

Gramsci, Antonio. *Selections from Prison Notebooks*, ed. and trans. Q. Hoare and G. Smith. New York: International Publishers, 1971.

Grandin, Greg. *Empire's Workshop: Latin America, the United States, and the Rise of the New Imperialism*. New York: Metropolitan Books, 2006.

Greene, John C. *Science, Ideology and World View*. Berkeley: University of California Press, 1981.

Grewal, Inderpal. *Transnational America: Feminisms, Diasporas, Neoliberalisms*. Durham: Duke University Press, 2005.

Groves, Harry E. *The Constitution of Malaysia*. Singapore: Malaysia Publications, 1964.

Gupta, Akhil. *Postcolonial Developments: Agriculture in the Making of Modern India*. Durham: Duke University Press, 1998.

Gurnah, Abdulrazak. *Admiring Silence*. New York: Free Press, 1996.

———. *Desertion*. New York: Pantheon, 2005.

Hale, Julian. *Radio Power: Propaganda and International Broadcasting*. Philadelphia: Temple University Press, 1975.

Hall, Catherine, ed. *Cultures of Empire: Colonizers in Britain and the Empire in the Nineteenth and Twentieth Centuries*. New York: Routledge, 2000.

Hall, Richard and Hugh Peyman. *The Great Uhuru Railway: China's Showpiece in Africa*. London: Gollancz, 1976.

Hall, Stuart. "When Was 'the Postcolonial'? Thinking at the Limit." In *The Postcolonial Question: Common Skies, Divided Horizons*, ed. Iain Chambers and Lidia Curti, 242–60. New York: Routledge, 1996.

Hamud, Randall B., ed. *Osama Bin Laden: America's Enemy in His Own Words*. San Diego: Nadeem Publishing, 2005.

Hardt, Michael and Antonio Negri. *Empire*. Cambridge: Harvard University Press, 2000.

Harris, Joseph E. *The African Presence in Asia: Consequences of the East African Slave Trade*. Evanston: Northwestern University Press, 1971.

Hartman, Saidiya. *Lose Your Mother: A Journey along the Atlantic Slave Route*. New York: Farrar, Straus and Giroux, 2007.

Harvey, David. *The Condition of Postmodernity*. Oxford: Blackwell, 2000.

———. *The New Imperialism*. Oxford: Oxford University Press, 2003.

Haskell, Thomas. "Capitalism and the Origins of the Humanitarian Sensibility, part 1." *American Historical Review,* 90, no. 2 (1985): 339–61

———. "Capitalism and the Origins of the Humanitarian Sensibility, part 2." *American Historical Review,* 90, no. 3 (1985): 547–66.

Henkin, Louis and Albert J. Rosenthal, eds. *Constitutionalism and Rights: The Influence of the United States Constitution Abroad*. New York: Columbia University Press, 1990.

Herring, George C. *From Colony to Superpower: US Foreign Relations Since 1776*. Oxford: Oxford University Press, 2008.

Hevi, Emmanuel. *An African Student in China*. New York: Praeger, 1963.

Hilsum, Lindsey. "Re-enter the Dragon: China's New Mission in Africa." *Review of African Political Economy*, nos. 104/5 (2005): 419–25

Ho, Engseng. *The Graves of Tarim: Genealogy and Mobility across the Indian Ocean*. Berkeley: University of California Press, 2006.

Ho, Fred and Bill V. Mullen, eds. *Afro Asia: Revolutionary Political and Cultural Connections between African Americans and Asian Americans*. Durham: Duke University Press, 2008.

Hobsbawm, Eric. *Nations and Nationalism Since 1780: Programme, Myth, Reality*. Cambridge: Cambridge University Press, 1992.

——. *Revolutionaries*. New York: New Press, 2001.

Hoffman, Stanley. "The French Constitution of 1958: The Final Text and Its Prospects." *American Political Science Review*, 53 (1959): 332–57.

Horne, Gerald. *Race Woman: The Lives of Shirley Graham Du Bois*. New York: New York University Press, 2000.

Horton, J. A. *Letters on the Political Condition of the Gold Coast*. London: W. J. Johnson, 1870.

——. *West African Countries and Peoples*. London: W. J. Johnson, 1868.

Howland, Douglas and Luise White, eds. *The State of Sovereignty: Territories, Laws, Populations*. Bloomington: Indiana University Press, 2008.

Human Rights Watch. *Sudan, Oil and Human Rights*. New York: Human Rights Watch, 2003.

Hutchison, Alan. *China's African Revolution*. Boulder: Westview, 1976.

Irele, Abiola. "Négritude—Literature and Ideology." *Journal of Modern African Studies*, 3, no. 4 (1965): 499–526.

Ismael, Tareq Y. "The People's Republic of China and Africa." *Journal of Modern African Studies*, 9, no. 4 (1971): 507–29.

——. *The U.A.R. in Africa: Egypt's Policy Under Nasser*. Evanston: Northwestern University Press, 1971.

Jackson, Henry F. *The FLN in Algeria: Party Development in a Revolutionary Society*. Westport, CT: Greenwood, 1977.

JanMohamed, Abdul R. *Manichean Aesthetics: The Politics of Literature in Colonial Africa*. Amherst: University of Massachusetts Press, 1983.

Jansen, G. H. *Nonalignment and the Afro-Asian States*. New York: Praeger, 1966.

Jayasuriya, Shihan De S. and Richard Pankhurst, eds. *The African Diaspora in the Indian Ocean*. Trenton: Africa World Press, 2003.

Jayawardena, Kumari. *Feminism and Nationalism in the Third World*. London: Zed, 1986.

Jenkins, R. and C. Edwards, *How Does China's Growth Affect Poverty Reduction in Asia, Africa, and Latin America?* Norwich: University of East Anglia, 2004.

Jennings, Ivor. *The Commonwealth in Asia*. Oxford: Clarendon Press, 1949.

Johnson, Chalmers. *The Sorrows of Empire: Militarism, Secrecy, and the End of the Republic*. New York: Metropolitan Books, 2004.

Johnson, D. H. *The Root Causes of Sudan's Civil War*. Oxford: James Currey, 2003.

Jones, Andrew F. and Nikhil Pal Singh, eds. *The Afro-Asian Century*, special issue of *Positions*, 11, no. 1 (2003).

Jones, Matthew. "A 'Segregated' Asia? Race, the Bandung Conference, and Pan-Asianist Fears in American Thought and Policy, 1954–1955." *Diplomatic History*, 29, no. 5 (2005): 841–68.

Joseph, Gilbert M. and Daniela Spenser, eds. *In from the Cold: Latin America's New Encounter with the Cold War*. Durham: Duke University Press, 2008.

Kahin, George McTurnan. *The African-Asian Conference: Bandung, Indonesia, April 1955*. Ithaca: Cornell University Press, 1956.

Kandiyoti, Deniz. "Bargaining with Patriarchy." *Gender and Society*, 2, no. 3 (1988): 274–90.

Kapur, Harish. *China and the Afro-Asian World*. New Delhi: Prabhakar Padhye, 1966.

Karlsson, Bengt G. and Tanka B. Subba, eds. *The Politics of Indigeneity in India*. London: Kegan Paul, 2006.

Kaunda, Kenneth. *Zambia Independence and Beyond. The Speeches of Kenneth Kaunda*, ed. and intro. by Colin Legum. London: Thomas Nelson and Sons, 1966.

Kelley, Robin D. G. *Freedom Dreams: The Black Radical Imagination*. Boston: Beacon Press, 2002.

―――― and Betsy Esch. "Black like Mao: Red China and Black Revolution." In *Afro Asia: Revolutionary Political and Cultural Connections between African Americans and Asian Americans*, ed. Fred Ho and Bill V. Mullen, 97–154. Durham: Duke University Press, 2008.

Kelly, John D. and Martha Kaplan. *Represented Communities: Fiji and World Decolonization*. Chicago: University of Chicago Press, 2001.

Kennedy, Dane. "Imperial History and Post-colonial Theory." *Journal of Imperial and Commonwealth History*, 24, no. 3 (1996): 345–63.

Khalidi, Rashid. *Resurrecting Empire: Western Footprints and America's Perilous Path in the Middle East*. Boston: Beacon Press, 2004.

Kidd, Benjamin. *The Control of the Tropics*. London: Macmillan, 1898.

Kimche, David. *The Afro-Asian Movement: Ideology and Foreign Policy of the Third World*. New York: Halstead Press, 1973.

Kindy, Hyder. *Life and Politics in Mombasa*. Nairobi: East African Publishing House, 1972.

Kirk-Greene, A. H. M., ed. *Africa in the Colonial Period III. The Transfer of Power: The Colonial Administrators in the Age of Decolonization*. Oxford: University of Oxford Inter-faculty Committee for African Studies, 1979.

Klare, Michael and Daniel Volman. "America, China and the Scramble for Africa's Oil." *Review of African Political Economy*, no. 108 (2006): 297–309.

Klein, Ira. "Indian Nationalism and Anti-industrialization: The Roots of Gandhian Economics." *South Asia*, 3 (1973): 93–104.

Knox, Robert. *The Races of Men: A Philosophical Enquiry into the Influence of Race Over the Destinies of Nations*. London: H. Renshaw, 1862.

Kotelawala, John. *An Asian Prime Minister's Story*. London: George G. Harrap and Co., 1956.

Kresse, Kai. *Philosophising in Mombasa: Knowledge, Islam and Intellectual Practice on the Swahili Coast*. Edinburgh: Edinburgh University Press for the International African Institute, 2007.

Krishnaswamy, Revathi and John C. Hawley, eds. *The Postcolonial and the Global*. Minneapolis: University of Minnesota Press, 2008.

Lake, Marilyn and Henry Reynolds. *Drawing the Global Colour Line: White Men's Countries and the International Challenge of Racial Equality*. Cambridge: Cambridge University Press, 2008.

Large, Daniel. "Beyond 'Dragon in the Bush': The Study of China-Africa Relations." *African Affairs*, 107, no. 426 (2008): 45–61.

Larkin, Bruce. *China and Africa, 1949–1970: The Foreign Policy of the People's Republic of China*. Berkeley: University of California Press, 1971.

Lazreg, Marnia. *The Eloquence of Silence: Algerian Women in Question*. New York: Routledge, 1994.

Le Bon, Gustave. *The Psychology of Peoples*. London: T. Fisher, 1899.

Le Sueur, James D., ed. *The Decolonization Reader*. New York: Routledge, 2003.

Leclerc, Gérard. *Anthropologie et colonialisme: Essai sur l'histoire de l'Africainisme*. Paris: Fayard, 1972.

Leed, Eric J. *No Man's Land: Combat and Identity in World War I*. Cambridge: Cambridge University Press, 1979.

Leslie, J. A. K. *A Survey of Dar es Salaam*. London: Oxford University Press, 1963.

Lewis, Martin W. and Kären E. Wigen. *The Myth of Continents: A Critique of Metageography*. Berkeley: University of California Press, 1997.

Lijphart, Arend, ed. *Parliamentary Versus Presidential Government*. Oxford: Oxford University Press, 1992.

Lofchie, Michael. *Zanzibar: Background to Revolution*. Princeton: Princeton University Press, 1965.

Loomba, Ania, Suvir Kaul, Matti Bunzl, Antoinette Burton, and Jed Esty, eds. *Postcolonial Studies and Beyond*. Durham: Duke University Press, 2005.

Loutfi, Martine. *Littérature et colonialisme: L'expansion coloniale vue dans la littérature romanesque française, 1871–1914*. Paris: Mouton, 1971.

Lu Duanfang. *Remaking Chinese Urban Form: Modernity, Scarcity and Space, 1949–2005*. New York: Routledge, 2006.

Luis-Brown, David. *Waves of Decolonization: Discourses on Race and Hemispheric Citizenship in Cuba, Mexico and the United States*. Durham: Duke University Press, 2008.

McClintock, Anne. "The Angel of Progress: Pitfalls of the Term 'Postcolonialism.'" *Social Text*, nos. 31/32 (1992): 84–98.

McMahon, Robert J. *Colonialism and the Cold War: The United States and the Struggle for Indonesian Independence, 1945–1949*. Ithaca: Cornell University Press, 1981.

Mackie, Jamie. *Bandung 1955: Non-alignment and Afro-Asian Solidarity.* Singapore: Didier Millet, 2005.

Maddox, Gregory H. and James L. Giblin, eds. *In Search of a Nation: Histories of Authority and Dissidence in Tanzania.* Athens: Ohio University Press, 2005.

Mamdani, Mahmood. *Citizen and Subject: Contemporary Africa and the Legacy of Late Colonialism.* Princeton: Princeton University Press, 1996.

———. *Good Muslim, Bad Muslim: America, the Cold War, and the Roots of Terror.* New York: Pantheon, 2004.

Maran, René. *Batouala,* trans. Barbara Beck and Alexandre Mboukou. London: Heinemann, 1973.

Martin, Esmond. *Zanzibar: Tradition and Revolution.* Zanzibar: Gallery Publications, 2007.

Martin, Lawrence W., ed. *Neutralism and Nonalignment: The New States in World Affairs.* New York: Praeger, 1962.

Massis, Henri. *Defense of the West.* London: Faber, 1927.

Mazrui, Ali. *Cultural Engineering and Nation-Building in East Africa.* Evanston: Northwestern University Press, 1972.

Mazrui, Alamin and Ibrahim Noor Shariff. *The Swahili: Idiom and Identity of an African People.* Trenton: Africa World Press, 1994.

Maung Maung, U. *Burma's Constitution.* The Hague: Martinus Nijhoff, 1959.

Mbembe, Achille. *On the Postcolony.* Berkeley: University of California Press, 2001.

Medeiros, E. S. and M. Taylor Fravel. "China's New Diplomacy." *Foreign Affairs,* 82, no. 6 (2003): 22–35.

Menon, Sridevi. "Where Is West Asia in Asian America? 'Asia' and the Politics of Space in Asian America." *Social Text,* 24, no. 1/86 (Spring 2006): 55–79.

Merchant, Carolyn. *The Death of Nature.* New York: Harper and Row, 1983.

Metcalf, Thomas R. *Imperial Connections: India in the Indian Ocean Arena, 1860–1920.* Berkeley: University of California Press, 2007.

Mezu, S. Okechukwu. *Léopold Sedar Senghor et la défense et illustration de la civilisation noire.* Paris: M. Didier, 1968.

Mignolo, Walter D. *The Idea of Latin America.* London: Blackwell, 2005.

———. *Local Histories/Global Designs: Essays on the Coloniality of Power, Subaltern Knowledges, and Border Thinking.* Princeton: Princeton University Press, 2000.

Miller, Christopher L. *The French Atlantic Triangle: Literature and Culture of the Slave Trade.* Durham: Duke University Press, 2008.

Misra, K. P., ed. *Non-alignment Frontiers and Dynamics.* New Delhi: Vikas Publishing House, 1982.

Mitchell, Timothy. *Colonising Egypt.* Berkeley: University of California Press, 1991.

Miyoshi, Masao, ed. *Learning Places: The Afterlives of Area Studies*. Durham: Duke University Press, 2002.

Mohanty, Charlotte, Ann Russo, and Lordes Torres, eds. *Third World Women and the Politics of Feminism*. Bloomington: Indiana University Press, 1991.

Monson, Jamie. *Africa's Freedom Railway: How a Chinese Development Project Changed Lives and Livelihoods in Tanzania*. Bloomington: Indiana University Press, 2009.

———. "Liberating Labor? Constructing Anti-hegemony along the TAZARA Railway." In *China Returns to Africa: A Rising Power and a Continent Embrace*, ed. Christopher Alden, Daniel Large, and Ricardo Soares de Oliveira, 197–220. New York: Columbia University Press, 2008.

Moore, David Chioni. "Colored Dispatches from the Uzbek Border: Langston Hughes' Relevance, 1933–2002," *Callaloo*, 25, no. 4 (2002): 1115–35.

———. "Is the Post in Postcolonial the Post in Post-Soviet? Notes Toward a Global Postcolonial Critique," *PMLA*, 116, no. 1 (2001): 111–28.

———. "Local Color, Global 'Color': Langston Hughes, the Black Atlantic, and Soviet Central Asia, 1932," *Research in African Literatures*, 27, no. 4 (Winter 1996): 49–70.

Morgan, D. J. *The Official History of Colonial Development. Volume 5: Guidance towards Self-government in British Colonies, 1941–1971*. Atlantic Highlands, NJ: Humanities Press, 1980.

Morley, David and Kuan-Hsing Chen, eds. *Stuart Hall: Critical Dialogue and Cultural Studies*. London: Routledge, 1996.

Mortimer, Robert A. *The Third World Coalition in International Politics*. New York: Praeger, 1980.

Motala, Ziyad. *Constitutional Options for a Democratic South Africa*. Washington, DC: Howard University Press, 1994.

Mudimbe, V. Y. *The Invention of Africa: Gnosis, Philosophy and the Order of Knowledge*. Bloomington: Indiana University Press, 1988.

Muekalia, D. J. "Africa and China's Strategic Partnership." *African Security Review*, 13, no. 1 (2004): 5–11.

Mullen, Bill V. *Afro-Orientalism*. Minneapolis: University of Minnesota Press, 2004.

Nandy, Ashis. *The Intimate Enemy: Loss and Recovery of Self Under Colonialism*. Delhi: Oxford University Press, 1983.

Natalegawa, R. M. Marty M., ed. *Asia, Africa, Africa, Asia: Bandung, towards the First Century*. Jakarta: Department of Foreign Affairs, Republic of Indonesia, 2005.

Nehru, Jawaharlal. *The Discovery of India*. New York: Penguin, 2004.

Ngũgĩ wa Thiongo. *Decolonising the Mind: The Politics of Language in African Literature*. London: James Curry, 1986.

Nixon, Rob. *Homelands, Harlem and Hollywood: South African Culture and the World Beyond*. New York: Routledge, 1994.

Nkrumah, Kwame. *Consciencism: Philosophy and the Ideology for Decolonization*. New York: Monthly Review Press, 1970.

———. *Neo-colonialism: The Last Stage of Imperialism*. New York: International Publishers, 1965.

Nwabueze, Benjamin Obi. *Constitutionalism in the Emergent States*. London: C. Hurst and Company, 1973.

———. *Presidentialism in Commonwealth Africa*. New York: St. Martin's, 1974.

Nyamweya, James. "The Constitution of Kenya." *Civilisations*, 14, no. 4 (1964): 331–41.

Nyerere, Julius K. *Freedom and Unity*. London: Oxford University Press, 1967.

———. *Ujamaa: Essays on Socialism*. Oxford: Oxford University Press, 1968.

Odinga, Ajuma Oginga. *Not Yet Uhuru: The Autobiography of Oginga Odinga*. New York: Hill and Wang, 1967.

Ogot, B. A. and W. R. Ochieng, eds. *Decolonization and Independence in Kenya, 1940–93*. Athens: Ohio University Press, 1995.

Ogunsanyo, Alaba. *China's Policy in Africa, 1958–71*. Cambridge: Cambridge University Press, 1974.

Onimode, Bade. *A Political Economy of the African Crisis*. London: Zed, 1988.

Orde-Browne, G. St. John. *The Vanishing Tribes of Kenya*. London: Seeley, Service, 1925.

Othman, Haroub, ed. *Babu, I Saw the Future and It Works: Essays Celebrating the Life of Comrade Abdulrahman Mohamed Babu 1924–1996*. Dar es Salaam: M and M Printers, 2001.

Ottoway, David and Marina Ottoway. *Algeria: The Politics of a Socialist Revolution*. Berkeley: University of California Press, 1970.

Ozouf, Mona. *Festivals and the French Revolution*, trans. Alan Sheridan. Cambridge: Harvard University Press, 1988.

Parker, Jason. "Cold War II: The Eisenhower Administration, the Bandung Conference and the Reperiodization of the Postwar Era." *Diplomatic History*, 30, no. 5 (2006): 867–92.

Patriarca, Sylvana. "Indolence and Regeneration: Tropes and Tensions of Risorgimento Patriotism." *American Historical Review*, 110, no. 2 (2005): 380–408.

Peaselee, Amos J. *Constitutions of Nations*. The Hague: Martinus Nijkoff, 1966.

Pennybacker, Susan D. "The Universal Races Congress, London Political Culture, and Imperial Dissent, 1900–1939." *Radical History Review*, issue 92 (Spring 2005): 103–17.

Petterson, Donald. *Revolution in Zanzibar: An American's Cold War Tale*. Boulder: Westview, 2002.

Prashad, Vijay. *The Darker Nations: A People's History of the Third World*. New York: New Press, 2007.

———. *Everybody Was Kung-fu Fighting: Afro-Asian Connections and the Myth of Cultural Purity*. Boston: Beacon, 2001.

Pratt, Mary Louise. *Imperial Eyes: Travel Writing and Transculturation*. London: Routledge, 1992.

Prestholdt, Jeremy. *Domesticating the World: African Consumerism and the Genealogies of Globalization*. Berkeley: University of California Press, 2008.

Prybyla, Jan S. "Communist China's Economic Relations with Africa, 1960–64." *Asian Survey*, 4, no. 11 (1964): 1135–43.

Rajan, M. S., V. S. Mani, and C. S. R. Murthy, eds. *The Nonaligned and the United Nations*. New Delhi: South Asian Publishers, 1987.

Ranger, Terence. "Nationalist Historiography, Patriotic History and the History of the Nation: The Struggle over the Past in Zimbabwe." *Journal of Southern African Studies*, 30, no. 2 (2004): 215–34.

Raphael-Hernandez, Heike and Shannon Steen, eds. *Afro-Asian Encounters: Culture, History, Politics*. New York: New York University Press, 2006.

Read, Alan, ed. *The Fact of Blackness: Frantz Fanon and Visual Representation*. Seattle: Bay Press, 1996.

Retort (Iain Boal, T. J. Clark, Joseph Matthews, and Michael Watts). *Afflicted Powers: Capital and Spectacle in a New Age of War*. New York: Verso, 2005.

Rich, Paul. "'The Baptism of a New Era': The 1911 Universal Races Congress and the Liberal Ideology of Race." *Ethnic and Racial Studies*, 7, no. 4 (1984): 534–50.

Risso, Patricia. *Merchants and Faith: Muslim Commerce and Culture in the Indian Ocean*. Boulder: Westview, 1995.

Robbins, Thomas and Roland Robertson, eds. *Church–State Relations: Tensions and Transitions*. New Brunswick: Transaction, 1987.

Robinson, Kenneth and Frederick Madden, eds. *Essays in Imperial Government*. Oxford: Basil Blackwell, 1963.

Rodriguez, Besenia. "'Long Live Third World Unity! Long Live Internationalism!': Huey P. Newton's Revolutionary Intercommunalism." *Souls: A Critical Journal of Black Politics, Culture and Society*, 8, no. 3 (2006): 119–41

Roy, Anjali Gera. "Bhangra Remixes." In *India in Africa, Africa in India: Indian Ocean Cosmopolitanisms*, ed. John C. Hawley, 95–116. Bloomington: Indiana University Press, 2008.

Romulo, Carlos P. *The Meaning of Bandung*. Chapel Hill: University of North Carolina Press, 1956.

Rubenstein, Alvin Z., ed. *Soviet and Chinese Influence in the Third World*. New York: Praeger, 1975.

Rupp, Leila. *Worlds of Women*. Princeton: Princeton University Press, 1991.

Saaler, Sven and J. Victor Koschmann, eds. *Pan-Asianism in Modern Japanese History: Colonialism, Regionalism and Borders*. London: Routledge, 2007.

Sadleir, Randal. *Tanzania: Journey to Republic*. New York: St. Martin's, 1999.

Said, Edward W. *Culture and Imperialism*. New York: Vintage, 1993.

Said, Mohamed. *The Life and Times of Abdulwahid Sykes (1924–1968): The Untold Story of the Muslim Struggle against British Colonialism in Tanganyika*. London: Minerva, 1998.

Salim, A. I. *Swahili-speaking Peoples of Kenya's Coast*. Nairobi: East African Publishing, 1973.

Schmalzer, Sigrid. "Labor Created Humanity: Cultural Revolution Science on Its Own Terms." In *The Chinese Cultural Revolution as History*, ed. Joseph Esherick, Paul Pickowicz, and Andrew Walder, 185–210. Stanford: Stanford University Press, 2006.

———. "On the Appropriate Use of Rose-colored Glasses: Reflections on Science in Socialist China." *Isis* 98, no. 3 (2007): 571–83.

Schmidt, Elizabeth. *Cold War and Decolonization in Guinea, 1946–1958*. Athens: Ohio University Press, 2007.

———. *Mobilizing the Masses: Gender, Ethnicity, and Class in the Nationalist Movement in Guinea, 1939–1958*. Portsmouth, NH: Heinemann, 2005.

Schueller, Malini Johar. "Articulations of African-Americanisms in South Asian Postcolonial Theory: Globalism, Localism and the Question of Race." *Cultural Critique*, 55 (Fall 2003): 35–62.

Scott, Alan, ed. *The Limits of Globalization: Cases and Arguments*. London: Routledge, 1997.

Scott, David. *Conscripts of Modernity: The Tragedy of Colonial Enlightenment*. Durham: Duke University Press, 2004.

———. *Refashioning Futures: Criticism after Postcoloniality*. Princeton: Princeton University Press, 1999.

Selected Documents of the Bandung Conference. New York: Institute of Pacific Relations, 1955.

Selected Works of Jawaharlal Nehru, ed. Ravinder Kumar and H. Y. Sharada Prasad. Delhi: JN Memorial Fund, 2000.

Senghor, Léopold Sédar. *Ce que je crois: Négritude, francité et civilisation de l'universel*. Paris: B. Grasset, 1988.

———. *Prose and Poetry*, selected and trans. John Reed and Clive Wake. Oxford: Oxford University Press, 1965.

———. *Selected Poems*. Oxford: Oxford University Press, 1964.

Shepard, Todd. *The Invention of Decolonization: The Algerian War and the Remaking of France*. Ithaca: Cornell University Press, 2006.

Shivji, Issa. *Pan-Africanism or Pragmatism? Lessons of Tanganyika-Zanzibar Union*. Dar es Salaam: Mkuki na Nyota Publishers, 2008.

Shohat, Ella. "Notes on the Postcolonial." *Social Text*, nos. 31/32 (1992): 99–113.

Silveira, Onésimo. *Africa South of the Sahara: Party Systems and Ideologies of Socialism*. Stockholm: Rabén and Sjögren, 1976.

Singham, A. W. and Tran Van Dinh, eds. *From Bandung to Colombo*. New York: Third Press Review, 1976.

Singham, A. W. and Shirley Hune. *Non-alignment in an Age of Alignments*. London: Zed, 1986.

Sinha, Mrinalini. *Specters of Mother India: The Global Restructuring of an Empire*. Durham: Duke University Press, 2006.

Sithole, Ndabaningi. *African Nationalism*. London: Oxford University Press, 1969.

Smith, William Edgett. *We Must Run While They Walk: A Portrait of Africa's Julius Nyerere*. New York: Random House, 1971.

Snow, Philip. *The Star Raft: China's Encounter with Africa*. London: Weidenfeld and Nicolson, 1988.

Sorum, Paul Clay. *Intellectuals and Decolonization in France*. Chapel Hill: University of North Carolina Press, 1977.

Spann, R. N., ed. *Constitutionalism in Asia*. Bombay: Asia Publishing House, 1963.

Springhall, John. *Decolonization Since 1945: The Collapse of European Overseas Empires*. New York: Palgrave, 2001.

Spruyt, Hendrik. *Ending Empire: Contested Sovereignty and Territorial Partition*. Ithaca: Cornell University Press, 2005.

Stargardt, A. W. "The Emergence of the Asian Systems of Power." *Modern Asian Studies*, 23, no. 3 (1989): 561–95.

Steinberg, Joel, ed. *In Search of Southeast Asia*. Honolulu: University of Hawai'i Press, 1985.

Stoler, Ann Laura, ed. *Haunted by Empire: Geographies of Intimacy in North America*. Durham: Duke University Press, 2006.

Stren, Richard. *Housing the Urban Poor in Africa: Policy, Politics and Bureaucracy in Mombasa*. Berkeley: Institute of International Studies, University of California, 1978.

Suffian, Tun Mohamed, H. P. Lee, and F. A. Trindade, eds. *The Constitution of Malaysia—Its Development: 1957–1977*. Kuala Lumpur: Oxford University Press, 1978.

Sutter, R. "Asia in the Balance: America and China's 'Peaceful Rise.'" *Current History*, 103, no. 674 (2004): 284–89.

Swift, Charles. *Dar Days: The Early Years in Tanzania*. New York: University Press of America, 2002.

Tagore, Rabindranath. *Diary of a Westward Voyage*. Bombay: Asia Publishing House, 1962.

———. *Letters from Abroad*. Madras: Ganesan, 1924.

――. *Nationalism*. London, Macmillan, 1917.

――. *Personality*. London: Macmillan, 1917.

Tambo, Oliver. "Afro-Asian Solidarity." In *Preparing for Power: Oliver Tambo Speaks*, compiled by Adelaide Tambo, 89–91. London: Heinemann, 1987.

Taylor, Ian. "The 'All-weather Friend'? Sino-African Interaction in the Twenty-first Century." In *Africa in International Politics: External Involvement on the Continent*, ed. I. Taylor and P. Williams, 83–101. London: Routledge, 2004.

――. *China and Africa: Engagement and Compromise*. London: Routledge, 2006.

――. "China's Foreign Policy towards Africa in the 1990s." *Journal of Modern African Studies*, 36, no. 3 (1998): 443–60.

――. "Taiwan's Foreign Policy and Africa: The Limitations of Dollar Diplomacy." *Journal of Contemporary China*, 11, no. 30 (2002): 125–40.

―― and P. Williams, eds. *Africa in International Politics: External Involvement on the Continent*. London: Routledge, 2004.

Thompson, D. "China's Soft Power in Africa: From the 'Beijing Consensus' to Health Diplomacy." *China Brief*, 5, no. 21 (2005): 1–4.

Thornton, John K. *Africa and Africans in the Making of the Atlantic World, 1400–1680*. Cambridge: Cambridge University Press, 1992.

Tönnies, Ferdinand. *Community and Civil Society*, ed. Jose Harris, trans. Jose Harris and Margaret Hollis. Cambridge: Cambridge University Press, 2001.

Triska, Jan F., ed. *Constitutions of the Community Party-States*. Palo Alto: Hoover Institution on War, Revolution, and Peace, 1968.

Tsing, Anna Lowenhaupt. *Friction: An Ethnography of Global Connection*. Princeton: Princeton University Press, 2005.

Tull, Denis M. "China's Engagement in Africa: Scope, Significance and Consequences," *Journal of Modern African Studies*, 44, 3 (2006): 459–79

Turner, Victor. *Dramas, Fields, and Metaphors: Symbolic Action in Human Society*. Ithaca: Cornell University Press, 1974.

――. *The Ritual Process: Structure and Anti-Structure*. Chicago: Aldine, 1969.

Udoma, Udo. *History and the Law of the Constitution of Nigeria*. Lagos: Malthouse Press, 1994.

United Nations Office of Public Information. *The Universal Declaration of Human Rights: A Standard of Achievement*. New York: United Nations Office of Public Information, 1962.

Universal Races Congress. *Record of the Proceedings of the First Universal Races Congress, Held at the University of London, July 26–29, 1911*. London: P. S. King and Son, 1911.

Van de Walle, N. *African Economies and the Politics of Permanent Crisis, 1979–1999*. Cambridge: Cambridge University Press, 2001.

van der Linden, Marcel. "Transnationalizing American Labor History." *Journal of American History*, 86, no. 3 (1999):1078–92.

van Onselen, Charles. *The Seed Is Mine: The Life of Kas Maine, a South African Sharecropper, 1894–1985*. New York: Hill and Wang, 1996.

Villard, André. *Histoire du Sénégal*. Dakar: M. Viale, 1943.

Von Eschen, Penny M. *Race against Empire: Black Americans and Anticolonialism, 1937–1957*. Ithaca: Cornell University Press, 1997.

Wake, C. S. "The Psychological Unity of Mankind." *Memoirs Read before the Anthropological Society of London*, 3, 1867–68: 134–47.

Wallerstein, Immanuel. *World-Systems Analysis: An Introduction*. Durham: Duke University Press, 2004.

Weber, Charlotte. "Unveiling Scheherazade: Feminist Orientalism in the International Alliance of Women." *Feminist Studies* 27, no. 1 (2007): 125–57.

Webster, John. *The Constitutions of Burundi, Malagasy and Rwanda*. Chicago: Program of East African Studies, 1964.

Wedell, George, ed. *Making Broadcasting Useful: The African Experience*. Manchester: Manchester University Press, 1986.

Weinbaum, Alys Eve. *Wayward Reproductions: Genealogies of Race and Nation in Transatlantic Modern Thought*. Durham: Duke University Press, 2004.

Weinstein, Warren, ed. *Chinese and Soviet Aid to Africa*. New York: Praeger, 1975.

Westad. Odd Arne. *The Global Cold War: Third World Interventions and the Making of Our Times*. Cambridge: Cambridge University Press, 2005.

Williams, William Appleman. *Empire as a Way of Life*. Oxford: Oxford University Press, 1980.

Wilson, Amrit. *US Foreign Policy and Revolution: The Creation of Tanzania*. London: Pluto, 1989.

Wilson, Kathleen, ed. *A New Imperial History: Culture, Identity and Modernity in Britain and the Empire, 1660–1840*. New York: Cambridge University Press, 2004.

Wohl, Robert. *The Generation of 1914*. Cambridge: Harvard University Press, 1979.

A World on the Move: A History of Colonialism and Nationalism in Asia and North Africa from the Turn of the Century to the Bandung Conference. Amsterdam: Djambaten, 1956.

Wright, Richard. *The Color Curtain: A Report on the Bandung Conference*. Jackson: University Press of Mississippi, 1995 [1956].

Wu, Judy Tzu-Chun. "Journeys for Peace and Liberation: Third World Internationalism and Radical Orientalism during the U.S. War in Vietnam." *Pacific Historical Review* 76, no. 4 (2007): 575–84.

Wylie, Diana. *Art and Revolution: The Life and Death of Thami Mnyele, South African Artist*. Charlottesville: University of Virginia Press, 2008.

Young, Crawford. *The African Colonial State in Comparative Perspective*. New Haven: Yale University Press, 1994.

———. *Politics in the Congo: Decolonization and Independence*. Princeton: Princeton University Press, 1965.

Young, Cynthia A. *Soul Power: Culture, Radicalism, and the Making of a U.S. Third World Left*. Durham: Duke University Press, 2006.

Young, Robert J. C. *Postcolonialism: An Historical Introduction*. Oxford: Blackwell, 2001.

Yousaf, Nahem. *Alex La Guma: Politics and Resistance*. Portsmouth, NH: Heinemann, 2001.

Yu Fai Law. *Chinese Foreign Aid: A Study of Its Nature and Goals, 1950–1982*. Fort Lauderdale: Verlag Breitenbach, 1984.

Yu, George T. "Africa in Chinese Foreign Policy." *Asian Survey*, 28, no. 8 (1988): 849–62.

———. "China's Failure in Africa." *Asian Survey*, 6, no. 8 (1966): 461–68.

———. "Dragon in the Bush: Peking's Presence in Africa." *Asian Survey*, 8, no. 12 (1968): 1018–26.

———. "Sino-African Relations: A Survey." *Asian Survey*, 5, no. 7 (1965): 321–32.

———. "Working on the Railroad: China and the Tanzania–Zambia Railway." *Asian Survey*, 11, no. 11 (1971): 1101–17.

———. *China's Africa Policy: A Study of Tanzania*. New York: Praeger, 1975.

Zhang Tieshan. *Youyi Zhilu: Yuanjian Tanzan Tielu Jishi* 友谊之路：援建坦赞铁路纪实 [*The Road of Friendship: The Memoirs of the Development Assistance of the Tanzania–Zambia Railroad*]. Beijing: Zhongguo Duiwai Jingji Maoyi Chuban She, 1999.

Zolberg, Aristide. *One-party Government in the Ivory Coast*. Princeton: Princeton University Press, 1964.

Zweig, D. and Bi Janhai. "China's Global Hunt for Energy." *Foreign Affairs*, 84, no. 5 (2005): 25–38.

Index

China (*continued*)
  strategic elements of African policy, 297–300
  support for Africa in UN, 293
  TAZARA workers trained in, 246–47
  treatment of foreign visitors, 238–39
  and world economy, 291–92
  Zanzibari delegations to, 208–10
Chinese history: related to African events and conditions, 205
Chinese-African Chamber of Commerce, 294
Christianity: and Western civilization, 114
Chu Tu-nan, 211; on shared heritage of Chinese and Africans, 205
citizenship: challenges to Muslim, in Kenya, 332, 334
civilizing mission ideology, 69–78
  critique of Georges Duhamel, 80–86
civil-rights movement, US: and global histories of Bandung, 355
class: and sisterhood, 156–57
Clinton, Bill
  and China as strategic partner, 291
  and Osama as America's public enemy number one, 320
Colombo Powers, 10
colonization: attributes valorized in, 73–75
colonized peoples: contrasted with Europeans, 71
colonizers: masculine bias of, 72–75
Colrane, Daniel, 275
communist constitutional model, 121–24
Communist Party of South Africa, 271, 275, 276
communitas, 3, 25–27, 42, 189, 343
communities, imagined, 3, 23–27
communities, represented, 3
communities of fate, political, 25
community, political, 22–27
  terminology of, 23

Comoros: constitution of, 130
Congo-Brazzaville: constitution, 130
constitution: as instrument of social transformation, 120–24
constitutional monarchy, 111–13
constitutions
  French influence on, 126
  and human rights, 124–31
  independence: influence of religion, 113–19
  postcolonial, 107–31
  and socialist ideology, 119–24
  in the West, 114–15
Coomaraswamy, Ananda: and preservation of Indian skills, 87
Cooper, Frederick
  on community, 24
  on discipline, 198
  on gatekeeper state, 19
  and postcolonial blame, 8–9
cosmopolitanism: of Mombasan Muslims, 327–34
counterterrorism: and Mombasan Muslims, 340
CPSA. *See* Communist Party of South Africa
Curie, Marie, 73

Dahomey: constitution of, 126, 130
Dalitbahujan, 56–57
Danner, Mark: and the *Spectacular*, 321
Dar es Salaam: influence of radio broadcasts from, 173–74
Darfur: genocidal campaign in, 301–2, 307, 310
debt, African: Chinese cancellation of, 293
Declaration of the Rights of Man, 126; and French colonies, 130
decolonization, 5, 6, 7, 8, 9, 19, 20, 55–64
  dialogical side of, 59–64
  and growth of independence constitutions, 107–9

feminism, international (*continued*)
and non-Western women, 149
feminism, Western: critique of,
150–51
festivals, Chinese
influence in Zanzibar, 221–23
and vision of the future, 199
See also halaiki
50 Cent, 323, 324, 340
First, Ruth: and transnational conversation on antiapartheid struggle,
269
fiscal transparency: and Chinese economic interests, 307
Forum on China–Africa Cooperation
(FOCAC), 1–3, 294
Foucault, Michel: and disciplinary
institutions, 199, 228
Friedrich, Carl
on independence constitutions, 110
and Western constitutions, 115
friendship: of Chinese and African
workers, 250

Gandhi, Leela: and rhetoric of futurity, 196–97
Gandhi, Mohandas
critique of industrial West, 100
discomfort with railways, 89
and limits of Western industrial
civilization, 92–93
Garvey, Marcus, 275
Gbenye, Christophe, 185
Geneva Accords (1954), 14
Ghana: governmental form, 111
Ghose, Aurobindo: as critic of the
West, 91–92
Gilbert, John: on TAZARA project,
251, 252
Gilbert, Sandra: on male combatants
in World War I, 82
Gilly, Adolfo: on Zanzibari Revolution, 216
Gizenga, Antoine, 185
Gleijeses, Piero: on Zanzibari Revolution, 216

global media: manipulation by bin
Laden, 321
Global War on Terrorism, 333, 339,
342, 343
globalization, 46–47, 56–58
and the humanities, 62–64
as liberation and subjugation, 61–62
Go, Julian: on postcolonial independence in Africa and Asia, 29–30
Goswami, Manu: and nation-state
system, 23
government: constitutional forms of,
111–13
Gramsci, Antonio: and elite emphasis
of civilizing mission ideology, 75
Group of 77, 18
Guantanamo Bay: detention of Muslims at, 336
Guenon, René, 86
Guevara, Che, 31, 201, 219, 324, 340,
345
Guinea: constitution of, 130
Gulf War, 336
Gumede, J. T., 275
Gurnah, Abdulrazak: on Zanzibari
politics, 203–4
Gurnah, Ahmed: on Zanzibari cosmopolitanism, 200

Haitian Revolution, 5
halaiki, 199, 221, 222, 223, 234
Hall, Stuart: and struggle against racism, 58
Hamad, Seif Sharif: on Zanzibari
nationalism, 202
Hamid, Abdul: on Malaysian constitution, 117
Hanga, Kassim, 216
Hardt, Michael
on discipline, 227–28
and globalization, 63
on nation and community, 24
Hartman, Saidiya: trip to Western
Africa, 358–59
Heidegger, Martin: and Europeanization of the earth, 56